Mapping the Nation

MAPPING

This series of readers, published in association with *New Left Review*, aims to illuminate key topics in a changing world.

Other titles in the series:

Perry Anderson and Patrick Camiller, eds,
Mapping the West European Left

Monica Threlfall, ed., *Mapping the Women's Movement*

Slavoj Žižek, ed., *Mapping Ideology*

Mapping
the Nation

Edited by
Gopal Balakrishnan

With an Introduction by
Benedict Anderson

PUBLISHED IN ASSOCIATION WITH
new left *review*

VERSO
London • New York

First published by Verso 1996

Verso
UK: 6 Meard Street, London W1V 3HR
USA: 180 Varick Street, New York NY 10014–4606

Verso is the imprint of New Left Books

ISBN 1–85984–960–1
ISBN 1–85984–060–4 (pbk)

British Library Cataloguing in Publication Data
A catalogue record for this book is available from the British Library

Library of Congress Cataloging-in-Publication Data
A catalog record for this book is available from the Library of Congress

Typeset by M Rules
Printed and bound in Great Britain by
Biddles Ltd, Guildford and King's Lynn

Contents

Introduction

Benedict Anderson

There is no disagreement that nationalism has been 'around' on the face
of the globe for, at the very least, two centuries. Long enough, one might
think, for it to be reliably and generally understood. But it is hard to think
of any political phenomenon which remains so puzzling and about which
there is less analytic consensus. No widely accepted definition exists. No
one has been able to demonstrate decisively either its modernity or its
antiquity. Disagreement over its origins is matched by uncertainty about its
future. Its global spread is read through the malignant metaphor of meta-
stasis as well as under the smiling signs of identity and emancipation; and
where did these processes begin – in the New World or the Old? Today, it
is possible to ask a new kind of question – 'how masculine is it?' – without
there being any obvious best answer. How is its universality to be reconciled with its necessary concrete particularity? What discipline helps
inquiry the most profoundly: history, psychology, political economy, sociology, anthropology, philosophy, literary criticism, or . . .? To add to the
unease: given what seems today the vast role that nationalism has played
over two centuries of world-politics, why have so many seminal thinkers of
modernity – Marx, Nietzsche, Weber, Durkheim, Benjamin, Freud, Lévi-
Strauss, Keynes, Gramsci, Foucault – had so little to say about it?

All these uncertainties mean that any anthology 'mapping the terrain'
of nationalism finds the authors more often with their backs to one
another, staring out at different, obscure horizons, than engaged in
orderly hand-to-hand combat. Hence any brief introduction can only
adumbrate some general contours.

The philosophical difficulties have been there all along. The Herder
who famously wrote that 'Denn jedes Volk ist Volk; es hat seine National

1

Bildung wie seine Sprache' was positioned to insist on the uniqueness of *every* people/*Volk* only as the author of a vast four-volume universal history entitled *Ideën zur Philosophie der Geschichte der Menschheit*. From the Enlightenment on up to very recent times the axiomatic frames in which the great European thinkers thought were universal – so to speak, *Menschheit* and/or *Weltgeschichte*. Hegel spent his whole industrious life along the little 500-mile axis between Stuttgart and Berlin, but three and a half centuries of print-capitalism in the post-Renaissance age of European expansion seemed quite naturally to bring all antiquities and all contemporary societies into his library for perusal, reflection and theoretical synthesis. In the age that was launched with the (not yet French) Revolution, all the key concepts were understood globally – progress, liberalism, socialism, republicanism, democracy, even conservatism, legitimacy and later fascism. Curiously enough, nationalism too, so that when the time was ripe no one thought there was anything strange about a 'League of Nations', and Lloyd George could nonchalantly describe Mazzini as the Father of this international organization. Nor did this kind of thinking stay confined to Europe. When, at the end of the 1980s, the great contemporary Indonesian writer Pramoedya Ananta Toer published his vast historical tetralogy on the origins of Indonesian nationalism, he could happily describe his hero as *anak semua bangsa* – child of all nations. Meanwhile, in the intervening half-century, across the globe, millions of people had sacrificed their lives for their nations' sakes. It was gradually becoming clear that it was impossible to think about nationalism except comparatively and globally: but it was also very difficult to feel it, and act politically on it, in any but particular terms.

This disjuncture, and the theoretical stumble that it causes, helps to explain some of the history of serious thinking about nationalism, its hiatuses and bursts of energy. During the long century of conservative intra-European peace (1815–1914) only occasionally, and to a few, did nationalism give much theoretical anxiety and the occasions are instructive. The present collection opens with two of the most intelligent of these interventions.

In the 1860s, at the height of British imperial power – but also after the Europe-wide upheaval of 1848, the revolutions led by Mazzini and Garibaldi against the Papacy and the Kingdom of Naples, the rise of the Fenians in Ireland and America, and the nationalist Juárez's successful checkmating of Archduke Maximilian's attempt to establish a Habsburg dynasty in Mexico City – the Naples-born Lord Acton (subsequently the first Catholic Regius Professor of History at Oxford), sounded the alarm bells. Enlightened defender of the universal principle of Legitimacy, he observed that what he called 'nationality' was of three subversive modern ideas the one 'most attractive at the present time, and the richest in promise of future power.'[1] In his view, 'those states are substantially the most perfect which, like the British and Austrian empires, include various distinct nationalities without oppressing them', because 'inferior races are raised by living in political union with races intellectually superior' and '[e]xhausted and decaying nations are revived by the contact of a younger vitality'. Against John Stuart Mill's claim in *Considerations on Representative Government* that 'it is, in general, a necessary condition of free institutions, that the boundaries of governments should coincide in the main with those of nationalities', Acton argued that this conception was a pernicious residue of the French Revolution, a variant on the general 'modern' tendency to found the State on speculative, abstract, monistic ideas (including, he noted sarcastically, the greatest happiness of the greatest number). Any such tendency inevitably led to revolutionary and absolutist politics and destroyed limited government and the pluralistic bases of true liberty. One can scarcely doubt that Acton would have regarded the murderous demise of former Yugoslavia in the name of 'ethnic cleansing' as confirmation of his worst forebodings, and that he would have looked with prophetic satisfaction at the emergence of the conservative European Community.

As the Great War loomed on the horizon, Otto Bauer, defender of universal socialism, and regular lecturer at Vienna's Arbeiterschule, penned a huge comparative tome which sought to show theoretically that, rightly understood, socialism and nationalism were perfectly compatible, and, practically, that the nationalist conflicts threatening the existence of the Austro-Hungarian Empire could be productively transcended in a projected supranational, socialist, Vereinigten Staaten von Gross-Oesterreich (VSGO).[2] (It is astonishing that in the ninety years that have passed since its initial publication, his influential magnum opus, *Die Nationalitätenfrage und die Sozialdemocratie*, has never been translated into English; hence the special importance to be attached to the substantial excerpts included in the present collection.) Against all reactionary ideas of the 'eternal *Volksgeist*' type – which, for example, had encouraged the nineteenth-century transformation of Tacitus' virtuous hero Arminius into the grotesque, gigantic 'Hermann'-*denkmal* in the Black Forest – he argued that nations were products of history, and built on centuries of social and sexual intermingling of different groups. Germans were a random mix of Slavs, Celts and Teutons, and early-twentieth-century Germans had far more in common with, and much more to learn from, contemporary French and Italians than they did with and from the subjects of the Holy Roman Empire. He went on, in a vein which partly foreshadowed the ideas of Ernest Gellner (see below), that the nation was a product of the Great Transformation, which dissolved all ancient, isolated communities into modern industrial societies, which require a solidarity based on an abstract, literacy-based high culture. Writing passionately on the basis of his experience at the Arbeiterschule, he argued that the brutality of capitalism had not only torn workers from their local peasant cultures, but had also deprived them of entry into these largely upper- and middle-class-created national cultures, through the exhausted, immiserated ignorance to which the factory system kept them chained. It was thus socialism's historic task to help them break out of this darkness into Enlightenment. At the same time, Bauer contested the idea, then held by many on the Left, that the victory of socialism would create a sort of flat, uniform cosmopolitanism. Distinguishing sharply between commonality and similarity, he stated that all modern nations experienced, for example, industrial capitalism in similar ways, but they did not experience it in common. Commonality, cutting across class lines, linked specific groups by what he called 'community of destiny', read not quasi-metaphysically as ancient doom, but as shared will towards the future. This will, subject to constant change in the real struggle for life, was precipitated through shared language and habits of everyday life, shared culture, and, eventually, shared political institutions, into what he called national character.[3]

Nothing could be more striking than Bauer's position in relation to Acton's and to the theses so forcefully propounded by Marx and Engels in *The Communist Manifesto* half a century earlier. Both Acton and Bauer wished to disconnect nationality from the state. The conservative Neapolitan Englishman saw nations (ahistorically and largely a-culturally) as 'merely natural', and thus requiring the imposition of an ethical Legitimist state above them; Habsburg rule was thus the threatened dike against the nihilist forces of modernity. Bauer, on the other hand, understood both nations and states as historically formed, but with national character and culture rather than the state as sources of value. The importance of the Habsburg Empire was thus that it formed a contingent historical shell of practices and institutions out of which a socialist federation of nationalities would emerge – on the road towards the eventual withering away of all states. Conversely, against the *Manifesto*'s view of the capitalist world market dissolving all national cultures, Bauer believed that progressive social development was increasing the density of contact between members of particular cultures, raising the level of those cultures, and promoting differentiation of human personalities; the function of socialism was not to counteract these tendencies but to spread the standardization of material life at the most advanced levels which capitalism had originally set in motion. (Thus only the bourgeois saw the nation under the sign of State Power.)

After 1918, everything seemed to change abruptly. The collapse of the Hohenzollern, Habsburg, Romanov and Ottoman empires ended the legitimacy of Legitimacy, and put paid to the dream of a United States of Greater Austria. Out of the peripheral debris emerged a welter of small, weak, mostly agrarian national states in Central and Eastern Europe, and a congeries of colonies and protectorates in the Near East. Even the victorious United Kingdom soon lost most of Ireland, while its German royal family naturalized itself as Windsors. The formation of the League of Nations, at which even the remaining imperial powers masqueraded as simple nations, seemed to create a new universal legitimacy.

But the truly decisive event was the ascent of the Bolsheviks to power in Petrograd, and their astonishing success in creating a stable anticapitalist order over much of tsardom's former domains. For although it eventually joined the League, the young, solitary Soviet Union did not regard itself as a nation-state, nor, on the whole, did its many enemies think of it as such. In the eyes of many, it seemed to have achieved something like Bauer's dream, transcending the problem of nationalism by formal recognition of the terrains and cultures of its major nationalities while subordinating them fully to a universal project. It was precisely this project that attracted the loyalties of millions of people scattered over most parts of the globe. Against Bolshevism were raised two rivalrous, countervailing universalisms: capitalist democracy/the 'West' on the one hand, and fascism on the other. While there is no denying that at the local level fascism exploited nationalism, it is essential to recognize its world-wide appeal as a supranational force against 'world-wide' Jewry, Bolshevism, liberalism, and so forth. Hence it was that the most important studies of nationalism in the interwar years, done by Hans Kohn, Carlton Hayes, and their students, were structured by the binary, universal opposition between 'good' (Western/democratic) and 'bad' (Eastern/authoritarian/fascist).[4] No matter that the good European capital cities of London, Paris and The Hague were the centres of vast extra-European imperial autocracies.

The destruction of Europe's fascist regimes, as well as that of militarist Japan, did not profoundly change the post-1918 picture. In spite of the fact that the Soviet Union became a part of the United Nations, which the United States now also joined, world-politics in the Cold War era were widely understood in supranational terms. True, Stalin decided against incorporating the parts of East and Central Europe he controlled into the Soviet Union, so that for the first time communist states appeared which were explicitly national in status; but these states were small and weak, and understood as minor, subordinate allies of the core.[5] (Until the late 1950s even vast China was widely thought of in this way.) On the other hand, the United States, which completely dominated Western Europe, was also seen, world-historically, less as a nation-state than as the domineering centre of a global anti-communist coalition.

The emancipation of the European colonies in Asia and Africa, between 1945 and 1975, did not for a considerable time alter these conditions, as these new nation-states were, like the new European nation-states of the interwar years, mostly weak, poor, agrarian, and rent by internal conflicts, many of which were read and manipulated along the prevailing world-axis.

The era in which we now live probably begins, at least symbolically, in the 1960s, signalled by the global reverberations of nationalism in two small, poor and peripheral states. Tiny Vietnam's heroic struggle against the colossal United States, graphically pictured round the world through the new medium of television, helped precipitate, as no other 'peripheral' nationalism had done, convulsions not only in America, but in France, Germany, Japan, and elsewhere, making 1968 a sort of 1848-style *annus mirabilis*. At the same time, Brezhnev's tanks brutally destroyed the nationalist Spring in communist-ruled Czechoslovakia, with comparable long-term consequences for the Soviet project. The same decade saw the rise in the United States: first of the Civil Rights movement, followed by a Black Nationalism which soon crossed national boundaries; the beginnings of a new-style feminist movement with increasingly global reach; the Stonewall Riot, which began the first-ever transcontinental movement for the emancipation of gays and lesbians – Queer Nation, for the nonce. In Old Europe too, the development of the supranational Community went hand in hand with the emergence of militant nationalisms against established nation-states – Northern Ireland, Scotland, Belgium, Catalonia, the Basque lands, and so on.[6] By the second half of the 1980s the Soviet Union was on its last legs, leaving what remains of twentieth-century communism to the rattled heirs of Deng Xiaoping. Meanwhile Japan, representing neither to itself nor to the outside world any universal project, had become the planet's second most powerful national economy – if it makes sense any longer to speak in such terms. It is hard to think of any previous era when so much changed politically, so rapidly, and in so many places; or in which there was so much uncertainty about the future.

But there is another transformation taking place, more quietly, but with enormous implications for what may be to come. Living, on the whole, the quiet life in eighteenth-century Königsberg, Kant could imagine commerce as the benign global force that would one day lead to Perpetual Peace among the Nations. (Meanwhile, that same 'commerce' was hauling millions of enslaved Africans across the Atlantic.) He could do so because industrial capitalism was only just beginning to appear on his horizon, the huge westward migrations from continental Europe had yet seriously to commence, and the railway was as yet undreamed of.

Hegel, younger, more familiar with the work of Adam Smith, and with better prophetic instincts, was alarmed early on by the social and political implications of the economic revolution getting under way, and among the purposes of his modern state were precisely the containment and domestication of the anomic forces that the market was beginning to unleash. By the next generation, List was thinking seriously about the kind of political changes that would be needed consciously to realign early capitalism with the modern state, in the form of national economies large enough to create enough power to sustain and police their frontiers. Even Marx, who understood better than anyone else the revolutionary global dynamic of capitalism, was not entirely immune to Listian assumptions. In the famous claim that 'The proletariat of each country, must, of course, first of all settle matters with its own bourgeoisie', we can be sure that these 'countries' were of the Listian type, rather than little Switzerland, Belgium or Portugal.

As late at least as the founding of the League of Nations, the conception of 'national economy' was generally accepted, and certainly underlay the whole doctrine of self-determination; it received its first undeniably deadly blow only with the World Depression, which struck all nations simultaneously, and which no raising of tariff walls seriously alleviated. National economy, however, also implied a certain geographical immobility of labour, and a certain boundedness to the communications systems underpinning it. (It is striking that the huge labour flows organized outside Europe within the colonial empires were then paid scant theoretical attention.) The very idea that the map of Europe could and should be drastically redrawn to provide more self-determination assumed that, say, Poles would henceforth stay put in Poland, reading Polish newspapers, participating in Polish politics, and building a Polish economy. Large sections of the organized Left accepted this frame of reference, not least because, the infant Soviet Union aside, experience seemed to have shown that the most significant long-term gains for the working class were achieved less on the factory floor than in *national* parliaments and through parliamentary legislation. Hence it was that, quite innocently and even unselfconsciously, the term '*national*-ization' was widely used to describe the actual or planned removal of sectors of the economy from the control of private property: it was, so to speak, a synonym of socialization. By then, however, the age of Ford, the automobile, radio and even aviation had arrived.

After the colossal devastation caused by the Second World War, it took a little time for these forces to make themselves fully manifest. The military successes of the Red Army brought Soviet power deep into the centre of Europe, and in Asia the most populous country on the planet, in Chinese Communist Party (CCP) hands, passed out of the reach of the

market. For political reasons, too, the state economies of the two communist-ruled giants resolutely prohibited the movement of labour outside
their productive spheres. Capitalist Western Europe found it impossible
to retain its extra-European empires. Common political and economic
weaknesses did for it something of what they had done for the small
German and Italian statelets in the mid nineteenth century. In this light
one can read the subsequent formation of the European Community as
Listianism updated for the era of late capitalism. In the newly independent ex-colonies of Asia and, later, Africa, the assumptions of 1918 came
into their own under the sign, among others, of 'nationalization'.

But by the 1970s and early 1980s, the dikes against the full force of late
capitalism seemed to be crumbling through processes with which we are
all familiar. Huge migrations from impoverished ex-colonial states into
the rich capitalist cores got under way, first into Western Europe, the
United States, and the former Dominions, at first, more recently into
Japan, the oil-rich Middle East, and the newly industrialized countries
(NICs) of East and South-East Asia. Stalin's and Mao's 'Continental
System' began leaking badly, and eventually collapsed. The electronic revolution created communications systems that escaped the control even of
the most powerful national states, permitting movement of finance capital on a scale and at a speed unimaginable even thirty years earlier.
Transnational systems of production came into increasing dominance,
and old-style Fordism began to give way to decentralized, out-of-country
production systems and sophisticated, highly flexible niche-marketing.
(One of the melancholy early indications of this was the global drug-
business which burst on the scene in the 1960s and seems still
uncontainable.) Cheap and fast transportation made completely
unprecedented world-wide population movements possible, no matter
what late-century labour-*Zollverein* systems were conceived.

As a result of these transformations, nationalism now appears in at least
two new guises, and with consequences of which no one can be sure. The
first is, of course, the creation of a congeries of weak, economically fragile
nation-states out of the debris of the Soviet system, some entirely new,
others residues of the settlement of 1918; in either case, from many
points of view, three-quarters of a century late. (But it can be argued that
these nationalisms are regional-specific and are unlikely to disturb global
trends.) The second is the impending crisis of the hyphen that for two
hundred years yoked state and nation. In the heyday of this hyphen,
when nationalist movements dreamed of achieving their own states, these
states were believed capable of providing prosperity, welfare and security,
as well as pride and international recognition. On the other hand, these
states were hypothetically guaranteed the obedience and undivided

loyalty of most of those viewing themselves as members of the nation. Nothing can be less certain than the long-term survival of these assumptions. Portable nationality, read under the sign of 'identity', is on the rapid rise as people everywhere are on the move.

Up until the eve of the Second World War, the rate of change in military technology was sufficiently ambling, and the costs of militaries were sufficiently modest that a reasonable number of nation-states felt they could be, even had to be, at some level competitive. (It was then still possible for Japan to come out of feudal nowhere to build a better fighter-plane than Ford's United States.) The great institutional innovation of the French revolutionaries and their Prussian antagonists – the mass conscript army – was still normal. Mass (male) citizen participation in national defence was a vital element in keeping the hyphen steadily in place. Almost all of this is now gone. Serious military innovation is affordable by only a tiny percentage of the world's two hundred or so nation-states, and the others tag along as small-game pirates, oligopolized consumers, or scavengers on the disorderly bargain-basement world-market. (It is reported, for example, that there are significant areas in the far west of China where the People's Liberation Army (PLA) cannot operate freely in the face of local warlords heavily armed with ex-Soviet munitions.) Technology has made the conscript army obsolete. States incapable of militarily defending their citizens, and hard put to ensure them employment and ever-better life-chances, may busy themselves with policing women's bodies and schoolchildren's curricula, but is this kind of thing enough over the long term to sustain the grand demands of sovereignty?

A final contextual consideration: up until 1945, political, social and economic conflicts, no matter how arduous, took place within a framework that one could only half-ruefully call utopian. On the Left it was possible, of course, to imagine a day when capitalism would be overcome and superseded. But even on the Right, destroying Bolshevism, or Jewry, had a plausible allure. The opening of the atomic age really ended this era. One might put it this way: by the 1960s, Washington really had the possibility of destroying Bolshevism in a few hours, and Moscow really had the capability of eliminating existing capitalism just as quickly. The negative millennium had for the first historical moment come into view. In the intervening years, to planetary atomic death have been added other kinds of global *memento mori* – depletion of the ozone layer, declining biodiversity, steepening demographic immiseration, epidemics such as AIDS.

If one recalls the political circumstances of Acton's and Bauer's historic interventions, one should not be too surprised that the post-1960s period has seen an explosion of sophisticated writing about nationalism. This is one reason why, after theirs, all the texts in this volume were composed in the last decade, and why they represent very different standpoints and concerns. Virtually all the authors are, or were, distinguished intellectuals, whose works are widely admired, so that it would be presumptuous to claim to 'introduce' them. But it may be useful to situate them against the landscape that I have sketched out above.

It could be said, without stretching the point too far, that the detonators were two Czechs of the generation born before the Second World War and the atomic age, one working in Prague and the other, for much of the time, in London. The greatly missed Ernest Gellner already in the middle 1960s began the elaboration of his influential and iconoclastic theory that nationalism is at bottom nothing more (or less) than a necessary and thoroughly functional response to the Great Transformation from static agrarian society to the world of industry and mechanical communication. It involved the spread of standardized 'high cultures' (masquerading as ur-national), instituted through vast state-arranged and state-financed educational systems to prepare people to survive under conditions in which the division of labour and social mobility were highly advanced. In the Euro-cosmopolitan spirit of the Enlightenment, Gellner understood nationalism globally, sociologically, from on high, and had little public time for the 'sentimentalities' associated with 'national cultures' (though he was known occasionally to turn to Czech folksongs when in private need of solace). Meanwhile, in Prague, Miroslav Hroch, teaching at Prague's ancient Charles University, published his pathbreaking historical-sociological comparative study of a very particular set of small-country nationalist movements in Central and Eastern Europe – in the era of Dubček's 'communism with a human face', and the violent response to it from Moscow. Perhaps characteristically, given the circumstances, Hroch stressed exactly what Gellner brushed aside – the variability of world-timing among these nationalist movements, as well as their very different social bases and economic circumstances. Furthermore, he insisted, contra Gellner, that nations are real anthropological formations, and that the connections between the rise of nationalism and modern industrial society have been weak and uncertain. We are fortunate in this volume to include not only a trenchant restatement of Hroch's general theses (and some pessimistic thoughts on Eastern Europe's future) but also Gellner's critical response and defence of his own position.

In the early 1970s, the time when Western Europe began to experience, against most previous expectations, nationalist 'revivals' – in Scotland, Belgium, the Basque lands, and perhaps especially in Ireland – Anthony Smith began writing, in a putatively post-imperial London, a long series of increasingly complex works on nationalism and nationality, also in a contra-Gellnerian spirit. While fully conceding that in some important respects nationalism is a modern phenomenon, he insisted that its appeal could not seriously be understood if it was treated functionally, and as arising *ex nihilo*. We include, therefore, a fine brief account of his historically considered argument that nationalism necessarily, and naturally, builds on much older ethnic communities, of which, perhaps not unfortuitously, the prime exemplars are the Armenians and the Jews.

By the 1980s, this cluster of positions came under critical review from a number of directions. We include here two important and contrasting contributions, so to speak, from Manchester and Calcutta. John Breuilly attacked both the sociologism of Gellner and the continuism of Smith by stressing the essentially political character of nationalism. He argued in effect that Gellner could not easily explain how the transition to nationalism actually occurred in 'late agrarian' society, and that Smith had no simple response to the question of why some ethnic communities 'went nationalist' while others did not, and under precisely what historical circumstances. He therefore laid great stress on the importance of political entrepreneurs, and on the concrete political interests expressed through them in contrasting institutional and geopolitical settings.

On the other hand, Partha Chatterjee, a member of the influential Subaltern Studies collective, attacked Gellner (and many others) by frontally raising the basic question of imperialism and colonial domination. The same 'Enlightened' industrial modernity which in Gellner's view had created nationalism was the basis for Europe's domination of the rest of the globe in the century and a half following the French Revolution. Nationalism had therefore to be understood as part and parcel of that domination. Its appearance in the late colonial world, and afterward, had to be read under the sign of inauthenticity, no matter how local leaders of the type of Nehru, Sukarno, and Nkrumah insisted on its integrity and autonomy. Nationalism was, outside Europe, necessarily a 'derivative discourse', blocking the way for authentic self-generated, autonomous development among communities which remained dominated by self-seeking, ultimately collaborationist 'nationalist' politicians, intellectuals, bureaucrats and capitalists. We include here a recent reformulation of his position, in which the prime target has shifted from Gellner to my book *Imagined Communities*, and in which elite nationalism in Asia and Africa receives a somewhat warmer evaluation than in his previous writing.

If the contributors briefly discussed above were basically concerned with the historical nature, the origins, and the rise, of nationalism, and thus belong in spirit to the era before the collapse of the Soviet Union, the remainder of our texts can be said to face towards the future of nationalism in the new world conjuncture.

The young scholar Gopal Balakrishnan, generationally Gellner's grandson, provides a pivotal linking contribution which begins with observations on the difficulties which Hegel and Marx faced in determining the role played by *particular peoples* in History conceived as a succession of universal social structures before moving on to a nuanced critique of *Imagined Communities*. His essay ends with some compelling reflections on the complex relations between nation and class, as bases of collective agency, in the politics of the advanced capitalist world.

Up until quite recently theoretical writing on nationalism ignored, overlooked, or marginalized the issue of gender. But over the past fifteen years this 'silence' has been irreversibly ended by a vast new corpus of feminist scholarship and theorizing. Two general features of this writing stand out: one is the emphasis on the ambiguity (to say the least) of women's relationships with nationalist projects, and the nexus of the nation-state with particular gender-regimes; the second is the difference between the experience of advanced capitalist societies in the 'West' (broadly conceived) and that of colonial, semi-colonial, and postcolonial worlds of Asia, Africa, and the Middle East.

Sylvia Walby, author of *Theorizing Patriarchy*, focuses primarily on the Western democracies, and is concerned with the way in which the modern nation-state, based on the principles of universal adult suffrage and formal equality before the law, has been transforming the nature of patriarchy from private to public. Access to nationhood and citizenship has undermined the control of individual male household heads over 'their' women, who are no longer excluded from the public sphere; but it has also encouraged the newer subordination of women, and the appropriation of their labour, by a male-dominated national collective. Out of this transformation have emerged new forms of public conflict over nationally legislated control, or attempted control, over women's fertility, 'family' responsibilities, access to 'national/masculine' spheres of employment such as the military, and so on.

The last four contributions move us back towards the European terrain with which this collection opens. A distinguished American cultural anthropologist specializing in, and suffering through, the Romania of Ceauşescu and his epigones, Katherine Verdery argues that the symbolism of the nation has been shifting its signification as modern states find it increasingly difficult to fulfil the promises of autonomy and wellbeing bequeathed to them as legitimating missions by the nineteenth century. At the same time, and partly for just this reason, the premium on a deeply interiorized, homogeneous identification between nation and person has been rising. Ethnic and racial stereotyping, xenophobia, sectarian 'multiculturalism' and the more brutal forms of identity politics seem to be the wave of the future; yet there is no escaping this development, since 'being born into something as a natural condition will remain fundamental to human experience . . .'

Verdery's cautious pessimism is here powerfully reinforced by Eric Hobsbawm, the most outstanding of living Anglophone historians. Born in the year of the Bolshevik Revolution, growing up in Vienna as Nazism's dark shadow moved across central Europe, he has lived through state-fascism's destruction, and also the collapse of the Soviet Union which largely made that wrecked triumph possible, and for which over many years he had strong, if critical, sympathies. A cosmopolitan Jewish polymath, who nonetheless remains strongly attached to the polyethnic United Kingdom which gave him refuge, he has been the most outspoken critic of the 'new nationalisms' of Europe, arguing that the Mazzinian age in which nationalism was integrative and emancipatory has long passed. He has even famously written that the extraordinary contemporary flood of sophisticated writing on nationalism is the best sign that his diagnosis is correct: Minerva's owl takes flight only at dusk.

At least since the late 1970s, Hobsbawm has been engaged in a sharp but illuminating debate with Tom Nairn, a fellow-Marxist, but also a Scottish nationalist, and the most penetrating critic of the decrepitude of his interlocutor's beloved United Kingdom. It is therefore fitting that this collection includes some recent reflections of the author of *The Breakup of Britain*. Coming from a very different position than that of Partha Chatterjee, Nairn's long-standing criticisms of the imperious pretensions of intellectual cosmopolitanism nonetheless resonate with some of the latter's themes. Here they are combined with an argument that it has been precisely the large 'integrated' multinational states – the huge dynastic realms of the nineteenth century of which the UK is the last limping survivor, as well as twentieth-century Big Germany, the United States, the Soviet Union, crypto-Ch'ing China, and ex-raj India – that have caused the greatest human destruction in our time. Hence what he regards as the general crumbling of a series of World 'Orders' decided by these political Godzillas is to be read as leading towards a more attractive, and more fruitful, anarchic Disorder, in which high nineteenth-century aspirations for total sovereignty make way for a complex interactive community of genuinely postimperial nationalities. He argues that the prime hope for this transformation is the deepening of democracy, of local political participation, and the institutionalization across the globe of a human rights regime.

No one in recent years has done more than the macrosociologist Michael Mann to provide us with a global-historical comparative understanding of the development of modern institutions, most particularly the

State. The core of his contribution here is an elegant, acutely detailed dis-
assembling of the myths, black and rosy-fingered, surrounding the
European Community. But his observations are embedded within a wider
perspective on the mature nation-state, which, with its attendant notions
of political and social citizenship, he views as a twentieth-century phenomenon constructed on the basis of prolonged, if compromised, class
struggle. His analysis shows why he can quote with such approval an
unnamed Belgian cabinet minister, who during the Gulf War, remarked
that the Community is 'an economic giant, a political dwarf, and a military worm'. He notes that 'most national politics concern taxes, income
policy, welfare policies, moral issues, and foreign crisises. These are not
perceived to be, and are not, the province of the EC.' And if supranational forces are in some ways reducing the full sovereignty of the
nation-state, that same state, he believes, is steadily increasing its power at
the expense of provincial, local, and private institutions and groups.
Mann also underlines the fact that, despite the extraordinary international mobility of *financial* capital today, the vast bulk of the nation's
production is destined for domestic markets, while 'transnational' corporations have their headquarters and research institutions in decidedly
national spaces.

From this he argues that, far from declining, the nation-state is still
'growing' on the world-stage, and that the poor countries of the world
suffer from a lack of effective nation-stateness. This lack it is their right-
ful ambition to overcome, although success may take arduous decades to
achieve. Yet, at the same time, he observes that if even the achievements
of Swedish social democracy are seriously threatened by 'transnational fiscal conservatism', socialists must 'lift their gaze from inside their own
nation-states to exercise power at the international level. . . . The class
movement which historically most strengthened the nation-state should
now begin to subvert it.'

Jürgen Habermas is surely the most widely influential political philosopher of our time. If Verdery can be read as a cautious and moderate
version of Hobsbawm's pessimism, we might here, for the nonce, take
Adorno's (and perhaps, oddly enough, Acton's) heir as expressing a
quieter partnership with the optimism of Nairn and Mann. Habermas is
fully aware of the destructive aspects of the globalization of financial and
labour markets, of the development of quasi-permanent underclasses in
late-late capitalist societies, and of the impotence of national states in con-
structively dealing with the many problems whose scale vastly outstrips
their territorial reach. He argues, however, that the political innovations
of the nineteenth century – above all, the modern republic, participatory
democracy, and constitutional politics (all of which Nairn also emphasizes) – need to be extended upwards towards the supranational sphere,

rather than spread downward towards hitherto caged nationalities. The European Community, with all its warts, is thus a step in the right direction, not least because it seems bound to enshrine, at some new level, the principle of multiculturalism – not as a congeries of irritable narcissisms, but as a rational integration of local cultural solidarities within, but sharply distinct from, the supra-ethnocultural 'republican' state-idea that was born from the Enlightenment.[7] This stance permits Habermas to speak about the possibility, emerging from the kinds of international meetings held recently on global issues in Geneva, Rio de Janeiro, Cairo and Beijing, of what he calls 'world domestic politics'.

It remains only to add, by way of appreciative postscript, our collective thanks for the imagination (and, in my own case, the fraternal patience and thoughtful suggestions) of Gopal Balakrishnan and Robin Blackburn, who put this collection intelligently together, and of my brother Perry, who, at somewhat longer distance, guided it towards its ultimate form.

Notes

1. The other two were egalitarianism, aimed at the principle of aristocracy, and communism (he was thinking of Babœuf rather than Marx), aimed against the principle of private property.

2. The specification of this United States of Greater Austria can be found in his *Werkausgabe*, Vienna 1975, vol. 1, p. 482.

3. Note that Bauer was careful not to speak of shared language as something unique to itself. He was quite aware of the many different nations that used Spanish and English as their shared languages, without making any monopoly claims to it. Similarly, he looked with equanimity on the prospect of forms of German being the common language of different European states, including the VSGO, without this involving the suppression of Czech or Hungarian. In all this we can see why, if for completely different reasons, the conservative Acton and the socialist Bauer attached such importance to the huge political realm centred in Vienna.

4. Kohn (1891–1971), raised in Czech-nationalist Prague under the Dual Monarchy, an activist in the Zionist youth movement, and subsequently a student of Near Eastern nationalist movements from a base in Jerusalem, published his first magnum opus, *Nationalismus*, in 1922. His near-contemporary Carlton Hayes (1882–1964), a long-time professor at Columbia University, published his first major work, *Essays on Nationalism*, in 1926. Oddly enough, he eventually served as Roosevelt's wartime ambassador to Franco's Madrid.

5. There are more than superficial parallels between the powerful, unanticipated reactions in Central and Eastern Europe to the short-lived, gigantic empires established, across a century and half, by Napoleon and Hitler. One key consequence of the Nazi assault was a fusion of communism and nationalism which would have made postwar incorporation into the Soviet Union far more implausible than it would have seemed between the wars. One can see comparable fusions in those areas of East and South-East Asia ruthlessly seized by Japanese militarism between 1937 and 1945. Mao, Tito, Ho Chi Minh, Kim Il Sung, and Enver Hoxha are exemplary in this regard.

6. The reasons for this emergence are too complex to explore here. It seems nonetheless plausible to link them with the postwar collapse of the colonial empires, which drastically

reduced the prestige and allure of the imperial centres, and removed, so to speak, the safety-valves that sent energetic young members of the 'nationalities' to Angola, Algeria, India, or the Congo. At the same time, membership in the Community made the absolutist claims of existing sovereignties in Western Europe much less convincing than hitherto.

7. Habermas publicly expressed his misgivings about the Kohlist reunification of Germany; it is hard not to see his appreciation of the Community's potential as a hope for the containment of Big German chauvinism.

Nationality

Lord Acton

Whenever great intellectual cultivation has been combined with that suffering which is inseparable from extensive changes in the condition of
the people, men of speculative or imaginative genius have sought in the
contemplation of an ideal society a remedy, or at least a consolation, for
evils which they were practically unable to remove. Poetry has always preserved the idea that at some distant time or place, in the Western islands
or the Arcadian region, an innocent and contented people, free from the
corruption and restraint of civilized life, have realized the legends of the
golden age. The office of the poets is always nearly the same, and there is
little variation in the features of their ideal world; but when philosophers
attempt to admonish or reform mankind by devising an imaginary state,
their motive is more definite and immediate, and their commonwealth is
a satire as well as a model. Plato and Plotinus, More and Campanella, constructed their fanciful societies with those materials which were omitted
from the fabric of the actual communities, by the defects of which they
were inspired. The *Republic*, the *Utopia*, and the *City of the Sun* were
protests against a state of things which the experience of their authors
taught them to condemn, and from the faults of which they took refuge
in the opposite extremes. They remained without influence, and have
never passed from literary into political history, because something more
than discontent and speculative ingenuity is needed in order to invest a
political idea with power over the masses of mankind. The scheme of a
philosopher can command the practical allegiance of fanatics only, not of
nations; and though oppression may give rise to violent and repeated out-
breaks, like the convulsions of a man in pain, it cannot mature a settled
purpose and plan of regeneration, unless a new notion of happiness is
joined to the sense of present evil.

17

The history of religion furnishes a complete illustration. Between the later medieval sects and Protestantism there is an essential difference, that outweighs the points of analogy found in those systems which are regarded as heralds of the Reformation, and is enough to explain the vitality of the last in comparison with the others. Whilst Wyclif and Hus contradicted certain particulars of the Catholic teaching, Luther rejected the authority of the Church, and gave to the individual conscience an independence which was sure to lead to an incessant resistance. There is a similar difference between the Revolt of the Netherlands, the Great Rebellion, the War of Independence, or the rising of Brabant, on the one hand, and the French Revolution on the other. Before 1789, insurrections were provoked by particular wrongs, and were justified by definite complaints and by an appeal to principles which all men acknowledged. New theories were sometimes advanced in the cause of controversy, but they were accidental, and the great argument against tyranny was fidelity to the ancient laws. Since the change produced by the French Revolution, those aspirations which are awakened by the evils and defects of the social state have come to act as permanent and energetic forces throughout the civilized world. They are spontaneous and aggressive, needing no prophet to proclaim, no champion to defend them, but popular, unreasoning, and almost irresistible. The Revolution effected this change, partly by its doctrines, partly by the indirect influence of events. It taught the people to regard their wishes and wants as the supreme criterion of right. The rapid vicissitudes of power, in which each party successively appealed to the favour of the masses as the arbiter of success, accustomed the masses to be arbitrary as well as insubordinate. The fall of many governments, and the frequent redistribution of territory, deprived all settlements of the dignity of permanence. Tradition and prescription ceased to be guardians of authority; and the arrangements which proceeded from revolutions, from the triumphs of war, and from treaties of peace, were equally regardless of established rights. Duty cannot be dissociated from right, and nations refuse to be controlled by laws which are no protection.

In this condition of the world, theory and action follow close upon each other, and practical evils easily give birth to opposite systems. In the realms of free-will, the regularity of natural progress is preserved by the conflict of extremes. The impulse of the reaction carries men from one extremity towards another. The pursuit of a remote and ideal object, which captivates the imagination by its splendour and the reason by its simplicity, evokes an energy which would not be inspired by a rational, possible end, limited by many antagonistic claims, and confined to what is reasonable, practicable, and just. One excess or exaggeration is the corrective of the other, and error promotes truth, where the masses are concerned, by counter-balancing a contrary error. The few have not strength to achieve great changes unaided; the many have not wisdom to be moved by truth unmixed. Where the disease is various, no particular definite remedy can meet the wants of all. Only the attraction of an abstract idea, or of an ideal state, can unite in a common action multitudes who seek a universal cure for many special evils, and a common restorative applicable to many different conditions. And hence false principles, which correspond with the bad as well as with the just aspirations of mankind, are a normal and necessary element in the social life of nations.

Theories of this kind are just, inasmuch as they are provoked by definite ascertained evils, and undertake their removal. They are useful in opposition, as a warning or a threat, to modify existing things, and keep awake the consciousness of wrong. They cannot serve as a basis for the reconstruction of civil society, as medicine cannot serve for food; but they may influence it with advantage, because they point out the direction, though not the measure, in which reform is needed. They oppose an order of things which is the result of a selfish and violent abuse of power by the ruling classes, and of artificial restriction on the natural progress of the world, destitute of an ideal element or a moral purpose. Practical extremes differ from the theoretical extremes they provoke, because the first are both arbitrary and violent, whilst the last, though also revolutionary, are at the same time remedial. In one case the wrong is voluntary, in the other it is inevitable. This is the general character of the contest between the existing order and the subversive theories that deny its legitimacy. There are three principal theories of this kind, impugning the present distribution of power, of property, and of territory, and attacking respectively the aristocracy, the middle class, and the sovereignty. They are the theories of equality, communism, and nationality. Though sprung from a common origin, opposing cognate evils, and connected by many links, they did not appear simultaneously. Rousseau proclaimed the first, Babœuf the second, Mazzini the third; and the third is the most recent in its appearance, the most attractive at the present time, and the richest in promise of future power.

In the old European system, the rights of nationalities were neither recognized by governments nor asserted by the people. The interest of the reigning families, not those of the nations, regulated the frontiers; and the administration was conducted generally without any reference to popular desires. Where all liberties were suppressed, the claims of national independence were necessarily ignored, and a princess, in the words of Fénelon, carried a monarchy in her wedding portion. The eighteenth century acquiesced in this oblivion of corporate rights on the Continent, for the absolutists cared only for the State, and the liberals only for the individual. The Church, the nobles, and the nation had no place in the popular theories of the age; and they devised none in their own defence, for they were not openly attacked. The aristocracy retained its privileges, and the Church her property; and the dynastic interest, which overruled the natural inclination of the nations, and destroyed their independence, nevertheless maintained their integrity. The national sentiment was not wounded in its most sensitive part. To dispossess a sovereign of his hereditary crown, and to annex his dominions, would have been held to inflict an injury upon all monarchies, and to furnish their subjects with a dangerous example, by depriving royalty of its inviolable character. In time of war, as there was no national cause at stake, there was no attempt to rouse national feeling. The courtesy of the rulers towards each other was proportionate to the contempt for the lower orders. Compliments passed between the commanders of hostile armies; there was no bitterness, and no excitement; battles were fought with the pomp and pride of a parade. The art of war became a slow and learned game. The monarchies were united not only by a natural community of interests, but by family alliances. A marriage contract sometimes became the signal for an interminable war, whilst family connections often set a barrier to ambition. After the wars of religion came to an end in 1648, the only wars were those which were waged for an inheritance or a dependency, or against countries whose system of government exempted them from the common law of dynastic States, and made them not only unprotected but obnoxious. These countries were England and Holland, until Holland ceased to be a republic, and until, in England, the defeat of the Jacobites in the year forty-five terminated the struggle for the Crown. There was one country, however, which still continued to be an exception; one monarch whose place was not admitted in the comity of kings.

Poland did not possess those securities for stability which were supplied by dynastic connections and the theory of legitimacy, wherever a crown could be obtained by marriage or inheritance. A monarch without royal blood, a crown bestowed by the nation, were an anomaly and an outrage in that age of dynastic absolutism. The country was excluded from the European system by the nature of its institutions. It excited a cupidity which could not be satisfied. It gave the reigning families of Europe no hope of permanently strengthening themselves by intermarriage with its rulers, or of obtaining it by request or by inheritance. The Habsburgs had contested the possession of Spain and the Indies with the French Bourbons, of Italy with the Spanish Bourbons, of the empire with the house of Wittelsbach, of Silesia with the house of Hohenzollern. There had been wars between rival houses for half the territories of Italy and Germany. But none could hope to redeem their losses or increase their power in a country to which marriage and descent gave no claim. Where they could not permanently inherit they endeavoured, by intrigues, to prevail at each election, and after contending in support of candidates who were their partisans, the neighbours at last appointed an instrument for the final demolition of the Polish State. Till then no nation had been deprived of its political existence by the Christian Powers, and whatever disregard had been shown for national interests and sympathies, some care had been taken to conceal the wrong by a hypocritical perversion of law. But the partition of Poland was an act of wanton violence, committed in open defiance not only of popular feeling but of public law. For the first time in modern history a great State was suppressed, and a whole nation divided among its enemies.

This famous measure, the most revolutionary act of the old absolutism, awakened the theory of nationality in Europe, converting a dormant right into an aspiration, and a sentiment into a political claim. 'No wise or honest man', wrote Edmund Burke, 'can approve of that partition, or can contemplate it without prognosticating great mischief from it to all countries at some future time.'[1] Thenceforward there was a nation demanding to be united in a State – a soul, as it were, wandering in search of a body in which to begin life over again; and, for the first time, a cry was heard that the arrangement of States was unjust – that their limits were unnatural, and that a whole people was deprived of its right to constitute an independent community. Before that claim could be efficiently asserted against the overwhelming power of its opponents – before it gained energy, after the last partition, to overcome the influence of long habits of submission, and of the contempt which previous disorders had brought upon Poland – the ancient European system was in ruins, and a new world was rising in its place.

The old despotic policy which made the Poles its prey had two adversaries – the spirit of English liberty, and the doctrines of that revolution which destroyed the French monarchy with its own weapons; and these two contradicted in contrary ways the theory that nations have no collective rights. At the present day, the theory of nationality is not only the most powerful auxiliary of revolution, but its actual substance in the movements of the last three years. This, however, is a recent alliance, unknown to the first French Revolution. The modern theory of nationality arose partly as a legitimate consequence, partly as a reaction against it. As the system which overlooked national division was opposed by liberalism in two forms, the French and the English, so the system which insists upon them proceeds from two distinct sources, and exhibits the character either of 1688 or of 1789. When the French people abolished the authorities under which it lived, and became its own master, France was in danger of dissolution: for the common will is difficult to ascertain, and does not readily agree. 'The laws', said Vergniaud, in the debate on the sentence of the king, 'are obligatory only as the presumptive will of the people, which retains the right of approving or condemning them. The instant it manifests its wish the work of the national representation, the law, must disappear.' This doctrine resolved society into its natural elements, and threatened to break up the country into as many republics as there were communes. For true republicanism is the principle of self-government in the whole and in all the parts. In an extensive country, it can prevail only by the union of several independent communities in a single confederacy, as in Greece, in Switzerland, in the Netherlands, and in America; so that a large republic not founded on the federal principle must result in the government of a single city, like Rome and Paris, and, in a less degree, Athens, Berne, and Amsterdam; or, in other words, a great democracy must either sacrifice self-government to unity, or preserve it by federalism.

The France of history fell together with the French State, which was the growth of centuries. The old sovereignty was destroyed. The local authorities were looked upon with aversion and alarm. The new central authority needed to be established on a new principle of unity. The state of nature, which was the ideal of society, was made the basis of the nation; descent was put in the place of tradition, and the French people were regarded as a physical product: an ethnological, not historic, unit. It was assumed that a unity existed separate from the representation and the government, wholly independent of the past, and capable at any moment of expressing or of changing its mind. In the words of Siéyès, it was no longer France, but some unknown country to which the nation was transported. The central power possessed authority, inasmuch as it obeyed the whole, and no divergence was permitted from the universal sentiment. This power, endowed with volition, was personified in the Republic One and Indivisible. The title signified that a part could not speak or act for the whole – that there was a power supreme over the State, distinct from, and independent of, its members; and it expressed, for the first time in history, the notion of an abstract nationality. In this manner the idea of the sovereignty of the people, uncontrolled by the past, gave birth to the idea of nationality independent of the political influence of history. It sprang from the rejection of the two authorities – of the State and of the past. The kingdom of France was, geographically as well as politically, the product of a long series of events, and the same influences which built up the State formed the territory. The Revolution repudiated alike the agencies to which France owed her boundaries and those to which she owed her government. Every effaceable trace and relic of national history was carefully wiped away – the system of administration, the physical divisions of the country, the classes of society, the corporations, the weights and measures, the calendar. France was no longer bounded by the limits she had received from the condemned influence of her history; she could recognize only those which were set by nature. The definition of the nation was borrowed from the material world, and, in order to avoid a loss of territory, it became not only an abstraction but a fiction.

There was a principle of nationality in the ethnological character of the movement, which is the source of the common observation that revolution is more frequent in Catholic than in Protestant countries. It is, in fact, more frequent in the Latin than in the Teutonic world, because it depends partly on a national impulse, which is only awakened where there is an alien element, the vestige of a foreign dominion, to expel. Western Europe has undergone two conquests – one by the Romans and one by the Germans – and twice received laws from the invaders. Each time it rose again against the victorious race; and the two great reactions, while they differ according to the different characters of the two conquests, have the phenomenon of imperialism in common. The Roman republic laboured to crush the subjugated nations into a homogeneous and obedient mass; but the increase which the proconsular authority obtained in the process subverted the republican government, and the reaction of the provinces against Rome assisted in establishing the empire. The Caesarean system gave an unprecedented freedom to the dependencies, and raised them to a civil equality which put an end to the dominion of race over race and of class over class. The monarchy was hailed as a refuge from the pride and cupidity of the Roman people; and the love of equality, the hatred of nobility, and the tolerance of despotism implanted by Rome became, at least in Gaul, the chief feature of the national character. But among the nations whose vitality had been broken down by the stern republic, not one retained the materials necessary to enjoy independence, or to develop a new history. The political faculty which organizes states and finds society in a moral order was exhausted, and the Christian doctors looked in vain over the waste of ruins for a people by whose aid the Church might survive the decay of Rome. A new element of national life was brought to that declining world by the enemies who destroyed it. The flood of barbarians settled over it for a season, and then subsided; and when the landmarks of civilization appeared once more, it was found that the soil had been impregnated with a fertilizing and regenerating influence, and that the inundation had laid the germs of future states and of a new society. The political sense and energy came with the new blood, and was exhibited in the power exercised by the younger race upon the old, and in the establishment of a graduated freedom. Instead of universal equal rights, the actual enjoyment of which is necessarily contingent on, and commensurate with, power, the rights of the people were made dependent on a variety of conditions, the first of which was the distribution of property. Civil society became a classified organism instead of a formless combination of atoms, and the feudal system gradually arose.

Roman Gaul had so thoroughly adopted the ideas of absolute authority and undistinguished equality during the five centuries between Caesar and Clovis, that the people could never be reconciled to the new system. Feudalism remained a foreign importation, and the feudal aristocracy an alien race, and the common people of France sought protection against both in the Roman jurisprudence and the power of the crown. The development of absolute monarchy by the help of democracy is the one constant character of French history. The royal power, feudal at first, and limited by the immunities and the great vassals, became more popular as it grew more absolute; while the suppression of aristocracy, the removal of the intermediate authorities, was so particularly the object of the nation, that it was more energetically accomplished after the fall of the throne. The monarchy which had been engaged from the thirteenth century in curbing the nobles, was at last thrust aside by the democracy, because it was too dilatory in the work, and was unable to deny its own origin and effectually ruin the class from which it sprang. All those things which constitute the peculiar character of the French Revolution – the demand for equality, the hatred of nobility and feudalism, and of the Church which was connected with them, the constant reference to pagan examples, the suppression of monarchy, the new code of law, the breach with tradition, and the substitution of an ideal system for everything that had proceeded from the mixture and mutual action of the races – all these exhibit the common type of a reaction against the effects of the Frankish invasion. The hatred of royalty was less than the hatred of aristocracy; privileges were more detested than tyranny; and the king perished because of the origin of his authority rather than because of its abuse. Monarchy unconnected with aristocracy became popular in France, even when most uncontrolled; whilst the attempt to reconstitute the throne, and to limit and fence it with its peers, broke down because the old Teutonic elements on which it relied – hereditary nobility, primogeniture, and privilege – were no longer tolerated. The substance of the ideas of 1789 is not the limitation of the sovereign power, but the abrogation of intermediate powers. These powers, and the classes which enjoyed them, come in Latin Europe from a barbarian origin; and the movement which calls itself liberal is essentially national. If liberty were its object, its means would be the establishment of great independent authorities not derived from the State, and its model would be England. But its object is equality; and it seeks, like France in 1789, to cast out the elements of inequality which were introduced by the Teutonic race. This is the object which Italy and Spain have had in common with France, and herein consists the natural league of the Latin nations.

This national element in the movement was not understood by the revolutionary leaders. At first, their doctrine appeared entirely contrary to the idea of nationality. They taught that certain general principles of government were absolutely right in all States; and they asserted in theory the unrestricted freedom of the individual, and the supremacy of the will over every external necessity or obligation. This in apparent contradiction to the national theory, that certain natural forces ought to determine the character, the form, and the policy of the State, by which a kind of fate is put in the place of freedom. Accordingly the national sentiment was not developed directly out of the revolution in which it was involved, but was exhibited first in resistance to it, when the attempt to emancipate had been absorbed in the desire to subjugate, and the republic had been succeeded by the empire. Napoleon called a new power into existence by attacking nationality in Russia, by delivering it in Italy, by governing in defiance of it in Germany and Spain. The sovereigns of these countries were deposed or degraded; and a system of administration was introduced which was French in its origin, its spirit, and its instruments. The people resisted the change. The movement against it was popular and spontaneous, because the rulers were absent or helpless; and it was national, because it was directed against foreign institutions. In Tyrol, in Spain, and afterwards in Prussia, the people did not receive the impulse from the government, but undertook of their own accord to cast out the armies and the ideas of revolutionized France. Men were made conscious of the national element of the revolution by its conquests, not in its rise. The three things which the Empire most openly oppressed – religion, national independence, and political liberty – united in a short-lived league to animate the great uprising by which Napoleon fell. Under the influence of that memorable alliance a political spirit was called forth on the Continent, which clung to freedom and abhorred revolution, and sought to restore, to develop, and to reform the decayed national institutions. The men who proclaimed these ideas, Stein and Görres, Humboldt, Müller, and de Maistre, were as hostile to Bonapartism as to the absolutism of the old governments, and insisted on the national rights, which had been invaded equally by both, and which they hoped to restore by the destruction of the French supremacy. With the cause that triumphed at Waterloo the friends of the Revolution had no sympathy, for they had learned to identify their doctrine with the cause of France. The Holland House Whigs in England, the Afrancesados in Spain, the Muratists in Italy, and the partisans of the Confederation of the Rhine, merging patriotism in their revolutionary affections, regretted the fall of the French power, and looked with alarm at those new and unknown forces which the War of Deliverance had evoked, and which were as menacing to French liberalism as to French supremacy.

But the new aspirations for national and popular rights were crushed at the restoration. The liberals of those days cared for freedom, not in the shape of national independence, but of French institutions; and they combined against the nations with the ambition of the governments. They were as ready to sacrifice nationality to their ideal as the Holy Alliance was to the interests of absolutism. Talleyrand indeed declared at Vienna that the Polish question ought to have precedence over all other questions, because the partition of Poland had been one of the first and greatest causes of the evils which Europe had suffered; but dynastic interests prevailed. All the sovereigns represented at Vienna recovered their dominions, except the King of Saxony, who was punished for his fidelity to Napoleon; but the States that were unrepresented in the reigning families – Poland, Venice, and Genoa – were not revived, and even the Pope had great difficulty in recovering the Legations from the grasp of Austria. Nationality, which the old regime had ignored, which had been outraged by the revolution and the empire, received, after its first open demonstration, the hardest blow at the Congress of Vienna. The principle which the first partition had generated, to which the revolution had given a basis of theory, which had been lashed by the empire into a momentary convulsive effort, was matured by the long error of the restoration into a consistent doctrine, nourished and justified by the situation of Europe.

The governments of the Holy Alliance devoted themselves to suppress with equal care the revolutionary spirit by which they had been threatened, and the national spirit by which they had been restored. Austria, which owed nothing to the national movement, and had prevented its revival after 1809, naturally took the lead in repressing it. Every disturbance of the final settlements of 1815, every aspiration for changes or reforms, was condemned as sedition. This system repressed the good with the evil tendencies of the age; and the resistance which it provoked, during the generation that passed away from the restoration to the fall of Metternich, and again under the reaction which commenced with Schwarzenberg and ended with the administrations of Bach and Manteuffel, proceeded from various combinations of the opposite forms of liberalism. In the successive phases of that struggle, the idea that national claims are above all other rights gradually rose to the supremacy which it now possesses among the revolutionary agencies.

The first liberal movement, that of the Carbonari in the south of Europe, had no specific national character, but was supported by the Bonapartists both in Spain and Italy. In the following years the opposite ideas of 1813 came to the front, and a revolutionary movement, in many respects hostile to the principles of revolution, began in defence of liberty, religion, and nationality. All these causes were united in the Irish agitation, and in the Greek, Belgian, and Polish revolutionists. Those sentiments which had been insulted by Napoleon, and had risen against him, rose against the governments of the restoration. They had been oppressed by the sword, and then by the treaties. The national principle added force, but not justice, to this movement, which, in every case but Poland, was successful. A period followed in which it degenerated into a purely national idea, as the agitation for repeal succeeded emancipation, and Panslavism and Panhellenism arose under the auspices of the Eastern Church. This was the third phase of the resistance to the settlement of Vienna, which was weak, because it failed to satisfy national or constitutional aspirations, either of which would have been a safeguard against the other, by a moral if not by a popular justification. At first, in 1813, the people rose against their conquerors, in defence of their legitimate rulers. They refused to be governed by usurpers. In the period between 1825 and 1831, they resolved that they would not be misgoverned by strangers. The French administration was often better than that which it displaced, but there were prior claimants for the authority exercised by the French, and at first the national contest was a contest for legitimacy. In the second period this element was wanting. No dispossessed princes led the Greeks, the Belgians, or the Poles. The Turks, the Dutch, and the Russians were attacked, not as usurpers, but as oppressors – because they misgoverned, not because they were of a different race. Then began a time when the text simply was that nations would not be governed by foreigners. Power legitimately obtained, and exercised with moderation, was declared invalid. National rights, like religion, had borne part in the previous combinations, and had been auxiliaries in the struggles for freedom, but now nationality became a paramount claim, which was to assert itself alone, which might put forward as pretexts the rights of rulers, the liberties of the people, the safety of religion, but which, if no such union could be formed, was to prevail at the expense of every other cause for which nations make sacrifices.

Metternich is, next to Napoleon, the chief promoter of this theory; for the anti-national character of the restoration was most distinct in Austria, and it is in opposition to the Austrian Government that nationality grew into a system. Napoleon, who, trusting to his armies, despised moral forces in politics, was overthrown by their rising. Austria committed the same fault in the government of her Italian provinces. The kingdom of Italy had united all the northern part of the Peninsula in a single State; and the national feelings, which the French repressed elsewhere, were encouraged as a safeguard of their power in Italy and in Poland. When the tide of victory turned, Austria invoked against the French the aid of

the new sentiment they had fostered. Nugent announced, in his pro-
clamation to the Italians, that they should become an independent
nation. The same spirit served different masters, and contributed first to
the destruction of the old States, then to the expulsion of the French, and
again, under Charles Albert, to a new revolution. It was appealed to in the
name of the most contradictory principles of government, and served all
parties in succession, because it was one in which all could unite.
Beginning by a protest against the dominion of race over race, its mildest
and least-developed form, it grew into a condemnation of every State that
included different races, and finally became the complete and consistent
theory that the State and the nation must be co-extensive. 'It is', says Mr
Mill, 'in general a necessary condition of free institutions, that the boundaries of governments should coincide in the main with those of
nationalities.'[2]

The outward historical progress of this idea from an indefinite aspiration to be the keystone of a political system, may be traced in the life of
the man who gave to it the element in which its strength resides –
Giuseppe Mazzini. He found Carbonarism impotent against the measures
of the governments, and resolved to give new life to the liberal movement
by transferring it to the ground of nationality. Exile is the nursery of
nationality, as oppression is the school of liberalism; and Mazzini
conceived the idea of Young Italy when he was a refugee at Marseilles. In
the same way, the Polish exiles are the champions of every national
movement; for to them all political rights are absorbed in the idea of
independence, which, however they may differ with each other, is the one
aspiration common to them all. Towards the year 1830 literature also
contributed to the national idea. 'It was the time', says Mazzini, 'of the
great conflict between the romantic and the classical school, which might
with equal truth be called a conflict between the partisans of freedom
and of authority.' The romantic school was infidel in Italy, and Catholic
in Germany; but in both it had the common effect of encouraging
national history and literature, and Dante was as great an authority with
the Italian democrats as with the leaders of the medieval revival at
Vienna, Munich, and Berlin. But neither the influence of the exiles, nor
that of the poets and critics of the new party, extended over the masses.
It was a sect without popular sympathy or encouragement, a conspiracy
founded not on a grievance, but on a doctrine; and when the attempt to
rise was made in Savoy, in 1834, under a banner with the motto 'Unity,
Independence, God and Humanity', the people were puzzled at its
object, and indifferent to its failure. But Mazzini continued his propaganda, developed his *Giovine Italia* into a *Giovine Europa*, and established
in 1847 the international league of nations. 'The people', he said, in his
opening address, 'is penetrated with only one idea, that of unity and

nationality. . . . There is no international question as to forms of government, but only a national question.'

The revolution of 1848, unsuccessful in its national purpose, prepared
the subsequent victories of nationality in two ways. The first of these was
the restoration of the Austrian power in Italy, with a new and more energetic centralization, which gave no promise of freedom. Whilst that
system prevailed, the right was on the side of the national aspirations, and
they were revived in a more complete and cultivated form by Manin.
The policy of the Austrian Government, which failed during the ten
years of the reaction to convert the tenure by force into a tenure by right,
and to establish with free institutions the condition of allegiance, gave a
negative encouragement to the theory. It deprived Francis Joseph of all
active support and sympathy in 1859, for he was more clearly wrong in his
conduct than his enemies in their doctrines. The real cause of the energy
which the national theory has acquired is, however, the triumph of the
democratic principle in France, and its recognition by the European
Powers. The theory of nationality is involved in the democratic theory of
the sovereignty of the general will. 'One hardly knows what any division
of the human race should be free to do, if not to determine with which
of the various collective bodies of human beings they choose to associate
themselves.'[3] It is by this act that a nation constitutes itself. To have a collective will, unity is necessary, and independence is requisite in order to
assert it. Unity and nationality are still more essential to the notion of the
sovereignty of the people than the cashiering of monarchs, or the re-
vocation of laws. Arbitrary acts of this kind may be prevented by the
happiness of the people or the popularity of the king, but a nation
inspired by the democratic idea cannot with consistency allow a part of
itself to belong to a foreign State, or the whole to be divided into several
native States. The theory of nationality therefore proceeds from both
the principles which divide the political world – from legitimacy, which
ignores its claims, and from the revolution, which assumes them; and for
the same reason it is the chief weapon of the last against the first.

In pursuing the outward and visible growth of the national theory we
are prepared for an examination of its political character and value. The
absolutism which has created it denies equally that absolute right of
national unity which is a product of democracy, and that claim of national
liberty which belongs to the theory of freedom. These two views of
nationality, corresponding to the French and to the English systems, are
connected in name only, and are in reality the opposite extremes of political thought. In one case, nationality is founded on the perpetual
supremacy of the collective will, of which the unity of the nation is the
necessary condition, to which every other influence must defer, and
against which no obligation enjoys authority, and all resistance is

tyrannical. The nation is here an ideal unit founded on the race, in defiance of the modifying action of external causes, of tradition, and of existing rights. It overrules the rights and wishes of the inhabitants, absorbing their divergent interests in a fictitious unity; sacrifices their several inclinations and duties to the higher claim of nationality, and crushes all natural rights and all established liberties for the purpose of vindicating itself. Whenever a single definite object is made the supreme end of the State, be it the advantage of a class, the safety or the power of the country, the greatest happiness of the greatest number, or the support of any speculative idea, the State becomes for the time inevitably absolute. Liberty alone demands for its realization the limitation of the public authority, for liberty is the only object which benefits all alike, and provokes no sincere opposition. In supporting the claims of national unity, governments must be subverted in whose title there is no flaw, and whose policy is beneficent and equitable, and subjects must be compelled to transfer their allegiance to an authority for which they have no attachment, and which may be practically a foreign domination. Connected with this theory in nothing except in the common enmity of the absolute state, is the theory which represents nationality as an essential, but not a supreme, element in determining the forms of the State. It is distinguished from the other, because it tends to diversity and not to uniformity, to harmony and not to unity; because it aims not at an arbitrary change, but at careful respect for the existing conditions of political life, and because it obeys the laws and results of history, not the aspirations of an ideal future. While the theory of unity makes the nation a source of despotism and revolution, the theory of liberty regards it as the bulwark of self-government, and the foremost limit to the excessive power of the State. Private rights, which are sacrificed to the unity, are preserved by the union of nations. No power can so efficiently resist the tendencies of centralization, of corruption, and of absolutism, as that community which is the vastest that can be included in a State, which imposes on its members a consistent similarity of character, interest, and opinion, and which arrests the action of the sovereign by the influence of a divided patriotism. The presence of different nations under the same sovereignty is similar in its effect to the independence of the Church in the State. It provides against the servility which flourishes under the shadow of a single authority, by balancing interests, multiplying associations, and giving to the subject the restraint and support of a combined opinion. In the same way it promotes independence by forming definite groups of public opinion, and by affording a great source and centre of political sentiments, and of notions of duty not derived from the sovereign will. Liberty provokes diversity, and diversity preserves liberty by supplying the means of organization. All those portions of law which govern the relations of men with each other, and regulate social life, are the varying result of national custom and the creation of private society. In these things, therefore, the several nations will differ from each other; for they themselves have produced them, and they do not owe them to the State which rules them all. This diversity in the same State is a firm barrier against the intrusion of the government beyond the political sphere, which is common to all, into the social department, which escapes legislation and is ruled by spontaneous laws. This sort of interference is characteristic of an absolute government, and is sure to provoke a reaction, and finally a remedy. That intolerance of social freedom which is natural to absolutism is sure to find a corrective in the national diversities, which no other force could so efficiently provide. The co-existence of several nations under the same State is a test, as well as the best security of its freedom. It is also one of the chief instruments of civilization; and, as such, it is in the natural and providential order, and indicates a state of greater advancement than the national unity which is the ideal of modern liberalism. The combination of different nations in one State is as necessary a condition of civilized life as the combination of men in society. Inferior races are raised by living in political union with races intellectually superior. Exhausted and decaying nations are revived by the contact of a younger vitality. Nations in which the elements of organization and the capacity for government have been lost, either through the demoralizing influence of despotism, or the disintegrating action of democracy, are restored and educated anew under the discipline of a stronger and less corrupted race. This fertilizing and regenerating process can only be obtained by living under one government. It is in the cauldron of the State that the fusion takes place by which the vigour, the knowledge, and the capacity of one portion of mankind may be communicated to another. Where political and national boundaries coincide, society ceases to advance, and nations relapse into a condition corresponding to that of men who renounce intercourse with their fellow-men. The difference between the two unites mankind not only by the benefits it confers on those who live together, but because it connects society either by a political or a national bond, gives to every people an interest in its neighbours, either because they are under the same government or because they are of the same race, and thus promotes the interests of humanity, of civilization, and of religion.

Christianity rejoices at the mixture of races, as paganism identifies itself with their differences, because truth is universal, and errors various and particular. In the ancient world idolatry and nationality went together, and the same term is applied in Scripture to both. It was the mission of the Church to overcome national differences. The period of her undisputed supremacy was that in which all Western Europe obeyed the same laws, all literature was contained in one language, and the political unit of Christendom was personified in a single potentate, while its intellectual unity was represented in one university. As the ancient Romans concluded their conquests by carrying away the gods of the conquered people, Charlemagne overcame the national resistance of the Saxons only by the forcible destruction of their pagan rites. Out of the medieval period, and the combined action of the German race and the Church, came forth a new system of nations and a new conception of nationality. Nature was overcome in the nation as well as in the individual. In pagan and uncultivated times, nations were distinguished from each other by the widest diversity, not only in religion, but in customs, language, and character. Under the new law they had many things in common; the old barriers which separated them were removed, and the new principle of self-government, which Christianity imposed, enabled them to live together under the same authority, without necessarily losing their cherished habits, their customs, or their laws. The new idea of freedom made room for different races in one State. A nation was no longer what it had been to the ancient world – the progeny of a common ancestor, or the aboriginal product of a particular region, a result of merely physical and material causes – but a moral and political being; not the creation of geographical or physiological unity, but developed in the course of history by the action of the State. It is derived from the State, not supreme over it. A State may in course of time produce a nationality; but that a nationality should constitute a State is contrary to the nature of modern civilization. The nation derives its rights and its power from the memory of a former independence.

The Church has agreed in this respect with the tendency of political progress, and discouraged wherever she could the isolation of nations; admonishing them of their duties to each other, and regarding conquest and feudal investiture as the natural means of raising barbarous or sunken nations to a higher level. But though she has never attributed to national independence an immunity from the accidental consequences of feudal law, of hereditary claims, or of testamentary arrangements, she defends national liberty against uniformity and centralization with an energy inspired by perfect community of interests. For the same enemy threatens both; and the State which is reluctant to tolerate differences, and to do justice to the peculiar character of various races, must from the same cause interfere in the internal government of religion. The connection of religious liberty with the emancipation of Poland or Ireland is not merely the accidental result of local causes; and the failure of the Concordat to unite the subjects of Austria is the natural consequence of a policy which did not desire to protect the provinces in their diversity and autonomy, and sought to bribe the Church by favours instead of strengthening her by independence. From this influence of religion in modern history has proceeded a new definition of patriotism.

The difference between nationality and the State is exhibited in the nature of patriotic attachment. Our connection with the race is merely natural or physical, whilst our duties to the political nation are ethical. One is a community of affections and instincts infinitely important and powerful in savage life, but pertaining more to the animal than to the civilized man; the other is an authority governing by laws, imposing obligations, and giving a moral sanction and character to the natural relations of society. Patriotism is in political life what faith is in religion, and it stands to the domestic feelings and to homesickness as faith to fanaticism and to superstition. It has one aspect derived from private life and nature, for it is an extension of the family affections, as the tribe is an extension of the family. But in its real political character, patriotism consists in the development of the instinct of self-preservation into a moral duty which may involve self-sacrifice. Self-preservation is both an instinct and a duty, natural and involuntary in one respect, and at the same time a moral obligation. By the first it produces the family; by the last the State. If the nation could exist without the State, subject only to the instinct of self-preservation, it would be incapable of denying, controlling, or sacrificing itself; it would be an end and a rule to itself. But in the political order moral purposes are realized and public ends are pursued to which private interests and even existence must be sacrificed. The great sign of true patriotism, the development of selfishness into sacrifice, is the product of political life. That sense of duty which is supplied by race is not entirely separated from its selfish and instinctive basis; and the love of country, like married love, stands at the same time on a material and a moral foundation. The patriot must distinguish between the two causes or objects of his devotion. The attachment which is given only to the country is like obedience given only to the State – a submission to physical influences. The man who prefers his country before every other duty shows the same spirit as the man who surrenders every right to the State. They both deny that right is superior to authority.

There is a moral and political country, in the language of Burke, distinct from the geographical, which may be possibly in collision with it. The Frenchmen who bore arms against the Convention were as patriotic as the Englishmen who bore arms against King Charles, for they recognized a higher duty than that of obedience to the actual sovereign. 'In an address to France,' said Burke,

> in an attempt to treat with it, or in considering any scheme at all relative to it, it is impossible we should mean the geographical, we must always mean the moral and political, country. . . . The truth is, that France is out of itself – the

moral France is separated from the geographical. The master of the house is expelled, and the robbers are in possession. If we look for the corporate people of France, existing as a corporate in the eye and intention of public law (that corporate people, I mean, who are free to deliberate and to decide, and who have a capacity to treat and conclude), they are in Flanders and Germany, in Switzerland, Spain, Italy, and England. There are all the princes of the blood, there are all the orders of the State, there are all the parliaments of the kingdom. . . . I am sure that if half that number of the same description were taken out of this country, it would leave hardly anything that I should call the people of England.[4]

Rousseau draws nearly the same distinction between the country to which we happen to belong and that which fulfils towards us the political functions of the State. In the *Émile* he has a sentence of which it is not easy in a translation to convey the point: 'Qui n'a pas une patrie a du moins un pays.' And in his tract on Political Economy he writes: 'How shall men love their country if it is nothing more for them than for strangers, and bestows on them only that which it can refuse to none?' It is in the same sense he says, further on, 'La patrie ne peut subsister sans la liberté.'

The nationality formed by the State, then, is the only one to which we owe political duties, and it is, therefore, the only one which has political rights. The Swiss are ethnologically either French, Italian, or German; but no nationality has the slightest claim upon them, except the purely political nationality of Switzerland. The Tuscan or the Neapolitan State has formed a nationality, but the citizens of Florence and of Naples have no political community with each other. There are other States which have neither succeeded in absorbing distinct races in a political nationality, nor in separating a particular district from a larger nation. Austria and Mexico are instances on the one hand, Parma and Baden on the other. The progress of civilization deals hardly with the last description of States. In order to maintain their integrity they must attach themselves by confederations, or family alliances, to greater powers, and thus lose something of their independence. Their tendency is to isolate and shut off their inhabitants, to narrow the horizon of their views, and to dwarf in some degree the proportions of their ideas. Public opinion cannot maintain its liberty and purity in such small dimensions, and the currents that come from larger communities sweep over a contracted territory. In a small and homogeneous population there is hardly room for a natural classification of society, or for inner groups of interests that set bounds to sovereign power. The government and the subjects contend with borrowed weapons. The resources of the one and the aspirations of the other are derived from some external source, and the consequence is that the country becomes the instrument and the scene of contests in which it is not interested. These States, like the minuter communities of the Middle Ages, serve a purpose, by constituting partitions and securities of self-government in the larger States; but they are impediments to the progress of society, which depends on the mixture of races under the same governments.

The vanity and peril of national claims founded on no political tradition, but on race alone, appear in Mexico. There the races are divided by blood, without being grouped together in different regions. It is, therefore, neither possible to unite them nor to convert them into the elements of an organized State. They are fluid, shapeless, and unconnected, and cannot be precipitated, or formed into the basis of political institutions. As they cannot be used by the State, they cannot be recognized by it; and their peculiar qualities, capabilities, passions, and attachments are of no service, and therefore obtain no regard. They are necessarily ignored, and are therefore perpetually outraged. From this difficulty of races with political pretensions, but without political position, the Eastern world escaped by the institution of castes. Where there are only two races there is the resource of slavery; but when different races inhabit the different territories of one empire composed of several smaller States, it is of all possible combinations the most favourable to the establishment of a highly developed system of freedom. In Austria there are two circumstances which add to the difficulty of the problem, but also increase its importance. The several nationalities are at very unequal degrees of advancement, and there is no single nation which is so predominant as to overwhelm or absorb the others. These are the conditions necessary for the very highest degree of organization which government is capable of receiving. They supply the greatest variety of intellectual resource; the perpetual incentive to progress which is afforded not merely by competition, but by the spectacle of a more advanced people; the most abundant elements of self-government, combined with the impossibility for the State to rule all by its own will; and the fullest security for the preservation of local customs and ancient rights. In such a country as this, liberty would achieve its most glorious results, while centralization and absolutism would be destruction.

The problem presented to the government of Austria is higher than that which is solved in England, because of the necessity of admitting the national claims. The parliamentary system fails to provide for them, as it presupposes the unity of the people. Hence in those countries in which different races dwell together, it has not satisfied their desires, and is regarded as an imperfect form of freedom. It brings out more clearly than before the differences it does not recognize, and thus continues the work of the old absolutism, and appears as a new phase of centralization. In those countries, therefore, the power of the imperial parliament must be limited as jealously as the power of the crown, and many of its functions must be discharged by provincial diets, and a descending series of local authorities.

The great importance of nationality in the State consists in the fact that it is the basis of political capacity. The character of a nation determines in great measure the form and vitality of the State. Certain political habits and ideas belong to particular nations, and they vary with the course of the national history. A people just emerging from barbarism, a people effete from the excesses of a luxurious civilization, cannot possess the means of governing itself; a people devoted to equality, or to absolute monarchy, is incapable of producing an aristocracy; a people averse to the institution of private property is without the first element of freedom. Each of these can be converted into efficient members of a free community only by the contact of a superior race, in whose power will lie the future prospects of the State. A system which ignores these things, and does not rely for its support on the character and aptitude of the people, does not intend that they should administer their own affairs, but that they should simply be obedient to the supreme command. The denial of nationality, therefore, implies the denial of political liberty.

The greatest adversary of the rights of nationality is the modern theory of nationality. By making the State and the nation commensurate with each other in theory, it reduces practically to a subject condition all other nationalities that may be within the boundary. It cannot admit them to an equality with the ruling nation which constitutes the State, because the State would then cease to be national, which would be a contradiction of the principle of its existence. According, therefore, to the degree of humanity and civilization in that dominant body which claims all the rights of the community, the inferior races are exterminated, or reduced to servitude, or outlawed, or put in a condition of dependence.

If we take the establishment of liberty for the realization of moral duties to be the end of civil society, we must conclude that those states are substantially the most perfect which, like the British and Austrian Empires, include various distinct nationalities without oppressing them. Those in which no mixture of races has occurred are imperfect; and those in which its effects have disappeared are decrepit. A State which is incompetent to satisfy different races condemns itself; a State which labours to neutralize, to absorb, or to expel them, destroys its own vitality; a State which does not include them is destitute of the chief basis of self-government. The theory of nationality, therefore, is a retrograde step in history. It is the most advanced form of the revolution, and must retain its power to the end of the revolutionary period, of which it announces the approach. Its great historical importance depends on two chief causes.

First, it is a chimera. The settlement at which it aims is impossible. As it can never be satisfied and exhausted, and always continues to assert itself, it prevents the government from ever relapsing into the condition which provoked its rise. The danger is too threatening, and the power over men's minds too great, to allow any system to endure which justifies the resistance of nationality. It must contribute, therefore, to obtain that which in theory it condemns – the liberty of different nationalities as members of one sovereign community. This is a service which no other force could accomplish; for it is a corrective alike of absolute monarchy, of democracy, and of constitutionalism, as well as of the centralization which is common to all three. Neither the monarchical nor the revolutionary, nor the parliamentary system can do this; and all the ideas which have excited enthusiasm in past times are impotent for the purpose except nationality alone.

And secondly, the national theory marks the end of the revolutionary doctrine and its logical exhaustion. In proclaiming the supremacy of the rights of nationality, the system of democratic equality goes beyond its own extreme boundary, and falls into contradiction with itself. Between the democratic and the national phase of the revolution, socialism had intervened, and had already carried the consequences of the principle to an absurdity. But that phase was passed. The revolution survived its offspring, and produced another further result. Nationality is more advanced than socialism, because it is a more arbitrary system. The social theory endeavours to provide for the existence of the individual beneath the terrible burdens which modern society heaps upon labour. It is not merely a development of the notion of equality, but a refuge from real misery and starvation. However false the solution, it was a reasonable demand that the poor should be saved from destruction; and if the freedom of the State was sacrificed to the safety of the individual, the more immediate object was, at least in theory, attained. But nationality does not aim either at liberty or prosperity, both of which it sacrifices to the imperative necessity of making the nation the mould and measure of the State. Its course will be marked with material as well as moral ruin, in order that a new invention may prevail over the works of God and the interests of mankind. There is no principle of change, no phase of political speculation conceivable, more comprehensive, more subversive, or more arbitrary than this. It is a confutation of democracy, because it sets limits to the exercise of the popular will, and substitutes for it a higher principle. It prevents not only the division, but the extension of the State, and forbids to terminate war by conquest, and to obtain a security for peace. Thus, after surrendering the individual to the collective will, the revolutionary system makes the collective will subject to conditions which are independent of it, and rejects all law, only to be controlled by an accident.

Although, therefore, the theory of nationality is more absurd and

more criminal than the theory of socialism, it has an important mission
in the world, and marks the final conflict, and therefore the end, of two
forces which are the worst enemies of civil freedom – the absolute monarchy and the revolution.

Notes

1. Edmund Burke, 'Observations on the Conduct of the Minority', *Selected Works*, vol. V,
p. 112.
2. J.S. Mill, *Considerations on Representative Government*, London 1861, p. 298.
3. Ibid., p. 296.
4. Edmund Burke, 'Remarks on the Policy of the Allies', *Selected Works*, vol. V, pp. 26,
29, 30.

The Nation
Otto Bauer

The Nation

National Character

Up till now science has left the nation almost exclusively to poets, journalists, and speakers at public meetings, in parliament and at the *bierkeller*. In a time of great national struggles, we have scarcely seen even the first approaches to a satisfactory theory of the essence of the nation. Yet such a theory is certainly needed. National ideology and national romanticism affect us all, and few of us can pronounce the word national in German without giving it a remarkably emotional tone. Whoever wants to understand and criticize national ideology cannot avoid the question of the essence of the nation.

Bagehot says that the nation is one of those many phenomena that we understand so long as we are not asked, but that we cannot explain in brief and succinct terms.[1] But science cannot rest content with an answer of this kind; it cannot abandon the question of the concept of the nation if it wants to speak of it. And this question is not so easily answered as may appear at first. Is the nation a community of people of the same descent? But the Italians are descended from Etruscans, Romans, Celts, Teutons, Greeks and Saracens, the French of today from Gauls, Romans, Britons and Teutons, and the Germans from Teutons, Celts and Slavs. Is it a common language that unites people into a nation? But English and Irish, Danes and Norwegians, Serbs and Croats speak in each case the same language yet are not on that account a single people. The Jews, on the other hand, have no common language yet are a nation. Is it consciousness of common membership that makes up the nation? But the Tyrolean peasant would then be no German, as he has never been conscious of belonging together with the East Prussians and Pomeranians, Thuringians and Alsatians. What exactly is it that the Germans are conscious of when they remember their Germanness? What makes them members of the German nation, belonging together with other Germans? An objective criterion for this togetherness must certainly first be present, before one can become conscious of it.

The question of the nation can only be approached from the concept of national character. Let us provisionally define national character as the complex of physical and mental characteristics that distinguishes one nation from others; beyond this, all peoples have those common characteristics that we mutually acknowledge as human, while on the other hand the particular classes, professions and individuals of each nation have individual properties, special characteristics, that distinguish them from one another. But it is clear that the average German is different from the average Englishman, no matter how much they may have in common as individuals, as members of the same class or the same profession; just as each English person shares a set of characteristics with another, no matter how separated they may be by individual or social differences. For the person who denies this, the nation is nothing; does the Englishman who lives in Berlin and speaks German thereby become a German?

It is no objection to the concept of national character that the differences of nations may be explained from the differences of their destinies, their struggle for existence, their social composition, as for example Kautsky seeks to explain the stubbornness and toughness of the Russians by the fact that the mass of the Russian people consists of peasants, and agriculture everywhere produces clumsy, but tough and stubborn natures.[2] This is not to deny the existence of a specifically Russian national character; it rather seeks to explain the national peculiarities of the Russians.

If many people hasten to explain the origin of national character yet are not prepared to dwell for a moment on this character itself, this is due to the misuse that is made of the concept.

First of all, national character is wrongly ascribed a persistence that the course of history serves to refute; it cannot be denied that the Teutons of Tacitus's time possessed a set of common characteristics that distinguished them from other peoples, such as the Romans, and as little can it be denied that the Germans of our time share certain traits of character that differ from other peoples, however these features may have arisen. But no one with any learning can deny on this account that the German of today has far more in common with the other civilized nations of his time than he has with the Teutons of Tacitus.

National character is changeable. The members of a nation are linked by a community of character in a certain definite era; in no way is the nation of our time linked with its ancestors of two or three millennia ago. When we speak of a German national character, we mean the common features of the Germans of a particular century or decade.

It has wrongly often been overlooked that as well as common national character there are a whole series of other commonalities of character, of which those of class and profession are by far the most important. The German worker shares certain features with any other German, and this joins the Germans in a national community of character. But the German worker has features in common with his fellow class members of all other nations, making him a member of the international character community of class. The German writer undoubtedly shares certain common character traits with the writers of all other peoples, thereby belonging to an international professional community.

It would be an idle question to ask whether class gives rise to a more intensive community of character than does nation, or vice versa. There is no objective standard that could measure the intensity of such communities.[3]

But the concept of national character is still more compromised by the way uncritical thought has held that it can explain a particular way of acting from national character itself, as for example the belief that the rapid change of constitution in France is explicable because the French, like their Gallic ancestors, are always 'seeking new things', as Caesar maintained.

The nation has a national character. But this national character only means a relative commonality of traits in the mode of behaviour of particular individuals; it is not an explanation of these individual modes of behaviour. National character is not an explanation, it is something to be explained. In establishing the variation of national character, science has not solved the problem of the nation, but simply posed it. How that relative community of character arises, how it happens that all members of a nation, for all their individual differences, still coincide in a series of features, and for all their physical and mental identity with other people still differ from the members of other nations – this is precisely what science has to grasp.

This task of causal explanation of the relative community of character among members of a nation is not solved but only bypassed if the actions of a nation and its members are explained in terms of a mysterious *Volksgeist* or soul of the people. National spirit is an old favourite of the Romantics. The historical school of law introduced it into science. It teaches that the national spirit produces in individuals a common conviction of justice, which is either in itself already law, or else the power that makes law.[4] It was subsequently believed that not only law, but all

actions and destinies of the nation could be understood as the manifestation or embodiment of the national spirit. A unique national spirit, a
national soul, is the substrate or substance of the nation, that which per-
sists through all change, the unity in all individual variety; individuals are
simply *modi*, mere phenomenal forms of this spiritual substance.[5] It is
clear that this national spiritualism is also based on mistaken thinking.

National spirit cannot explain the community of national character,
since it itself is nothing but national character transformed into a metaphysical being, into a spectre. National character itself, however, as we
already know, is no explanation of the mode of behaviour of any individual, but only the knowledge of relative similarity of behaviour of fellow
nationals at a definite period of time. It is no explanation; it rather
requires explanation. And this, the explanation of the community of
national character, is the task of science.

Natural Community and Cultural Community

The sharp demarcation of national individualities could never be understood in terms of natural community alone. For every natural community
is governed by the tendency of progressive differentiation. Moritz Wagner
has pointed out how spatial separation leads to the origin of new species.
Now the Germanic tribes are certainly descended from a common ancestral stock. The descendants of this ancestral people, however, spread
themselves over a wide area by migration. The conditions of life under
which the particular tribes lived became quite diverse – different for the
Alpine dwellers than for those of the plains, different for the inhabitants
of the Bohemian mountain fringe than for those of the coast. The different conditions of life then produced in the tribes different particular
characters. These differences were not levelled out, as spatial separation
prevented intermarriage betwen the different tribes. In this way the different tribes necessarily developed into different peoples, whose
inherited peculiarities were eventually quite distinct. As in ancient times
the Celts, Teutons and Slavs arose from a common ancestral stock, so the
Germanic people necessarily split up into a number of independent
peoples, and these too were immediately subject to the process of differentiation, in turn dividing over the centuries into various branches
completely different from one another. History, however, shows that this
process of differentiation was countered by an opposite process of unification. Thus the Germans of today are a nation in a quite different
sense from in the Middle Ages. The Germans of the Baltic coast are
today far more connected with the Germans of the Alps than they were in
the fourteenth century. The unification of the tribes into a people cannot
be conceived in terms of the natural facts of heredity, which can only

explain the division of one people into segments, and never the creation of a nation from different tribes; this unification can only be conceived in terms of the effective influences of common culture. We will discuss in more detail below the rise of a uniform nation out of tribes which live in diverse conditions of existence and are not linked by intermarriage.

If, therefore, the nation is considered on the one hand as a natural community, on the other hand as a community of culture, this is still not to focus on the various causes that determine national character. Human character is never explained by anything other than human destiny; national character is never anything but the precipitate of a nation's history. The conditions under which human beings produce their subsistence and distribute the product of their labour determine the destiny of each people; on the foundation of a definite mode of production and distribution a specific mental culture also arises. The history of a people as determined in this way then has a double effect on its descendants: on the one hand, by the cultivation of definite physical properties through the struggle for existence and the transmission of these properties to descendants by natural heredity; on the other, by the production of particular cultural values and their transmission to descendants by upbringing, by custom and law, by the effect of communication between people.

If we turn now to consider the nation as a cultural community, that is, to show how national character is determined by the common cultural values transmitted from earlier generations, we stand on a much firmer basis than if we seek to explain the rise of this community of character from the natural inheritance of physical properties. For if in the one case we are confined to relatively few firm observations, and for the rest have to resort to hypotheses, in the other case we stand on the firm ground of human history.

Modern Capitalism and the National Cultural Community

The abolition of feudal law removed all the obstacles that had formerly blocked the operation of capitalist forces on the rural population. In the meantime, however, these powers had undergone a change of nature, their force of attack strengthened by the change in the productive forces they could make use of. From cooperation, the simple combination of labourers performing similar work, from the manufacturing workshop based on division of labour among craftsmen, the capitalist enterprise had advanced to the factory, with the machine at its service. The spinning jenny, the mechanical loom and the steam engine became tools of industrial capital. Equipped with these new weapons, capital now set out right away to revolutionize all social relations across the country.

All these tremendous changes brought about, on the one hand, a completely new spatial and professional distribution of the population, and, on the other, a fundamental change in the economic position of the peasantry and hence in their psychology. The peasant's son no longer has a place on the land; his father can no longer use him in autumn to thresh the corn, for the corn is now threshed on the harvest field by the steam thresher; he can no longer set him to work at the loom in winter, for the mechanical loom has put an end to this old domestic industry; so the peasant's son leaves the land and moves to the great regions of industry. The agricultural population does not increase, but the number of those in industry and commerce grows all the more quickly. Tremendous numbers of people gather in the big cities, in the great industrial zones. Those peasants who are left on the land, however, are confined purely to farming. They no longer consume the products of their own labour, but produce for the market and with the money they receive buy those industrial products that they need.

Do we need to explain what all this means for the cultural community of the nation? The rural population is uprooted by capitalism, torn away from the soil to which it had been tied since the people first settled, torn from the narrow limits of the village bounds. Their sons move into the town, where the population is drawn from far-flung parts of the country, mutually influencing one another and mixing their blood, where in place of the old traditions, the monotony of the old peasant life endlessly recurring with the change of seasons, they encounter the vivaciously pulsing life of the metropolis, which destroys all traditional views – a new and ever-changing world. They are thrown hither and thither with the ups and downs of the trade cycle. What a difference between the modern metal worker, for example, working today for an iron magnate on the Rhine and tomorrow being dispatched to Silesia by a wave of industrial migration, who weds in Saxony and brings up his children in Berlin, and his grandfather, who spent his life from birth to death in a remote Alpine village, saw the local town maybe twice a year when there was an annual fair or a big church festival, and did not even know the peasants in the next village, as a mountain range made communication difficult between the two.

These psychological transformations which capitalist development has produced have changed our entire education system, while they in turn would not have been possible without the development of this system in the first place. Education has become a necessary instrument of modern development: modern capitalism needed a higher level of popular training, as without this the complicated administration of large-scale business would be impossible; the modern peasant needed education, if he was to develop into a modern farmer; the modern state needed it, if it was to create local administration and the modern army. The nineteenth century thus saw an imposing development of basic education. We need not dwell on what it means for the community of national culture if the school reader gives the child of the East Prussian worker and the child of the Tyrolean peasant the same elements of education, the same fragments of our mental culture, in the same uniform German language.

What school begins, the army continues. The conscription system had to reach its logical conclusion in universal military service. The modern army was born on the battlefields on which the French Revolution defeated the absolutist powers of the old Europe – a people's army at least in its composition, if not yet in its organization and aim. Military service tears the peasant's son away from the narrow realm of the village, brings him together with companions from the town and from other parts of the country, exposes him to the influence of the population of the garrison town. In this way the military revolutionizes people's minds quite against all intention. It is no coincidence that in Gerhart Hauptmann's *Die Weber* ('The Weavers', 1892) the man who kindles the flickering spark of rebellion into a flame is a soldier just returned home from the city.

And the effect that school has on the child and military service on the youth is completed by that democracy has on the grown man. Freedom of association, of assembly and of the press becomes the means of bringing the great questions of the day into every peasant village and every workshop, making the great affairs of the world into a particular fate and effective cultural influence for each individual man. Universal suffrage, which calls all to take part in decision, forces the parties to struggle to the last man, and in their political slogans all the great achievements of our whole history, our whole civilization, wrestle for each peasant and each worker; each speech in the assembly, each page of the newspaper, brings a piece of our mental culture to the last voter. No matter how different in origin, wealth, profession or political views, they are all embraced in a cultural community, because all are subject – the object of all parties' struggles – to similar cultural influences, and in the individuality of each single person the similar cultural influences become effective and are hardened into character.

But of all the historical movements that produce the modern nation of the capitalist age, by far the most important is the workers' movement. Its direct effect alone is immense. It is this that has achieved by its struggle a reduction of the working day at least sufficient for a part of our national culture to reach the workers, that has raised workers' wages to a level at which utter physical and mental impoverishment does not completely exclude them from the cultural community of the nation. It has done more: by awakening fear in the owning classes threatened by socialism, it has forced these into struggle. The bourgeois and even the *junker* must seek to have an effect on the masses. They too seek to organize workers for their own ends, to unite artisans and peasants for a struggle against the working class. The struggle over the great question of property thus rages through the whole of society, a battle for every single man. Books, associations and newspapers convey the arguments of all political parties to each individual member of the people. No matter in how diluted a form, through the struggle of parties a fragment of the flow of our culture permeates to each individual, becomes effective in his character, and unites us all into a cultural community composed by similar cultural influences.

The Teutons in the age of Caesar were a cultural community: but this ancient community broke up with the settlement of the nation that went with the transition to agriculture. In place of the national community, locally tied communities emerged: sharply different from place to place, valley to valley. Only the ruling and owning classes were still united into a nation by higher culture. Modern capitalism, however, for the first time, has again produced a truly national culture of the whole people, which oversteps the narrow limits of the village bounds. It has brought this about by uprooting the population, severing their local connections, and redistributing them by place and occupation in the process of form-ing modern classes and professions. It has achieved this by means of democracy, which is its creation, by popular education, universal military service and equal suffrage.

The development of the productive forces signals a powerful rise in the productivity of human labour. But only a small part of the growing wealth that stems from this work comes into the possession of the masses that create it. Property in the means of labour has become an instrument for drawing off a large part of the ever-increasing wealth. Only in one part of the working day does the worker create the goods that become his own; the rest of the working day he creates the wealth that becomes the possession of the owners of the means of labour. Material goods, however, are always transformed into mental culture. Thus it is the law of our age that the labour of some becomes the culture of others. The fact of exploitation, of surplus labour, which is expressed in the phenomena of long working hours, low wages, poor food and overcrowded housing for the worker, puts a barrier on how far the broad mass of working people can be educated to take part in the nation's mental culture. The fact of exploitation thus also restricts the development of the nation into a cul-tural community; it obstructs the involvement of the worker in the national cultural community; and what holds true for the worker holds also for the peasant exploited by merchant and mortgage capital, and for the artisan subject to the capitalist trader. From early childhood to old age they are at work; in late evening they seek vainly for rest in the cramped household that all too many must share; worry for the daily maintenance of life leaves them not a moment free. What can these people know of the forces at work in us more fortunate ones, that combine us into a nation? What do our workers know of Kant? Our peasants of Goethe? Our artisans of Marx?

But it is not only through exploitation itself, but also through the need to defend this exploitation, that capitalism inhibits the development of the entire people into a community of national culture. It has indeed built elementary schools as far as it needed them, but it refrains from creating a genuine national education that could give the masses full possession of intellectual culture. This is not only because, in order not to reduce its ability to exploit children, it sets too narrow a limit on school time, skimps on the costs of education and would sooner spend its wealth on the instruments of its power, but above all because the masses brought up to full participation in the culture of the nation would not tolerate its rule for a day longer; it fears the elementary school, as this educates its opponent, and it seeks therefore to reduce this to its own means of power. Capitalism necessarily brought in general military service, but it did not create a people's army. It locks its soldiers in barracks, seeks to keep them as far removed as possible from the influence of the population, and seeks to create in them by external insignia, by removal in space, and by the suggestion of its ideology, the sense of a special status that keeps them at a distance from the life of the masses. Capitalism created democracy. But while democracy was once the bourgeoisie's youthful dream, it is now the fear of its old age, as it has become an instrument of power for the working class. Freedoms of press, assembly and association are feared by an obsolete capitalism as so many weapons of its enemies. It therefore does what it can to restrict the development of the nation. Capitalism cannot let the nation fully emerge as a cultural community, since every fragment of mental culture becomes a power in the hands of the working class, a weapon to be one day wielded against it.

We should certainly rejoice in every attempt to convey to the workers a part of our science and art. Only blind enthusiasts will forget, however, that while the individual worker of unusual talent can become a person of culture even today, the full possession of our cultural values must necessarily remain closed to the mass today. Anyone who has ever seen how our workers, after a nine- or ten-hour day of physical work, exert themselves to acquire a portion of the tremendous wealth of our intellectual culture, how they struggle with the tiredness that would close their eyes, how they wrestle with the fearful obstruction of poor education which makes every strange word a difficulty for them, how they try to grasp social laws without having heard of natural laws or learned mechanics, how they want to understand the exact laws of economics though they have never learned mathematics – anyone who has seen this will not dare hope to succeed in making our culture a possession of these exploited people. Only flatterers of the proletariat can say to the workers that today, as proletarians, they can understand all science and enjoy all beauty. It is the great pain of the working class that they cannot manage this, that they are excluded from the most valuable treasure of our national spiritual culture, though even the simplest handyman contributed to bringing it about. It is still as ever the case that similar culture makes only the masters into a national community, while the working, exploited and oppressed masses, without whose hands' work this culture could not have existed for a day, could never have arisen, are fobbed off with a wretched fragment of this wealth. But of course, the day is nearer than ever before when these masses will be in a position to lay their hands on this great abundance, in order to make this mental culture, the creation of the work of the whole people, also the possession of the whole people. Only on this day, however, will the national cultural community first come fully into existence.

The Realization of a National Cultural Community by Socialism

The spatial redistribution of the population has dramatically transformed the character of the German nation. Have we not become quite different people by being uprooted from the soil that we tilled, the woods and meadows that we wandered through, and installed in the big cities with their housing barracks, the industrial zones with their soot and smoke, in which the last flower and tree perish in an air heavy with coal? How different are those who grow up in our industrial towns from the village dwellers of earlier times. But did the nation consult and decide on this transformation of its whole being, which amounts to a transformation of its character? By no means. True, the redistribution of the population is effected via human consciousness, decided by human will, but not by the will of the nation, rather by the self-will of millions acting independently; decided by countless capitalists figuring on paper where production costs might be lowest and profits highest; decided by innumerable workers, who find out where a job is vacant, where a wage can most readily enable them to spend their life with their loved ones. And the result of these individual decisions, guided by quite other considerations, is a transformation in the existence of the whole nation, a transformation in the essence of its culture, a transformation in its character. Who gave these individuals the power to make the whole nation into something different from what it was before? The law did; private property in means of labour means precisely that the nation has given its fate out of its own hands, entrusting it to the will of individuals. These individuals, however, decide not the fate of the nation, but only their own individual fate, and they know nothing of the effects that their decisions have on the overall existence of the nation. Yet through nothing more than millions of such individual decisions, unconcerned with the nation and knowing nothing of it, the fate of the nation is determined. And if the man of science discovers that behind the apparent accident of individual wills acting independently there are in fact laws that are ultimately responsible for effecting this redistribution of the population and thus transforming the character of the nation, these are still laws of which those who made their decisions knew nothing, laws that in the fine expression of the young Engels, operated 'without the consciousness of the participants'.

It is quite different in a socialist society. The creation of new jobs, the spatial distribution of the population, then become the conscious act of the organized society. It must be decided by the organs of society, discussed by the individuals who form these organs, and its effect must be investigated. The redistribution of population thus becomes a conscious act. The future society will discuss and decide whether to build a new shoe factory in a mining district, for example, where production costs are low, or in a pleasant wooded landscape, where the workers involved in shoe production can lead the most healthy and pleasant life. The effect on the character of the nation, the determination of the transformations of this character, is something that society then takes back for itself, and the future history of the people becomes the product of its conscious will. In this way the nation of the future will achieve what the nation in commodity-producing society can never achieve: to form itself, to shape its own fate, and consciously determine the future transformations of its character. Only socialism gives the nation for the first time its complete autonomy, genuine self-determination, removing it from the effect of forces that it is unaware of and from whose operation it is alienated.

But the fact that socialism makes the nation autonomous, and its destiny the product of its own conscious will, means that socialist society will see an increasing differentiation of nations, a sharper definition of their specificities and a sharper separation of their characters. This judgement will surprise many people; both friends and opponents of socialism hold it as certain that socialism will level the diversity of nations, reducing the distinctions between them if not abolishing these altogether.

It is certainly true that the material cultural content of different national cultures will be equalized in socialist society. This work has already been begun by modern capitalism. The precapitalist peasant produced and lived for whole centuries in the manner handed down by his ancestors, without adopting any of the advances of his neighbours; he used the same wretched plough, although a few miles away he could have discovered a better one that would have secured him a much higher yield. Modern capitalism, on the other hand, has taught nations to learn from one another; each technical advance becomes in a few years the property of the whole world, each change in the law is studied and copied by neighbouring peoples, each trend in science and art influences the civilized peoples of the whole world. There can be no doubt that socialism will tremendously increase this cosmopolitan tendency of our culture and will equalize incomparably more quickly the material cultural contents, that nations will learn far more from one another and will take from each other whatever corresponds to their needs. But it would be hasty to conclude from this that the levelling of material cultural contents will then make each nation the same.

New ideas will not be able to conquer a socialist society in any other way than by seeking to conquer each individual member who has been raised by socialist national education as a highly developed personality in full possession of national culture. This means, however, that a new idea cannot just be adopted, but must be deliberately taken up, adapted to and incorporated into the whole mental being of millions of individuals. Just as no individual tacks something new onto his own mental existence in a simple mechanical way, but rather incorporates it, adjusts it to his own personality, mentally digests it by a process of apperception, so too will the whole nation not just take up something new in a simple way, but rather by elaborating it, adapting it to its being, and altering it in the process of adoption by millions of minds. Through this great fact of national apperception, any idea that one nation takes over from another must always be first adapted to the nation's entire being, and be changed by it before it is adopted. This means that nations will not simply take over from one another new literature or art, new philosophy or social doctrine, but always adopt these in a further elaborated way. Adaptation to the existing mental culture of the nation, however, means linkage, incorporation into the entire history of the nation. Just as today it is much harder for the English or French or German people to take over unchanged a new world of mental values from another people than it is for the Japanese or Croatians, for example, so in socialist society no new piece of mental culture will be able to gain entry into a nation without linking up to its national culture, placing itself in connection with this, and being co-determined by it. Thus autonomy of national cultural community in socialism necessarily means, despite the equalization of material cultural contents, a growing differentiation of the mental cultures of nations.

Drawing the entire people into a national cultural community, the attainment of full self-determination by the nation, growing mental differentiation of the nations – this is what socialism means. The complete cultural community of all members, as this existed in the era of clan communism, will be restored by the communism of great nations after the millennial era of class division, the division between members of the nation and those it left behind.

The Concept of Nation

We can now proceed to draw general conclusions from the facts adduced, and thus define the concept of nation that was our objective. At the start of our investigation we conceived the nation first of all as a relative community of character. We can now specify more precisely the nature of this community.

At the outset of our work we provisionally described national character as the totality of physical and mental characteristics that are peculiar to a nation, that unite its different members and divide them from other nations. These various characteristics, however, are in no way of equal value.

One part of national character is certainly the differential determination of the will. Will is expressed in any process of learning as attention, which selects from the mass of phenomena experienced only certain ones, and apperceives only these. Will is expressed still more directly, however, in any decision: a German and an Englishman will act differently in the same situation; they will tackle differently the same work; in pursuit of enjoyment they will choose different pleasures; if they are equally well off, they will prefer different ways of life and satisfy different needs – this is certainly the essence of national character.

We previously asked how such a community of character arises, and answered that similar effective causes have produced similarity of character. We thus defined the nation as a community of destiny.

It is now necessary to grasp the concept of community of destiny more precisely. Community does not mean just similarity. Germany, for example, underwent capitalist development in the nineteenth century just as England did. The forces acting in this direction were the same in the two countries, and the decisive influence on people's character. Yet the Germans did not thereby become Englishmen. Community of destiny does not mean just subjection to a common fate, but rather common experience of the same fate in constant communication and ongoing interaction with one another. English and Germans have both experienced capitalist development: but at different times, in different places, and only in loose connection with one another. Thus, while the same driving forces may have made them more similar to each other than they previously were, they would never make them into one people. Not similarity of destiny, but only common experience and suffering of destiny, a community of destiny, creates the nation. Community, to cite Kant, means 'general mutual interaction' (third analogy of experience: foundation of community). Only this destiny experienced in general mutual interaction, in constant connection with one another, produces the nation.

That the nation is not the product of mere similarity of destiny, but that it arises from and consists in the community of destiny, the constant interaction of those who share this destiny, distinguishes the nation from all other communities of character. One such community of character is that of class. The proletarians of all countries bear similar character traits. For all their variation, the same class situation has etched similar features on the character of the German and English, the French and Russian, the American and the Australian worker: the same joy in struggle, the same revolutionary sentiment, the same class morality, the same political desire. But what has created community of character here is not a community of destiny but a similarity of destiny. For whatever links of communication there may be between German and English workers, these are far looser than those that connect the English worker with the English bourgeois – who both live in the same town, read the same posters on the walls, the same newspapers, take part in the same political or sporting events, and occasionally either speak to each other or at least both speak to the same individuals, the various intermediaries between capitalists and workers.

It could perhaps be said that the effective influences of way of life, of destiny, determine the workers of various nations more intimately than the various classes of one and the same nation, and that therefore in terms of character too the workers of different countries are more similar to each other than are the bourgeois and workers of the same country. But for all this, what divides the character community of nation from that of class is that the one arises from a community of destiny, the other simply from a similarity of destiny.

The nation can thus be defined as a community of character that grows out of a community of destiny rather than from a mere similarity of destiny. This is also the significance of language for a nation. It is with the people I stand in closest communication with that I create a common language; and it is with the people with whom I share a common language that I stand in closest communication.

We have discovered two ways through which the effective causes, the conditions of the human struggle for existence, weld people together into a national community of destiny. The first of these is that of natural inheritance. The nation here is a community of descent: it is maintained by common blood, as the popular expression has it, by a commonality of germ plasm, as science teaches. But the members linked by common inheritance remain a nation only so long as they remain in a community of communication with one another, so long as they maintain their common blood by intermarriage. If the sexual connection between the members of the nation ceases, then the tendency immediately arises for the previously uniform population to develop into new and mutually distinct communities of character. What is needed for the continuity of the nation as natural community is not only commonality of blood by common descent, but also the maintenance of this commonality by an ongoing mingling of blood.

But the character of the individual is never simply the totality of hereditary properties; it is always determined also by the culture that is transmitted to him and works on him: by the education he enjoys, the law to which he is subject, the customs by which he lives, the ideas of god and the world, of what is proper and improper, beautiful and ugly, that are handed down to him, by the religion, philosophy, science, art and politics that have their effect on him – above all, however, by what governs all these phenomena, that is, the way in which in the midst of his fellow nationals he leads his struggle for existence, and gains his necessities of life. We thus arrive at the second great means by which the struggle for existence determines the individual: by the transmission of cultural goods by word of mouth.

The great instrument of this communication is language: it is the instrument of education and of all economic and all intellectual communication. The effective range of culture is marked by the possibility of understanding through language. The community of communication is a close one only as far as the community of language extends. Communication community and language reciprocally determine each other: language is the condition for all close communication, and for this very reason the necessity of communication generates common languages, while with the break-up of the communication community language too gradually differentiates. I can, of course, learn a foreign language without thereby becoming a member of the foreign nation, since the foreign language never subjects me to cultural influences in the same way as the mother tongue. The culture transmitted by the mother tongue influenced my childhood, the years of strongest receptivity, and formed my initial character; all later impressions, so far as they are adopted and adapted to an already existing individuality, undergo a change in the very process of adoption.

On top of this, it is rare for the foreign language to become the possession of the individual in the same complete way as the mother tongue, and the most refined and intimate effects are generally lost: even for an educated German, English and French literature rarely has the same force as does German. It is unthinkable that a nation should maintain itself in the long run as a community of culture without the community of language, this most important instrument of human communication. Community of language, on the other hand, is still no guarantee of national unity: despite common language, Danes and Norwegians experience a difference in culture, as do the Catholic Croats and Orthodox Serbs. But to the degree that the culturally divisive effect of religion disappears, Serbs and Croats will develop into a nation, by virtue of the community of communication mediated by a common language and the similar cultural influences under which they live. This indicates the national significance of the victory of a uniform language over dialects: the necessity of closer communication created the uniform language, and the existence of linguistic unity then subjects all who master it to a similar cultural influence. The reciprocal effect of the two unites them into a cultural community.

Is humanity really now divided into nations in such a way that each individual belongs to one nation, and no one belongs simultaneously to several? The merely natural linkage of a person to two nations by descent alters nothing in the strict differentiation of nations. In border lands where two nations abut on one another, people are often variously mingled, so that the blood of both nations flows in the most diverse mixtures in their veins. Despite this, there is as a rule no fusion of nations. Here it is precisely the difference of cultural community that sharply divides the nations despite this mingling of blood. The national struggles in Austria offer an example of this. Anyone who sees in the struggle between Germans and Czechs a racial struggle only displays their historical ignorance. Among the peasantry, perhaps, Germans and Czechs may have preserved their blood in a more or less pure state, but the strata that wage the national struggle and that it is waged over – the intelligentsia, the petty bourgeoisie, the working class – have mingled their blood by intermarriage for centuries, so that there can no longer be any talk of a German or a Czech nation in the sense of a natural community. For all that, the nations have in no way fused together. The difference of culture transmitted by language makes them persist as independent nations sharply divided from one another.

It is quite different if an individual gains an equal or nearly equal share in the culture of two or more nations. There are also such individuals, in no small number, in the border regions, and zones where several nations live side by side. From childhood on they speak the language of two nations: they are almost equally influenced by the destinies of two nations, by the cultural peculiarities of two nations, and so in character they grow into members of both nations, or if you like, into individuals who belong fully and completely to neither nation. For the individual on whom the culture of two or more nations has its effect, whose character is influenced equally strongly by the different national cultures, does not simply combine the character traits of two nations, but rather possesses a quite specific character of his own, just as a chemical combination displays different characteristics from each of its component elements. This is also the deepest reason why the individual who is culturally the child of many nations is generally little loved, an object of suspicion, and in times of national struggle even condemned as a traitor or transgressor: the mixture of cultural elements creates a new character, and the cultural amalgam of two nations appears accordingly as a foreigner, as much so as someone who belongs entirely to a different nation.

If this antipathy to cultural half-breeds is understandable, we should not let it lead us astray. It is very often the greatest individuals who combine in them the culture of two or more nations. Our men of science, our great artists, very often experience several circles of national culture with almost equal strength. In such a man as Karl Marx, the history of four nations – Jews, Germans, French and English – congealed into an individual characteristic, which is precisely why his personal work could flow into the history of all the great nations of our time; the history of any civilized nation during the last few decades is incomprehensible without his work.

The cultural effect of several national cultures on the same individual, however, happens only as an individual, not a mass phenomenon. Even the massive adoption of foreign cultural elements by a whole nation never completely abolishes national character, but at most reduces its differences. For the foreign elements never work on individuals with the same force as the original national culture: they are never adopted unchanged, but undergo in the very process of adoption an alteration and adaptation to the already existing national culture. This is the phenomenon of national apperception which we have already discussed.

Our investigation has shown us that the effectiveness of the common culture that constitutes the nation differs widely according to different social constitutions. There are basically three types of national cultural community that we have already acquainted ourselves with.

The first type, represented in our historical presentation by the Teutons in the era of clan communism, shows us a nation in which all members, bound by common blood, are also linked by the common culture inherited from their ancestors. We have repeatedly mentioned how this national unity breaks down with the transition to a settled existence: the inherited features differentiate as intermarriage ceases between locally distinct tribes subject to differing conditions of existence; the inherited common culture then also develops differently in the different tribes. The nation thus bears within it the germ of its decay.

The second type of nation is represented by a society based on differentiation of social classes. The mass of the people continue to undergo the above process of differentiation: without common sexual intercourse, they become physically more distinct; no longer bound by any tie of communication, the original common language develops into various local dialects; subject to different conditions in the struggle for existence, they develop diverse kinds of culture, which in their turn produce differences of character. The mass of the people thus steadily lose their national unity, the more so as the original commonality of inherited features is lost in the course of the centuries, and the original common culture is overlaid and fragmented by the later arising difference of cultural elements. What holds the nation together is no longer the unity of both blood and culture among the masses, but rather the cultural unity of the ruling classes, which sit over these masses and live off their labour. They and their dependants are linked together by sexual relations and by cultural communication of various kinds: thus the knights of the Middle Ages, the educated classes of modern times, form the nation. The broad masses, however, by the work of whose hands the nation is maintained – peasants, artisans, workers – are simply left behind as far as the nation is concerned.

The socialist society of the future presents the third and final type, once again uniting all fellow nationals into an autonomous national unity. Here, however, it is no longer common descent, rather common education, work, and cultural enjoyment, that compose the nation. This nation, therefore, is no longer threatened with the danger of decay, but community of education, participation in cultural goods, close connection in the common life and in social labour give the nation secure guarantee of national unity.

The nation for us is thus no longer a rigid thing, but a process of becoming, whose nature is governed by the conditions under which people struggle for their necessities of life and to maintain themselves. And since the nation does not yet arise at a stage when people only seek their sustenance and do not produce it, where they secure their necessities of life by simply taking possession and occupying unowned wealth where they find it, but only at a stage at which man wins from nature by labour the goods that he needs, so the origin of the nation, and the particularity of each nation, is determined by the mode of labour of the people, by the means of labour they use, the productive forces they master, and the relationships they enter into in the productive process. To grasp the origin of the nation, and of each individual nation, as a part of the struggle of humanity with nature – this is the great problem that Karl Marx's historical method has enabled us to solve.

For national materialism,[6] the nation is a piece of a peculiar material substance with the secret power of producing out of itself the community of national character. For this theory, therefore, the history of humanity becomes a history of the struggles and minglings of persistent and unchanging racial and hereditary substances. This unscientific approach has experienced a remarkable rebirth in recent years – especially under the influence of Gobineau – but Darwinism has effectively countered it.

National spiritualism, on the other hand, has made the nation into an esoteric 'spirit of the people', the history of the nation into the self-development of this spirit, and world history into a struggle marked by the propensity of different popular spirits for mutual friendship or enmity. But if, for example, Lamprecht still places the development of national consciousness at the centre of his history of the nation, and believes in this way he has found a general law of development of the popular spirit, even he goes on to explain the transformations of national consciousness, the developments of the popular souls from the 'symbolic' age through to the 'age of irritability' (*Reizsamkeit*), in terms of changes in the nation's economy; the development of these souls is for him no longer the driving force of development, but rather the result of changes in the form of labour. If he is still not content with understanding the nation in its becoming in terms of the development of human productive forces, the law-like transformation of production relations, but on top of this seeks to bring the development of national consciousness, the 'soul of the people', under general laws that cannot explain a single extra historical fact but can only describe the general features of the development, what is involved here is not anything like laws, but rather, as Simmel puts it, mere 'preparations for laws', 'provisional generalizations of the typical phenomena of history, preliminary orientations on the mass of particular facts'.[7]

Prepared for on the one hand by Darwinism, which has superseded national materialism, and on the other hand by historical research, which has replaced the explanation of historical evolution in terms of the mystical popular spirit by demonstration of the economic processes that determine the evolution of the nation, the materialist conception of history can comprehend the nation as the never completed product of a constantly ongoing process, whose ultimate driving force is the conditions of human struggle with nature, the transformations of human productive forces, the changes in human relations of labour. This conception makes the nation for us into a historical entity.

Difference in national character is an empirical fact that can be denied only by a doctrinaire notion that sees simply what it wants to see, and does not see what everyone else does. Yet, despite this, time and again efforts have been made to deny difference in national character and maintain that what distinguishes nations is no more than their language. This opinion is found among many theorists who base themselves on Catholic doctrine. It was taken over from the humanist philosophy of the

bourgeois Enlightenment, and was similarly appropriated by many socialists, who sought to use it to support a proletarian cosmopolitanism that,
as we shall see below, represents the initial and primitive position of the
working class towards the national struggles of the bourgeois world. This
supposed insight into the inessentiality of the nation is perpetuated in
Austria today in the linguistic usage of the social-democratic press, which
loves to speak of comrades of German and Czech 'tongues', instead of
German and Czech comrades. The idea that national differences are
nothing but differences of language rests on the atomistic-individualistic
conception of society, which sees society as the mere sum of externally
connected individuals, and hence the nation as the mere sum of people
linked externally, that is, by language.

Our insight into the essence of the nation, however, not only makes it
impossible to deny in individualistic fashion the reality of national character; it also makes impossible the far more dangerous misuse of this
concept. National character is indeed nothing more than the orientation
of the will determined in the individual member by the community of
destiny he shares with all other members. Once it has arisen, national
character appears as an autonomous historical power. If theory teaches us
to understand it as the precipitate of relations between individuals, immediate experience rather sees it as governing and controlling these
relations. This is the fetishism of national character. Our theory demol-
ishes this ghost with one blow. It is no longer something esoteric that
national character appears to determine the desire and action of the
individual member, once we recognize that each member is the product
of his nation and that national character is nothing more than the specific orientation of the will that community of destiny generates in each
member as his individual property. And national character ceases to
appear as an independent power as soon as we grasp it as the precipitate
of national history. We understand now that the seemingly autonomous
historical efficacy of national character conceals nothing more than the
fact that the history of past generations, the conditions of their struggle
for existence, the productive forces they mastered, the relations of production they entered into, continue to determine the behaviour of their
natural and cultural progeny. In this way, however, national character
also loses its substantial character, that is, the appearance it has of something enduring and persisting in the flux of phenomena. Nothing but a
precipitate of history, it changes with every hour, with every new event
that the nation experiences, is as changeable as the events it reflects.
Placed back in the midst of world events, it is no longer a persistent
being, but rather a constant becoming and perishing.

But our theory still has a further task to perform, on which former
attempts to determine the nature of the nation have all foundered. The

question here is to distinguish the concept of the nation from the narrower local and tribal communities within the nation. To be sure, community of destiny has joined the Germans into a community of character. But is this not also true of the Saxons or Bavarians, the Tyroleans and Styrians, indeed of the inhabitants of each single alpine valley? Have the different ancestral destinies, differences of settlement and division of the land, its fertility and the climate not made Zillertalers and Passeirers, 'Vintschgers' and 'Pusterers' into sharply marked communities of character? Where can we draw the line between those communities of character that are considered independent nations, and those that we see as narrower associations within the nation?

At this point we have to recall that we have already come across these narrower communities of character as products of the break-up of the nation resting on common descent. After the progeny of the Germanic tribes separated from one another in space, were tied to the soil by agriculture, and led their lives without communication or intermarriage, they grew ever more different. Despite issuing from a common natural and cultural community, they were on the way towards forming autonomous natural and cultural communities that were sharply distinct from each other. Each of these narrower associations has a tendency to develop into a particular nation of its own. The difficulty of delimiting the concept of these narrower communities of character from that of the nation thus rests on their representing progressive stages in national development.

This tendency to national fragmentation is opposed, as we have already seen, by a counter-tendency, which seeks to bind the nation more closely together. But this counter-tendency is initially effective only for the ruling classes. It binds the knightly estate of the Middle Ages, the educated classes of the early capitalist age, into a close nation sharply separated off from all other communities of character, bringing this into close economic, political and social communication, creating for it a common language, and facilitating the effect of the same intellectual culture and customs. It is initially the ruling classes that this close tie of a cultural community links into a nation. No one can be in doubt whether a cultivated person is German or Dutch, Slovene or Croat; national education and the common national language sharply demarcate even the most closely related nations from one another. But whether the peasants of a particular village should be classed as low Germans or Netherlanders, Slovenes or Croats, is a decision that always remains somewhat arbitrary. It is only the circle of full members of the nation that is sharply circumscribed, not that of those whom the nation has left behind.

Modern capitalism gradually distinguishes even the lower classes of the people ever more sharply into separate nations, for they too gain a place in national education, in the cultural life of their nation, in the uniform national language. The tendency towards unity also takes root in the working masses. But only socialist society will see it prevail. It will demarcate the entire people, by the difference of national education and custom, as sharply from one another as only the educated classes of the different nations are separated today.

In a society based on private property in the means of labour, the ruling classes – first the knightly estate, today the educated – form the nation as the totality of those in whom the same culture, formed by the history of the nation, transmitted by its common language and national education, produces an affinity of character. The broad masses, on the other hand, do not form the nation – no longer, as the original tribal community no longer binds them closely enough together, and not yet, as the community of education that is coming into being still does not bring them fully into its reach. The difficulty of finding a satisfactory definition of the concept of nation, on which all previous attempts have come to grief, is thus historically determined. The nation was sought in the present class society, in which the old sharply bordered tribal society has fragmented into an endless number of local and tribal groups, while the new community of education that is coming into being cannot yet unite these small groups into a national whole.

Thus our search for the essence of the nation discloses a grandiose historical picture. At the beginning – in the age of clan communism and nomadic agriculture – the uniform nation as a community of descent. Then, since the transition to settled agriculture and the development of private property, the division of the old nation into the cultural community of the ruling classes on the one hand, and those left behind by this process on the other – these last locked into narrow local circles, the fragmentation products of the old nation. Further, with the development of social production in capitalist form, the broadening of the community of national culture – the working and exploited classes remain the backward of the nation, but the tendency towards national unity on the basis of national education becomes gradually stronger than the particularist tendency to the break-up of the old nation based on community of descent into ever more sharply distinguished local groups. Finally, once the society of social production sheds its capitalist shell, the resurrection of the uniform nation as a community of education, work and culture.

The national conception of history, which sees the driving force of events in the struggles of nations, seeks a mechanics of nations. Nations appear to it as elements that are no further resolvable, as rigid bodies that knock against each other in space, and act on each other by pressure and thrust. We, however, resolve the nation itself into a process. For us history no longer reflects the struggles of nations, but the nation itself appears as the reflection of historical struggles. For the nation has no appearance save in the national character, in the nationality of the individual; and the nationality of the individual is no more than one side of his determination by social history, his determination by the development of the processes and relations of labour.

National Consciousness and National Sentiment

As long as someone knows only members of his own nation, he will be aware not of his coincidence with them, but only of his difference from them. If my communication is only with Germans, and I hear only from Germans, I have no occasion at all to become aware of the fact that the people I know are alike to me in one respect, that is, in being German, but I see only the differences. This one is Swabian, and I am Bavarian; this one is a bourgeois, I am a worker. Only when I get to know foreign nationals do I become aware that these people are foreign to me, while I am linked with those I previously communicated with, and with millions of others, through the tie of membership of a nation. Knowledge of foreign life is the precondition of all national consciousness. It is no accident that our oldest celebrated glorification of the German people begins with the words: 'Many lands have I seen . . .' National consciousness thus arises first of all among the merchants, the soldiers, the workers who find themselves in foreign lands; it is most widespread in border regions, where several nations are adjoined.

The nation as a community of character governs the action of its individual members even if they are not aware of their nationality. The individual's nationality is indeed one of the means by which socio-historical forces govern the decisions of the individual. But the individual becomes aware of this determination by nationality only if he has recognized himself as belonging to a nation. Only national consciousness makes nationality into a conscious driving force of human behaviour, and especially of political behaviour.

This is certainly why national consciousness has been ascribed such great significance for the preservation and essence of the nation. In national consciousness has been sought precisely the constitutive characteristic of the nation: a nation is allegedly the totality of those people who are aware of their membership of it and their difference from other nations. Thus Rumelin writes, for example, 'My people are those whom I see as my people, whom I name as my own, with whom I know myself linked by indissoluble ties.' This psychological theory of the nation seemed more acceptable when no one was able to find an objective characteristic of the nation, as all attempts to discover the tie that binds nation into community either in language or in common descent or in membership of a state seemed to founder on the diversity of national phenomena. And yet this psychological theory of the nation is not only unsatisfactory, but completely incorrect. It is unsatisfactory, for even on the assumption that it were true that the nation is formed by those people aware of their common membership, the question would still arise as to why I feel a common membership with these particular people and not with others. What, then, are the 'indissoluble ties' by which I know myself bound together with my fellow nationals? If I become aware of my nationality, what actually is it that I become aware of? What is it that compels me to know myself as one with the Germans forever, and not with the English or French?

Today, moreover, it may well be said that anyone at all who belongs to the cultural community of a nation is also aware of this membership. But this expansion of national consciousness is essentially a product of our capitalist age, which with its unprecedented wealth of communications has brought nations into so close a connection that no one who has a share in the culture of his nation remains completely ignorant of other nations. Even someone who has never seen anyone from a different nation face to face still learns about foreign nations from literature, from the newspaper – if only in caricatures – and a consciousness of his own nationality grows out of this knowledge of others. Only in such an age could the erroneous view arise that it is national consciousness that combines people into nations.

This driving force of love for one's own nation has a different strength among different classes and individuals. The national feeling of peasants has no stronger roots than those of the hatred of someone closely tied to his inheritance and tradition towards everything foreign. The national sentiment of the modern bourgeoisie and industrial workers is completely different. The eternal novelty that the big city, changing fashion, the newspapers, place before their eyes, has long since accustomed them to view foreign things without such strong feelings of displeasure. Love for one's own nation for them has different sources from hatred of foreign characteristics.

One of these sources is the fact that the idea of one's own nation is bound up in space and in time with other ideas, whose structure of feeling is transferred to the idea of the nation. If I think of my nation, I remember my homeland, my parents' house, my first childhood games, my old schoolmaster, the girl whose kiss once thrilled me, and from all these ideas a feeling of pleasure flows into the idea of the nation I belong to.

But there is more. National consciousness for me is not knowledge of something outside myself, but rather the knowledge of my own nationality, of my own kind. When I become aware that I belong to a nation, I realize that a close community of character ties me to it, that its destiny forms me and its culture defines me, that it is itself an effective force in my character. The nation is not something alien to me, rather a part of myself that returns to me in the nature of others. Thus the idea of the nation is bound up with the idea of my ego. If someone slights the nation, they slight me too; if the nation is praised, I have my share in this praise. For the nation is nowhere but in me and my kind. The strongest feeling of pleasure is thus bound up with the idea of the nation. It is not, as has sometimes been maintained, real or ostensible community of interest with fellow nationals, rather awareness of the tie of community of character, that nationality is nothing but my own kind, that accompanies the idea of the nation with a feeling of pleasure, and arouses in me love of the nation.

There is yet a further driving force of national sentiment: it arises from the enthusiasm that, as Goethe writes, history arouses. In the telling of history, the idea of the nation is linked with the idea of its destiny, with the memory of heroic struggles, relentless wrestling for knowledge and art, with triumphs and defeats. The whole rapport that someone today may feel with the struggling people of the past is then transformed into love for the bearer of this motley fate, the nation. It is at root not a new element that is introduced here, but only an extension of the two last named; as the idea of the nation owes a good part of its wealth of senti-ment to its close connection with the idea of my own youth, so too its connection with the idea of those people whom history teaches us to love and admire kindles new love for it. And as I learn to love the nation if I recognize in its specificity my own nature, so does its history grow dearer to me if I believe I find in its destinies back to the dawn of time the forces that have etched the essential features of successive generations through to my own. All that romantic delight in the distant past thus becomes a source of love for the nation. And this is why a national work of art – such as Wagner's *Die Meistersinger* – can have a national effect: because it teaches me to love a piece of the history of the nation and through it the nation itself.

The tale of the nation's history produces above all the lively national sentiment of the intelligentsia. But the more that universal education, newspapers, lectures and books rehearse the fortunes of the nation, the more this evokes a national sentiment towards the history of the nation among the broad masses.

The national sentiment that arises on this basis then leads to a peculiar national valuation of things. For as the idea of the German people is bound up with a feeling of pleasure, the next step is for me to refer to as 'German' whatever arouses such a feeling in me. If I call someone a 'real German', this is no longer just giving information of his nationality, but a form of praise. 'Good German' becomes a term of praise, 'un-German' a term of abuse.

Science enables us to explain the rise of national sentiment out of national consciousness, and the rise of this remarkable national valuation out of national sentiment. Still more, it enables us to criticize national valuation. And this is a task of no small significance. For only a criticism of national ideology can generate the atmosphere of sobriety in which alone a dedicated investigation of national policy is possible.

The Critique of National Values

Man is not only a being of knowledge, who becomes aware of his causal connection with his nation; he is, above all, a being of desire and action, who sets goals for himself and selects means to these goals. This fact gives rise to a further valuation that enters into conflict with national valuation. What is the relationship between this rationalistic mode of valuation and the national valuation arising from national sentiment?

Rationalist evaluation and national valuation may coincide. When Lessing, for example, combated the influence of French culture on German education, this arose from a national valuation, taking the form of a battle to preserve or restore national specificity. But Lessing's struggle also corresponded to a rationalistic valuation; the courtly culture of the French was not suited to the newly arisen German bourgeoisie; it contradicted both their ideal of the beautiful and their ideal of the proper. If the great representatives of the German bourgeoisie at that time defended German ways against foreign influences, this was because German ways appeared to them more valuable, of higher standing, because German culture was for them a better means to their supreme goal, to their ethical and aesthetic ideal. Thus rationalist and national valuation coincided.

But if these two modes of valuation coincide, this is a historical accident, and in no way something necessary. For national specificity is a product of the fortunes of the nation; and these fortunes are governed not by a rational world spirit that brings what is reasonable into existence and makes what exists reasonable, but rather by the blind necessity of the struggle for existence.

This antithesis of national and rationalistic valuation that is active in each individual obtains great social importance through the fact that class and political antagonisms draw strength from this clash of valuations.

National specificity is at any time the product of the inherited social constitution. If revolutionary movements arise that seek to overthrow the existing order of society and replace it by a new one, those interested in the maintenance of present conditions, that is, the ruling and owning classes, are quick to point out that national specificity is created and conditioned by the existing order of society, and that any overthrow of their rights and their property would destroy or change this traditional national specificity. They thus make national valuation into an instrument of their class struggle.

But if all classes that fear for their supremacy and their possessions seek to maintain national specificity, and claim to protect national values, all upward-striving classes, who still seek to gain power in society, are on the other hand rationalist. For rather than treasuring all that has been historically transmitted, this is precisely the object of their attack. National specificity for them, therefore, is nothing but the specificity of those classes that dominate and exploit the nation; the national institutions that supposedly alone correspond to national character and enable its preservation are for them the bulwarks of the rule and exploitation of the classes they oppose. What contempt the German democrats before 1848 had for those who sought to justify the intolerable political and social conditions of Germany as the expression of a 'Christian-German popular spirit', for the national-historical school that 'legitimizes the pettiness of today by the pettiness of yesterday, a school that declares every cry of the living flesh against the knout as rebellious, as long as the knout is a warranted, hereditary, historical knout'.[8] If national valuation is beloved and dear to all conservative classes, so the valuation of all revolutionary classes is rationalistic.

This holds true also for the working class of today. In the words of the young Marx this is

> a class with *radical chains*, a class of bourgeois society that is not a class of bourgeois society, an estate that is the dissolution of all estates, a sphere which possesses a universal character by its universal suffering, and makes no special claim to justice because it is no particular injustice that is done to it, but injustice in general . . .'[9]

For the same reason that the working class is not yet a class of the nation, it is also no longer a national class. Excluded from the enjoyment of cultural values, these values are for it an alien possession. Where others see the shining history of national culture, it sees the misery and serfdom of those on whose broad shoulders all national culture has rested since the decline of the old clan communism. It sees its ideal not in the maintenance of national specificity, but rather in the overthrow of the entire former constitution of society, which alone can make it into a member of the nation. Thus the working class wields the knife of criticism against everything that is historically transmitted. Nothing is valuable to it simply because it is handed down, but must rather prove its value by serving its own class struggle. Indeed it laughs at all those who seek to resist its class struggle by claiming that this contradicts the specificity of the nation, as only its class struggle can make it into a member of the nation. Since the national cultural values are not in the possession of the proletariat, national valuation is not the proletarian valuation. If the working class is excluded from national culture, this is a source of suffering, but by the same token the workers' dignity is also rooted in this. Their grandfathers were chased from house and home by landlords seeking to extend their domains; their fathers had to leave the peasant village where their ancestors had lived for centuries, perhaps since the nation first settled, and were thus uprooted and torn away from all tradition; they themselves are subject to the changing influences of the big city, drawn into all currents of the day, thrown hither and thither to all parts of the country by the play of the trade cycle. The working class has thus become rootless, freer from the laming power of all tradition than any class before it. It has similarly come to embody a rationalism for which nothing is holy simply because it is old and handed down, because it is familiar, but which, rejecting everything that is simply transmitted by history, knows no other measure than the goal for which it struggles, and the means it must choose to this goal. Everything new is welcome to it; from the ambit of the new and strange it selects what seems suitable for it; traditional national specificity appears to it as nothing, as a traditional limitation. The Russian worker takes his ideals from Germany, the German learns new methods of struggle from the Belgians and Russians, he copies the English in his trade unions, and the French in his political struggle. Each new current immediately arouses his attention – indeed he is often inclined to overvalue it simply because it is new, unprecedented, unfamiliar, precisely because it contradicts what others mean by national cultural possession and national specificity. There is no class that is inwardly more completely free from national valuation than the proletariat that has been freed from all tradition by the destructive power of capitalism, excluded from the enjoyment of national cultural goods, and that rises up in struggle against all powers historically handed down.[10]

But the more rational the proletariat becomes, the more national valuation is cherished by its immmediate opponent, the bourgeoisie – even if this valuation sounds peculiar in the mouths of capitalists. For it is capital whose effects have destroyed the traditional national specificity of each nation, and altered each nation in its whole being. While the bourgeoisie was young, it had no truck with national valuation; at that time it despised the traditional ruins of history and dreamed of the social edifice it would construct according to the plans of its own class reason. But the more power the proletariat wins against the bourgeoisie, the more sympathetic does the national mode of valuation, and all historicism, grow to the bourgeoisie.

The bourgeoisie of today treasures all historic survivals, as it owes its own rule only to historic survival; and as it treasures everything historical, so it also treasures what is historical in itself, nationality. Thus it becomes ever more the defender of national specificity, adapts itself ever more to national valuation, believing it can defend the traditional order of society as arising from national specificity and needing this for its own maintenance. It is no accident that bourgeois theorists today once more take pains to make the preservation of national specificity an ethical duty, that national spiritualism again celebrates its resurrection, that in jurisprudence and political economy the historical school dominates our universities and that our fictional literature and art disclose national peculiarity.

National valuation and rationalist valuation spring from different aspects of human existence; they necessarily arise in each individual, and exist in every one of us in mutual conflict. But through class struggle this internal antagonism within us becomes an external antagonism in society. National valuation becomes increasingly the valuation of the ruling and possessing classes, and rationalist valuation the valuation of the working class. From different values, too, arise different politics.

National Policy

Can the nation completely renounce the striving to maintain its specificity? Is this not the same for the nation as the drive for self-preservation is for every living being? Does not cultural cosmopolitanism, which, instead of preserving national specificity, seeks to learn from all nations what is valuable and use it for one's own nation, threaten the demise of separate national existence? Does it not seek to reduce humanity to a grey mixture in which all national diversity disappears?

We have already repeatedly adduced against this view our observation of national apperception. We know that each nation in the course of the centuries has adopted elements of civilization from a wide range of foreigners. The old Teutons first found themselves under the strong influence of Roman culture. Christianity brought them Oriental, Greek and Roman elements. In the age of landed property, the cultural influence of southern France was extraordinarily strong; at the time of the Crusades this was combined with Italian and Oriental effects. With capitalist commodity production Italian humanism and the Italian Renaissance had their effect on Germany. The following centuries again saw strong French influence. The reawakening bourgeoisie stood under the influence of classical antiquity, of French, English and Dutch science and art. The nineteenth century, indeed, saw the most varied nations, even from distant parts of the globe, increase our cultural wealth. And despite all this, it is impossible to speak of a disappearance of national specificity! The explanation of this is national apperception: no nation adopts foreign elements unaltered; each adapts them to its whole being, and subjects them to a change in the process of adoption, of mental digestion. Elements of French culture became something quite different in the heads of the English and in the heads of the Germans. The equalizing of the material contents of culture in no way means setting aside national specificity. Indeed, awareness of the specificity of the nation has never been more evident than in our own day, though undoubtedly each nation today learns far more and more quickly from other nations than at any time in the past.

When the Western bourgeoisie waged its great battles of class struggle against the absolutist state and the landlord class, while in Germany the backwardness of economic development and political oppression still held back the bourgeoisie, Madame de Staël once said that anyone in Germany who did not concern themselves with the whole world had nothing to do there. At that time the German intelligentsia acquired the entire knowledge of their time; modern natural science built up in Holland, England and France, French and English political doctrine, and the philosophy based on both branches of science, were all adopted in Germany. But the concepts taken over from the nations of the West at this time were developed quite differently in Germany than in France or England. For here the direct class struggle, which in Germany was not yet possible, did not divert attention from principles, the necessity of practical utilization did not compel any compromise between idea and reality, as it did early on in England, and after the Revolution also in France. Thus Germany became the classical country in which principles were thought through, deductions drawn out to a conclusion. This is the basis on which our philosophy grew to maturity, to that consistent rationalism that believed even the slightest action could be justified only by inserting it into a great system of ends. Only in Germany could someone like Vischer say that he could not imagine how anyone could act in politics without having studied and thought through Hegel's *Logic*. And this way of thinking did not remain confined to the narrow stratum of the intelligentsia. In diluted form it made its way into the broad masses; the schoolteacher, the priest, the press, the beginnings of political agitation gradually made this a way of thinking of the masses. 'It is visible,' wrote Fichte, 'and I believe generally understood, that all the efforts of the time were bent to banning obscure sentiments and establishing the rule of clarity and knowledge alone.' It is impossible to understand the revolution of 1848 without due attention to this national specificity of the Germans of that time. Still today there is a tinge of this way of thinking in the German workers; it justifies Engels's well-known saying that the

German workers are the heirs of German classical philosophy, the German socialists the descendants of Kant, Fichte and Hegel.

But capitalism and the constitutional monarchy dominated by *Junkers* and bourgeois have completely altered this entire specificity of the German people. A barren empiricism and historicism, a delight in value-less detailed research, the worship of success, that *realpolitik* which, as Marx put it, takes for reality the closest thing it sees under its nose, characterizes the intellectual life of present-day Germany. Bourgeois rationalism is no longer possible, proletarian rationalism is forbidden by the bourgeoisie by means of the state it controls, which tries to exclude each individual of 'dubious sentiment' from all practical effectiveness. The spiritual kin of our academic youth of the 1830s and 1840s are the Russian intelligentsia of today rather than the present Germans. And even this transformation of national specificity is in no way confined to the academically educated upper stratum; the new spirit is seeping into the broad masses through many channels. Revisionism in German social-democracy is its child; it arises from an abandonment of all 'impractical' principles, a politics of opportunism that has chased out the old rationalism, a belief that action is no longer to be justified as means to a higher end that theory has established, but rather by immediately visible success, however small.

So thoroughly have a few decades of capitalist development transformed the national specificity of the people. But do the German people no longer have a national specificity? Have the Germans thereby turned into English or Americans? A change in national specificity in no way means the surrender of this specificity.

This insight, then, gives rise to the idea of a different national policy. Our concern should not be whether future generations will be similar to those living now, but rather that our descendants, bound by a community of character, should still form a nation. But how large will the circle be of those forming this future nation? Deliberately planned action towards the goal that the entire people should have a share in the community of national culture, be defined by national culture and thus linked into a national cultural community, also deserves to be called a national policy. To distinguish it from conservative national policy, I call it evolutionary national policy. It is evolutionary, as it breaks with the idea that our task is the changeless preservation of the historically arisen specificity of the nation; it opposes this incorrect idea with that of the development and evolution of the national character. But there is a still deeper sense in which this can be called an evolutionary policy, as not only does it not prevent the further development of the national character, but it alone seeks to make the whole people into the nation, to have them develop themselves into the nation. For it the question is not just that of the development of the nation, but rather the development of the whole people into the nation.[11]

This evolutionary national policy is then the policy of the modern working class. The working class, of course, pursues its policy not for the sake of the nation, but for its own sake. But since the proletariat necessarily struggles for possession of the cultural goods that its own work creates and makes possible, so the effect of this policy is necessarily that of calling the whole people to participate in the national cultural community and thus making the totality of the people into the nation for the first time.

The opposition between conservative and evolutionary national policies is also evident in the attitude towards local and tribal groups within the nation. From the standpoint of national valuation it is only consistent to seek also to maintain these peculiarities, to encourage dialects in a struggle against the uniform language, to preserve traditional costumes. For us, on the other hand, such peculiarities within the nation appear an obstacle to the community of culture; if the standard German language is a foreign language for someone, they can have no share in our national literature, science and philosophy, cannot be formed by our traditional culture, and are not integrated into the German community of character. Certainly the study of dialects deserves all attention, and aesthetic satisfaction in local peculiarity is quite understandable; but we should not forget that all such peculiarity, which arose from the local boundedness of the peasant and has been effectively challenged by capitalism, by the free movement of wage-labour, by democracy and modern education, is an obstacle to the national cultural community and thus right away an obstacle to the unity of the nation. If conservative national policy wants to preserve and support these peculiarities also within the nation, it is literally anti-national: romantic pleasure in all traditional peculiarity tears apart the cultural unity of the nation. It is not by uncritically admiring and seeking to preserve all traditional ways, but rather by struggling to ensure that every member of the people takes up the culture of the nation and thus becomes the product, the child, of the nation, that we pursue our national policy.

The National State

The Principle of Nationality

The transformation of the traditional state system was effected in the nineteenth century in the name of the principle of nationality. Each nation should form one state, each state embrace only one nation. The struggles for German unity and Italian freedom, the liberation of Greece,

Romania, Serbia and Bulgaria from Turkish domination, the struggle of the Irish for home rule and of the Poles for the restoration of their state, the breakaway of the Latin American states from Spain, are all forms of the great struggle to realize the principle of nationality.

This phenomenon is so striking that many theorists have made the desire to live together in an independent political community into a constitutive characteristic of the nation. Thus for Renan,[12] or for Kirchhoff,[13] the nation is a totality of people who seek to live together in an independent community, to defend this community, and are ready to sacrifice for this community. What we have here is a psychological theory of the nation. But while the theory that seeks to make national consciousness, knowledge of common membership, the hallmark of the nation is already familiar to us, and is intellectualist, the doctrine that finds the essence of the nation in the desire for political unity and freedom is for its part voluntarist.[14]

Thus the nation is frequently understood as nothing more than the totality of state citizens, or the totality of inhabitants of an economic space. In Germany the policy called 'national' is one that seeks to grant the existing class state the means of power it demands: soldiers, cannon, warships; in France it means the politics of 'revanche' and colonial expansion. The term 'national economy' is used not to refer to the economy of the nation – for example of Germans in different countries – but rather to the economy of the German economic space, which in no way includes all Germans, and beside Germans also includes French, Danes, Poles and Jews, as well as smaller numbers belonging to the most diverse nations. 'Protection of national labour', likewise, does not mean, for example, the protection of German workers in Austria or the United States, but rather the protection of work performed in the German economic space, and so on. We have nothing to do with the nation understood in this sense. This use of language rests on a confusion of the nation with the population of the political and economic area.[15]

Often as the relation of nation and state is discussed, theory is generally content with maintaining that it is 'natural' for every nation to seek to become a state. In this way, however, the task of science is again not solved, but only posed. We have to ask why it appears to people 'natural' or reasonable that each nation, and only a nation, should form a political community. The principle of nationalities evidently includes two demands: first, the desire for national freedom, the rejection of foreign rule, the demand for 'each nation a state', and second, the desire for national unity, the rejection of particularism, the demand for 'the whole nation one state'. The question now is to explain why these demands arose in the nineteenth century, and became powerful enough to overthrow the traditional system of states.

The impulse to the nation-state movement was certainly given by the demand for rejection of foreign rule. When such rule means at the same time oppression and exploitation of the whole nation, the demand to reject it requires no explanation.

Petty bourgeois, peasants and workers in any state, even a national state, stand under alien rule; they are exploited and oppressed by land-lords, capitalists and bureaucrats. But this alien rule may be concealed: it is not apparent but must be grasped. Rule by an alien nation, on the other hand, is apparent and immediately visible. If a worker comes into an office or stands before a court, he does not understand that it is an alien power that rules him through the officials and judges; for officials and judges present themselves as organs of his nation. But if the official and judge belong to a different nation, if they speak a foreign language, then the fact of subjection of the mass of the people to an alien power is visibly apparent and hence intolerable. The peasant's son also serves in the army of the national state as an instrument of alien power. But this alien power, the ruling classes whose purposes the army serves, knows very well how to conceal this fact; it knows how to make people believe the army is an instrument of power of the entire nation. If, however, the officers belong to a foreign nation, and give their orders in a foreign language, then even the peasant's son who has to obey these orders perceives right away that he is in thrall to an alien power. In a uniform national society, the capitalist and feudal lord appear as organs of the nation, its representatives whom the nation has entrusted with the task of managing production and distribution; but if they belong to a foreign nation, the peasant perceives when liable for corvée service, and the wage-worker right away, that they have to work in the service of a foreigner, to the profit of someone else. This is the great significance of foreign rule, that it makes immediately visible and apparent, and thus intolerable, the exploitation and oppression which in other cases must first be understood.

The demand to cast off foreign domination can be seen as the driving force of all nation-state movements of the nineteenth century. The conspiracy of the absolute princes of Europe against the French Revolution threatened the French people with the danger of bowing to foreign will, sacrificing to foreign power the freedom they had fought for, so the revolutionary struggle of the French became a national struggle. Then, when the armies of Napoleon conquered Germany, the demand for national freedom burned here too: Arndt, the hater of the French, preceded Schenkendorf, the herald of the Kaiser. The freedom struggles of the Italians, Irish and Poles, of the Greeks and the Slavs of the Balkan peninsula, were likewise struggles against foreign rule. From hatred of foreign rule grew the yearning for national freedom expressed by 'Young Europe'.

The forces unleashed by modern capitalism, however, worked in the same direction. Capitalism needs a large and populous economic space; the necessity of capitalist development thus struggles against the political fragmentation of the nation. If the capitalist states were bound together by free exchange of goods, welded into a single economic space, then capitalism could perfectly well put up with the fragmention of the nation into a number of independent states. In reality, however, the state in the capitalist world almost always becomes a more or less independent economic space: by protective duties, taxation policy, railway tariffs and different legislation, exchange between states is restricted. The great mass of goods produced in a state serve the needs of the consumers who live there. The demand of capitalism for a large economic space thus becomes the demand for a large state. Let us try and sketch out the reasons that made the development of the large state a necessity in the nineteenth century.

The more populous an economic space, the more numerous and large can be the factories in which each commodity is produced. Factory size, as is well known, means a reduction in production costs, a rise in the productivity of labour. But a larger number of similar-sized factories has the same effect: first because division of labour and specialization can develop within the plant, significantly increasing labour productivity; there is no doubt, for example, that the extraordinarily rapid industrial development of the United States of America was very largely promoted by the fact that the size of the economic space there enables a far more developed division of labour than in the European states. Further, a larger number of similar-sized factories makes possible improvements in communications, which yet again reduce the production costs. Where a large number of factories exist side by side, canals and railways are built, whereas for a few factories either these facilities are not built at all or else the transport costs are higher per unit of freight because of less intensive use.

All these reasons are so forceful that small states can never be satisfied with being independent economic spaces, but must strive even against the most widespread protectionist efforts for trade with other countries. But for a small economic space, this trade meets major problems.

First of all, differences in currency and taxation, in civil law and procedure, set obstacles to trade between states. Then each state establishes its own news network, so that knowledge of the market in a foreign state is rarely so precise as that of the home market. Further, only the large state is able to regulate the transport system and set railway tariffs; the small state, which shares a railway line with a series of other small states, can make communications harder, but cannot promote economic development by a planned tariff policy.

By treaties of all kinds, states seek to overcome these obstacles:

common currencies, trade agreements, customs unions, treaties over law enforcement, trade marks, models and patents, intergovernmental regulation of railway tariffs, all serve this end. But even in negotiating these treaties with neighbouring states, the small economic space is at a disadvantage:

> The foreign trade of a space of restricted size is large in relation to its production, hence it is very important for such a country. For the larger foreign states, however, from which it imports goods and to which it seeks to export, this trade is of little significance in relation to their own production. The small state has less success therefore in defending its interests in agreements, and in getting other states to adapt their trade policy to its needs.[16]

But the smaller state is not only economically weaker; it is of course also politically weaker, and yet capitalism always needs the strong arm of the state in order to carry through its drive for expansion. How could German capital seek profitable investment in foreign countries, or German merchants travel in foreign markets, if they were not protected by the war-making power of their state? The small state, which is unable to provide its citizens abroad with sufficient protection, thus appears to the capitalists an inadequate and unsatisfactory instrument of their rule. All the more so, in that the small state is also generally a very expensive instrument. For, other conditions being equal, the administration of a large state is cheaper than that of a small one, and the burden of taxation accordingly less.

The nations of the nineteenth century saw all these advantages of the large state directly before them; it was generally acknowledged how France had blossomed since the customs barriers that had divided the provinces from each other had been dismantled. No wonder the demand grew stronger among Germans and Italians to make their respective countries each into a large and single economic space.

We thus see the German bourgeoisie taking the lead in the struggle to establish a large German economic space. Under Friedrich List it struggled for the *Zollverein*, and for a German railway network. In 1833 Prussia joined together with the two Hessens, Bavaria, Würtemberg and Saxony into a single customs zone. In 1847, after long interruption, a unitary German legal code was re-established, containing an agreement on currency exchange, which led to German trade law being applied to all German states – something that sheds a bright light on the driving forces of the unification movement.

The superiority of large economic spaces, however, only explains the fact that the Germans demanded a large state; but why precisely a national state? Why should the boundaries of the nation become the boundaries of the state? Here the operation of economic requirements combines with the effects of political transformations.

We have already mentioned more than once that the bourgeoisie was rationalistic as long as it struggled against the traditional political order. The bourgeoisie in battle against the absolutist state, with the freedom of its leading lights restricted by this state, its sons thrown into prison, its press gagged, its writings prosecuted and its associations dissolved – this bourgeoisie distrusted the state of historic tradition and demanded instead the natural state, the state of reason. This distrust of everything transmitted by history was further nourished by the transformations of the Napoleonic age. When the peace of Luneville brought such a number of German petty states to an unlamented end, why should the surviving states continue to exist? And when, following the wars of liberation, the Congress of Vienna set out to revise the map of Europe and reorder the system of states, it appeared contrary to common sense to imagine the way to further development with the antiquated equipment of former times. So the idea of the natural state, the rational state, was further strengthened. But what are the natural boundaries of the state?

On this question, the national consciousness and national sentiment expanded by bourgeois development and reinforced by the Napoleonic Wars pointed to the nation as the 'natural' foundation of the state and formulated this idea as the principle of nationality: each nation its state! And each state only one nation! For the landlords and peasants, territory is the foundation, and the natural limits of territory are the natural frontiers of the state; for the bourgeois and workers of the capitalist epoch, however, the state is above all an organization of men for their common purposes; what separates people must thus divide states. The state commands me from outside, the nation lives within me, a living and effective power in my character as determined by its fortunes. Thus the nation appears a natural model, the state an artificial product.

Herder expresses this idea very clearly. The nation is a natural growth:

> A people is as much a plant of nature as a family, only one with many branches. Nothing seems so directly opposed to the purpose of government as the unnatural expansion of states, the uncontrolled mingling of human varieties under one sceptre.[17]

Let us try to separate the different thoughts that are summarized in this statement. Its foundation is evidently the demand that the state as the product of human will should be adapted to and follow nature. It was the age of Rousseau that renewed the old demand of the Stoics, *naturam sequi*. Nature is unchanging, given, the state is changeable, labile; hence the state must adapt to the claims of nature.[18] The state must thus follow the nation, and unite politically the nation, the whole nation, and nothing but the nation.

Is it correct that the nation is a natural creation, but the state an artificial product? For us this distinction no longer has the traditional sense. The old antithesis, surviving from the days of Plato and Aristotle, between a political rationalism that views the state as an artificial product to be constructed by human will according to the demands of reason, and a political naturalism that views the state as a creation of nature, governed by 'great eternal iron laws', has been overcome in the modern theory of knowledge. We know today that what is involved here is simply a difference in perspective, and not an exclusive alternative. If we pursue science, then the state for us is a product of nature as much as any other phenomenon, and governed by laws; our task is to investigate the laws that govern the rise, change and demise of states. If we pursue politics, on the other hand, and seek to reorder the state, it is then evidently for us a product of human will, the object of our activity. For the politician, however, the nation is also a creation of his will, a product of artifice: for it can be the object of his endeavour to maintain or to change the national character, to widen or constrict the circle of the nation's members. If both state and nation can, on the one hand, be considered a product of nature, which is grasped under laws as an object of science, and, on the other, can become an artificial object, which is an object of our will, is there then any sense left in Herder's idea that the state as the artificial product should follow and adapt to the nation as natural growth?

Notes

1. Walker Bagehot, *Der Ursprung der Nation*, Leipzig 1874, p. 25.
2. Karl Kautsky, *Neue Zeit*, vol. 23, 2, p. 464.
3. This question, whether the German worker has more character traits in common with the German bourgeois or with the French worker, does not coincide with that of whether the German worker is to follow a politics of class or of nation, whether he is to unite with the proletarians of all countries against international capital or with the German bourgeoisie against other peoples. The resolution of this question depends on quite other considerations than establishing the intensity of the different communities of character.
4. On the defects of this view, especially for the question of the origin of law, see Rudolf Stammler, *Wirtschaft und Recht*, Leipzig 1896, pp. 315 ff.
5. Fichte takes this metaphysical concept of the nation still more deeply when he says:

> The totality of those who continue living together in the society, persisting in producing themselves both naturally and mentally, a totality that altogether stands under a certain particular law of development of the divine out of it, is a people. It is the commonality of this particular law that in the eternal world and hence also in the temporal world unites this quantity into a natural totality permeated by itself.

Johann Fichte, *Reden an die deutsche Nation*, Leipzig 1909, p. 116. In this conception, each person is nothing but one of the countless modes of appearance of the divine, but the divine stands under different laws and only those forms of appearance of the divine that stand under the same law form the nations. The national spirit is one form of appearance of the divine; the individual is one form of appearance of the national spirit. Fichte ends up with this metaphysic of the nation, although previously (p. 52) he comes very close to the correct empirical concept of the nation. It is characteristic of this post-Kantian dogmatic idealism that even when it managed to conceive a phenomenon correctly in an empirical and historical sense, it was not satisfied with this, but rather sought to make the empirical phenomenon it had correctly specified scientifically into a phenomenal form of metaphysical being distinct from this.

6. Here Bauer is referring to the view which holds that national populations are biological unities. [Editor's note]

7. Georg Simmel, *Die Probleme der Geschichtsphilosophie*, Leipzig 1905, pp. 84 ff.

8. Karl Marx, 'Critique of Hegel's *Philosophy of Right*. Introduction', *Early Writings*, London 1990, p. 245.

9. Ibid., p. 256.

10. It may possibly surprise many people that I speak of the proletariat as the embodiment of rationalism, since the theory of the proletariat, i.e. Marxism, precisely escaped from rationalism in social science, and taught us for the first time to understand everything that exists in its historical determinacy. What is important to distinguish here, however, is that Marx taught *science* to grasp existence and becoming in its historical dependence and determinacy. He did not thereby withdraw the traditional from rationalist criticism, holding it to be justified by showing its historical origin. No one combated this nonsense more sharply than he did! It was none other than Marx who rather taught us to understand proletarian rationalism historically, in its origin.

11. It goes without saying that the term 'evolutionary' here is in no way in opposition to 'revolutionary'. A revolution, a sudden transfomation, is only a particular method, a means of development, a phase of evolution.

12. Ernest Renan, *Qu'est-ce qu'une nation?*, Paris 1882.

13. Alfred Kirchhoff, *Zur Verständigung über die Begriffe 'Nation' und 'Nationalität'*, Halle 1905.

14. We can now group the theories of the nation that we have discussed as follows: (1) metaphysical theories of the nation: national spiritualism and national materialism; (2) psychological theories of the nation: psychological-intellectualist and psychological-voluntarist; (3) the empirical theory of the nation, which is satisfied with enumerating the 'elements' that are essential to the nation. To these theories we oppose our own doctrine of the nation as the community of character growing out of a community of destiny, a doctrine deriving from the materialist conception of history.

15. On the distinction between people and nation see the work by F.J. Neumann referred to above.

16. Richard Schüller, *Schutzzoll und Freihandel*, Vienna 1905, p. 247.

17. Johann Herder, *Ideen zur Geschichte der Menschheit*, book 9, iv.

18. In Herder's conception this is evidently nature in the narrower sense: the nation for him is a community of descent. In principle, however, this line of thought is unchanged if we let the nation proceed from the human struggle of existence not only by natural inheritance, but also by the transmission of cultural values.

3

From National Movement to the Fully-formed Nation:
The Nation-building Process in Europe
Miroslav Hroch

The nation has been an inseparable accompaniment of modern European history. It is not difficult to ironize over the record of 'nationalism' in past and present, to criticize its role and to award good or bad marks to different groups, personalities or even nations, in the process. There is a public that finds this procedure to its taste, but it is not to be confused with a scientific approach to the subject. Historians are not judges; their task is to explain actual historical transformations. There has been a significant amount of new literature on nations and nationalism in recent years, much of it produced by social scientists developing theoretical frameworks, and then illustrating their generalizations with selected examples. Historians prefer to start with empirical research, and then move to broader conclusions. My own work has not sought to advance a theory of nation-building, but rather to develop effective methods for the classification and assessment of experiences of nation-building as a process set within a wider social and cultural history – treated not as so many singular and unrepeatable events, but as part of a broad transformation of society that is amenable to controlled generalizations.[1] But it is important to stress at the outset that we are very far from being able to explain all the major problems posed by the formation of modern nations. Every historian of national movements agrees there are numerous data gaps in our understanding of them. In this sense, all defensible conclusions remain no more than partial findings, and all 'theories' should be taken as projects for further research. Polemically, one might say that at the moment we have an overproduction of theories and a stagnation of comparative research on the topic.

Nation and Civil Society

This misfortune is, I think, in part due to a widespread conceptual confusion. For today the process whereby nations were formed in Europe is typically represented as the unfolding or spread of the ideas of 'nationalism'. This is perhaps especially true of recent Anglo-Saxon literature.[2] In my view, this is a basically misleading way of looking at the subject. For the diffusion of national ideas could only occur in specific social settings. Nation-building was never a mere project of ambitious or narcissistic intellectuals, and ideas could not flow through Europe by their own inspirational force. Intellectuals can 'invent' national communities only if certain objective preconditions for the formation of a nation already exist. Karl Deutsch long ago remarked that for national consciousness to arise, there must be something for it to become conscious of. Individual discoveries of national sentiment do not explain why such discoveries recurred in so many countries, independently of each other, under different conditions and in different epochs. Only an approach that looks for the underlying similarity of reasons why people accepted a new national identity, can shed light on this problem. These reasons may be verbalized, but below the level of 'high politics' they are often unverbalized.

Now the 'nation' is not, of course, an eternal category, but was the product of a long and complicated process of historical development in Europe. For our purposes, let us define it at the outset as a large social group integrated not by one but by a combination of several kinds of objective relationships (economic, political, linguistic, cultural, religious, geographical, historical), and their subjective reflection in collective consciousness. Many of these ties could be mutually substitutable – some playing a particularly important role in one nation-building process, and no more than a subsidiary part in others. But among them, three stand out as irreplaceable: (1) a 'memory' of some common past, treated as a 'destiny' of the group – or ar least of its core constituents; (2) a density of linguistic or cultural ties enabling a higher degree of social communication within the group than beyond it; (3) a conception of the equality of all members of the group organized as a civil society.

The process whereby nations were built, around such central elements, was not preordained or irreversible. It could be interrupted, just as it could also be resumed after a long hiatus. Looking at Europe as a whole, it is clear that it went through two distinct stages, of unequal length. The first of these started during the Middle Ages, and led to two quite different outcomes, which provided contrasting starting-points for the second stage, of a transition to a capitalist economy and civil society. At that point the path to a modern nation in the full sense of the word proceeded from either one or the other of two contrasted socio-political situations (though, of course, there were transitional cases). Over much of Western Europe – England, France, Spain, Portugal, Sweden, the Netherlands – but also farther east in Poland, the early modern state developed under the domination of one ethnic culture, either in absolutist form or in a representative-estates system. In the majority of such cases, the late feudal regime was subsequently transformed, by reforms or revolution, into a modern civil society *in parallel* with the construction of a nation-state as a community of equal citizens. In most of Central and Eastern Europe, on the other hand, an 'exogenous' ruling class dominated ethnic groups which occupied a compact territory but lacked 'their own' nobility, political unit or continuous literary tradition. My own research has been concerned with this second type of situation. It is an error, however, to think that it never existed in Western Europe as well. The plight of the 'non-dominant ethnic group' has come to be identified with lands in Eastern and South-Eastern Europe – as the fate of Estonians, Ukrainians, Slovenes, Serbs or others. But there were originally many similar communities in Western and South-Western Europe too. There, however, the medieval or early modern state assimilated most of them, although a significant number of distinctive ancient cultures persisted through such processes of integration – Irish, Catalan, Norwegian and others (in Eastern Europe, the Greeks perhaps form an analogy).[3] There was also an important set of transitional cases, in which ethnic communities possessed 'their own' ruling class and literary traditions, but lacked any common statehood – the Germans and Italians, or later (after the loss of their commonwealth) the Poles.

Now in the second type of situation, on which my own work has concentrated, the onset of the modern stage of nation-building can be dated from the moment when selected groups within the non-dominant ethnic community started to discuss their own ethnicity and to conceive of it as a potential nation-to-be. Sooner or later, they observed certain deficits, which the future nation still lacked, and began efforts to overcome one or more of them, seeking to persuade their compatriots of the importance of consciously belonging to the nation. I term these organized endeavours to achieve all the attributes of a fully-fledged nation (which were not always and everywhere successful) a *national movement*. The current tendency to speak of them as 'nationalist' leads to serious confusion. For nationalism *stricto sensu* is something else: namely, that outlook which gives an *absolute priority to the values of the nation over all other values and interests*. It was far from being the case that all the patriots in the national movements of Central and Eastern Europe in the nineteenth or early twentieth century were nationalists in this, accurate sense of the word. The term can scarcely be applied to such representative figures as the

Norwegian poet Wergeland, who tried to create a language for his country, the Polish writer Mickiewicz who longed for the liberation of his homeland, or even the Czech scholar Masaryk, who formulated and realized a programme of national independence after having fought all his life against Czech nationalists. Nationalism was only one of many forms of national consciousness to emerge in the course of these movements. Nationalism did, of course, often later become a significant force in this region, just as it did further west in the region of state-nations, as a type of power politics with irrationalist overtones. But the programme of the classic national movement was of another kind. Its goals covered three main groups of demands, which corresponded to felt deficits of national existence: (1) the development of a national culture based on the local language, and its normal use in education, administration and economic life; (2) the achievement of civil rights and political self-administration, initially in the form of autonomy and ultimately (usually quite late, as an express demand) of independence;[4] (3) the creation of a complete social structure from out of the ethnic group, including educated elites, an officialdom and an entrepreneurial class, but also – where necessary – free peasants and organized workers. The relative priority and timing of these three sets of demands varied in each case. But the trajectory of any national movement was only consumed when all were fulfilled.

Between the starting-point of any given national movement and its successful conclusion, three structural phases can be distinguished, according to the character and role of those active in it, and the degree of national consciousness emergent in the ethnic group at large. During an initial period, which I have called Phase A, the energies of the activists were above all devoted to scholarly inquiry into and dissemination of an awareness of the linguistic, cultural, social and sometimes historical attributes of the non-dominant group – but without, on the whole, pressing specifically national demands to remedy deficits (some did not even believe their group could develop into a nation). In a second period, or Phase B, a new range of activists emerged, who now sought to win over as many of their ethnic group as possible to the project of creating a future nation, by patriotic agitation to 'awaken' national consciousness among them – at first usually without notable success (in one sub-stage), but later (in another sub-stage) finding an increasingly receptive audience. Once the major part of the population came to set special store by their national identity, a mass movement was formed, which I have termed Phase C. It was only during this final phase that a full social structure could come into being, and that the movement differentiated out into conservative-clerical, liberal and democratic wings, each with their own programmes.

Four Types of National Movement

The purpose of this periodization, as I proposed it, was to permit mean-ingful comparisons between national movements – that is, something more than mere synchronic surveys of what was happening at the same time in different lands of Europe in the last century, namely the study of analogous forms and phases of historical development. Such comparison requires the selection of a limited set of specific dimensions in terms of which different national movements can be analysed. The more complex the phenomenon to be compared, the greater the number of such per-tinent dimensions, of course. But it is normally advisable to proceed gradually, accumulating comparative results step by step, rather than introducing too many dimensions all at once. Here are some of the most significant markers, certain of which I or others have explored, while oth-ers remain topics for future research: the social profile and territorial distribution of leading patriots and activists; the role of language as sym-bol and vehicle of identification; the place of the theatre (also music and folklore) in national movements; the salience or otherwise of civil rights as a demand; the importance of historical awareness; the position of the school system and the spread of literacy; the participation of the churches and the influence of religion; the contribution of women as activists and as symbols. Above all, however, what emerged from my own work was the central significance for any typology of national movements in Central and Eastern Europe (but not only there) of the *relationship* between the transition to Phase B and then to Phase C, on the one hand, and the transition to a constitutional society based on equality before the law, on the other hand – what is often generically called the moment of 'bourgeois revolution'. Combining these two series of changes, we can distinguish four types of national movement in Europe:

1. In the first, the inception of national agitation (Phase B) occurred under the old regime of absolutism, but it acquired a mass character in a time of revolutionary changes in the political system, when an organized labour movement was also beginning to assert itself. The leaders of Phase B developed their national programmes in condi-tions of political upheaval. This was the case with Czech agitation in Bohemia, and with the Hungarian and Norwegian movements, all of which entered Phase B around 1800. The Norwegian patriots gained a liberal constitution and declaration of independence in 1814, while the Czechs and Magyars developed – albeit in very different fashion – their national programmes during the revolutions of 1848.

2. In the second, national agitation likewise got under way under the old regime, but the transition to a mass movement, or Phase C, was

delayed until after a constitutional revolution. This shift of sequence could be caused either by uneven economic development, as in Lithuania, Latvia, Slovenia or Croatia; or by foreign oppression, as in Slovakia or the Ukraine. Phase B can be said to have started in Croatia in the 1830s, in Slovenia in the 1840s, in Latvia at the end of the 1850s, and in Lithuania not till the 1870s – reaching Phase C in Croatia not before the1880s, in Slovenia in the 1890s, and in Latvia and Lithuania only during the revolution of 1905. Forcible Magyarization checked the transition to Phase C in Slovakia after 1867, as did oppressive Russification in the Ukraine.

3. In the third type, the national movement acquired a mass character already under the old regime, and so before the establishment of a civil society or constitutional order. This pattern produced armed insurrections, and was confined to lands of the Ottoman Empire in Europe – Serbia, Greece and Bulgaria.

4. In the final type, national agitation first began under constitutional conditions, in a more developed capitalist setting, characteristic of Western Europe. In these cases, the national movement could reach Phase C quite early, as in the Basque lands and Catalonia, while in other cases it did so only after a very long Phase B, as in Flanders, or not at all – as in Wales, Scotland or Brittany.

None of the steps traced so far – from definition to periodization to typology – is, of course, an end in itself. They do not explain the origins or outcomes of the various national movements. They are no more than necessary starting-points for the real task of all historical research: causal analysis. What explains the success of most of these movements in the epoch that ended at Versailles, and the failure of others? What accounts for the variations in their evolution and upshot? If the fashionable idea that nations in Europe were invented by nationalism is clearly unfounded, mono-causal explanations fare little better. Any satisfactory account will have to be multi-causal, and move between different levels of generalization; and it will have to extend across a chronologically lengthy span of uneven European development.

Antecedents to Nation-building

Any such explanation must begin with the 'prelude' to modern nation-building that lies in the late medieval and early modern epochs, which was of great moment not only for the state-nations of the West, but also for those ethnic groups that remained or became dominated by 'external' ruling classes in the centre and east of the continent, or elsewhere. In historical reality, of course, there were many transitional cases between these two ideal-types. A large number of medieval polities with their own written languages did not develop successfully into state-nations, but on the contrary lost their autonomy partly or completely, while their populations generally retained their ethnicity. This was true of the Czechs, Catalans, Norwegians, Croats, Bulgarians, Welsh, Irish and others. Even in cases of typologically rather 'pure' non-dominant ethnic groups – for example, the Slovenes, Estonians or Slovaks – we cannot dismiss their common past as a mere myth. More generally, the legacy of the first stage of a nation-building process, even if aborted, often left significant resources for the second. These included, in particular, the following:

1. Very often, certain relics of an earlier political autonomy remained, though appropriated by members of estates belonging to the 'ruling' nation, and generated tensions between the estates and absolutism that sometimes provided triggers for later national movements. This partern could be observed in many parts of Europe during the late eighteenth century – for example, in the resistance of the Hungarian, Bohemian and Croatian estates to Josephine centralism, the reaction of the nobility in Finland to Gustav III's neo-absolutism, the opposition of the Protestant landowners in Ireland to English centralization, or the response of the local bureaucracy in Norway to Danish absolutism.
2. The 'memory' of former independence or statehood, even situated far in the past, could play an important role in stimulating national historical consciousness and ethnic solidarity. This was the very first argument employed in Phase B by patriots in the Czech lands, Lithuania, Finland, Bulgaria, Catalonia and elsewhere.
3. In many cases, the medieval written language had more or less survived, making it easier to develop the norm of a modern language with its own literature, as proved to be the case with Czech, Finnish and Catalan, among others. However, the contrast between cases of this legacy and its absence was much exaggerated in the nineteenth century, when it was sometimes claimed it corresponded to a distinction between 'historical' and 'unhistorical' peoples, whereas in fact its salience was limited to the tempo at which historical consciousness of the nation now arose.

What is clear in all cases, however, is that the modern nation-building process started with the collection of information about the history, language and customs of the non-dominant ethnic group, which became the critical ingredient in the first phase of patriotic agitation. The learned researchers of Phase A 'discovered' the ethnic group and laid a basis for the subsequent formation of a 'national identity'. Yet their intellectual activity cannot be called an organized social or political movement. Most of the patriots articulated no 'national' demands as yet. The conversion of their aims into the objectives of a social movement seeking cultural and political changes was a product of Phase B and the reasons why this occurred still remain in large measure an open question. Why did scholarly interests become emotional attachments? Why should affection or loyalty to a region pass into identification with an ethnic group as a nation-to-be?

The Role of Social Mobility and Communication

As a first approach, one might single out three processes as decisive for this transformation: (1) a social and/or political crisis of the old order, accompanied by new tensions and horizons; (2) the emergence of discontent among significant elements of the population; (3) loss of faith in traditional moral systems, above all a decline in religious legitimacy, even if this only affected small numbers of intellectuals (but not just those influenced by Enlightenment rationalism, also other dissenting currents). In general, it is clear that future research must pay more attention to these various facets of crisis, and to the competence or willingness of patriots to articulate responses to them in national – rather than simply social or political – terms. If certain groups of intellectuals now launched a true national agitation, this then initiated the critical Phase B. But this did not automatically mean the birth of a modern nation, which required further conditions for its emergence. For we must ask under what circumstances such agitation was ultimately successful, in passing over into a mass movement of Phase C capable of completing the national programme?

Various theories have been advanced by social scientists to explain this transformation, but it is difficult to be satisfied with them, because they do not correspond to the empirical facts. Ernest Gellner, for example, attributes the growth of 'nationalism' essentially to the functional requirements of industrialization.[5] Yet most of the national movements in Europe emerged well before the arrival of modern industry, and usually completed the decisive Phase B of their development before they had any contact with it – many of them, indeed, in overwhelmingly agrarian conditions. But if such flaws are common to much of the sociological literature, we cannot, on the other hand, simply confine ourselves to inductive descriptions of the kind favoured by a traditionalist historiographer. Let us then look at two factors, designated by different terms by different authors, but in substance enjoying a certain consensus in the field. Adopting Karl Deutsch's vocabulary, we can term these social mobility and communication.[6] Here the situation seems on the surface relatively straightforward. We can confirm that in most cases members of patriotic groups belonged to professions with quite high vertical mobility, while in no case were they dominated by recruits from groups with low social mobility, like peasants. A high level of social mobility thus seems to have been a favourable condition for acceptance of patriotic programmes in Phase B. So far, so good. Unfortunately, however, we know that it often also facilitated successful upward assimilation of members of the same groups into the ranks of the ruling nation. Similarly, social communication as the transmission of information about reality, and of attitudes towards it, certainly played an important role in the advent of modern capitalist society – and if we analyse the occupations of the patriots, we will arrive at the conclusion that national agitation appealed most readily to those within the non-dominant ethnic group who enjoyed the best channels of such communication. A territorial analysis yields the same result: those regions with the densest networks of communication were most susceptible to such agitation. Thus far, Deutsch's view seems to be corroborated – that the growth of national movements (he spoke of nationalism) went hand in hand with the advance of social communication and mobility, themselves processes within a more general transformation of society.[7]

Yet it is still necessary to check this hypothesis against historical reality in at least two limiting cases. At one extreme, we have to hand the example of the district of Polesie in interwar Poland, an area with minimal social mobility, very weak contacts with the market, and scant literacy. When its inhabitants were asked in the census of 1919 what was their nationality, most of them just replied: 'from hereabouts'.[8] The same pattern prevailed in Eastern Lithuania, West Prussia, Lower Lusatia, and various Balkan regions. But what of the opposite situation? Can an intensive growth of communication and a high rate of mobility be considered causes of a successful Phase B? By no means – the experience of such lands as Wales, Belgium, Britanny or Schleswig shows, on the contrary, that these could coexist with a weak response to national agitation, in conditions where a maturing constitutional order proved more important.

Crisis and Conflict

There must then have been another weighty factor, besides social change and high levels of mobility and communication, that typically helped to lend impetus to a national movement. I have termed this factor a nationally relevant conflict of interests – in other words a social tension or collision that could be mapped onto linguistic (and sometimes also religious) divisions. A common example in the nineteenth century was the conflict between new university graduates coming from a non-dominant ethnic group, and a closed elite from the ruling nation keeping a hereditary grip on leading positions in state and society.[9] But there were also clashes between peasants belonging to the subaltern group and landlords from the dominant one, between craftsmen from the former and large traders and manufacturers from the latter, and so on. It is important to stress that these conflicts of interest which bore on the fate of national movements cannot be reduced to class conflicts – for the national movements always recruited members from several classes and groups, so that their interests were determined by a broad spectrum of social relations (including, of course, class relations).

Why were social conflicts of this kind articulated in national terms more successfully in some parts of Europe than in others? Paradoxically, we may say that in the nineteenth century national agitation often started earlier and made more headway in those areas where the non-dominant ethnic groups as a whole, often including their leaders, had scant political education and virtually no political experience, because of the absolutist oppression under which they had grown up. Bohemia or Estonia are two among many examples. In these circumstances, there was little room for the more developed forms of political discourse or argument. On both sides of a given conflict, it was easier to articulate social contradictions or hostilities in national categories – as dangers to a common culture, or particular language, or ethnic interest. This is the main reason why West European national movements reveal a typological deviance (see Type 4, above). It was the higher levels of political culture and experience that allowed conflicts of interest in most Western zones to be articulated in political terms. Thus Flemish patriots were from the outset of Phase B divided into two camps – liberal and clerical – and most Flemish electors expressed their political preferences by voting for the Liberal or Catholic parties, leaving only a small minority for the Flemish Party proper. The same phenomenon can be observed in Wales or Scotland today. In these conditions, the national programme could not easily win a mass following, and in some cases never achieved a transition to Phase C. The lesson is that it is not enough to consider only the formal level of social communication reached in a given society – one must also look at the complex of contents mediated through it (even if these are in part unconscious). If the national slogans and goals used by agitators to articulate social tensions do in fact correspond to the immediate daily experience, to the level of schooling, and the system of symbols and stereotypes current in the majority of the non-dominant ethnic group, Phase C can be attained in a relatively short time.

The pattern of a successful national movement thus invariably includes at least four elements: (1) a crisis of legitimacy, linked to social, moral and

cultural strains; (2) a basic volume of vertical social mobility (some educated people must come from the non-dominant ethnic group); (3) a
fairly high level of social communication, including literacy, schooling
and market relations; and (4) nationally relevant conflicts of interest.
Such a model does not pretend to explain everything in the long and
complex history of national movements. Let me illustrate this with an
indication of some of the problems that remain unsolved for us today,
despite the plethora of new 'theories of nationalism'.

Gaps Revealed by the Model

My own comparative research has focused on the range of social con-
stellations at work in Phase B of the national movements of
nineteenth-century Europe. So far, no analogous studies have been made
of Phase C.[10] Here too comparative analysis is badly needed, not only of
the social groups mobilized once the national programme acquired a
mass appeal, but also of the relative importance of the three principal
components of its own agenda. There was no single ideal combination of
these. What we need to explore are the interrelationships between the
cultural, political and social aspirations in the national programmes of
the time, as well as the inner structure of each, and the specific demands
that issued from them. We already know these could vary widely.
Furthermore, once political demands gained salience in the national
programme, the movement itself inevitably became a battlefield for the
pursuit of power, not only in struggle against the ruling nation, but within
the leaderships of the national movement as well. Under these conditions, leadership of the national movements typically passed from
intellectuals to professional strata in a wider sense.

Another vital field for comparative research is a social physiognomy of
the leading patriots – above all, the national intelligentsias in the region.
Some preliminary comparisons I have undertaken of Czech, Polish,
Slovak and German intellectuals in this period suggest that there are so
far unexploited opportunities here for interpretation of national stereotypes, of the political culture and social sentiments of the patriots. The
striking differences in the social origins of German and Czech intelligentsias of the time cast a new light on the national movements of each
group in Bohemia.[11] But we should also note that so far little work has
been done on those intellectuals who, by reason of their education and
ethnicity, could have participated in the national movement, but did not
do so. We need to know more about these nationally unconcerned or
assimilated intelligentsias as well.

A final and substantial lacuna in contemporary research on the
national movements of the last century may seem unexpected. Much

irony has been expended on the historical legends and fictive pasts purveyed by the patriots of the time.[12] But we do not in fact know very much
about the real role of history in the emergence and growth of national
movements. For, of course, there was a genuine fund of historical experience on which many of them could draw – all the materials deposited by
the first, pre-modern stage of the nation-building process itself; and then
there were the various forms in which these subsequently found reflection in the consciousness of the non-dominant ethnic group. Typically,
the kind of historical thought that arose at the beginning of the national
movement was very different from the sort that developed towards its
end. Here comparisons between Western and Eastern Europe, ruling
nations and ruled nations, are likely to be instructive. Setting German
and Czech historical novels of this period side by side, as I have recently
done, yields suggestive results: while most of the former take their heroes
from the ranks of (mainly Prussian) rulers and nobles, the same social
layer is only rarely represented in the latter.[13]

The 'New Nationalisms' Recapitulate the Old

To what extent is the model outlined so far, which was developed out of
work on the national movements of nineteenth-century Europe, helpful
for understanding the 'new nationalisms' of Central and Eastern Europe
today? The conventional view that current turmoil is the result of the
release of irrational forces that were long suppressed – 'deep-frozen' as it
were – under communism, and are now in full revival after a lapse of fifty
years, is evidently superficial. Such a conception is extravagant – closer to
the world of fairy-tales than of historical processes. It is much more plausible to see the forces reshaping Central and Eastern Europe during the
last decade as 'new national movements', whose goals offer many analogies with those of the nineteenth century, as well as some significant
differences.

The most striking resemblance between the two lies in the contemporary reproduction of the same triptych of aspirations which composed
the national programme a hundred years ago. The specific goals sought
are naturally not identical to those of the earlier national movements, but
the general thrust is closely related. Once again, linguistic and cultural
demands have surfaced with force – above all, of course, in the territories
of the former Soviet Union. There, official policy had never suppressed
local languages in the way tsarist rule often did – indeed it had helped to
promote these in the interwar period, when Ukrainian, Byelorussian,
Caucasian and Central Asian vernaculars had become languages of
school instruction and publication. But in the Western lands acquired
after the war, no such policies were pursued, as Russian was increasingly

imposed as a language of public life. Hence the importance of linguistic issues today in this zone, where Estonia has declared knowledge of its language to be a condition of civil rights, or Moldavia has reclaimed the Latin alphabet. In the countries to the west of the Bug and the Dniester, linguistic demands have been less salient. But here too among the first signs of the break-up of Yugoslavia was the campaign to separate Croat as a fully independent language from Serb, in the seventies and eighties; likewise the Institute of Slovak Literature (Matica) has led the way in pressing linguistic arguments for national independence in Slovakia.

If the significance of the linguistic component varies from region to region today, the political component is in every case central. The two main goals articulated here each have their parallel in the past. On the one hand, the call for democracy corresponds to the demand for civil rights in the programme of the 'classical' movements. On the other hand, the desire for full independence recalls the drive for ethnic autonomy in the nineteenth century. In most cases, although not all (Slovenia, Croatia or Slovakia), the pre-war experience of independent statehood furnishes the decisive model here. By 1992, political independence has, of course, been fully reasserted over most of East-Central Europe; while in the former USSR, the constituent union republics are all now at least juridically sovereign states. In these conditions, energies turn to the direction now to be taken by the independence gained – that is, the question of policies towards external neighbours, and to domestic minorities.

Finally, the new national movements exhibit a social programme of a distinct kind, in conditions where there is typically a rapid exchange of ruling classes. The leaders of these movements aim for a very specific goal: to complete the social structure of the nation by creating a capitalist class corresponding to that of Western states, in which they would come to enjoy a salient position themselves. Here too the formal analogies with the past are striking.

Beyond these, moreover, there are a series of further significant resemblances. In the nineteenth century, the transition to Phase B occurred at a time when the old regime and its social order were on the verge of disintegrating. As traditional ties weakened or dissolved, the need for a new collective identity brought together people from different social classes and then political currents into one national movement. In the same way today, after the breakdown of communist rule and central planning, familiar ties have crumbled, leaving a generalized anxiety and insecurity in which the national idea takes over the role of collective integration. In conditions of acute stress, people characteristically tend to over-value the protective comfort of their own national group.

Identification with the national group in turn includes, as it also did in the last century, the construction of a personalized image of the nation.

The glorious past of this personality comes to be lived as part of the individual memory of each citizen, and its defeats resented as failures that still touch them. One result of such personalization is that people will regard their nation – that is, themselves – as a single body in a more than metaphorical sense. If any distress befalls a small part of the nation, it can be felt throughout it, and if any branch of the ethnic group – even one living far from the 'mother-nation' – is threatened with assimilation, the members of the personalized nation may treat it as an amputation of the national body.

The personalized national body needs, of course – as in the nineteenth century – its own distinct space. Now, as then, claims to such space tend to be based on appeals to two different criteria, whose relationship is often highly contentious: on the one hand, to the principle of an area defined by the ethnic homogeneity of its population, as a common linguistic-cultural group; and on the other hand, to the notion of a historic territory with its own traditional borders, which often include other ethnic groups with minority status. In the nineteenth century, the second criterion acquired especial importance for so-called 'historical nations'. Thus Czechs deemed all the lands inside the frontiers of Bohemia and Moravia their national body; Croats viewed all three parts of the medieval kingdom as their property; Lithuanians regarded the Polish-Jewish city of Wilno as their true capital. Today, this pattern is potentially even more widespread, since besides those nations which were deemed 'historical' in the past century, there are others that acquired the relevant kind of history before the war – when the Estonians or Latvians gained an independent state, or even during it – when Slovaks and Croats secured protectorates under a Nazi licence. In these conditions, leaders of the new national movements are once again inclined to declare state borders to be national boundaries and to treat ethnic minorities in 'their' territory as outsiders, whose identity can be neglected or whose members expelled. Psycho-geography is once more playing an important role in Europe, as children in elementary schools constantly contemplate official maps of their country.[14]

Ethno-linguistic Demands and Problems of Demotion

Why, it may be asked, do ethnic and linguistic arguments so frequently become uppermost in the programme of many of the new national movements in Central and Eastern Europe – just at a time when the Western world is trying to bid farewell to ethnicity as an organizing principle of economic life? The experience of the classic national movements of the region suggests an explanation.[15] When their agitation first started in the nineteenth century, the members of the non-dominant ethnic group had no political education, nor any experience of public activity in civil society. Appeals to the political discourse of civil or human rights could hardly be effective, in these conditions. To a Czech or an Estonian peasant, 'freedom' meant the abolition of feudal exactions and the ability to use their own farmland without impediment, not a parliamentary regime. The reality of a common language and customs could be much more readily grasped than remote conceptions of constitutional liberty. Today, in a somewhat analogous fashion, after fifty years of dictatorial rule, an education in civil society is still largely missing, and linguistic and cultural appeals may once more act as substitutes for articulated political demands – we can see this in the former republics of Yugoslavia, in Romania, in the Baltic states. This can in practice happen even where official discourse resounds with talk of democracy and civil rights.

Linguistic and ethnic demands do not, of course, everywhere have the same importance. But in many of the republics of the former Soviet Union, in particular, the idiom of the dominant nation often remained a symbol of political oppression, whatever the formal position of the main local language. In the nineteenth century, much of the struggle waged by the national movements of the time against the German-speaking bureaucracy of the Habsburg Empire, or the Russian bureaucracy of the tsarist empire, or the officialdom of the Ottoman Empire, revolved around linguistic issues. Today too, the vernacular of any small nation fighting for its independence is automatically regarded as the language of liberty. At stake here, however, are more than questions of prestige and symbolism. The unwillingness of members of the dominant nation to accept real linguistic equality has always put the non-dominant ethnic group at a material disadvantage. German- and Hungarian-speakers under the Dual Monarchy refused to learn or use the languages of other ethnic groups living on 'their' territory. Then, with the break-up of the empire and the emergence of new independent states in 1918–19, many of them suddenly found themselves reduced to the status of official minorities. But they characteristically were still unwilling to accept the predominance of the language of the small – but now dominant – nations under whose rule they lived: Czechs, Romanians, Poles and others. This was an explosive situation, whose consequences became fateful with the advent of the Third Reich in Germany. Today a similar process of demotion is occurring, as – in particular – Russians in the outlying republics become minorities in the independent states under construction by national movements. The historical parallels between the position of the *Volksdeutsche* and that of – so to speak – the '*Volksrussen*' are striking and disquieting.

The Specificity of the Post-communist Conjuncture

What of the role of nationally relevant social conflicts in contemporary conditions? Theoretically, we might suppose that these would not arise where clashes of interest can find straightforwardly political or social expression. Yet, although our knowledge here remains quite limited, it is already clear that some such conflicts are becoming nationally pointed. The cases where a local intelligentsia confronts a nomenclature elite of another ethnic origin, which refuses to learn the local language – the paradigmatic Baltic situation – are in this respect not the most widespread. In fact, the majority of social conflicts that are nationally relevant today are quite distinct from the classic nineteenth-century situation, and bear witness to the profound dissimilarity between the social structures of Central and Eastern Europe of today and yesterday.

For the current situation in the region is in many respects a unique one in European history. The old order, based on a planned economy and rule by a nomenclature, has suddenly disappeared, leaving a political and social vacuum. In these conditions new elites, educated under the old regime, but now at the head of the national movement, have rapidly occupied leading positions in society. The educated strata of the non-dominant ethnic groups strove towards similar goals in the nineteenth century, but they had to contend with the established elites of the ruling nation for every position, and a condition of their success was acceptance of the traditional forms of life, moral codes and rules of the game of the class above them. Today, by contrast, vertical social mobility into the highest levels of wealth or power is subject to no traditional usages, but often appears to be simply the result of individual or national egoisms. The vacuum at the top of society has created the possibility of very swift careers, as a new ruling class starts to take shape, recruited from a confluence of three principal streams – apprentice politicians (some of them former dissidents), veteran bureaucrats (the more skilful managers from the old command economy), and emergent entrepreneurs (sometimes with dubious capital resources). The fight within, and among, these groups for positions of privilege has so far yielded the most intense conflicts of interest in post-communist society; and wherever members of different ethnic groups live on the same territory, it generates the leading tensions of a nationally relevant character today.

The hazards in this situation are significantly increased by another salient difference between the contemporary and the earlier constellation. In the nineteenth century, nationally relevant conflicts of interest typically sprang from processes of economic growth and social improvement – pitting traditionalist artisans against modernizing industrialists, small peasants against large landlords, or modest entrepreneurs against big bankers, for respective shares of a cake that was increasing in size. Today, however, conflicts of this sort are notoriously unfolding against a background of economic depression and decline, in which the cake is becoming smaller. In these circumstances, it is no surprise that the gamut of conflicts within the national movement itself is notably wider than in the past. One result is that the broad spectrum of political positions represented by the programmes of even the (genuinely) 'nationalist' parties of the hour, who can differ widely on methods and goals, make it more difficult to speak of a single national programme. At the same time, the qualitatively higher degree of social communication assured by the modern electronic media enables a much faster conversion of national agitatation into mass sentiment. The possibilities for popular manipulation and invention of national interests where there are none become greater. Control of the mass media in Central and Eastern Europe is a vital stake in the struggle for power, for professional use of them confers extraordinary power on the controllers. We have by no means seen the full consequences here.

There is, however, a further difference in the present conjuncture that may work to counteracting effect. During the nineteenth century, the national movement and nation-building process, and nationalism too, were common to every part of Europe. The new national movements of Central and Eastern Europe, by contrast, appear on the scene at a time when the idea of European integration has become a historical reality in the Western part of the continent. The form it may take remains, of course, highly contested, as two opposite tendencies dispute the constitutional future of the EC – one seeking to make of Europe a continent of citizens irrespective of their ethnicity, the other holding fast to traditional ethnic identities and trying to construct Europe as a unity of separate nation-states. Whatever the outcome of this conflict, it cannot be ignored that the leaders of all the new national movements in the former communist zone proclaim their desire to enter the field of a unified Europe. In this respect we can speak of two (subjectively) complementary processes of group identification in Central and Eastern Europe: the national, based on the historical experience of the different ethnic groups in the area and giving rise to the conflicts mentioned above, and the European, reflecting new horizons and hopes. Were we to apply the terms of our periodization of the classic national movement to the process of European integration itself, we would no doubt find a successful second stage of Phase B in Western Europe, while only the very beginning of Phase B is visible in Central and Eastern Europe – where it is in any case important to distinguish economically opportunist declarations of adherence to European ideals from cultural or political aspirations to them.

Prospects of Catastrophe?

What is likely to be the impact of the new national movements in the former communist zone on the continent as a whole? The tragic processes under way in what was only yesterday Yugoslavia make the dangers of the conjuncture all too evident. Uncompromising concentration on the ethnic attributes of the nation leads quickly to nationalist politics in the true sense of the word. Once this dynamic is unleashed, moralist or humanist appeals typically prove vain – not because of any lack of talent among those who make them, but because once these new movements have acquired a mass character, they can be neither deflected by rational argument nor suppressed by political force (which may even provoke their radicalization), as the experience of their predecessors shows. How far do they thereby threaten, not only the integration, but the stability of Europe?

Everyone knows that the most disastrous consequence of the classic national movements of the region was their role in helping to precipitate the First World War. Today, critics of the 'new nationalism' in Central and Eastern Europe warn of the dangers of a repetition of this fatal sequence. What they forget, however, is that it was the nationalist policies of the Great Powers which essentially brought about the war – the conflicts between small states and their nationalist politicians were little more than kindling used by these Powers. Contemporary 'ethno-nationalism' is mainly a phenomenon of small ethnic groups or nations, which are far from possessing major international weight. The conflicts to which it gives rise are indeed factors of regional instability, but they do not endanger the peace of Europe in the same way as at the turn of the century – or at any rate, they will not do so as long as none of the Great Powers tries to profit from them. This seems a remote prospect at present, since all the major European states save Russia are now joined within the European Community. Nevertheless, it would be unwise to discount entirely the possibility of some interested politicians or parties in the leading Western states using certain of the new national movements to enlarge their own sphere of influence. German initiatives in Slovenia and Croatia have been interpreted by some in this light. There is, of course, a further problem now haunting the region, one that recalls the interwar period rather than the last century. This is the position of minorities within the post-communist states. Such minorities are of two types. The first comprises ethnic groups living in relatively compact areas within a state dominated by another nation, who at the same time belong to a nation on the other side of the frontier: for example, the Magyars in Slovakia or Transylvania, the Serbs in Croatia, the Poles in Moravia, the Russians in Estonia, the Albanians in Kosovo. The second numbers ethnic populations dispersed within a state that is not their own, such as the Slovaks or Germans in Hungary, the Romanians in Serbia, the Turks in Macedonia, the Gypsies everywhere. In either case, minority movements may arise similar in form to national movements, but with the critical difference that they cannot hope to achieve an independent nation-state. The utmost goals of these movements can be political autonomy or border-revision. But such objectives may, of course, on occasion be more explosive than the aims of the new national movements themselves.

In conclusion, it may well be asked: on the basis of our knowledge of the classical national movements of nineteenth-century Europe, what could be thought alterable and what unalterable in the dynamic of the new movements? The basic precondition of all national movements – yesterday and today – is a deep crisis of the old order, with the breakdown of its legitimacy, and of the values and sentiments that sustained it. In the case of the current movements, this crisis is combined with economic depression and the threat of widespread social decline, generating increasing popular distress. But in both periods, a third crucial element of the situation is a low level of political culture and experience among the broad mass of the population. The coincidence of these three conditions – societal crisis, economic recession, political inexperience – is specific to the contemporary conjuncture, when its effects have been intensified by the great increase in the density and speed of social communication. Once the ruling order – absolutism or communism – underwent a certain liberalization, social or political movements against it were inevitable. These became national, if two further factors intervened: the existence of real deficits for a full national life, and of significant tensions that could be articulated as national conflicts, within a pattern of uneven development. Once such national movements acquire a mass character, whether in the past century or this one, they cannot be stopped by governmental ban or use of force. At most, they can today be inflected by civic education in schools and the media, perhaps today in a putatively 'European' direction, and by official measures to ensure a reasonable ethnic balance in public employment. The limitations of such measures are only too evident. The one truly effective remedy for the dangers of the present situation is, alas, the most utopian: a resolution of the economic crisis of the region, and advent of a new prosperity.

Notes

1. See this author's *Social Conditions of National Revival in Europe. A Comparative Analysis of the Social Composition of Patriotic Groups among the Smaller European Nations*, Cambridge 1985, and *Nardodni Hnuti v Evrope 19. Stoleti*, Prague 1986.

2. The term 'nationalism' itself entered into scholarly currency rather late – perhaps no earlier than the work of the American historian Carlton Hayes, above all with his *Historical*

Evolution of Modern Nationalism, New York 1931. Its usage still remained fairly rare in inter-war Europe, as can be seen from A. Kemiläinen's survey *Nationalism. Problems concerning the Word, the Concept and the Classification*, Jyväsklä 1964. The first significant European scholar to deploy the notion for a systematic analysis was E. Lemberg, *Der Nationalismus*, 2 vols, Hamburg 1964.

3. Thus if we compare the incidence of national movements in Western and Eastern Europe in the nineteenth century, the number is about the same. But the proportions change if we ask how many autonomous medieval cultures were either integrated or extinguished in each region. For in the West, only some of these cultures survived to form the basis of later national movements: others – Niederdeutsch, Arab, Provençal, etc. – did not. The Western monarchies generally proved much more capable of assimilating 'non-state' cultures and communities than the Habsburg, Romanov or Ottoman empires.

4. There were national movements which developed the goal of independence very early – for example, the Norwegian, Greek or Serb. But there were many more that came to it only rather late, and in the exceptional circumstances of the First World War – among them the Czech, Finnish, Estonian, Latvian, and Lithuanian movements; while others – the Slovene or Byelorussian – did not formulate it even then. The Catalan case provides a vivid example of the way in which even a powerful national movement need not pose the demand for an independent state.

5. See *Nations and Nationalism*, Oxford 1983, *passim*.

6. See Deutsch's work *Nationalism and Social Communication*, Cambridge, Mass., 1953. Other scholars have also stressed the importance of social communication for an understanding of national sentiment, without adopting Deutsch's perspective or terminology. See, for example, Benedict Anderson, *Imagined Communities. Reflections on the Origins and Spread of Nationalism*, London 1983 – enlarged edn 1991.

7. Otto Bauer was the first to understand the relation of the nation-building process to the general capitalist transformation of society; O. Bauer, *Die Nationalitätenfrage und die Sozialdemokratie*, Vienna 1907.

8. This episode is not analysed in Western literature; see J. Tomaszewski, *Zdziejów Polesia 1921–1939*, Warsaw 1963, pp. 25, 32ff.

9. I first pointed out the importance of this nationally relevant conflict in my book *Die Vorkämpfer der nationalen Bewegungen bei den kleinen Völkern Europas*, Prague 1968. For more detailed subsequent analysis of the problem of unemployed intellectuals see A.D. Smith, *The Ethnic Revival in the Modern World*, Cambridge 1981.

10. The shortage of case studies of this problem explains why Eric J. Hobsbawm could not analyse the social structure of Phase C in his latest work, *Nation and Nationalism 1789–1945*, Cambridge 1990.

11. Some partial results published in Miroslav Hroch, 'Das Bürgertum in den nationalen Bewegungen des 19. Jahrhunderts – ein europäischer Vergleich', in Jürgen Kocka, ed., *Bürgertum in 19. Jahrhundert*, Volume 3, Munich 1988, pp. 345ff.

12. For a typical example of such a facile response, see W. Kolarz, *Myths and Realities in Eastern Europe*, London 1946.

13. *Die bürgerliche Belletristik als Vermittlerin des bürgerlichen Geschichtsbewusstsein: deutsches und tschechiches Geschichtsbild im Vergleich*, Bielefeld, ZIF, 1987.

14. On psycho-geography as a factor of national identity, see F. Barnes, ed., *Us and Them: The Psychology of Ethnonationalism*, New York 1987, pp. 10ff.

15. The present national movements of 'East' and 'West' are distinctly less comparable today than they were before 1918. Western national movements (for example, the Catalan, Basque, Welsh, Breton or Scots) are still typically engaged in a Phase C, or even a Phase B that started in the nineteenth century – whereas the majority of Eastern movements (for example the Czech, Estonian, Lithuanian or Polish) achieved national independence after the First World War, while others (for example the Byelorussian or Ukrainian) are now resuming an interrupted Phase B, or (like the Slovak or Croatian) Phase C.

4

The Coming of Nationalism
and Its Interpretation:
The Myths of Nation and Class

Ernest Gellner

This is a theoretical essay. It purports to offer a general theoretical account and explanation of a very significant social transformation, namely, the coming of nationalism in the course of the nineteenth and twentieth centuries. The claims made are the following:

1. A major and distinctive change has taken place in the social conditions of mankind. A world in which *nationalism*, the linking of state and of 'nationally' defined culture, is pervasive and normative is quite different from one in which this is relatively rare, half-hearted, unsystematized and untypical. There is an enormous difference between a world of complex, intertwined, but not neatly overlapping patterns of power and culture, and a world consisting of neat political units, systematically and proudly differentiated from each other by 'culture', and all of them striving, with a great measure of success, to impose cultural homogeneity internally. These units, linking sovereignty to culture, are known as nation-states. During the two centuries following the French Revolution, the nation-state became a political norm. How and why did this happen?
2. A theoretical model is available which, starting from generalizations which are eminently plausible and not seriously contested, in conjunction with available data concerning the transformation of society in the nineteenth century, does explain the phenomenon in question.
3. Most, though not all, of the relevant empirical material is compatible with this model.

These are strong claims. If sustained, it means that the problem under discussion – nationalism – unlike most other major problems of historical social change, does have an explanation. Most of the other major trans-formations which have occurred in history have also repeatedly provoked attempts at explication. But the explanations offered only consist of spe-cifying interesting possibilities, or provide plausible partial contributions to a final answer. They are seldom definitive and sufficient and convin-cing. By contrast, a cogent, persuasive explanation of nationalism is available.

The Model

It is best to begin with the specification of the model. It specifies two dif-ferent, very generic types of society. The argument focuses on the difference in the role of structure and culture in the two distinct types of society.

Agro-literate Society

Agro-literate society is defined by a number of characteristics. It is a soci-ety based on agriculture (including pastoralism), in other words on food production and food storage. It is endowed with a fairly stable tech-nology: though innovations and improvements can and do occur from time to time, they are not parts of some sustained process of discovery and invention. The society is free of the general idea (so pervasive and commonplace now, amongst *us*) that nature forms an intelligible system susceptible to exploration, which when successful engenders a powerful new technology. The vision on which this society was based was *not* that of an ever-increasing comprehension and mastery of nature (as ours is), jus-tifying the expectation of perpetual improvement in the human condition. Rather, the vision presupposed a stable partnership between nature and society, in which nature not merely provides a modest but fairly constant material provision, but also somehow underwrites, justifies the social order, and mirrors its arrangements.

The consequences of the possession of a stable technology, and no more, are various. Given the relative inelasticity of the supply of food, *and* the existence of a definite, and none too high, ceiling on food-production, the values of the members of the society are generally directed towards coercion and hierarchy. What really matters for a mem-ber of such a society is that he be well placed on its hierarchical scale, rather than that he should *produce* copiously and efficiently: and being an effective producer is not the best way (or perhaps is not a good way at all) of enhancing one's status. A characteristic value of such a society is 'nobil-ity', which means a conjunction of military vocation and ascribed high status.

This orientation follows from the basic logic of the situation in a society with a fairly stable productive potential: there is nothing much to be gained by attempts to increase production, but the individual, and also any sub-group, has everything to gain from a favoured position *within* society. Increased production will only benefit the privileged power-holders, rather than the person responsible for the increase; but *becoming* one of the power-holders does benefit the successful aspiring individual himself. So he must strive to enhance his power and status, and should not waste effort on increasing output.

This tendency is much reinforced by the second trait following from a stable technology – a Malthusian condition. The possibilities of increasing food production are limited, those of population growth are not. The units of which this kind of society is composed tend to value offspring, or at any rate male offspring, as a source of labour-power and defence-power. However, the high valuation of offspring must at least intermittently bring the total population close to the limit, or beyond the limit, of the available food supply. All this, in turn, reinforces the martial and hierarchical orientation of the society: when hunger comes, it does not strike at random. It strikes in accordance with rank. Men starve in accordance with status, lower orders starving first. This is ensured by the socially controlled access to the guarded storage-centres of sustenance. In North Africa, a most suggestive term for central government is in use: *Makhzen.* It has the same root as *magazine.* The government controls and *is* the storehouse.

Some of the self-maintaining mechanisms operative in this kind of society are indicated in Diagram 4.1 below.

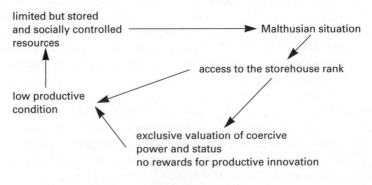

Diagram 4.1

The consequence of this situation is that an agro-literate society constitutes a complex system of fairly stable statuses. The possession of a status, and access to its rights and privileges, is by far the most important consideration for a member of such a society. A man is his *rank*. (This is quite different for the society which was to replace it, in which a man is his *culture*, and/or his bank balance, and where rank is ephemeral.)

How was the earlier system maintained? In general, there are two possibilities of maintaining order: coercion and consent. Those who would disturb the existing system of roles and modify them in their own favour are prevented from doing so, either by menaces, and possibly by the actual execution of threats, or by inner restraints, by causing them to internalize a system of ideas and convictions which then inhibits deviant conduct. In practice, each of these two mechanisms operated. The two mechanisms are not separated, but work in conjunction. They are intertwined so intimately that it becomes impossible to disentangle their contributions to the maintenance of the social order.

Which of the two factors is the more important? This is an exceedingly difficult question. There is no reason to suppose that a single answer applies to all circumstances. Marxism is most naturally interpreted as a doctrine which would ascribe the greatest influence on a social order neither to coercion nor to ideology (castigating both of these affirmations as 'Idealism'), but to *production* instead. But it is less than clear just what a direct determination of the social order by the productive system, unmediated by either coercion or ideas, could possibly mean. Tools and techniques on their own cannot make men conform to the rules of distribution: this can only be done through either coercion or consent, or a fusion of both. How does a mode of production engender its own mode of coercion? It is difficult not to suspect that Marxism owed some of its appeal and persistence to its lack of clarity on this point.

The ideological system of a society does not merely contribute to the stability of the system by persuading its members that the system is legitimate. Its role is far more pervasive and complicated than that. It also makes possible the very implementation of coercion, by providing coercers with principles of organization and of resolving internal disputes, without which a mere chaotic, unorganized collection of coercers would lose much of its effectiveness.

This type of society is endowed not only with a more or less stable agricultural base, but also with literacy. Writing is a technique which makes possible the recording and retrieval of data, ideas, information, formulae and so forth. Pre-literate society is not devoid of techniques of preservation of affirmations and meanings: important formulae can also be maintained by ritual and repetition. But writing greatly enlarges the scope of preservation and transmission of ideas, affirmations, information, principles.

Writing tends to increase the status-differentiation of this kind of society. It is a skill which requires sustained and fairly prolonged initiation, known as 'education'. An agrarian society is not endowed with either the resources or the incentives for disseminating this skill very widely, let alone universally. The possession of such skills distinguishes those who possess them from those who do not. Literacy becomes a badge of rank, as well as constituting a guild mystery. This status-differentiating use of writing may be reinforced by further devices, notably the use of dead or special languages for written messages, which thereby become distinct from spoken ones not just in virtue of being written, but also of being written in another tongue. The awe of writing hinges on mystery, not on intelligibility. The cult of clarity comes late in the history of mankind, never prevails fully, and constitutes one further revolution.

Most ordinary members of this kind of society acquire their 'culture', their stock of ideas and symbols, 'on the job', in the course of the very process of living, as part of the daily interchange between kinsmen, neighbours, masters and disciples. In this way, a living culture, un-codified, not frozen in script, without a rigid formalized set of rules, is transmitted simply as part of an on-going 'way of life'. But skills such as lit-eracy are not normally transmitted in that manner. Instead, they are transmitted in the course of prolonged and specialized training, incul-cated, not by ordinary people in the course of doing ordinary things, but by full-time specialists, dedicated to perpetuating and exemplifying su-perior norms.

There is a profound difference between a culture transmitted simply in the course of living, 'on the job', informally, and culture transmitted by full-time specialists, committed to doing very little else, who in so doing, carry out a formal, well-defined duty, specified in some detail in norm-ative texts, which are fixed, and cannot easily be manipulated by individuals. The former is liable to be flexible, changing, and regionally diversified, very pliable, sometimes to an extreme degree. The latter can be made rigid, resistant to change, standardized over an extensive ter-ritory.[1] It can be sustained by an impressive corpus of writing and reasoning, and be possessed of theories which further legitimize its own messages. Its doctrine may contain a theory specifying the origin of important truth – 'Revelation' – which then in turn reconfirms its *other* theories. A theory of revelation is part of this creed, and the creed is vin-dicated by the revelation. The circle is closed and complete.

This kind of society is characterized by a tension between a high cul-ture, transmitted by formal education, enshrined in texts, and setting up socially transcendent norms, and, on the other hand, one or more low cultures, incarnated only in living practice, and not in that disembodied form of speech known as writing, and hence incapable of rising above actual practice. So what is typical of this kind of society is a discrepancy, and sometimes conflict, between a high and a low culture, which can of course assume a variety of forms: the high culture may strive to impose its norms on the low, or the members of the low may strive to assume as many of the characteristics of the high as possible, in order to enhance their own standing. The former is typical of Islam, the latter of Hinduism. But neither endeavour is likely to be very successful. The characteristic end product is a marked cultural differentiation between 'high' and 'low' styles, frequently to the point of mutual unintelligibility. The unintelligibility is functional. A man can hardly strive to elevate himself into a condition which he simply does not understand, or defy a doctrine he knows to be beyond his humble comprehension. Cultural differences define positions within society; they control access to them and inhibit escape from them, far more than they define the limits of the society as a whole. It is only in the transition from agrarian to industrial society that culture ceases to be the device which defines specific social positions and allocates individuals to them, and becomes, instead, the boundary-demarcation of large and internally mobile social unity, *within* which individuals have no fixed position, and are rotated in the light of the requirements of production.

If this overall model of the old Agraria be accepted as valid, what are the consequences for the relationship between culture on the one hand, and political legitimacy and boundaries of states on the other? The answer must be that generally there will be *very little* such connection between the two spheres.

A society of this type is constantly given to as it were secreting, engendering, elaborating cultural differentiations within itself. It constitutes a system of differentiated ranks and statuses, and these need to be recognized, highlighted, externalized. This is what culture is. The Russian cultural historian Yuri Lotman reports an eighteenth-century Russian nobleman who had a different mode of address to various people in accordance with just how many 'souls' they owned. He deployed a varied repertoire of differential greetings, sensitive to various sizes of human holdings. A character in a novel by Graham Greene notes the disrespect in the tone of the bank clerk addressing him, and reflects inwardly that he would be treated better if only his overdraft were significantly larger.

This kind of acute semantic sensitivity to nuances of status and property helps eliminate ambiguity and diminish friction. No status differences without externalization! No visible marks without status warrant! As major breaks occur in the stratification of society, culture signals those chasms by similarly dramatic discontinuities of dress, speech, comportment, consumption. Peasants are quite liable to speak a language literally different from that of gentry, burghers or bureaucracy. Notoriously, in nineteenth-century Russia, the upper strata of society differentiated themselves from the rest by an extensive use of French. It has been claimed that at the time of Italian unification in 1861, only 2.5 per cent of the Italian population actually spoke 'proper' Italian.[2] Agrarian society engenders estates, castes, guilds, status of all kinds, and these require a cultural expression. Cultural *homogeneity* by contrast has little, if any, function in it. On the contrary, attempts to standardize cultural bearing constitute an offence, sometimes in a perfectly literal, penal sense. To attempt to emulate the bearing of distant ranks is a violation of the protocol and of the command structure of the society. It is a form of insolence which can hardly be allowed to go unpunished. The offender is fortunate if he receives only informal punishment.

There is also a strong tendency towards so to speak lateral differentiation, in addition to functional and vertical differentiation. Not only do men tend to acquire distinctive styles so as to protect themselves against emulation from below, or to refrain from giving offence upwards; there is also a tendency for rural communities to acquire cultural distinctiveness in comparison with geographic neighbours of similar status. In illiterate peasant communities, dialects generally vary from village to village. The insulated style of life encourages a kind of cultural and linguistic drift, and divergence ensues even when it had not been present at first.

Rulers seldom have the incentive to impose cultural homogeneity on their subjects, and often, on the contrary, derive much benefit from diversity. Cultural specificity helps allocate people to their social and geographical niche, inhibits the emergence of far-flung and possibly dangerous identities and loyalties. 'Divide and rule' policies are easier to implement if culture in any case already divides the population. Rulers are interested in the taxes, tithes, rents, corvée of their subjects, but seldom in either their souls or their culture. In agrarian society, culture divides rather than unifies. Occasionally, there are tendencies toward cultural homogenization. These may be due to an effective imperial bureaucracy or to a soteriological-universalist world religion (which insists on saving human souls *as such*, rather than ministering to social ranks or segments), or to a combination of the two. But bureaucratic centralization and religious universalization and institutionalism, especially in that accentuated form known as a Reformation, are precisely amongst the social features which prepared or induced the passage to a post-industrial and nationalism-prone world.

The overall conclusion must be that in such societies, shared culture is seldom a plausible basis for the formation of political units.[3] The term 'nation', if used at all, is more likely to denote a loose corporate body, the politically enfranchised gentry of a given territory, those committed to take part in politics, than literally the sum total of participants in a culture. The Polish 'nation', for instance, was once the collectivity of enfranchised gentry of the Polish republic, and included persons of Ukrainian speech, but not peasants of Polish stock and language. The term denotes a political and not a cultural category of persons.

Political units in such a society have a strong tendency to be either smaller or larger than cultural units. Tribal segments, city states, seldom exhaust the culture which they practise, but rather, they share it with a much wider area; empires, on the other hand, are circumscribed only by military resistance or by geographical obstacles, but have not the slightest inclination to restrict themselves to some single culture. The Muslim conqueror of North Africa is said to have ridden his horse into the Atlantic to show that he could go no further – but he was unperturbed by the cultural and linguistic distance of the Berber indigenous population.

People in this kind of society have plural and nested and cross-cutting memberships and loyalties, some of them perhaps vaguely related to what later comes to be called nationality, but most of them bearing no relation to it. There is great cultural diversity, and there are complex political units and groupings, but the two sets of linkages have no clear or important relationship to each other. Political hierarchies and cultural networks simply are not mediated and united by something called 'nationality'.

Of course, linguistic and cultural differentiation may be used to mark off not merely nuances of status, but a more general membership of, say, the dominant administrative-military class. In so far as a language is then a token of the political unit controlled by that class, we may occasionally have something which, at least superficially, resembles modern nationalism. But this is not a general phenomenon, and the differences between it and genuine modern nationalism are more important than the similarities.

Advanced Industrial Society

A type of society now exists in the world (and is spreading fast) which is radically different from agro-literate society, as described. Its economic foundation is altogether different: it is self-consciously based on sustained, continuous innovation, and on an exponential growth in productive resources and output. It is committed to a theory of knowledge which makes nature intelligible without recourse to Revelation, and thus also renders nature effectively manipulable and a source of ever-growing affluence. At the same time, nature is no longer available as a source of legitimating principles of the social order. In fact, economic growth is the first principle of legitimacy of this kind of society: any regime which fails to attain and maintain it is in trouble. (The second principle of legitimacy is nationality, which constitutes our theme.)

This society is no longer Malthusian: economic growth eventually out-strips demographic growth, which, for independent reasons, diminishes, or disappears altogether. Its culture no longer values offspring so highly, if at all: sheer labour power or brawn is of little consequence, either for authorities or for individuals, either productively or militarily. (It is true that early industrialism engenders conscription and mass peasant armies, and peasants are valued as cannon-fodder. But in the age of the Falkland and Gulf wars, numbers count for little, whereas technological sophist-ication and training become decisive.) Human beings are usable only if educated, and education is expensive. Quality not quantity of personnel counts, and quality depends on the machinery of cultural production of men, in other words on 'education'. Offspring are not valued by author-ity for their military or productive potential, or by parents as a form of insurance. Offspring are expensive and must compete, often unsuccess-fully, with other forms of satisfaction and indulgence.

The nature of work has also changed radically. In agrarian society, 'work', essential but not at all prestigious, was predominantly physical, manual labour, and in the main was connected with agricultural pro-duction. It amounted to the application of human muscle to matter, with some limited assistance from animal power, and some mechanical devices based on the utilization of water or wind. All this changed completely in advanced industrial society. Physical work in any pure form has all but dis-appeared. What is still called manual labour does not involve swinging a pick-axe or heaving soil with a spade, which on the whole people only do for recreation: it generally involves controlling, managing and maintain-ing a machine with a fairly sophisticated control mechanism. But for most people, 'work' is even further removed from the coal-face of nature, so to speak. It involves the rapid manipulation of meanings and people through computers, or, at worst, telephones and typewriters and faxes, computerized tills, and so on.

All this has profound implications for culture, for the system of sym-bols in use. Such rapid interchange of messages between anonymous, distant interlocutors simply cannot tolerate the dependence of meaning on local dialectal idiosyncrasy, and still less on context, let alone highly specific context. Context is erased by the very method of communication. So meaning cannot be transmitted by the body posture, identity, tone, location of the speaker, or the timing or context of delivery. Status can neither contribute to meaning, nor be reinforced by it. The medium does not convey it. All those elements – posture, tone et cetera – were, in the actual folk language, a kind of phoneme: they contributed to the determination of sense. But these were phonemes with a strictly and nar-rowly limited use and validity, like an unconvertible municipal currency. A universal communication system requires that only tokens endowed with a universal, standardized, context-free significance be used.

It is now essential that the meaning is carried by the message alone, and be *internal* to it. Both the emitting and the receiving centre must be trained to attend to message alone, in accordance with shared rules concerning what is and what is not part of the message. Men must be able to isolate the elements which generally contribute to the determination of meaning, and to ignore local idiosyncratic context. The acquisition of such a fine and well-tuned and standardized sensitivity to what is and what is not relevant, is not at all an easy matter. It presupposes sustained schooling and great semantic discipline. It calls for the conceptual equivalent of military drill: finely tuned responsiveness to formalized words of command with sharply defined rules of implementation – though the range of these possible commands is immeasurably greater than the one available in the military idiom. The meaning must be clear, the range of comprehended meaning very large, probably infinite.

What all this amounts to is that, for the very first time in the history of mankind, a high culture becomes the pervasive, operational culture of an entire society. Men can respond to the full, infinite range of meanings contained in language, instead of merely responding, like a peasant recruit, to a finite list of words of command, and those only when yelled by a man with the appropriate insignia, and in the recognized context. The implications of this are tremendous and still have not been fully appreciated and explored. The importance of universal education – presupposed by the very basic organization of society – goes far beyond woolly and pious commendations of the broadening of cultural horizons (assuming this takes place at all). Those implications include the pervasiveness of nationalism, which is our theme. A high culture is an orderly, standardized system of ideas, serviced and imposed by a corps of clerics with the help of writing. Roughly speaking, the syllogism runs: work has become semantic, and work requires impersonal, context-free communication between individuals, members of a broad mass. This can only be done if the members of that broad mass share the same rules for formulating and decoding messages. In other words, they must share the same culture, and it will be a high culture, for this standardized skill can only be acquired in formal schooling. Conclusion: the entire society must be pervaded by one standardized high culture, if it is to work at all. Society can no longer tolerate a wild proliferation of internal subcultures, all of them context-bound and severely inhibited in their mutual intercommunication. Access to the appropriate high culture, and acceptability within it, is a person's most important and valued possession: it institutes a pre-condition of access not merely to employment, but to legal and moral citizenship, to all kinds of social participation. So a person identifies with his or her high culture, and is eager that he or she inhabits a political unit where various bureaucracies function in that same cultural idiom. If this is not so, he will hope that either the boundaries or his own location change, so that it should *become* so. In other words, he or she is a nationalist.

There is a further factor making for the standardization of culture. Not wealth as such, but *growing* affluence is the key validating principle. This society is based not merely on mass affluence but, above all, on economic growth. It is the anticipation of continuous improvement which has come to legitimate the social order. If once upon a time a good harvest was the mark of a good king, now it is the sustained raising of industrial productivity which signifies a sound regime. The waste land with an impotent king is now one with a zero or negative rate of growth. The ruler's virility is expressed in expanding productivity. The idea of progress is the philosophical expression of this attitude.

The price of growth is innovation and the perpetual and continuous transformation of the occupational structure. This society simply cannot constitute a stable system of ascribed roles, as it did in the agrarian age: the important roles are positions in bureaucracies, productive and other, and the bureaucratic structures are unstable, and they must be such. (It is the stability of certain defective structures, for example communist hierarchies, which is a sign, and probably the cause, of their low effectiveness.) Moreover, the high level of technical skill required for at least a significant proportion of posts (probably not the majority, but in any case for a significant minority of them) means that these posts have to be filled 'meritocratically', by competence, rather than in the old habitual way, that is by birth and ascription, and with a view merely to the perpetuation of a stable structure and the reinforcement of its loyalties.

All this renders the society basically egalitarian: it cannot easily ascribe rank, for such permanent rank would often come into conflict with the standing entailed by the actual occupational effectiveness of the person in question. The need to fill posts in the light of performance and competence is incompatible with the old principle of filling them in terms of permanent, ascribed, deeply internalized rank. The society is egalitarian because it is mobile, and not mobile because egalitarian, and it *has* to be mobile. All this has totally reversed the long-term trend towards ever-increasing inequality, which had previously accompanied the movement towards increasing complexity of societies, prior to the coming of the industrial-scientific age.[4] The egalitarianism which the new order displays does not exclude, of course, tremendous inequalities in wealth, power and life-chances. But a base-line egalitarianism is nonetheless accepted as the norm by the society, and it is not devoid of a certain reality. It does possess a genuine social authority and effective social meaning.

The inequalities which do exist are gradual and continuous, rather than being marked by theoretically quite uncrossable chasms between estates or castes; they are, so to speak, statistical, consisting of the probabilities of success or fortune, rather than of formal, definitive exclusions or entitlements, as used to be the case; and the differences are not internalized in the souls of the beneficiaries and the victims of the inequality. They are not self-justifying, but require pragmatic justification. If excessive, they are held to be scandalous. Privileges tend to be camouflaged rather than flouted. The very rich are different from us, said Scott Fitzgerald to Ernest Hemingway. Yes, they have more money, replied Hemingway. Hemingway was not altogether wrong, even if Fitzgerald had a point. Hemingway expressed the modern vision, for which external status does not enter the soul; Fitzgerald was a romantic attached to the old world, in which it did. The world has moved, in large measure at least, from Fitzgerald to Hemingway, as de Tocqueville had insisted. Men differ in their externals not their internals.

But above all, the formal rules of operation of the society, at work and in politics, both permit and, above all, *require* members of the society to have the same culture. The flow of context-free information is required for the running of the society in all its aspects. The information network requires that anyone can be slotted in at any point: it is no longer possible to reserve positions for pre-specified categories of people. The sockets of the information network are standardized for all users, and not status-specific. Anyone not competent to take part in this flow of signals is an obstacle and an irritant, and provokes reactions of hostility and exclusion, and is liable to suffer humiliation.

How should one best sum up the implications of such a social organization for the relationship of culture on the one hand, and society and polity on the other?

So this kind of society not merely permits but positively requires homogeneity of culture. It must be a culture of a specific kind, that is, a 'high' culture (needless to say, the term is used here in a sociological and not in an evaluative sense). It must be standardized and disciplined. All this can only be achieved by sustained education, and this kind of society is indeed marked by the near-complete implementation of the ideal of universal education. Men are no longer formed at their mother's knee, but rather in the *école maternelle*.

The standardized educational system which processes the totality of the human material which goes to make up the society, which turns the biological raw material into an acceptable and serviceable cultural product, is enormous, and exceedingly expensive. A large part of its cost tends to be taken up by the state or by its local sub-units. In the end, only the state, or the public sector in a slightly wider sense, can really shoulder this onerous responsibility, and only the state can perform the task of quality control in this most important of all industries, that is, the production of socially acceptable, industrially operational human beings. This becomes one of its main tasks. Society must be homogenized, *gleichgeschaltet*: and the only agency capable of carrying out, supervising or protecting this operation is the central state. Given the competition of various states for overlapping catchment areas, the only way a given culture can protect itself against another one, which already has its particular protector-state, is to acquire one of its own, if it does not already possess one. Just as every girl should have a husband, preferably her own, so every culture must have its state, preferably its own. The state-cultures live in competition with each other. So this is the end product: a mobile, atomized, egalitarian society with a standard culture, where the culture is a literate, 'high' one, and where its dissemination, maintenance and boundaries are protected by a state. Stated even more briefly: one culture, one state. One state, one culture.

The theory of nationalism proposed here is materialist (though by no means Marxist), in so far as it derives the phenomenon to be explained from the basic manner in which society ensures its own material self-perpetuation. The earlier society based on agricultural production and on a stable technology was more or less doomed to a military-clerical ethos, to hierarchy, dogmatism, cultural plurality, a tension between a high and a low culture, and a political system based on power structures and religious ideology, but generally indifferent to cultural similarities. It proliferated differences, related to social positions, but not to political boundaries. The new society, based on expanding technology, semantic not physical work, on pervasive impersonal and often anonymous communication by means of context-free messages, and on an unstable occupational structure, is destined for a standardized, educationally transmitted high culture, more or less completely and pervasively diffused amongst all its members. Its political or authority structures will be legitimated by two considerations – whether they can ensure sustained economic growth, and whether they can engender, diffuse and protect the culture which is the idiom of the society in question. Polity and high culture will thus become intimately linked, and the old links between polity and faith or dynasty will be dissolved, or reduced to a merely decorative, rather than genuinely functional, status. The state is a protector of a culture and not a faith.

The argument establishing this link seems to me virtually Euclidean in its cogency. It seems to me impossible to be presented with these connections clearly and not to assent to them. Spinoza claimed that it is impossible to state a truth clearly without granting it assent. Alas, this is not generally true; but in this case at least, the connection does seem to me luminously manifest. (That, at any rate, is how the matter appears to me. As a matter of regrettable fact, an astonishing number of people have failed to accept the theory even when presented with it.)

It is no doubt exceedingly presumptuous to compare oneself to Euclid, or to hope that Euclidean cogency is ever available in the social sphere. My excuse is that I make the point with irony, and more in self-criticism than in vainglory. The argumentation does seem to me to have Euclidean force, but I also note that the world we live in is only in part Euclidean. There are many cases which illustrate the argument, but there are also many which fail to support it. This requires investigation. There is something odd about an argument which is cogent but whose conclusions are (in even partial) conflict with the facts. Perhaps – though that remains to be seen – the recalcitrant facts can be explained away as corollaries of other, complicating factors, not included in the initial model, but operative and significant in the real world.

Refinement of the Theory

The original formulation of our position only specified two abstract ideal types, an agrarian society which is not nationalism-prone, or, rather, is liable to be positively nationalism-resistant, and a fully industrial society, which could hardly be organized on any base other than a national one. It presupposes, within each political unit, a standardized culture (or the other way round – it presupposes that each standardized culture would strive to attain its own state). But this formulation said nothing about the *path* by which societies or polities moved from the first of these two conditions to the second. Any properly worked theory will, of course, need to do precisely this. It is part of the present theory that nationalism manifests itself in its most acute form not at the terminus, but at some of the points of the transition between the two social types.

One can postulate five typical stages on the path from a world of non-ethnic empires and micro-units to one of homogeneous nation-states:

1. Baseline. A world exists where ethnicity is still not yet self-evidently present, and where the idea of any link between it and political legitimacy is almost entirely absent.
2. A world which has inherited and retained most of its political boundaries and structures from the previous stage, but within which ethnicity as a political principle – in other worlds, nationalism – is beginning to operate. This is the stage of Nationalist Irredentism. The old borders and polities are under pressure from nationalist agitation.
3. National Irredentism triumphant and self-defeating. Plural empires collapse, and with them the entire dynastic-religious style of political

legitimation, and it is replaced by nationalism as the main effective principle. A set of smaller states emerge, purporting to fulfil the national destiny of the ethnic group with which they are identified. This condition is self-defeating, in so far as these new units are just as minority-haunted as the larger ones which had preceded them. The new units are haunted by all the weaknesses of their precursors, plus some additional ones of their own.

4. *Nacht und Nebel.* This is a term employed by the Nazis for some of their operations in the course of the Second World War. Under cover of wartime secrecy, or in the heat of conflict and passion, or during the period of retaliatory indignation, moral standards are suspended, and the principle of nationalism, demanding compact homogeneous ethnic groups within given political-territorial units, is implemented with a new ruthlessness. It is no longer done by the older and benign method of assimilation, but by mass murder or forcible transplantation of populations.

5. High level of satiation of the nationalist requirement, plus generalized affluence, plus cultural convergence, leads to a diminution, though not the disappearance, of the virulence of nationalist revendications.

Each of these stages requires some more detailed comments.

Baseline

Europe on the eve of the French Revolution did not in fact closely resemble the ideal-typical 'steady state' agrarian society, as described. For over a millennium, there had been economic growth, and sustained political and ideological change. There was extensive urbanization, fairly centralized polities had to a large extent replaced feudal fragmentation, and states were endowed with an effective bureaucratic apparatus. The Reformation had profoundly altered the rules of the game of cognitive and legitimative activities, and introduced the idea of direct private appeal to a socially independent fount of authority: initially scripture and private conscience, and eventually individual reason or experience. The scientific revolution had begun, shortly to be followed by the working out of its philosophical presuppositions and sequences. The Enlightenment had formulated a vision of the world and society which was secular, individualistic, and naturalistic. The economic and even the military centre of gravity of Europe had moved to its north-west corner, where a civil society, practising the separation of powers, was well established in England and Holland. Surprisingly, the liberal states proved to be militarily at the very least equal, or superior, to centralized, war-orientated monarchies. In the eighteenth century, the nation of shopkeepers repeatedly defeated the larger nation of military aristocrats. (The latter could prevail only when in alliance with another set of shop-keepers across the ocean.) In extensive parts of north-west Europe, the pattern of kinship and household formation was individualistic, with late marriage based on individual choice by partners, rather than committed to the perpetuation of relations between larger kin groups.[5] In many areas, literacy and its use for secular purposes were very widespread. In all these ways, and no doubt in many others, Europe had long ago begun to move in the direction of that modern world which was to emerge and become so conspicuous in the nineteenth century.

Nevertheless, when it came to the determination of political units and their boundaries, and establishing their legitimacy, the world which was challenged by the French Revolution, and which was re-established after the defeat of Napoleon, continued to be governed by dynastic principles. The position of monarchs had actually been strengthened by the after-math of the Reformation and of the Wars of Religion, by abrogating the idea of an overall interstate arbiter of legitimacy, and thus rendering the sovereignty of an independent state and ruler absolute. Much of the modernization carried out in the eighteenth century was the work of 'enlightened' absolutist monarchs, rather than of some more broadly based movements. It is true that royal absolutism had been challenged, both in political theory and in practice; but the English, after an experi-ment with a Commonwealth and a Restoration, in the end found their liberties best ratified by a suitably restrained monarchy, rather than by its abolition. The Dutch Republic drifted towards a personal monarchy. Republican and elective institutions were rare, few of the erstwhile city states survived, and the participatory form of government was on the whole restricted to smaller and less important entities. It is true that a *new* republic also emerged, and was successfully established towards the end of the eighteenth century in defiance of one powerful West European monarchy, though aided by another – but that was on the other side of the ocean.

The majority of agrarian polities had been monarchic, but the drift towards industrial society eventually also led to a move towards demo-cracy. The inherent impulsion of industrial society towards egalitarianism may provide part of the explanation for this. The monarchical tendency of agrarian society is probably a consequence of the general logic of power situations: in all conflicts, it is desirable for the victor to eliminate the loser 'for keeps' so as to preclude a return match, and it makes sense for all others to seek the favours of the victor, thereby strengthening him further. The logic of this snowball effect is operative in most circum-stances, and explains the pervasiveness of monarchy in agrarian society, though there are exceptions, such as pastoralists in open country, or peasants in mountainous terrain, or, sometimes, trading communities. All of these may escape the force of this argument, and find themselves endowed with participatory and internally balanced political institutions. Pastoralists escape central domination thanks to the mobility of their wealth, and are impelled to communalism by the need to defend themselves as collectivities; mountain peasants are endowed with forts by nature; and traders need elbow-room for individual initiative if they are to be effective, and suborning them is counter-productive.

Industrialization, on the other hand, means the dominance of wealth-acquisition over power-acquisition. Wealth leads to power, and the contrary process, though not absent, is less overwhelming. The snow-balling of power ceases to operate, and the snowballing of wealth (contrary to Marxist predictions) does not take place. So power and wealth tend to become far better diffused.

One may add that government in an agrarian society does not require great talents or training, nor does it often permit their deployment if they happen to be available. To put this point more simply, any fool can be a king or a baron. Some personal qualities – ruthlessness, aggressiveness, courage, cunning – may be an advantage, but the equipment required for facing the decisions which have to be taken are such as to allow the filling of these posts at random, for example by heredity, which is the simplest, and commonest, manner of filling social slots in the agrarian world. In general, one may suppose that such a principle operates unless a society is loose and devoid of structure, or unless *special* factors operate so as to ensure the filling of positions in the light of some other consideration (for example, the need of specific suitability for the complex and highly specific tasks which are to be performed).

Roughly speaking, the agrarian world fills social roles at random, and also attributes this allocation of positions to higher, transcendent authority. The deity is often credited with the supervision of recruitment to high office. By contrast, industrial society, at least in principle, fills them in terms of efficiency and performance, and justifies the procedure by human convenience. The shift to democracy can in part at least be explained as the effect of this general tendency on the problem of the filling of high posts in society and polity. When there is, at least in principle, equal access to most posts, it is difficult and illogical to restrict participation in decisions to some special segment of the population.

The theories of accountable, participatory, limited, plural et cetera government, which anticipated, accompanied or ratified the political changes of the eighteenth and nineteenth centuries, did not possess an agreed coherent theory concerning the precise nature and limits of the *unit* which was to be endowed with government. Society was to be democratic: but just *which* society was it to be? This question was not yet at the centre of attention. That there were indeed societies was something taken for granted; the question was just how they were to be run, on what principles and under whose rule, rather than precisely how they were to be delimited.

In the course of the nineteenth century, history gave an answer to a question which had hardly been asked – what exactly are the units which are to be endowed with government? It turned out to be – *nations*. But the unit which, in the modern world, is called a 'nation' does not altogether resemble anything known previously. It is a large body of anonymous individuals, either initiated into a high culture which defines that nation, or, at the very least, initiated into a low culture which has a recognized connection with the high culture in question, which constitutes its plausible human catchment area, and which predisposes its practitioners to enter the particular high culture in question, as probationary members. Units so defined had scarcely existed before. Now they have become the norm of political propriety. All other units have become anomalies.

At the beginning of the modern world, in 1815, whether they existed or not (and on the whole, as yet they did not), nations were not yet taken into consideration in the marking out of the new frontiers. And yet the world was such that it was soon to become ready to listen to those who would soon preach that *this* was how the world should be run: that legitimate political units were only those which were based on the nation, whatever that might be.

Irredentism

The age of nationalism or irredentism is the period during which there is much striving on behalf of the implementation of the ideal of One Culture, One State. The old world of endless cultural diversity and nuance, only very loosely connected, if indeed connected at all, with political boundaries, acquires an air of political impropriety, illegitimacy. It is to be replaced by a world in which each culture has its own political roof, and in which political units and authorities are only legitimated by the fact that they protect and express and cherish a culture. An enormously complex linguistic or cultural map of Europe of (say) 1815, within which linguistic-cultural boundaries hardly correlated at all with political ones, is to be replaced by a new map on which, by say 1948, the correlation, whilst not absolute, is very marked.

There are various methods by means of which this congruence could *in the end* be secured.

1. People can be changed. They can acquire the culture – including the self-image fostered by that culture, and the capacity to project that

image and have it accepted – even if they had started from some other culture, some other set of internalized and projected images. The baseline from which they start may be a sub-culture or dialect reasonably close to the, as it were, terminal culture, or it may be distant. The process may be largely spontaneous and even barely conscious, or it may be accompanied by directions from political and educational authority, or it may be directed by freelance, independent cultural activists, acting independently of political authorities or even in defiance of them.

2. People can be killed. Persons held unsuitable for incorporation in the desired homogeneous 'ethnic' socio-political unit, can be gassed, shot, starved et cetera.

3. People held unsuitable for incorporation in the unit to be established in a given territory can be moved from that territory to some other place (whether or not that other place is occupied by a political unit welcoming them). The moves in question can be wholly compulsory, as when gendarmes simply pack off people in cattletrucks or lorries, or they may be voluntary in a sense, as when populations move of their own accord under threat of danger and harassment.

4. Frontiers can be adjusted with a view to combining culturally similar populations within single political units. Given the complexity of the ethnographic map of Europe in the nineteenth century, there are limits to what can be achieved by such a method, *unless* accompanied by the use of some or all of the preceding methods.

All these methods have in fact been used, sometimes also in combination or in succession. In the Age of Irredentism – stretching from 1815 to 1918 – on the whole, the relatively benign methods 1 and 4 were employed. Methods 2 and 3, though not unknown, only came into their own at the later stage (*Nacht und Nebel*). One way of establishing a typology of the manner in which the world-without-nationalism has been transformed into a nationalist world is in terms of the concrete method used for the tidying up of the ethnic-political map.

It is worth noting that irredentism, whilst strong, was far from all-powerful. It made the period 1813–1914 turbulent, but nevertheless it did not succeed in making many changes. Eastern Europe continued to be divided between three poly-ethnic empires. In that period, irredentism succeeded in creating five or six new buffer states in the Balkans, united Germany and Italy, and produced one change in Scandinavia and another in the Low Countries. But clearly, it did not sweep all before it – till 1918. The brutal methods were in fact not much used in this period: it was a period of assimilation, and also of counter-assimilative 'awakening', that is, of nationalist agitation encouraging people to form new state-cultures on the basis of the raw material of uncodified peasant cultures, as an alternative to entering cultures *already* linked to a state apparatus. The idiom of 'awakening' was deeply characteristic of the self-perception of this movement. It insinuated the existence of permanent but somnolent 'rational' entities, requiring a waking agent. The truth of the matter is rather that these entities were being created, not woken.

Irredentism Triumphant and Self-defeating

The Great War of 1914–18 brought to an end the Age of Nationalist Irredentism by conceding many of its demands, at any rate when made by the victors or their protégés. Given the nature of the ethnographic map of Europe, satisfying some demands inevitably meant thwarting others. The greatest impact of this was in what we shall call the third time zone, in the area of highly complex multi-ethnic empires. Two of them in particular disappeared by 1918, presumably for ever, as a result of, at first, the two minor Balkan wars, and then the First World War.

The obliterated empires were replaced by smaller political units, self-consciously defined and legitimated by the nationalist principle. Each such new state was meant to provide political protection for a 'nation', that is, a culture which was to provide the crucial moral identity for those who accepted it. The state is, awkwardly, the expression and agency of a nation, rather than of the totality of its citizens.

The principle of 'national self-determination' was implemented in the course of the peace-making procedures, and was intended to provide the outcome with its legitimacy. The implementation was, of course, not even-handed: the victors, and the clients of victors, naturally did rather better out of it all than did the losers, or those with inadequate clout in the negotiating process. However, the unfairness of some of the new boundaries did not constitute the only weakness of the new international order. Given the complexity and ambiguity of ethnic boundaries, *any* boundaries were bound to be offensive to some, and to be unjust by some perfectly plausible criteria. Given the complexity of the ethnic map of Eastern Europe, no uncontentious, manifestly just political map was possible.

The real weakness of the new system followed from all this. The new states were smaller and hence weaker than the empires which they had replaced. But this diminution in size and strength was not compensated by a greater homogeneity and hence greater cohesion: not at all. They were as haunted by irredentist minorities as the dismantled empires, those much-abused 'prisonhouses of nations'; perhaps they in turn should have been called the provincial or county goals of minorities. And the *nouvelles minorités*, so to speak, those who suddenly had minority status and hence irredentist sentiment thrust upon them, were often members of the previous culturally dominant ethnic or linguistic group, not habituated to such a lowly position, and hence more liable to resent it, and better equipped to resist it. They could find help and encouragement in their home state, which was dedicated to their own culture. They at any rate did not need to reconstruct, revive or invent past national greatness: it was, only too painfully, a matter of living recollection.

So, to sum up, the new order set up in the name of the Nationalist principle had all the weaknesses of the system it replaced, plus some additional ones of its own. Its weaknesses were soon and rapidly demonstrated. With the consolidation of an ideocratic dictatorship in Russia, and the establishment of an overtly nationalistic one in Germany, the entire edifice crumbled with amazing speed. Polish military resistance was to be measured in weeks, Yugoslav (official) and Greek resistance in days, and the other new national states did not resist at all (with the most remarkable and successful exception of Finland). Hitler and Stalin carved up the territories which separated them, with great ease and little opposition, at any rate from the state structures.

Nacht und Nebel

What was to follow was the period in which the benign method of securing homogeneity – namely assimilation – was replaced on a terrifying scale by two less benign methods – mass murder, and forcible transplantation of populations. This had already befallen some groups much earlier, notably the Armenians, and forcible population transfers also occurred in the wake of the Turkish-Greek war in the early 1920s. But the really extensive use of these methods came to be seen – or rather, initially, hidden – during the Second World War, and in the course of the period of retaliation immediately following it. Wartime secrecy, and then the indignation and temporary Victors' Licence which followed the end of the war, made possible the deployment of methods hardly thinkable in more normal circumstances.

Mass murder and then forcible deportation (accompanied by a certain amount of incidental murder) tidied up the ethnic map of large parts of Eastern Europe, though certainly not all of it. The mass extermination was directed above all at certain populations held to be specially ill-suited to inhabit a Europe destined to exemplify the nationalist ideal of homogeneous communities, joyfully celebrating a shared culture, proud and secure in the knowledge that they were under the protection of a political organization committed, above all things, to the safeguarding and perpetuation of that culture. Dirt has been defined as matter in the wrong place: minorities, in this New Europe, were cultures in wrong places. But there were certain cultures which were in the wrong place *wherever* they found themselves: they constituted, so to speak, a kind of universal dirt, or, rather, absolute dirt, a form of pollution which could not be purified by any relocation. They exemplified that severance from both folk roots and biological vitality which is the mark of cerebral intellectualism, individualist calculation, abstract and universalist identity and aspiration. Diaspora nations, especially when socially located in the commercial, financial and later intellectual and creative zones of society – and thereby separated from the earthy vigour of physical work directly at grips with nature – incarnated that cerebral pathogenic cunning which was, for romantic-biological communalism, deeply antithetical to health and community. This is certainly what the Nazis (of a wide variety of nationalities) felt about the Jews. They constituted an offence against the principle of nationality, against the essentially ethnic and communal nature of man, tied to blood and land, and they did so not by virtue of being in the wrong place, but simply by virtue of existing at all.

The metaphysics of this kind of mass murder is extremely interesting, and constitutes an integral and significant part of the intellectual history of Europe. The original metaphysics of romantic nationalism had been relatively gentle and benign. It claimed only that it was legitimate, or preferable, for men to find fulfilment in an idiosyncratic folk culture, in the song and dance of the village green, rather than in emulating some formal, cold rules of courtly conduct. If the folk culture was a little less disciplined than the formal model of the court, if the dance was wilder and the drink coarser and stronger, and the gastronomy less refined, this in itself was not, as yet, lethal for anyone. The newly commended folk culture was often even held to be gentler than the aristocratic style it was to replace, with its roots in a professional warrior class. But there was already an inescapable shift towards the valuation of feeling rather than reason. This expression of feeling on the part of the less powerful strata of society, deprived of access to the more powerful weaponry and devoid of extended and disciplined, centralized organization, was, however, not yet really all that menacing.

But beware. The gentle communalism, committed to nothing more than a romantic idealization of peasant life and the folksong, is now supplemented by a new creed which says that true humanity, real fulfilment, lies in feeling, and that cold ratiocination is deadly, corrosive, pathogenic, unhealthy. The antithesis of the healthy peasant is the urban trader, whose work consists of calculation and of manipulation, and not in healthy, physical, vigorous, and cooperative action in the fields. The communalistically inspired argument can also, by about the middle of the nineteenth century and thereafter, be reinforced by another one, drawn from Darwinism. Vigour, assertion and feeling are good not merely because they are parts of a beautiful ethnic culture, but because they further that competition which aids the survival of the fittest, and which leads to genuine beauty. How ugly those urban traders, with their flabby bodies and shifty eyes, and how beautiful the yeoman! How repulsive the self-tormenting thinkers, how handsome the confident warriors! Significantly, these sentiments were on occasion internalized not only by the killers, but also by some of their victims.

When anti-intellectualistic, anti-cerebral romanticism blends with the revaluation of aggression and compassion, it thereby loses its erstwhile innocuousness. And now, consider the endowment of this cluster of sentiments and ideas with formal organization and political clout. This is precisely what the advance of nationalism does for it.

Nationalism presents itself as the reaffirmation of the culture of the village green against the cold putative universalism of some courtly or industrial or bureaucratic language: the village against Versailles or the Hofburg and the Viennese coffeehouse – or against Manchester. But in fact, villagers themselves seldom if ever have the confidence, the resources, the organizational or conceptual means, or even the inclination, to fight for their own culture against city, court, or industrial complex. They have more earthy concerns, and if they rebel it is seldom for a culture. The people who do organize and agitate for a culture are the atomized, anonymous members of an industrial or industrializing society, eager not to be disadvantaged in the new world by being of the 'wrong' culture, anxious that the culture in terms of which they themselves operate, and the culture defining the dominant political unit in which they live, should be one and the same, so as to give them maximum professional prospects and psychic comfort.

What form does their organization take? The cult of action and feeling which is inherent in populist romanticism turns the sports or gymnastic association into the paradigmatic form of nationalistic club. It is the *Turn-Verein* which, above all, provides nationalism with its sacraments. Gymnastics is quite specially suitable, more so than competitive and individualistic sports. Gymnastics is the most Durkheimian of sports, providing modern society with a ritual in which the solidarity of very large, anonymous, but co-cultural societies can be celebrated. Czech nationalism, for instance, is almost synonymous with the Sokol (Falcon) organization: to say that a man was a Sokol was equivalent to saying that he was a patriot, though, ironically, the founders were two Germans. The Czech nation worshipped itself at the *Slet* (rally). When the communists took over after the coup of 1948, they decided, wisely from their viewpoint, to take over the Sokol organization rather than to suppress it or fight it.

So nationalism came to be an ideology which combined the erstwhile gentle cult of the life of the village green, with a vitalist metaphysics of assertion and physical vigour, and with a distrust of ratiocination if not a positive hostility to it. Darwin as interpreted by Nietzsche complements Herder. Natural selection was the means to health and excellence, whereas universalism and bloodless, cosmopolitan intellectualism and compassion were the path to ugliness and disease. It was assumed that natural selection would operate primarily not on individuals, or the human species as a whole, but on what seemed to correspond to species within the human race, namely nations. Nations were assumed to be the permanent real categories of the social world: if they had not manifested themselves politically in earlier periods, this was only because they had been 'asleep', and the nationalist saw himself as, above all, an *awakener*. To oppose conflict and ruthlessness in the dealings between nations was to align oneself with pathogenic forces of degeneration. These values and sentiments and ideas were carried and implemented by young men trained not so much by academic schooling as by the shared disciplined exercises of collective physical action. In that age, nationalists made rather good soldiers. The chances were that they were in good physical shape, had taken a lot of exercise, done a lot of hiking, or even rock-climbing, had a keen eye, were good shots, and were used to responding to crisp words of command. Love of nature and of communal, energetic activity was unwittingly paramilitary. In modern times, the parts of Europe which constitute what might be called the zone of romantic and nature-friendly populism, on the whole did better on the battlefield than populations more committed to other and more refined styles of joy.

This virulent style of nationalism, going so far beyond that which is merely required by the need for culturally homogeneous, internally mobile socio-political unity (that is nation-states), reflects and expresses what one might call the Poetry of Unreason. Communality, discipline, hierarchy and ruthlessness are good, and constitute the true fulfilment of human needs, not *despite* the fact that they are anti-rational, but *because* they are such. Bloodless, barren universalistic reason was in conflict with real deep springs of human conduct, if not actually at the service of pathogenic ones (roughly, Nietzsche's view). When the German army conquered Europe around 1940, it impressed those it conquered not merely by its might, but also by its beauty. ('How beautiful they are', Sartre makes a French prisoner of war remark, as he looks at his captors, in Sartre's novel depicting the fall of France.) This endowed the conquest with a certain legitimacy. The German soldier fought well not merely because he knew that he would be shot if he did not: he was also moved by a powerful national *esprit de corps*. Romantic *Kameradschaft* complemented Prussian discipline. The achievement of Nazism and its re-ritualization of politics was to endow an anonymous and industrial

Gesellschaft with the powerful and effective illusion that it was a genuine *Gemeinschaft*. It combined the efficiency of both industrial and absolute-monarchy discipline with the (idealized) affect-saturated cohesion of the localized kin group.

So this is the scenario: a purging of the joyful cohesive communal nation-state not merely of intrusive minorities, but above all of those eternal-universal minorities whose intellectualism and/or commercialism made them inherently unfit to be a member of *any* folk culture, let alone of 'ours'. So the exterminations which took place in the 1940s, though secret, were not, so to speak, shifty, underhand and opportunist. They were carried out, or ordered, to a considerable extent by people who were doing what they were doing not out of individual self-interest, but in fulfilment of a duty, for the general good, in pursuit of purification and beauty. It was indeed secret: mass murder continued to be sufficiently appalling to make it politically preferable to hide it. But if the secrecy was a means, the act itself was not. It was *wertrational*, it was the fulfilment of an end held to be inherently valuable. One of the Nazis who commented on the extermination project invoked the name of Kant, and what he said was not absurd: it was done for a principle, not from self-interest. Indeed it did not advance, but hampered, the interests of those who perpetrated it. To ignore this, or to deny or obfuscate it out of shame and embarrassment, is to distort and obscure an important point in the history of European thought and feeling.

One of the best known commentators on twentieth-century totalitarianism, Hannah Arendt, has argued that the ideology of Nazism is somehow quite discontinuous with European thought, that it has emerged unheralded and unprecedented from some dark conceptual underworld.[6] This seems to me altogether false. The particular blending of elements – a repudiation of universalism, a valuation both of culture and cohesion and of competitive ruthlessness, of discipline and hierarchy rather than market anarchy within society, plus a few other themes – all this, of course, is far from being the sum total of the European intellectual tradition, but it does not stand outside it either. In its naturalism, it is a continuation of the Enlightenment, and in its communalism and cult of idiosyncrasy, it is part of the Romantic reaction to it.

But what all this amounts to is this: the fourth stage of the development of nationalism, that of the tidying up of the ethnic map by unimaginably brutal means, was not something accidental, a chance by-product of the opportunity (under cover of wartime secrecy) to be less scrupulous and publicly well-behaved than is customary when under general observation and scrutiny. On the contrary, it was something which was inscribed on the agenda, so to speak, of European thought. On the complex ethnic map of Europe, especially Central and Eastern Europe, *any* solution of the problem of political boundaries was bound to thwart *many*. The fury aroused by the prolonged frustrations was now aided by a social metaphysic which commended brutal solutions anyway, and it was implemented by a temporarily victorious movement genuinely committed to that metaphysic, and in possession of the will and the means to carry out its requirements.

Diminution of Intensity of Ethnic Sentiment

A new age began in 1945. Those who had embraced the romantic cult of aggression – and of ethnic community – had been defeated, ironically, at the very court they had themselves chosen and declared to be ultimate and valid: trial by combat. That was the negative lesson. But fairly soon it was to be followed by a complementary positive lesson. The postwar period turned out to be one of sustained and unprecedented prosperity, the age of generalized, or at any rate very widespread, affluence. But some were to be more affluent than others: the greatest affluence came to those who had *lost* in the war, and were thereby deprived of the opportunity for further cultivation of collective aggression, and who had also been ruthlessly shorn of much territory. From the very viewpoint of success and of natural selection, the warrior ethic turned out to be rather less than commendable. But on the positive side the commercial-productive ethic also turned out to have great charms, and success in that field was clearly seen to be independent of the possession of territory. Consumerism made greater inroads on the traditional ethos of 'honour' than commercialism alone had ever done. *Lebensraum* turns out to be an irrelevancy. So peasant land-hunger came to be seen to be as antiquated as the cult of military valour. Contrary to what Marx had said, *consume* rather than *accumulate* was Moses and the Prophets of the new order.

These considerations undermine the vigour of expansionist nationalism. In so far as it was rational, or claimed to be such, it assumed that the possession of territory was the mark or the precondition of national greatness and/or prosperity, and it had now become clear that this was not so. The non-rational elements, the high valuation of aggression and martial virtues, is also undermined by consumerist values. So much for the level of ideology. But, of course, the main sphere of operation and transmission of nationalist sentiment is not the ideological, but the level of ordinary, daily, personal life. People really become nationalists because they find that in their daily social intercourse, at work and at leisure, their 'ethnic' classification largely determines how they are treated, whether they encounter sympathy and respect, or contempt, derision and hostility. The root of nationalism is not ideology, but concrete daily experience. A member of culture A, involved in constant dealings with economic, political and civic bureaucracies employing culture B, is exposed to humiliations and discrimination. He can only escape by becoming either an assimilationist or a nationalist. Often he vacillates between these two strategies.

It is at this level that nationalism receives diminished impetus during the later and prosperous stages of industrialism. For one thing, there is an element of truth in the 'Convergence thesis' concerning industrial societies. It may or may not apply to cultures which are very distant from each other: cultures of European and East Asian advanced industrial societies may well fail to resemble each other, even when based on similar technology, and in possession of comparable standards of living. But if the cultural baseline is reasonably similar to begin with, as for instance is the case of most or all European nations in relation to each other, then the attainment of the late industrial stage of industrial competence and affluence also brings with it a quite considerable cultural convergence. The youth culture of Atlantic societies, for instance, is remarkably similar, and incidentally it was in this very field that the Soviet Union first humbly capitulated to the West, long before beginning to do so in other spheres with the coming of perestroika. Soviet Pepsi-Cola and longing for blue jeans preceded the Soviet love affair with the idea of the market. Amongst advanced industrial nations with a reasonably close cultural starting-point, differences tend to become phonetic not semantic: people have and conceive and handle the same 'things' (generally made in the same way or even in the same places), and characterize them by the same concepts, but express these with words differing only in the sounds they use, rather than in their content.

Our theory of nationalism linked its emergence to the transformation of work: shared culture becomes important when work ceases to be physical and becomes semantic. Members of the same interacting community must share one and the same standardized code, and a man is identified by the code in teens of which he can operate. But if this is so, why should nationalism diminish again when the semanticization of work reaches its height, and why should it have been most acute when this was only in its beginnings? And why should a *universal* phenomenon manifest itself as insistence on *distinctive* ethnic units? The answer lies in the unevenness of industrialization, which maximizes inequalities and tensions in the early stages, at the points of entry into the world of semantic work. It is then that it is in the interests of somewhat later entrants to organize their own state-culture unit.[7]

So, the other factor conducive to the lessening of the intensity of ethnic sentiment in daily life is the diminution of economic distance. This must be compared with the situation which had prevailed during the period when nationalist sentiment was liable to be at its strongest, that is, during the early stages of industrialization. At that stage, economic differences between the early entrants into the system and others more privileged are enormous. Early migrants into the industrial workforce, inhabiting rapidly erected slums or shantytowns, deprived of virtually any material or moral or political resources, really do have nothing other than their labour power to sell, and are obliged to sell it on the worst possible terms, barely if at all above the level required for merest survival. They note the difference between their own condition and that of those more fortunate, and the class hatred postulated by Marxism, and also noted by ideologically more disinterested observers such as de Tocqueville, does indeed emerge. But, contrary to the predictions of Marxism, it does not persist and grow, unless it is endorsed with a, so to speak, ethnic *prise*. If the unfortunates are in a position to note that the more fortunate ones are culturally distinct from themselves, say in their speech, whether or not these differences are as yet linked to some ethnonym, then powerful sentiments, duly to be labelled national ones, rapidly emerge and persist. The impoverished ones have their own condition highlighted by the existence of others who are less unfortunate, and if those others are also distinct culturally, the unfortunates soon note that those who exploit them, or at any rate surpass them economically, are also those who add insult to injury by spurning them. They can spurn them generically, if indeed there is some generic cultural *differentia* which makes it possible to identify them as a human category. So, cultural *differentiae* become significant as catalysts of social cleavages and antagonisms, *if* they more or less coalesce with the marked, but culturally unhallowed economic differences, so characteristic of early industrialism. Generic contempt and privilege then engender a new generic identity. The new hatred arises on both sides of the great barrier. For the better-placed category, the culturally distinguishable poor constitute a menace, not only to the social order as a whole, but also in daily life. They are dirty and violent, they make the city unsafe, and they constitute a kind of cultural pollution.

During the later stages of industrialism, things are quite different. There are still enormous economic inequalities, and these sometimes correlate with cultural ones, and then become septic. Cultural category A is in general better off than category B, generating resentment among the B and fear among the A. But if both categories find themselves at a relatively high level, which is generally the case under late industrialism, though in 'objective', material terms those surviving differences may still be great, subjectively they matter much much less. Hence the intensity of resentment generated is also correspondingly less. The difference between objectively appalling poverty and mild prosperity is something tremendous; the difference between considerable prosperity and *very* considerable prosperity is psychologically far less great. Under conditions of advanced industrialism, differences between cultural categories tend to be of the latter rather than the former kind. The only categories of persons who are then massively underprivileged tend to be not cultural, 'ethnic' ones, but, so to speak, medical or personal ones – people with serious medical handicaps, isolated persons, and so forth. But such categories do not generate a 'nationalism'. (This general point does not, of course, apply to late labour migrants, who tend to be both underprivileged and culturally distinguishable, and who, of course, do generate virulent national sentiments on both sides.)

So, although a shared, context-free, education-based high culture continues to be the precondition of moral citizenship, of effective economic and political participation, under late industrialism, it need no longer generate intense nationalism. Nationalism can now be tamed, as religion has been tamed. It is possible to move a person's ethnicity from the public sphere to the private sphere, to pretend that it is only his own business, like his sex life, and something which need not interfere in his public life, and which it is improper to drag in. But this is really a pretence, which can be indulged if one dominant culture is appropriated by all and is usable as a kind of general currency, permitting people to be bi-cultural and use another one, if they so wish, in their homes and other restricted areas.

When the process of making work semantic reaches its apogee, it also has the tendency to endow advanced industrial cultures with the *same* meanings, to promote a convergence which, jointly with generalized affluence, diminishes conflict. It is *early* industrialism which both engenders maximum economic jealousy and resentment, and promotes the social imposition of high cultures which have not yet come to resemble each other.

All kinds of, as it were, federal or cantonal arrangements now become possible in the later stage. Political boundaries become less important, less obsessional and symbolic: it is no longer a matter of deep concern that 'our' border should be on a certain river or that it should follow the crest of a certain mountain range. Bitter tears are no longer shed, nor passionate poetry written and recited, concerning the failure of the customs barrier to be located on that beautiful waterway or that dramatic mountain range, for the attainment of which our boys bled so bravely. It now seems sufficient that mobility and access to the advantages be more or less evenly distributed among cultural categories, and that each culture has its secure home base where its perpetuation is assured by its own university, national museum, national theatre, TV network and so forth. Solutions of roughly this form seem to have been attained, or to be close to attainment, in a number of areas: which of course does not mean that they will be attained in general or universally.

The stages here described are the so to speak 'natural' steps along a path from the agrarian world, in which culture underwrites hierarchy and social position, but does not define political boundaries, to the industrial world in which culture *does* define boundaries of states, but where it is standardized, and hence insensitive, non-discriminating with respect to social position. It is hard to see how the transition could follow any other trajectory. In the beginning, there were dynastic or religious units, co-existing with and superimposed on local communal ones. Then came irredentism, seeking congruence of culture and state, and bound to be frustrated in most cases, because the complexity of the ethnic map simply does not allow the fulfilment of all the ethnic aspirations at once. Nationalism is not a zero-sum game, it is a minus-sum game, because the majority of cultures-participants is *bound* to lose: there are simply too many cultures, as it were potential state-definers, for the amount of space available on this earth for viable states. So, *most* of the cultures are bound to go to the wall and fail to attain their fulfilment, that is, the marriage of the culturally defined nation with its own state, which is what nationalist theory anticipates and ardently desires. But the anger and fury engendered during this process, in conjunction with the Darwinian cult of ruthlessness, the Nietzschean endorsement of deep feeling as against reason, and the widespread social dislocation, lead very naturally to the kind of murderous excess witnessed in Europe above all in the 1940s, but not unknown at other times. Finally, with the coming of generalized affluence and the diminution of cultural distance through late industrialism and a universal market and standardized lifestyle, there comes a certain diminution of intensity of national sentiment.

That, in brief, is the trajectory one would naturally expect, and which, in many areas, one does indeed find. But the schema is by no means universally applicable, even in Europe. It may fail to find complete fulfilment in actual history for a variety of reasons. In Europe, the underlying mechanism played itself out in different ways in various time zones, and these differences deserve to be noted.

1. Centralization *by* the state. A political unit may exist which was established by dynastic politics in the pre-nationalist era, but which happens to correspond – all in all, though, of course, never completely – to a homogeneous cultural area The territory it occupies contains a variety of local dialects (that is, languages without an army and navy) which are, however, close enough to the language employed by the state apparatus in question, to be treated as its 'dialects'. The speakers of these dialects may come to be persuaded that the formal and standardized speech which they are now encouraged to adopt, and obliged to use in writing and in dealings with the bureaucracy, is the 'proper' variant of the speech

they employ at home.[8] That is how one *should* speak. The cultural habits of such populations, and their genetically transmitted traits, are such that they can be incorporated in the 'national' self-image of the dominant high culture without contradiction and without too much strain. This kind of situation on the whole prevailed along the western, Atlantic seaboard of Europe. Strong dynastic states based on London, Paris, Madrid and Lisbon had existed since early modern times, if not longer, and could transform themselves into homogeneous nation-states (though adjustments had to be made in Ireland, and minor internal organizational changes elsewhere as well). A centralized culture is established *against* peasants, and not on the basis of their culture. Peasants have to be turned into real citizens, rather than being used for the definition of a new national culture. Hence ethnography is here irrelevant to nation-building. There is no call to record that which you wish to destroy. It is only when a new national culture is being constructed on the basis of an existing unselfconscious peasant mode of life, that the latter becomes of absorbing interest for nationalist scholars.

2. Immediately to the east of the zone of strong dynastic states, which only needed to 'civilize' their peasants, there is another time zone, of what one might call unificatory nation-state building. Here we find a strong, confident, self-conscious high culture (or rather, to be precise, two of them). A standardized and normative German speech has existed since the collective crusading push by Teutons into Eastern Europe, or, at the very latest, since the Reformation. A literary movement around the turn of the eighteenth and nineteenth centuries finally consolidated it. The Italians have possessed a normative, standardized literary language since the late Middle Ages, the early Renaissance. Admittedly, this normative variant of the language might only be used by a minority (in Italy, it has been claimed that this minority remained tiny well into the nineteenth century), and fail to penetrate the lower orders of society or of outlying regions.

But the main problem facing such a culture was the provision of a single and shared political roof for the entire zone, in which this culture was indeed already dominant, rather than creating a new culture. Once this was achieved, the problem faced was identical with that faced by the first zone: civilize the peasant savage. But political unification had to come first, and was at the very centre of attention: high cultural diffusion or 'education' came second. In this kind of state-nation-building, thinkers, poets and propagandists, though neither absent nor unimportant, were less crucial than statesmen, diplomats and soldiers. What needed to be done in this zone was to unify a patchwork of mini-states or medium states, and, in some cases, expel alien rulers from key positions.

Achieving all this involved altering the balance of power of Europe in some measure, and acting against some powerful vested interests. This could hardly be done without some degree of violent conflict, and this kind of unification was indeed secured by war, and greatly aided by diplomacy.

3. The next time zone further east is the one which has supplied the best-known image of 'nation-building': cultures exist, or are held to exist, which neither have their own state and merely require to 'educate' the lower orders, nor merely need to unify a multiplicity of political units (possibly also needing to expel some rulers thereof); on the contrary, cultures are found which do not possess a political unit at all, and which are not endowed with their own codification, their own internal authoritative norms. Plural folk cultures need to be replaced by normative high cultures *and* endowed with a political cover.

Within this category, it is usual to distinguish between 'historic' and 'non-historic' nations. The former once possessed a state but lost it; the latter never had one at all. The former require a 'rebirth' of a political unit which once existed, but has been somehow eliminated in the course of dynastic or religious conflicts. The latter require the creation of a political unit which is to be defined in terms of culture alone, without support from history. The difference between these two types is probably not as important as is often supposed.

What is important about this species is that it requires 'awakeners', activists-propagandists-educators, committed to reviving the glories of the past, or alternatively to bringing the nation to consciousness simply by virtue of its cultural existence, without the blessings of previous political history. Either way, these men have to act in a freelance manner, or, if organized, under the guidance of organizations not endowed with the support of the existing political authorities. They do not as yet have a state to help them do it. It is this above all which distinguishes this pattern from 'centralization from above'.[9]

4. Finally, there is the fourth time zone. This shared the fate of the third time zone in so far as it passed through the first two stages between 1815 and 1918, experiencing dynastic/religious politics and the irredentist reaction to them. In fact, in 1815, Eastern Europe was divided between three empires, and the tsarist empire seemed set for the same trajectory as the Habsburg and Ottoman empires. All three empires had for a time, on the whole, resisted the nationalist onslaught – the Ottoman Empire less successfully than the other two – and all three of them, notwithstanding the fact that they were on opposed sides in the war, went onto the rubbish heap of history in 1918.

But thereafter, the land of Orthodoxy and Autocracy followed quite a different path from the territories of the other two empires, which now went ahead under the inspiration of a varied set of ideological cocktails. Within these, nationalism was the only stable and ubiquitous ingredient. In these small successor states, nationalism was blended, variously, with populism, democracy, fascism, clericalism, modernization, dynasty, et cetera. The blends were not unduly impressive, at any rate as intellectual products.

The situation was quite different in the lands of the Tsar of All the Russias. Within a few years of a shattering military defeat, the empire was re-established under new management and under a new ideology, one which was no feeble and opportunist cocktail, but, on the contrary, constituted one of the most powerful and moving belief systems ever created.[10] With hindsight, it is easy to see that Marxism was tailor-made for the needs of the anguished nineteenth-century Russian soul. This soul had been crucified between the desire to emulate and catch up the West, and the messianic-populist aspiration for a total, and yet locally rooted, fulfilment. Marxism claimed, on the one hand, to be scientific and materialistic, and thereby to embody and unmask the secret which had made the West rich and strong, and to provide a formula for a shortcut which would lead to an overtaking of the West and to even greater power and wealth. But on the other hand, it also promised an eventual total fulfilment, one wholly free of exploitation and oppression and the moral defects and the compromises and tawdriness associated with the Western form of industrialism. In this total consummation, miraculously and mysteriously, the yearning of the human soul for community, and the desire for individual independence, would be satisfied all at once. Man would be both wholly free and yet at one with his fellows. This was the manifest destiny of all mankind, and its accomplishment was only thwarted by defects of social organization which Marxism had at long last effectively diagnosed, and which it would in the fullness of time remedy. In its form, this programme was to be implemented by a dedicated, disciplined and ruthless Secular Order, whose possession of the absolute truth made redundant any preoccupation with formal procedural propriety and checks. Indeed, it felt obliged to disregard the requirement of merely formal justice (which it held to be a tool of bourgeois domination) in the interests of the class credited with the mission of liberating mankind. Its possession of substantive justice meant that it had little or no need of that formal justice which had only been used to mystify and to thwart real fulfilment.

This doctrine and spirit, superimposed on a country which had in any case long been endowed with centralist and authoritarian and messianic traditions, and one faced with tremendous tasks in its struggle for modernization and for military security, led to horrifying consequences which are well known and hardly need to be rehearsed once again. But from the viewpoint of tracing the story of the implementation of the nationalist principle in European society, a few of the salient points of this development need to be re-stated. First of all: the shortcut in the end proved to be quite spurious, and, far from leading to an overtaking of the West, actually led to a widening of the economic gap and to increasing retardation. The strength of the ideology and of the institutions it engendered did, however, prevent the lands of the tsar from following, for seventy years, the same path as that followed by the erstwhile lands of the Habsburgs and the Ottomans. The faith eventually evaporated, not under the impact of the terror of the Stalin years – which, evidently, it could morally accommodate – but under the impact of the squalor of the Brezhnev era of stagnation.

My own guess is that the first secular faith to become a state religion lost its hold over the faithful, not because it was secular and thereby more open to refutation by historic fact (faiths tend, if anything, to be strengthened by such trials), but because it over-sacralized the world, and granted the faithful no retreat into a profane realm, in which they could rest during periods of diminished zeal. Through Hegel, Marxism is descended from Spinoza, and it is implicitly pantheistic and sacralizes all life. It has been claimed that societies cannot live without the sacred, but the fate of Marxism shows that they cannot live without the profane either. A faith which turns the economy into a sacrament cannot easily survive a prolonged period of manifest economic squalor and sluggishness. As long as the members of the apparat murdered each other, faith remained vibrant; but when they started bribing each other instead, faith evaporated. When a failure of international competitiveness – economic and military – obliged the system to seek to reform itself through liberalization, it was discovered that no one believed any more. The Nazis had believed in war and were eliminated in a violent trial by combat; the Bolsheviks believed in the verdict of the economy, and were eliminated in an economic contest.

At this point, the societies caught within this system resumed the development which had been frozen seventy (or, in some areas, forty) years earlier. But the development was resumed on a social base altogether different from that which had been left behind seventy years ago: although there was considerable *relative* economic failure in comparison with the West, there had also been tremendous development compared with the past. There was now near-universal literacy, extensive urbanization, and a certain modest, but nonetheless significant, economic sufficiency, large enough at any rate for many people to have a good deal to lose.

The system could now slot itself into the development which it had not been allowed to follow at any one of the three remaining stages: it could

indulge in irresponsible irredentism and the setting up of new political
units (which reproduce, on a smaller and hence even more vulnerable
scale, the ethnic conflicts of the disintegrating imperial unit); or it could
pass to the murderous stage of *Nacht und Nebel*, with killing and forced or
encouraged migration; or it could reach out to that stage of diminished
ethnic hatred which, one hopes, goes with very advanced industrialism.
There is clear evidence for each of these three possibilities, and as yet it
is too early to say which one of them will predominate; we can only say
with confidence that none of them will be wholly absent. But which one
will prevail – that is the crucial question concerning the development of
the Soviet Union or its succession in the 1990s.

One should add that the schema of the four time zones needs a certain
modification if it is to correspond to historic reality: there is an extensive
area between the Baltic, the Adriatic and the Black Sea, which belonged
to the third zone in the interwar period, but was forcibly transferred to
the fourth zone by the advancing Red Army in 1944–45, and remained
there till 1989.

An Alternative Vision

The periodicization proposed here differs significantly from that offered
in the highly influential and powerfully argued and well-documented
work of Miroslav Hroch.[11] As Eric Hobsbawm observes, 'the work of
Hroch . . . opened the new era in the analysis of the composition of
national liberation movements.'[12] Hroch represents an interesting
attempt to save both Marxism *and* the Nationalist vision of itself, and this
constitutes part of his interest: nations really exist and express themselves through nationalist striving, instead of being engendered by it and
being its creation. At the same time, the transition between the past
Marxist 'modes of production' remains the basic event of the time, and
the (autonomous?) nationalist development is plotted against that event.
Hroch's outstandingly well-documented argument deserves full examination, though I disagree with him on both counts: nations do not 'really
exist' (they only emerge as a special form of correlation of culture and
polity under certain economic conditions); and the Marxist feudal-
ism/capitalism transition is acceptable only if re-interpreted as the
transition from the agrarian to the industrial world.
    So, Hroch's typology or periodicization is engendered by the super-
imposition of two sets of distinctions. One of them is defined in terms of
the stages of the overall social order; the other, in terms of the successive
character of the national movement itself. The first distinction is binary:
it refers to the distinction between feudalism and absolutism on the one

hand, and capitalism on the other. The book was written from an avowedly Marxist viewpoint, though at the time it was written and published, it could hardly have seen the light of day in Prague had it not been formulated in that way. This does not necessarily imply that the Marxism of the argument was less than sincere; that is a question which it would seem to be inappropriate to raise here. At the same time, this is obviously a part of the background of the book, and it cannot be ignored.

This use of the Marxist theory of historical stages calls for some comments. Hroch, as stated, combines 'feudalism' and 'absolutism' in *one* 'stage'.[13] It is no doubt possible to include both of them with a broader, generic 'feudalism': within both of them, status is linked to land. Within each, there is a sharply differentiated system of ranks, connected with unsymmetrical obligations and duties, and organized in a pyramid with a monarchical apex. In each, there is an ethos of martial valour, a low valuation of productive work, and an even lower or ambiguous valuation of commerce and trade. The terminology of rank under centralized absolutism is the same as in, and is indeed inherited from, feudalism in the narrower sense. So they do share certain important features.

But the differences are at least as great and as important as the similarities. An absolutist state relies largely on a standing and professional army, within which the nobility may serve as officers, but to which they do not normally bring their own entire social units 'in arms'. The 'regiment' of a given nobleman, or one named after him, is in fact a standard unit subject to standardized rules of equipment, organization and command, and it is not the nobleman's household, estate and retinue reorganized for campaign, and run in terms of its own local, particularistic traditions. The absolutist monarch controls the territory over which he is sovereign, and legal and political authority in outlying or inaccessible regions is not delegated to nobles with a local power-base. As Adam Smith noted in connection with Cameron of Lochiel, such delegation, unsanctioned by law, did in fact occur in the pre-1745 Highlands, but it is precisely this which made the Highlands untypical and exceptional in an otherwise centralized state.[14] Under absolutism, the *noblesse d'épée* is complemented and in some measure replaced by a *noblesse de robe* – in effect, a bureaucracy. Under the Tudors, a new nobility with a service ethos complemented and replaced an independent, territorially based aristocracy.

It is significant that the name of de Tocqueville does not occur in Hroch's bibliography. The idea that the French Revolution completed, rather than reversed, the work of the centralizing French monarchy receives no discussion. The French Revolution is in fact mentioned only once (though the generic notion of 'bourgeois revolution' occurs far more frequently and plays an important role in the argument). When the

French Revolution is mentioned by name, it occurs in the context of a methodological discussion, and of an affirmation of the author's then commitment to a Marxist view of history, and to seeing *class*, rather than so to speak surface social position, as ultimately significant.[15]

But it is hard not to suspect that at this point at least this author's indisputably most important argument suffers not from an excess but from a lack of Marxism. The assumption of a generic (and homogeneous?) social baseline, a catch-all feudalism-absolutism, prevents one from even raising the question of the relation of the rise of nationalism to *earlier* structural changes in European society. But it clearly is, at the very least, necessary to ask the question concerning the connection between nationalism and that earlier transition from a politically fragmented genuinely feudal society, within which bureaucracy is largely absent, or at best present in or drawn from the Church, to that later 'absolutist' society, in which a secular bureaucracy is already prominent.[16] In that later social order, widespread administrative use of writing already begins to engender that linkage of a centralized polity and a literate, normative, codified high culture which lies close to the essence of the nationalist principle. Nationalist movements did not yet emerge in this period, but it is certainly arguable that it prepared the ground for them, through the centralization, bureaucratization and standardization which it practised. Whether or not this is so, it should be possible at least to ask the question. Though I subscribe to the view that, on the whole, nationalism in the form in which we know it is a phenomenon of the last two centuries, nevertheless it must be a defect of a theory of nationalism if, starting so uncompromisingly from an implicitly generic baseline of 'absolutism-feudalism', it actually inhibits the formulation of any questions concerning possible earlier roots.

There are other candidates for this role of early progenitors or harbingers of nationalism, notably the Reformation and, to a lesser extent perhaps, the Renaissance. The Protestant use of vernacular languages and the diffusion of literacy, and the direct contact of the believer with the Sacred Word (in an idiom intelligible to him) clearly has an affinity with the social profile of nationalism. The creation of national rather than international clergies, or the diffusion of the clerkly status throughout the whole of society, cannot be irrelevant to the eventual emergence of the nationalist ideal of one culture, one state, one society. The fragmentation of the universal political system, the diffusion of sovereignty, cannot but be a significant part of the pre-history, if not the history, of nationalism. When Bernard Shaw causes his version of St Joan to be burned as a Protestant by the Church and as a nationalist by the English, was he being altogether anachronistic? The absence of the name of Jan Hus from the index of a Czech book on nationalism is also strange.

So one can only repeat the point that, in a curious way, this remarkable work in part suffers from not an excess, but an insufficiency of Marxism. The major social transition to which its argument links nationalism is simply the move from absolutism-feudalism to capitalism, and it altogether ignores earlier, and possibly relevant, transitions. A person like the present writer, who does believe that nationalism is essentially linked to the coming of industrialism, cannot wholly disagree with such an approach, and does not really object to the use of 'capitalism' where 'industrialism' would be more appropriate: that is simply a part of the Marxist idiom, and made mandatory by that repudiation of the convergence-of-capitalist-and-socialist-industrialism thesis to which Marxism was committed; but one can easily carry out one's own translation of the terminology here. Nevertheless, one feels that the convention that the world began in the late eighteenth century is here carried to excess.

In this connection, it is also worth noting that the discussion of the implications for nationalism of the transition from capitalism to *socialism* is equally absent. Its handling would, of course, have been extremely delicate. Work attempting to handle the role of ethnicity in Soviet society (that of the late Yulian Bromley) is, however, cited.

The basic logic of Hroch's approach, then, is to relate nationalism to a single and stark transition, namely, that from pre-industrial to capitalist society. What exactly is it that is then so related to the underlying single great change in social ecology and structure?

The answer is – the phenomenology of nationalism. Here Hroch operates with not a binary but a three-term classification, a three-stage account of the development of nationalism. Hroch distinguishes between stage A, that of scholarly interest in and exploration of the culture of a nation, stage B, of nationalist agitation – the intellectuals no longer restrict themselves to ethnography, but promote national awareness amongst the population whose national culture they investigate – and finally stage C, the emergence of a mass national movement.

This typology is inspired by and specially applicable to (as the author recognizes) the emergence of 'small' nations not already endowed with, so to speak, their own and distinctive political roof. So, by implication – though the author does not formulate it in any way – the two dimensions formally introduced (traditional/capitalist, and the three stages of national awakening) are *also* related to a third dimension, along which we have the distinction large and state-endowed nations, as against small and 'oppressed' ones. In this last dichotomy, state-endowment would seem to be more important than size in a literal sense, in so far as the Danes appear to be consigned to the 'large nation', which can hardly be correct in some simple numerical sense.[17] This makes the Danes a large nation, and the Ukrainians a small one.

Formally speaking, this dimension or variable does not enter the argument, in so far as the official, declared subject of Hroch's inquiry is precisely nationalism amongst 'small' nations, that is, nations which need to *acquire* their political unit. However, notwithstanding the fact that this – the nationalism of 'small' nations – is the formal subject-matter of the book, it is I think natural, appropriate and illuminating to re-interpret the argument as a general treatise on nationalism, in which the focus on 'small oppressed' nations covers an approach which treats them as one distinctive variety of nation-formation in general. The theory implied then in fact covers both species, 'great' and 'small' alike.

However, officially, at the heart of the book there is the relationship between the twofold classification of societies, and the threefold classification of stages of nationalism. The manner in which these two overlap with each other then leads Hroch to propose four types of nationalism.[18]

The first type he calls the 'integrated type' of development. The transition from scholarly interest to active agitation precedes the industrial and bourgeois revolutions. The completion of the 'formation of a modern nation' follows these, and is in turn followed by the emergence of a working-class movement.

The second species he calls the 'belated type': national agitators replace scholars before the coming of the bourgeois and industrial revolution, and the emergence of a working-class movement precedes or is contemporaneous with the transition from agitation to mass nationalism, and the formation of a full modern nation only follows all the other processes considered.

The third variety he calls the 'insurrectional type'; agitators replace scholars already under feudal society, and a modern nation is actually formed under feudalism: 'The national movement had already attained a mass character under the conditions of feudal society.' The nation is formed before the emergence of bourgeois society.[19]

Finally, there is the fourth species, which he calls 'disintegrated': in this variety, even the early forms of nationalist activity only follow the bourgeois and industrial revolutions, and the nationalist agitation is not necessarily replaced by a mass movement at all. The generalization which seems to follow (and the author articulates it, though not quite in these words) is that very early industrialization can be fatal for nationalism.

An interesting and distinctive aspect of Hroch's approach is the importance of phase A in nation-formation, which he describes as follows: 'The beginning of every national revival is marked by a passionate concern on the part of a group of individuals, usually intellectuals, for the study of the language, the culture, the history of the oppressed nationality' (*National Revival*, p. 22). Hroch rightly notes that these ethnic explorers are quite often not members of the ethnic group in question:

the awakening does not necessarily or exclusively come, so to speak, from within. There often are vicarious 'awakeners'.

The presence and salience of this state could usefully be made into a *variable* in a general theory of nationalism, embracing 'large' and 'small' nations alike, rather than being, as it is in Hroch's argument, a *constant* in the study of 'small' nations (by which Hroch as stated means not size, but the absence of an indigenous ruling class and state). If we adopt such an approach, we can both see that, *and why*, this stage is so prominent in some of the European time zones, and absent in others. In the westernmost time zone, national unity is forced not with but against the peasantry. 'Peasant' is a term of abuse, not of endearment, in such societies.[20] National unity and the sense of nationhood are formed in a 'Jacobin' spirit, around an already existing and expanding set of central institutions, and the high culture associated with it. Peasant regional idiosyncrasy is an offensive hindrance, and it is to be ironed out as quickly as possible by an educational system which holds this to be one of its most important objectives. In the second time zone, populist romanticism is encountered, especially in Germany: the fragmented political units preceding national unification often practised alien speech and manners in their courts, and the local culture is stressed in opposition to this alien style. Nonetheless, a sense of national unity is forged against and not in support of regional dialects and lifestyles, and ethnography is not the handmaiden of nationalism. When Mussolini encouraged Italians from the south and from Veneto to settle in the Val d'Aosta, he was, all at once, combating both the good French speech of the Savoyard ruling class, habituated to seek their brides in Chambéry rather than in Italy, *and* the idiosyncratic local dialect of the Valdotain peasantry.

It is in the third time zone that this ethnographic 'phase' is pervasively and inherently present. Here, a national and state culture is created not in opposition to peasant idiosyncrasy, but on the basis of it. Of course, it has to be sifted and distilled and standardized; but nonetheless, it must first of all be investigated in its raw state, if it is ever to be streamlined and codified, and to provide the base for a new high culture around which a nation and state are to be created. The much-used distinction between historic and non-historic nations matters relatively little: it does not make too much difference whether the dialect-group in question had, long ago, been linked to a political unit and its own court culture, or whether it had never had such a standing. This makes some difference to the content of national myth which is to be created: the Czechs or Lithuanians can look back to medieval glories, whereas the Estonians, Latvians, Byelorussians or Slovaks cannot Only peasant folklore or the odd social bandit, but no monarchs or imperial exploits, can enter their mythology. But this hardly matters much.

The fourth time zone possesses features both of the first and the third zones. Ethnic exploration, in the form of Slavophile populism, not only existed, but was extremely important and prominent. But its point was not to create a national identity as a basis for a new state: a state already existed, and was linked to a national church, which seems to have done a good job in creating a national cultural identity. The celebrated 'going to the people' was concerned more with the definition or modification or re-establishment of the 'true content' of the national culture than with its actual *creation*. Was this culture to be based on the values of peasant lifestyle and religiosity, or on the elite or courtly orientation, with its orientation towards strong Westernizing themes? Amongst the other, non-Russian ethnic groups of the empire, on the other hand, the parallel with the third zone largely prevails. This is also the part of Europe much of which, in or around 1945, so to speak 'changed zones'. The countries forcibly converted to communism with the help of the Red Army in the later 1940s were in zone 3 till then, but were absorbed into zone 4 thanks to communism – that is, the nationalist trajectory was interrupted between about 1945 and 1989. It expressed itself dramatically in Yugoslavia in 1991.

One can sum up all this as follows: the nation-states which replaced dynastic-religious ones as the European norms in the two centuries following the French Revolution, could grow around pre-existing states and/or high cultures, or they could as it were roll their own culture out of existing folk traditions, and then form a state around that newly created normative great tradition. In the latter case, a consciousness and memory had to be created, and ethnographic exploration (in effect: codification and invention) was mandatory. This is Hroch's 'phase A'. But in the former case, folk tradition, instead of having to be endowed with memory, had to be consigned to oblivion, and be granted the gift not of memory, but of forgetting. The great theoretician of this path of nation-formation is, of course, Ernest Renan.[21] In the East they remember what never occurred, in the West they forget that which did occur. It was Renan who urged the French, in the interest of consistency, to abjure the political use of ethnography and ethnology: the boundaries of France never became ethnic, and they continue to invoke geopolitics and choice, rather than folk culture. It was also he who eloquently expounded the idea that the basis of national identity is not memory but amnesia: in the national Jacobin French state, Frenchmen were induced to forget their origins, in contrast to the non-national Ottoman Empire, where the very bases of social organization ensured that every man knew his ethnic-religious origin. To this day, Ottoman legislation survives in Israel, thanks to a parliamentary balance which makes the religious vote valuable for most coalitions, and so helps ensure that a man can only marry in terms of his pre-modern, communal identity, by using its church.

So ethnographic research is relevant in some but not all European contexts of nation-building: in others, its absence, or at least its political irrelevance, is just as important. Western nationalism ignores and does not explore folk diversity. So the options are – created memory, or induced oblivion. The great irony occurred in the history of social anthropology: through the enormously influential work of Bronislaw Malinowski, who virtually created and defined the British and Imperial school in this discipline, the kind of cultural-holistic ethnography, initially practised in the interests of culture-preservation and nation-building in the East, was adapted in Western science in the name of, and for the sake of, empiricist method.[22]

However, the main centre of Hroch's remarkable work lies not in his characteristically Central European stress on the contribution of ethnography to nation-building, but in his manner of relating the general story of the transformation of the European socio-economic system to the rise of nationalism. Here, in effect, he faces one of the most persistent and deep issues in this field: is it nations, or is it classes, which are the real and principal actors in history?

Admittedly, he proclaims his intention to start from Marxist principles: 'We shall not disguise the fact that the generalizing procedures we use in investigating hidden class and group interests and social relations are derived from the Marxist conception of historical development '[23] Yet interestingly, his formal position also firmly disavows any reductionism with respect to nations: 'In contrast with the subjectivist conception of the nation as the product of nationalism, the national will and spiritual forces, we posit the conception of the nation as a constituent of social reality of historical origin. We consider the origin of the modern nation as the fundamental reality and nationalism as a phenomenon derived from the existence of that nation.'[24] This affirmation could hardly be more clear or categorical. Nations or, strangely, 'the *origin* of the modern nation' (emphasis added), are part of the basic social ontology, and not merely a historical by-product of structural change, although it also appears (p. 4) that the characteristics which define a nation are not stable.

So his position in the book might be described as semi-Marxist: on the one hand, nations are granted an independent historical importance and reality, and are not reduced to a reflection of changes in class structure, but nevertheless they remain at the centre of the stage. Yet the transition from feudalism/absolutism to capitalism also retains its central position. A discussion of the subsequent transition to socialism is largely avoided – which is understandable, though in an oblique way it remains

present through the importance attributed to the emergence of a militant working-class movement, presumably meant to usher in a new era. It
is neither affirmed nor denied that this working-class movement will
eventually prevail and lead to a new social formation altogether. There is
nothing in the book to preclude anyone from supposing that this will
happen. Given the fact that the book was written and published under a
regime which was formally committed to the view that it had happened,
and did not permit any public denials of such a claim, the sheer fact
that there is no actual and explicit affirmation of it is not without some
interest.

So the overall conclusion of the book seems to be that, on the one
hand, nations do have an independent and irreducible existence, and
that, nonetheless, the main historical reality remains the kind of change
in class relations postulated by Marxism. History would seem to have *two*
themes – class conflict *and* the reality of nations. So the emergence of
modern nations must be related to this great transformation – a task the
book then carries out with an unrivalled empirical and conceptual thor-
oughness. Neither of the two movements – the transition to
industrialism (capitalism, in the book's terminology), the other to
nationalism – is said to explain the other. The book conspicuously steers
clear of any reductionism: both Marxists and nationalists are granted
their respective realms, but neither is allowed to claim domination of the
other. By implication, the two realms are declared to be independent.
This seems to me mistaken: both are in reality aspects of *one single
transition.*

But in the light of the actual more concrete findings of the book, can
these conclusions really be sustained? Or is it the case that these
admirable analyses and documentation in fact support quite a different
conclusion? Such a conclusion would, on the one hand, be far more
reductionist *vis-à-vis* nations, and refrain from endorsing their ultimate
reality; on the other hand, it would also take far less seriously the Marxist
theory of social transition. It would be silly to be dogmatic on these complex matters, or to disagree with Hroch's contention that there is much
more work to be done; nonetheless, I am inclined to argue that, even or
especially in the light of evidence adduced by Hroch, the rival conclusion
does seem to be borne out by the facts.

This rival conclusion could run more or less as follows: the pre-
industrial world (feudalism/absolutism in Hroch's terminology) is
endowed with a complex patchwork of cultures, and very diverse political
formations. Some cultures pervade the ruling strata and the political
apparatus of a state. These cultures eventually define, in his terminology,
'great nations' (though actual size in the literal sense seems to be irrelevant). Other cultures (those of 'small' nations) are not so favourably

located. They do not include rulers and occupants of key political posts amongst their fellow practitioners of the same culture. They must *create* their high culture, before they can even begin to strive for a state which would then protect it.

Hroch agrees that genuine modern nationalism does not occur in the earlier, pre-industrial stage, and that territorial movements (*Landes-patriotismus*) in this period should not be counted as a form of nationalism, contrary to the views of authors such as Hans Kohn.[25] The real national principle comes to operate only in a new social order, with its greatly increased social mobility and the enormously increased import-ance of high, literate culture. Thus far, we seem to be in agreement.

The pre-industrial world is characterized by strata which, as it were, 'know their place': in other words, estates. The industrial world by con-trast is characterized by strata which do *not* know their place, in other words, by 'classes'. Their places are not frozen. If this transition is the essence of the 'bourgeois revolution', then this revolution, at any rate, really does take place. But is there any example of the series of trans-formations of class relations, as postulated by Marxism, actually being completed? And why should we treat it as independent of nationalism and of *its* phases?

What *has* in fact happened is that national revolutions did occur in those cases in which class and cultural differences overlapped: classes without cultural differences attained nothing, and cultural ('ethnic') dif-ferences without class differences also achieved nothing. It was only their conflation which had a true revolutionary potential. In Hroch's own words:

> Class struggle on its own led to no revolutions, and national struggle without conflict between strata in a mobile industrial society was similarly ineffec-tive . . . conflicts of interest between classes and groups whose members were divided at the same time by the fact that they belonged to different linguistic groups had indisputable significance for the intensification of the national movement. The polarity of material contradictions therefore ran parallel to differences of nationality, and as a result of this conflicts of interest were artic-ulated not (or not only) at the social and political level appropriate to them but at the level of national categories and demands. (p. 185)

So, class conflict only really took off if aided by ethnic/cultural differ-ences. But equally (pp. 185 and 186): '. . . where the national movement was not capable of introducing into national agitation . . . the interests of specific classes and groups . . . it was not capable of attaining success.' So national movements were effective only if sustained by class rivalry. So classes without ethnicity are blind, but ethnicities without class are power-less. Neither classes nor nations on their own engender structural

changes. It is only their conflation which, in the conditions brought
about by industrialism, does so.

Or again (p. 189):

> the members of the new intelligentsia of the oppressed nationality in so far as
> they did not assimilate – were faced with an obstacle which impeded . . . their
> chance of rising to a higher social position. As soon as membership of a small
> nation began to be interpreted . . . as a group handicap, it began to function
> as a source of transformation of the social antagonism into a national one. It
> is the presence of cultural barriers to the mobility inherent in industrial soci-
> ety which leads to social transformation. Industrial society leads not to class
> war but to the emergence of homogeneous nation states.

So, in the end, we are faced with a picture which in effect treats neither
classes nor nations as given. Standardized cultures become politically significant in the new industrial world, but, of the very many available
cultures, the ones selected for the new role are those which overlap with
important economic cleavages, engendered by the turbulent passage to
industrial society. This is precisely the theory we have been arguing.

Industrialism engenders mobile, culturally homogeneous units. It
leads to nationalist revolutions when class and cultural differences overlap. Hroch's strategy of relating these to each other, as if they were
independent, is unworkable. They are politically effective if, and only if,
they are *jointly* present. He himself spells this out. Class conflict on its own
fails to engender revolutions. As the overwhelming majority of cultural
differences also fail to find political expression, and cannot and do not
find political expression, there is no case for reifying nations either.
Before the event, we can only identify countless cultural differentiations,
and we simply cannot tell just which will turn into 'nations'. *After* the
event, we know which nation *happened* to crystallize, but this does not justify saying that the nation in question 'was there' from the start, ready to
be 'awakened'. Neither national nor class ideology should be taken at
face value. Both antagonistic classes and antagonistic nations are explicable, though not in Marxist fashion. They are only effective in conjunction.
This is the truth of the matter.

Hroch's work is valuable not only for the outstanding and unrivalled
richness of its empirical material, and the ingenious manner in which it
is used for the deployment of the comparative method; it is also valuable
for its underlying theoretical purpose. That aim seems to me deeply mis-
guided, but the determined effort to implement it is valuable precisely
because it enables us to see its weaknesses. What Hroch in effect tries to
do is to confer scholarly respectability on two of the great myths of the
nineteenth and twentieth centuries, namely Marxism and nationalism.
He does this by retaining the Marxist theory of historic stages (or rather,

a truncated segment thereof), and to relate it to a schema of national awakening, specially applicable to what we have called Europe's third time zone. The nationalist myth is also endorsed by attributing some kind of genuine independent and pre-existent reality to the nations which *did* succeed in 'waking up'.

This vision is in the end indefensible. History in general is *neither* the conflict of classes *nor* that of nations. In general, it is rich in countless kinds of conflict, not reducible to those two alleged basic forms of conflict. Pre-industrial society is exceedingly rich in status differences, but there is nothing to support the argument that, under the surface, these are reducible to generic 'classes' defined by their selection to the means of production, and that the underlying process, in the end governing all else, is the conflict of these 'classes'. Nor are these persistent compact 'nations' waiting for the alarm-bell. Under the impact of a certain kind of socio-economic form, best described as 'industrialism', both classes (loose and unhallowed strata in a market society) *and* nations (anonymous, self-conscious, culturally defined human categories) emerge and become politically significant, and engender changes in boundaries *when the two converge*. Economic tension signalled and underscored by cultural differences is politically potent, and it does radically reorder the map. Cultural homogeneity is imposed, and when cultural boundaries more or less converge with economic differences, related to the point of entry into industrialism, *new* boundaries emerge. Neither economic tension nor cultural difference on its own achieves anything, or, at any rate, not much. Each of them is a product rather than a prime mover. The socio-economic base is decisive. That much is true in Marxism, even if its more specific propositions are false.

The genuine reality underlying the historic development seems to me to be a transition between two quite different patterns of relation between culture and power. Each of these patterns is deeply rooted in the economic bases of the social order, though not in the way specified by Marxism.[25] In the pre-industrial world, very complex patterns of culture and power were intertwined, but did not converge so as to form national-political boundaries. Under industrialism, both culture and power are standardized, and they underwrite each other and they converge. Political units acquire sharply defined boundaries, which are also the boundaries of cultures. Each culture needs its own political roof, and states legitimate themselves primarily as protectors of culture (and as guarantors of economic growth). This is the overall pattern, and we have also sketched out the manner in which its specific manifestation appears differently in various parts of Europe.

Neither classes nor nations exist as the inevitable and permanent furniture of history. This does not exclude the possibilities that, in certain specific circumstances, the dominant conflict may not occur between large anonymous groups defined by shared culture (nations), or large anonymous groups defined by their place in the productive process (classes, in the Marxist sense). What it does exclude is the doctrine that either classes or nations provide the units for some kind of permanent conflict which is the key to history. *Neither* in fact provides such a permanent underlying theme. Agrarian society is endowed with both complex stratification and complex cultural diversity, but neither engenders major and decisive groupings. Under industrialism, economic polarization occurs for a time, and cultural standardization occurs for a *longer* time. When they converge, they decisively transform the map. All in all, this theory is better compatible with Hroch's own data than is his own general theory, which, interestingly, attempts to perpetuate at the same time both the 'class' and the 'nation' interpretations of history. But we have no further need of either of these two myths.

Notes

1. Cf. J. Goody, *The Logic of Writing and the Organisation of Society*, Cambridge 1986.
2. Eric J. Hobsbawm, *Nations and Nationalism since 1780*, Cambridge 1990.
3. For the presentation of a contrary view, see A.D. Smith, *The Ethnic Origin of Nations*, Oxford 1986.
4. Cf. G. Lenski, *Power and Privilege: Theory of Social Statification*, New York 1966.
5. Cf. Alan Macfarlane, *The Origins of English Individualism*, Oxford 1978.
6. Hannah Arendt, *The Origins of Totalitarianism*, New York 1951.
7. Cf. Roman Szperluk, *Communism and Nationalism*, Oxford 1988.
8. Cf. E. Weber, *Peasants into Frenchmen*, London 1979.
9. The contrast between the second and third zones underlies the distinction central to John Plamenatz's remarkable essay, 'Two Types of Nationalism', in E. Kamenka, ed., *Nationalism. The Nature and Evolution of an Idea*, London 1976. Plamenatz contrasts the relatively benign and liberal nationalism of nineteenth-century unificatory movements with the arduous and often brutal operations of those who had to *forge* a national culture where it did not yet exist, rather than merely endowing an existing one with its political roof.
10. The fact that some of the other ideologies were hotchpotches without much merit as intellectual constructions was not in itself necessarily a disadvantage, from the viewpoint of their social and political effectiveness and usefulness. For instance, the Kemalist aspiration to modernize and secularize Turkey was rather rigid in its scholastic secularism. It was carried out in the *ulama* spirit, so to speak; it was deeply marked by the very thing it opposed. It reproduced some of its traits in a secular idiom, and it involved the Turkish elite in an unnecessarily painful *Kulturkampf*. Nevertheless, in the end it proved superior to Marxism and more durable, precisely because it did not tie the hands of the elite in social and economic policies. Its lack of a clear social doctrine eventually proved a great advantage.
11. Miroslav Hroch, *Social Preconditions of National Revival in Europe*, Cambridge 1985.
12. Hobsbawm, *Nations and Nationalism*.
13. Hroch, *National Revival*, pp. 10 and 25. For instance, on p. 25 he refers to 'the period when the decisive feature of social conflict was the struggle against feudalism and absolutism'.
14. Cf. Adam Smith, *The Wealth of Nations*.
15. Hroch, *National Revival*, p. 17.
16. Perry Anderson, *Lineages of the Absolutist State*, London 1974.

17. Hroch, *National Revival*, p. 8.

18. Ibid., p. 27ff.

19. The author's European orientation seems to prevent him from considering the parallel case of nationalist sentiment in societies which are partially feudal, but still have significant tribal traits – e.g. Somalis, Kurds, possibly some ethnic groups in the territory of the USSR.

20. In Angus Wilson's insightful novel about historians, *Anglo-Saxon Attitudes*, there is a perceptive account of the incomprehension occurring between two middle-class women, one French, the other Scandinavian. For the Frenchwoman, 'peasant' is a pejorative notion, and she simply cannot grasp the admiring, nostalgic, romantic-populist use of the idea by the other lady.

21. Ernest Renan, *Qu'est-ce qu'une nation?*, Paris 1882. Republished in *Ernest Renan et l'Allemagne*, E. Burc, ed., New York 1945.

22. Cf. R. Ellen, E. Gellner, G. Kubica, J. Mucha, eds., *Malinowski between Two Worlds*, Cambridge 1988.

23. Hroch, *National Revival*, p. 17.

24. Ibid., p. 3.

25. On the Marxist ontology of nations and classes, see Roman Szporluk, *Communism and Nationalism*, New York/Oxford 1988.

5

Approaches to Nationalism

John Breuilly

Introductory Comments

In this essay I will consider critically how nationalism has been defined and interpreted by historians. I will go on to suggest why approaches which consider nationalism as an aspect of modernity are to be preferred to other approaches. I will then explore further one such approach, which focuses on the relationship between nationalism and the development of the modern state, providing some examples of the insights that such an approach can yield.

One should be clear about what justifies 'theory' in relation to the subject of nationalism. First, theory has itself to be subject to some kinds of tests against evidence. So it is crucial that theory be framed in such a way as to allow of such tests. There are problems with this. A general concept which helps frame an approach to a subject cannot be falsified in the same way as a particular statement about a specific event. It is more a question of the use to which such concepts can be put in arriving at particular statements. Without some clear definitions and concepts it is impossible to identify and study even one particular case. The danger of untheorized history is that it either smuggles in unacknowledged definitions and concepts or substitutes ill-focused narrative for clear analytical description and explanation. Theory which cannot be used in historical work is valueless; historical work which is not theoretically informed is pointless.

The first problem we confront is what we mean by nationalism. A major difficulty in the way of clear debate is that different theorists and historians mean different things by the term. Very broadly I can see three different areas of interest: doctrine, politics, sentiments.

Nationalism probably has to be defined in the first place as a doctrine, as an -ism. However, that may be a very loose definition and serve as little more than the departure point for studies of politics or sentiments. On the other hand, in the work of writers such as Kedourie and Talmon, it is the emergence of the doctrine and then the political uses to which the doctrine is put which is at the centre of attention.[1] The kind of theory and history which is consequently produced is concerned with ideas and with those who generate such ideas, above all intellectuals or a whole group defined as an intelligentsia. What is more, classification of nationalism into different types is, in this approach, achieved by distinguishing between various kinds of doctrines such as liberal nationalism and integral nationalism.[2]

There is nothing intrinsically wrong with this view of nationalism. The problems arise when those who employ this approach to the subject seek to extend their type of understanding into nationalism as politics or as sentiments. To see nationalist politics as the work of intelligentsias and national sentiments as the achievement of political movements which serve nationalist doctrines, as such writers frequently do, can easily be shown to have little value. Nationalist politics are frequently dominated by other groups; the emergence of national sentiments has to be related to far more complex changes than the diffusion of a doctrine from its intellectual creators to broader populations.

At the other extreme nationalism is seen in terms of the development of national sentiments or 'national consciousness' within a broad population.[3] This population is frequently referred to as the 'nation', though how far one should equate the nation with groups which consciously share a sense of national identity is, as we shall see, a difficult issue. Again, there is nothing intrinsically wrong with this approach. The kind of work to which it gives rise focuses on such subjects as the breakdown of local and regional autonomy within a 'rational' territory – seen in terms of political centralization, the penetration of market relations, the growth of geographical and social mobility, and the spread of cultural homogeneity. Alternatively, national sentiment is seen as a reaction against these trends when they represent the efforts of more dominant cultural groups which come to be seen as foreign.

Again, there is nothing wrong with this focus in principle. But, also again, problems arise when this approach is extended to the other ways in which nationalism can be identified. Thus nationalist ideas or politics are seen as the products of a rising sense of national identity within the nation – perhaps representing the interests of key groups involved in the work of centralization or market penetration or expressing the values of a range of groups made nationally conscious by transformations in economy, communications, and politics. Yet we know that nationalist doctrines and nationalist politics frequently arise in societies and regions where much of the population lacks any strong or distinct sense of national identity. We also can point to cases where there are widely shared national sentiments but where these have not been associated either with the elaboration of nationalist doctrines or the emergence of significant nationalist political movements.

Finally, there is the focus upon politics. This is the approach I adopt but it is important to recognize its limitations. In itself the significance and achievements of a nationalist political movement tell one nothing either about the history of nationalist doctrine or of the degree to which national sentiments are diffused throughout the population which the nationalist movement claims to represent. I would argue, however, that usually historians take the subject of nationalism to be important because there has been a significant nationalist movement. Few would study the work of intellectuals who elaborate nationalist doctrines and supporting myths if these had not been used in a politically significant way. As for national sentiments, these are so diffuse and varied that they normally are only selected for study by historians when they are mobilized by a political movement.

There are a range of other terms which are closely linked to nationalism and which need to be distinguished from it. I see little analytic value in distinguishing 'patriotism' from 'nationalism'. The first tends to become a term of praise; the second a term of abuse. Insofar as the terms 'nation' and 'nationality' and 'national group' have any meaning apart from a conscious sense of identity amongst a group of people (that is, national sentiment) this must refer to some traits members of the nation are deemed to share irrespective of their self-identity. There are those who try to correlate nationalism – in any of its three basic forms – with such objective group characteristics, but the arguments have never been persuasive and always have to be accompanied by the recognition of many 'exceptions'. Equally, I would distinguish between terms such as *ethnie* and ethnicity on the one hand and nationalism on the other, especially if the former are taken to refer to objective group characteristics.

A second definitional question concerns the content of the assertions of a nationalist doctrine or the goals of a nationalist political movement or the values associated with national sentiments. Clearly, for example, a commitment to the territorial expansion of the nation-state and to the expulsion of 'aliens' from the national territory are very different. The same people may share both concerns but it is not necessary that they do, and in many cases it can be shown that they do not. One nationalist doctrine may assert that the nation is a matter of active, subjective commitment while another may insist that the nation is a racial or linguistic or religious community constituted independently of the opinions of its members.

My concern is with nationalism as politics. So far as the content of that politics is concerned, I define that as the making of the following claims:

1. There exists a nation – a special group which is set apart from all other human beings.
2. Political identity and loyalty are, first and foremost, with and to the nation.
3. The nation should have political autonomy, normally in the form of a sovereign state.[4]

I would argue that political movements making such claims are peculiarly modern, essentially movements of the last two centuries. In that time they have become the most important of all political movements and have made a major contribution towards redrawing the political map of the world. They have also helped establish the dominant political idea of modern times, which is that the world is largely divided into a series of states, each of which represents a nation, and that insofar as this is not the case in some parts of the world, it should become the case.

The most important purpose of any general theory of nationalism is to explain why such movements have come to be so important in modern times.

Very broadly I would distinguish between four approaches to nationalism: the primordial, functional, narrative, and modern. In turn I divide the modern – the only general approach which is, I will argue, valid – into a number of different approaches.

Primordial, Functional and Narrative Approaches

Primordial

The crudest form the primordial approach can take is that provided by nationalists themselves. The basic idea is that their nation has existed for a long time. One can trace back its history over centuries. There were earlier periods when the nation knew greatness; earlier heroes and golden ages which can inspire members of the nation in the present.

The problem with this approach is that it is so clearly at variance with the evidence. Nationalism as doctrine is very modern, even if perhaps Kedourie goes too far when he claims that it was 'invented' at the beginning of the nineteenth century.[5] Nationalism as politics is also very modern. Until the eighteenth century political action was justified in dynastic or religious terms, although at times a subordinate reference to national identity can be discerned.[6]

A more acceptable version of this approach has recently been propounded by Anthony Smith.[7] Smith argues that ethnic identity is not a recent invention. Rather there were *ethnies* which can be traced back – at least for Europe and the Middle East – centuries, if not millennia. He defines *ethnie* as 'named human populations with shared ancestry myths, histories and cultures, having an association with a specific territory and a sense of solidarity'.[8]

Smith argues against theorists such as Gellner, whose model of an agrarian empire had no place, or at best a marginal place, for such senses of identity which encompassed different estates within a particular region.[9] Instead he argues that the agrarian empire model does not comprehend all the features of agrarian societies. There are other kinds of societies (city-states, autonomous peasant communities). There are also more complex relations between different groups than can be allowed for in the agrarian model. He then goes on to classify different types of *ethnie*, for example distinguishing between lateral-aristocratic and vertical-demotic types. One can see how such a distinction could link closely between that made, for central Europe, between 'historic' and 'non-historic' nations, between dominant culture groups such as the Magyars and subordinate culture groups such as the Slavs.[10]

Smith recognizes that there are no direct or determinist links between these *ethnies* and modern nations. Modern nations possess, in addition to the characteristics of *ethnies* identified above, legal, political and economic unity. He knows that many *ethnies* did not go on to become modern nations. In a more recent book,[11] he has made clear the many transformations of modernity which are required to turn an *ethnie* into a nation. But he does wish to insist that the objective reality of a past *ethnie* does matter for modern nations. Without what he terms the 'myth-symbol complexes' which generate and express ethnic identity, modern nationalism would be rootless and arbitrary. The modern nationalist intellectual or politician elaborates upon existing ethnic identities. The stronger and more persistent such identities, the more successful will be modern nationalism.

In a way Smith appears to have found a sensible middle way between nationalists who simply assert the continuous history of the nation and those who regard the nation as a peculiar and modern construct. However, without disputing his case that ethnic identity does have some meaning in past times and that it can impose limits upon claims made in modern nationalism, I do not see this approach as very helpful to any understanding of nationalism.

First, it is vital to understand the functions and meanings of ethnic identity. What I find significant, even in Smith's own arguments, is that pre-modern ethnic identity is non-institutional. It is interesting that the three elements of modern nationality which Smith regards as absent in pre-modern *ethnies* are legal, political and economic identity. Yet these are the principal institutions in which national identity can achieve form. The problem with identity established outside institutions, especially those institutions which can bind together people across wide social and geographical spaces, is that it is necessarily fragmentary, discontinuous, and elusive. This would apply, for example, to ethnic identity in relation to kinship groups. Usually where one does locate pre-modern references to ethnic identity, these are related to broader institutions, usually church or dynasty. However, these institutions carry at their heart an alternative, ultimately conflicting sense of identity to that of the ethnic group.

It is difficult to know what function 'ethnic statements' had for particular priests or kings, but one can imagine that only for so long as such statements did have a function would they be made.[12] It is also just about impossible to know what meaning such statements, and associated myths and symbols, had for the majority of the people who in some way participated in those institutions. We can, perhaps, identify common cultural patterns at a broader level (for example, in artistic styles) but we do not know what that meant in terms of a sense of identity and also we cannot be sure that the pattern is not principally a product of our particular aesthetic categories.

Second, it is the discontinuities with modern national identity that I find most striking. It is, of course, true that nationalist intellectuals and politicians seize upon myths and symbols inherited from the past and weave these into arguments designed to promote national identity and justify national claims. However, it is very difficult to correlate their degree of success with the 'objective' importance of such myths and symbols. We know that in many cases modern nationalists have invented myths; one thinks, for example, of the epic of Ossian, which has played so important a role in modern Welsh nationalist thought. Obviously, given that nationalists took history seriously, the exposure of this epic as a contemporary work seriously embarrassed nationalists, but that has more to do with the nationalist view of history than with the power of ethnic identity. What is more, it is clear that modern nationalism transforms such myths and also that it ignores those which cut across its own purposes. It is also clear that many powerful nationalist movements of modern times have succeeded despite having very little in the way of a rich national history. Can one seriously claim that Libyan identity is somehow less well established than Egyptian identity; or that of Slovaks is less strong than that of Hungarians? In some cases, the development of a rich 'myth-symbol complex' does not take easily recognizable 'intellectual' forms and is divorced from the high cultural focus which informs most historical work. For example, the walls of many buildings in Protestant as well as Catholic parts of Belfast are covered in graffiti which develops a strong sense of identity but which, in the Protestant case, has little reflection in the work of intellectuals.

Clearly there does have to be *something* to which nationalists can appeal. There is no point in making great play with language and language differences if, in fact, there are no distinct languages. To that extent one can claim that the Romanian language is one of the objective bases on which Romanian nationalism is built. Even here, however, I would focus on discontinuity. The codification of a number of spoken dialects into a written language is a creative and modern achievement which can produce different results according to scholarly procedures and political interests. The idea that language is a basis for making political distinctions is modern. Only when language was rendered institutionally significant in the three modern components of nationality – law, polity, and economy – did it acquire political significance. An official language policy, such as that of Joseph II, compelled Magyar-speakers to shift from the *lingua franca* of Latin and stress their Magyar language against German. The expansion of a structure of 'public opinion', expressed by the increase in popular newspapers, periodicals and pamphlets, and frequently linked to the growing importance of elected assemblies in the affairs of state, also made the selection and standardization of language important. An expanded role for courts using one vernacular language, especially in the spoken form, made the choice of language a matter of more popular concern. The extension of market relations, and especially the coming together of different language or ethnic groups into the same areas (usually towns, but also mining settlements), could have the same effect. Finally, and modern, was the development of mass education. Joseph II's encouragement of the use of the vernacular language in elementary education, for example, both boosted the interest in the use of Slav languages and Romanian, and was seen as a threat by Magyar-speakers.

In other words, language becomes significant not merely as a repository of the national culture and memory, as a storehouse of myths, but also as a matter of political, economic, legal and educational interest. I would argue that when it is *nothing more* than the former, it does in fact have very limited significance to any but self-selected cultural elites. Sometimes, as in Ireland, such elites take power and use the state to enforce a language policy, but it is clear that this has had a very limited impact. English is the dominant language, even though the schools all teach the Gadhelic language. In Scotland and Wales, where state power is hardly used to the same degree (more in Wales than Scotland), the Gadhelic and Welsh languages only survive as language of the community in highland regions; otherwise they are preserved only by minorities of cultural enthusiasts. In all other cases the language disappears. That there was such a language, with such a potential national identity attached to it, is then forgotten because there is no one left to develop that potential, in either theory or practice. Forgetting as well as remembering is an important part of how the case for the ancient origins of modern nations is argued.

The only supra-local institutions in agrarian societies which could codify and reproduce the 'myth-symbol complexes' of ethnic identity were churches and dynasties. Yet these are precisely the institutions which are threatened by modern nationalism. In a few cases in late medieval and early modern Europe one does find dynasties developing a 'rational' image, usually as an instrument in conflict with institutions which make universalist claims such as the Catholic Church or the Holy Roman Empire. However, I would argue that such a policy had very limited success until linked to the expanding role of institutions which could also oppose monarchical power, such as the English parliament.[13]

More significant and difficult to understand is the relationship between religion and ethnic identity. I would agree with Gellner's argument that agrarian empires in which an extensive church develops are characterized by clerisies who codify doctrines which claim universal validity.[14] These religions, especially if they are of a proselytizing kind like Christianity or Islam, cannot accept the local and inward-looking character of ethnic identities. At most they can use such identities as means of penetrating communities in order to undermine or subordinate local supernatural beliefs and their custodians.

Yet it is clear that churches have been a major vehicle for the development of modern national identity. In the Habsburg Empire, for example, the Greek Orthodox and Uniate churches played a central role in the development of a Romanian nationalist movement. In the Ottoman Empire autonomous Christian institutions were crucial for the early development of the Greek, Bulgarian, and Serbian national movements.[15]

Partly this is a consequence of the *failure* of the universalist creed. The Ottomans abandoned an Islamic proselytizing mission in their European territories. The only formal regional autonomy they allowed was to Christian churches. These were natural institutional rallying points for autonomist movements in the nineteenth century which responded to the decay and disintegration of the Ottoman Empire.

In the case of most of Europe the failure of universal Christianity was the Reformation. The stress on the use of the vernacular language and the opposition to the hierarchical power of the clergy helped give churches a closer connection to the laity and to particular language groups. In largely peasant communities such as the Romanians, the existence of grudgingly tolerated churches of their own, with a small clerisy, could again provide a rallying point for later movements of national autonomy.

Generally, therefore, I would conclude that the primordial view of nationality has little value. Pre-modern ethnic identity has little in the way of institutional embodiment beyond the local level. Almost all the major institutions which construct, preserve and transmit national identities, and which connect those identities to interests, are modern: parliaments, popular literature, courts, schools, labour markets, et cetera. The only two pre-modern institutions which could have played such a role – dynasties and churches – stand in a highly ambivalent relationship to ethnic identity. Only where such dynasties or churches come into conflict with other, usually more powerful, dynasties and churches, does one find them becoming the vehicle of national identity. Even then, monarchs, court officials and clergy remain highly suspicious of appeals to nationality and, once a national movement acquires more widespread support and modern institutions, frequently come into conflict with more 'advanced' rationalists. This has very clearly been the case, for example, in Ireland. National identity is essentially modern, and any useful approach to the subject must begin from this premiss.

Functional

There is an almost infinite variety of functions which can be attributed to nationalism.[16]

First, there are psychological functions.[17] It is often argued that people require 'identities'. Nationalism can provide for such a need. Such an argument is frequently linked to an account of identity crises, such as those caused by the decline in religious belief and in the erosion of tradition. People who are uprooted from their villages, separated from their families and their priests, and moved to anonymous townships, can find some comfort in the identity offered by nationality. What is more, in this alien world, confronting a mixture of language and ethnic groups, they become sharply aware of their own identity in linguistic and ethnic terms.

There are many problems for the historian with this approach. The idea of 'identity need' is itself problematic and liable to circular reasoning. (If people stress a particular identity, that shows they 'need' that identity, but that is the only way in which that need manifests itself.) It is not obvious that the kinds of ethnic conflicts associated with modern urban growth stand in any very direct relationship to the development of nationalism. In many cases, for example in the United States of America, they remain largely separate. Nationalism is often supported by groups and individuals who do not seem especially exposed to such upheavals. If one can find more limited explanations for the resort to arguments about ethnic or language identity (for example, in order to exclude outsiders from scarce resources such as jobs or housing), then this will be preferable to the broad identity-need argument.[18] That will mean there is a danger of resorting to such an argument only when more specific and testable explanations have failed.

Above all, the problem with this kind of argument is the need to historicize it. One has to link the identity crisis to some specifically modern change (religious decline, industrial-urban growth) in order to account for the fact that the commitment to national identity is peculiarly modern. But accounts of this kind move beyond the limits of functional explanation. For example, Gellner's argument that culture replaces social structure as the provider of identity is not so much an argument about the 'function' of culture under modern conditions, but rather about the different meaning that culture and identity come to have in a modern world.[19] It may well be that there are then a series of more specific functions that national identity claims can serve, such as job reservation or political mobilization, but these are only possible given the overall character of modernity and the place of culture as a source of identity in modern conditions.

Precisely the same kind of case can be made against other functional arguments. One kind of Marxist explanation – that nationalism serves a function for class interests – can be treated in this way. It is clear that in some cases bourgeois groups have made a connection between their interests and nationalist arguments. It is, of course, equally clear that in some cases bourgeois interests are opposed to particular kinds of nationalism (which in turn can be linked to the interests of other classes). The argument can only be taken further by asking why, in the historical epoch of capitalism, a new kind of ideology was related to class interest. Why could not the bourgeoisie use older ideologies of religion and dynasty for their purposes? The answer must be that there is something different about the structure of the bourgeoisie as a class and its relations with other classes and the state compared to the situation of earlier ruling classes. One might go on to argue, for example, that the separation of economic and political power lies at the heart of this difference from earlier epochs. A bourgeoisie cannot develop a political identity and capacity through existing political institutions; instead ideas of representing a new way of life (self-help, enterprise), frequently embodied in cultural institutions (dissenting religious groups, professional associations, educational bodies, et cetera), and then of being 'represented' politically, through parliaments and a structure of public opinion, come to be central. The bourgeoisie 'rule' by means of 'influence', both economic and cultural, rather than as direct holders of power. One can then move from that to the central role of cultural-political identities, especially that of national identity, and how these are transmitted both to other classes and to the state.

I would not say that these arguments are valid, only that one has to move from a functional account to a structural account which links the central role of the national idea to modernity.

The same logic works for other functional arguments, for example that the 'function' of nationalism is to promote modernization. There is no question that nationalism has been used in this way (though it has also been used for other, often anti-modernization, purposes). However, it is clear that nationalism was, originally, one aspect of an unintended modernity. Only later, when ideas of both modernity and nationalism were firmly established, could people consciously use the idea of nationalism in an attempt to promote modernization. Even then, of course, one has to distinguish sharply between such an intention and how far or why that intention was successfully realized.

This raises a more general objection to functional accounts, which is that they can answer 'how' questions but not 'why' questions. One way in which a functional account can be made into an explanation is with reference to deliberate intention. Someone intends to use nationalism for the purpose (= function) concerned. The other way is that one can specify some feed-back operation which reinforces a particular function; for example, competition functions to develop an economy by means of mechanisms such as bankruptcies which eliminate less efficient firms and thereby release resources which enable new firms to enter the competition. The problem is, however, to explain how such relationships come into existence. Nationalism cannot originate as a deliberate project of modernization unless one attributes phenomenal clairvoyance as well as power to nationalists; equally it cannot 'function' in this way until it has become a normal component within a new set of social arrangements. Therefore, one is forced to go beyond functional explanations to structural accounts which see nationalism as one component of modernity.[20]

Narrative

Many historians take the rise of nationalism for granted. Given that, they can simply tell the story of this rise. This can be done at the level of particular cases or more generally.

Thus a typical 'national' history begins with the traditional, prenational state of affairs. For example, histories of Germany will begin with the Holy Roman Empire of the seventeenth and eighteenth centuries. The historian will point to the many weaknesses of the traditional, imperial institutions and of the multitude of small political units. Then he will turn his attention to newer, more dynamic groups and institutions – in this case the territorial states (especially Prussia) and the bearers of modern ideas and practices (entrepreneurs, educated officials). The story-line is how the traditional institutions more or less quickly crumble in the face of the modern forces; in turn the modern forces converge upon and reinforce each other. There are critical periods of rapid advance (1813–15, 1848, 1866–71), interrupted by periods of stagnation or even steps backwards, although even during these periods the forces of the national movement are building up. Nationalists, of course, played a major role themselves in elaborating such stories. Elements of the story were already being composed before the *dénouement*. Von Treitschke and von Sybel, for example, were already reinterpreting German history before Bismarck's unification, although those interpretations did not directly underpin the particular form of unification. Analogies were drawn from earlier histories (for example, the interpretation by Droysen of Alexander the Great which clearly cast the crude Macedonian conqueror of the more civilized parts of Greece in the role of a Prussia).

Furthermore, the narrative form, with its assumption of a beginning, middle and end, could actually become an important component of the national movement, presenting it as a form of progress with the end still to be realized in the future. Later, more celebratory and conservative narratives might be written; though equally critical forms of nationalism would continue to present the story as one still to be finished. In this way, the narrative mode could buttress liberal, conservative and radical forms of nationalism.

Finally, academic historians without any direct political interests would pare away the more obviously propagandist and partial features of the nationalist accounts. However, they frequently accepted the narrative as the proper form of an historical account, the national as providing the boundaries and identity of their subject matter, and the emergence, expansion and success of national movements as the principal story.[21]

This can also be the form taken by broader histories of Europe or the modern world. It is quite likely to be reinforced by the current breakdown of the last multinational empire, the Soviet Union and its satellite states of Eastern Europe, and we will be bound to be regaled by many accounts which will insist on seeing the Soviet Union as an artificial barrier in modern history which held up the consummation of the national story in Eastern and Central Europe.

The problem, of course, is that a narrative explains nothing. It is built on highly dubious assumptions.[22] Frequently, for example, it is assumed that the history of the modern world is the story of the 'rise' of the 'modern' and the 'fall' of the 'traditional'. But it is quite clear that the meaning and content of national ideas at the beginning of such a history

were very different from what they were at the end. A German 'nationalist' in 1800 stood for quite different things from his counterpart in
1870.[23] Once one grasps that modernization involves the *transformation of
everything*, then it is clear that it cannot be understood as one constant –
the 'modern' – growing at the expense of another constant – the
'traditional'.

Second, narrative tends not to bring out the contingency of outcomes.
It is, of course, impossible to prove that things could have been otherwise;
as impossible to prove that things had to be the way they were. But it is
not difficult to show that things did not turn out the way many wanted or
expected at the time, and that at least should give pause for thought.
Many contemporaries, for example, did not think that Austria would
rapidly capitulate to Prussia in 1866. There is no obvious connection
between that capitulation and the development of German nationalism.
A narrative which assumes victory, and bases its idea of what Germany was
and would become on that assumption, ignores this sense of contingency
and possibility. Yet, equally, a narrative which portrays this as an accident
(fortunate or unfortunate) would be in danger of rendering nation-state
formation as something fortuitous.[24]

It is clear that narrative must be theorized in order to provide an intelligible account of what is happening, in order for the reader to see why
nationalism and nation-state formation (but not necessarily every nationalism and every conceivable nation-state formation) are such pervasive
features of modernity. To achieve such theorization one has to see how
the idea of nationalism relates to the general process of modernization.

Conclusion

There are many insights and partial truths contained within primordial,
functional and narrative accounts of nationalism. However, they are all
inadequate as departure points for the understanding of nationalism.
What is needed is a framework which begins with an account of the place
of the national idea within modernity. I will now turn to consider a number of approaches which begin in this way.

Nationalism and Theories of Modernity

Just as the concerns with nationalism as doctrine, as politics, and as
broadly shared sentiments involve a progressive extension of the subject,
so one can focus on more or less broad aspects of modernity. There are
those who focus upon the transformations amongst elites which lead to
the production and reception of nationalist ideas. I would include the
important comparative work of Miroslav Hroch in this category.[25] There

are those, including myself, who focus upon transformations in the nature of power which lead to the production and reception of nationalist politics. There are those who focus upon societal transformations which lead to the production and reception of nationalist sentiments amongst broad strata of the population. I would include the work of Ernest Gellner in this category.

Transformation of Consciousness and Nationalist Ideas

For the first kind of work I will select the book by Benedict Anderson, *Imagined Communities*.[26]

Anderson's departure point is the question posed by the title of his book. The nation is an imagined community. This particular imagining is modern. This does not mean that the nation is contrasted with 'real' communities; all communities are imagined. What needs to be understood is why this particular style of imagining has come about.

What is distinctive about this style of imagining is that people imagine the nation to be a limited, exclusive community, that it is (or should be) sovereign, and that it is a community worthy of sacrifice, ultimately the sacrifice of one's life. These points overlap quite closely with the definition I gave earlier of the core doctrine of nationalism.

Anderson accordingly devotes his study to propounding a view of how such a style of imagining came about. Especially important in that account are the experiences of cultural and political elites in the colonial peripheries of imperial states, in particular under the impact of capitalism, the development of vernacular languages, and what Anderson calls 'print culture'.

I do not have space here to provide a detailed consideration of the way in which Anderson develops this argument. I would only say that it is developed quite brilliantly and persuasively, although I think his argument works better for certain cases (Latin America, British East Africa, French Indo-China), is less convincing in other cases (Russia, India), and in my view would confront grave problems for many European cases. The reason for this is that Anderson's argument works best when there is a close link, even an identity, between groups which develop cultural conceptions of nationality and the groups, often originally collaborators with the imperial state, which are at the centre of nationalist politics. It also works better for subordinate cultural groups at the periphery of large multinational states than for dominant cultural groups at the centre of such states.

This, in turn, points to a problem with Anderson's approach and any other approach of this kind. It can explain how new kinds of ideas about communities and how they should be organized can be developed amongst certain cultural elites. It cannot explain why these should evoke any response from those in power or from broad strata of the population. And indeed, one can locate various examples of elites developing such ideas, constructing new 'myth-symbol' complexes, and these remaining marginal to politics and society.

If one believed in a 'stage-theory' of nationalism which begins with the elaboration of ideas, moves into the construction of political movements, and culminates in becoming the accepted sentiments of a whole society – then at least such an approach might help explain how the first step comes to be taken. However, I think there are problems with such a stage-theory. For example, there are cases where an elaborate nationalist vision has to be developed *after* the formation of a nationalist political movement or has to be borrowed from abroad. I would argue that those who put together the effective politics of resistance to the Ottoman Empire in the Greek peninsula, for example, found it expedient to pre-sent their politics in terms of a Hellenic vision which had largely been elaborated by Western Europeans and which had an important influence upon Western public opinion and governments.

One might conclude that an approach designed to explain the development of new political ideas cannot simultaneously account for the development of new political movements or social sentiments. There is much to be said for that view, and I shall argue that the same points apply to approaches which focus on the state or on society. Nevertheless, I would reiterate an earlier point: that we are largely interested in such ideas because they become politically significant. I would also argue that unless and until such ideas get 'fixed' by becoming part of a political movement which must negotiate with governments and build support within society, they will tend to be rather vague and discontinuous.

For example, one finds various conceptions of German nationality amongst cultural elites between 1800 and 1830. The way in which Anderson has approached nationalism could be fruitfully applied to the process by which these conceptions developed. But there was something very unworldly about these conceptions; they were not disciplined and shaped by anything other than purely intellectual principles. When, however, a liberal nationalist movement began to take shape and sought to influence governments, to build on existing institutions such as the Customs Union, and to mobilize support within German society, so did the nationalist conception(s) take on a more definite form, a form which was then hardened in the work of political publicists. In other words, the nationalist 'imagining' is changed in intellectual character through becoming part of the political process.

Societal Transformation

Anderson refers to the spread of capitalism but it forms merely a back-drop to his main account. Hroch much more satisfactorily relates the construction of an elite nationalism to capitalist developments by means of rigorous comparison and detailed study of the regions and groups which take the lead in such nationalist movements.

But apart from understanding the political dimension which also shapes nationalism, there is the problem of explaining why nationalism should become a broadly accepted and supported idea. I have already argued that any account which sees this in terms of nationalism being functional for this or that group interest does not go far enough.

Gellner provides the kind of analysis which does go far enough. He has argued at the most general level that culture both becomes a separate sphere in modern society and also, in a mobile and rapidly changing industrialization process, can come to furnish a basis of identity which roles in social structures can no longer provide. Add to this his points about how industrial society, mass education and the construction of a sphere of popular culture all help to produce a 'standard' national culture and one has a powerful set of terms for understanding why national identity should be modern, peculiar but also very widespread.

Again, as with Anderson, let me immediately grant the power, signific-ance, and persuasiveness of the argument. There are particular points I would question – for example, concerning the explanation of the origins of a system of mass education. Gellner sees this as due to the need for a minimally qualified labour force (for example, basic literacy). Clearly such an argument supports his general case about the specialization of culture and the pressure towards a standardized national language. This appears to be a functional explanation, with the kinds of problems to which I have already referred. It is quite clear that in many cases there were other intentions behind the extension of schooling such as discip-line, humanitarianism, and concern with a new youth problem created by the changing relationship between home, age and work. It is difficult to pinpoint a mechanism which 'selects' mass education against other pos-sibilities. Given that, it is difficult to accept a straightforward link between industrial society's 'need' for a labour force that has been exposed to mass schooling, and the 'provision' of that schooling.

However, I would largely agree with the argument that there is a close, indeed necessary, connection between the formation of indus-trial societies and of 'standard' national cultures. This is as much to do with market relations and the increasing downward penetration of state institutions such as courts, armies based on conscription and welfare bureaucracies as it is to do with the undeniable advance of mass elementary schooling. The idea that most social transactions in industrial societies take place within 'cultural zones' which are increasingly defined by the national idea is a very powerful one.

The main problem I have is relating the argument to nationalism. First, much nationalist doctrine and many nationalist political movements flourished in societies which had yet to undergo this transformation to industrialism. Second, only parts of the world have undergone this transformation, yet one can find the development of broadly shared national sentiments in parts of the world which have still not reached this stage. Commercial agriculture, mass education, and modern systems of communication can all produce many of the effects Gellner relates to industrialism. Even if dependent upon industrialism elsewhere (both as a model and as the provider of resources) this does weaken the relationships which are specified in Gellner's theory. So there are two points here: there are means of diffusing a national culture in non-industrial societies; and there are politically significant forms of nationalism in non-industrial societies. One can add a third point – that nationalism as a specific political movement is often quite weak in culturally homogeneous industrial societies living in modern nation-states. Clearly, therefore, one has to separate a number of different things here. In particular, the relationship between nationalism (as opposed to participating in a broadly shared national culture) and industrialism is nowhere near as strong as Gellner's account suggests.

I do not doubt that national cultures are most developed in industrial societies, and that this has a major impact upon the character of nationalism in such societies. However, it seems to me that the fit between such societies and nationalism – whether as doctrine, as politics, or as shared sentiments – is a very loose one.

Nationalism and Political Modernization

My own preference is to begin with a consideration of nationalism as politics. Political movements can be connected to political doctrines on the one hand. (What are the sources of the ideas employed by nationalist movements?) They can also be connected to broadly shared sentiments on the other hand. (How far are nationalist movements able to mobilize a broad base of support and what role does its appeal to national sentiments play in that mobilization?) One should stress, however, that in particular cases the connection may well be a negative one. A nationalist movement may ignore nationalist intellectuals and draw instead upon religious values, and it may achieve success more through elite contacts and relationships with governments than by mobilizing mass support. Finally, such mobilization as does take place may be based upon an

appeal to sectional interests or non-nationalist values rather than nationalist propaganda and commitment.

However, as I have already argued, nationalist political action does
tend to create a more coherent set of doctrines and sentiments and also
makes it easier to assess their importance. The exigencies of political
action, whether of opposition movements or governments, disciplines
ideas and points them to practical goals, and also channels diffuse sentiments in a particular direction. One can have a fairly easy measure of the
importance of the subject by asking how much support such political
movements are able to tap within their society and how powerful they are,
whereas it is notoriously difficult to estimate the significance of ideas or
sentiments 'in themselves'. Political movements usually leave a rich variety of sources for the historian which can insure against empty
speculation or misleading generalization from a very narrow base of evidence. For all these quite practical reasons, I think there is much to be said
for approaching nationalism in the first instance as politics.

The next step is to relate this to a framework in which the emergence
of nationalism is connected to the process of modernization. In general
terms I would concur with Gellner's views on modernity. In particular, I
would start with the idea of modernization as involving a fundamental
change in the *generic division of labour*.[27] By this term, in contrast to the
more specific *economic division of labour*, is meant that the very broadest
categories of human activity – coercion, cognition and production (or in
more conventional terms: power, culture and economy) are redefined
and placed in a different relationship to one another. Above all I would
draw attention to what I would call a transition, in Europe, from a corporate to a functional division of labour. By a corporate division of labour
I refer to a society with a very complex range of functions but where a
bundle of different functions are carried out by particular institutions,
usually on behalf of some distinct group. For example, the ideal-typical
guild performs economic functions (regulating production and distribution of particular goods and services); cultural functions (taking care
of the general as well as vocational education of apprentices, organizing
the major recreational and ceremonial activities of members of the guild,
even enforcing religious observance); and political functions (running
courts which impose and enforce penalties upon members, having automatic membership of town governments). Churches, lordships, peasant
communes and even the monarch in his capacity as privileged landowner
also exhibit such multi-functional characteristics. One should not portray
such a division of labour as in any way consensual or 'organic'. There are
many points of conflict; in some functions particular institutions claim
universal or at least over-arching powers (churches and religious doctrines; monarchs and the law) although they usually depend upon other

institutions actually to carry out those functions at lower levels. There are also disputes over the boundaries of competence to be drawn between different institutions and there are internal conflicts within various institutions. Furthermore, this notion of a corporate division of labour should be seen as an ideal-type. In reality there are many deviations from that type. Certainly by the late eighteenth century such a division of labour was subject to incisive intellectual critiques and, in many parts of western and central Europe, was crumbling.

The critiques – especially those associated with rationalist creeds such as the Enlightenment, physiocracy and classical political economy – envisaged a different division of labour, one whereby each of the major social functions was concentrated into particular institutions. Thus economic functions would be disentangled from other functions and concentrated into individuals and firms operating in a free market. Churches would become free associations of believers. Power would be exercised by specialized bureaucracies under the control of elected parliaments or enlightened despots. There were great variations in the critiques which sometimes might raise up one of these functions above the others (classical political economy and the market; Jacobins and the polity) but they all pointed to this basic transformation.

Historically such a transformation did not proceed smoothly. Furthermore, the different elements of the transformation developed at different speeds and times and in different ways. To link this framework to nationalist politics one needs to focus upon one aspect of the transformation. This is the development of the modern state. Here, for want of space, I will just make a series of assertions about the main lines of this development in Europe.

The modern state originally developed in a liberal form – that is, it involved a concentration of 'public' powers into specialized state institutions (parliaments, bureaucracies), while leaving many 'private' powers under the control of non-political institutions (free markets, private firms, families, et cetera). That involved a double transformation of government: institutions such as the monarchy *lost* 'private' powers (for example, the principal source of revenue from royal lands and the granting or possession of monopolies); other institutions such as churches, guilds, and lordships lost their 'public' powers to government. In this way a clear and distinct idea of the state as 'public' and 'civil society' as 'private' was elaborated and seemed to have some hold upon reality.

This idea was reinforced by related changes in relationships between states. First, the development of an explicit idea of the state as the sole source of political functions was associated with a modern idea of sovereignty. All powers of coercion had to rest with the state. This also required a much clearer definition than hitherto of the boundaries of the state, particularly as the process of modern state formation in Europe was something which went on in the context of competition between a number of states. It is interesting, for example, that one of the issues at dispute when the war between France and *ancien régime* states broke out in 1792 was the source of power over enclaves within France which owed some allegiance to the Holy Roman Empire.[28] The modern conception of France as a tightly bounded space within which the French state was sovereign was opposed to an older conception of power as varying bundles of privileges related to different groups and territories. Clear and distinct ideas of the state as sole source of sovereignty and as a bounded territory are hallmarks of the modern state.

The breakdown of corporate ties meant that within both state and civil society there was a new emphasis upon people as individuals rather than members of groups. The main problem for those seeking to establish as well as those trying to understand political order in such situations came to be how to make the state–society connection; how to maintain some harmony between the public interests of citizens and the private interests of selfish individuals (or families). Nationalist ideas could be related to both of the major forms taken by attempts to solve this problem: one imposing citizenship ideals upon society; the other imposing interests (individual or class) within civil society upon the state.[29]

First, there was the political solution of citizenship. A society of individuals was simultaneously defined as a polity of citizens. It was through participation in liberal and democratic institutions that a sense of commitment to the state could be generated. The 'nation' in this sense was simply the body of citizens. What mattered was the political rights, not the cultural identities, of those who were citizens. This idea of nationality was what underlay the programmes of the eighteenth-century patriots. It could stress participation and the cultivation of political virtue. In its most extreme form, as expressed by Rousseau and practised by Robespierre, it threatened to obliterate the notion of 'freedom' as privacy beyond the state by defining freedom solely as participation in the implementation of the 'general will'.[30]

The second 'solution' was to stress the *collective* character of *society*. At first, this was principally an argument of political elites confronted both by an intellectual problem (how did one legitimize state action?) and by a political problem (how could one appeal to social groups to support one's politics?). In a way it was a matter of contingency that, in many cases, as Gellner has argued, 'culture' also came to be increasingly standardized under modern conditions, cutting across different social groups. Now the arguments of nationalism could serve to provide a sense of identity in place of the social criteria (mainly those of privilege) employed in a corporate society.

Liberalism, the first major political doctrine of modernity, found it difficult to come to terms with the idea of collective or community interests which should be accorded political recognition.[31] Equally, however, many groups could not be reconciled to the abstract, rational character of liberalism, especially if formal participation rights masked real, socially structured inequality. Such groups might be attracted to a nationalism which could turn cultural identity into a political programme. Furthermore, under modern conditions it has been both possible and necessary to develop political languages and movements which deliberately appeal to a wide range of groups occupying a particular territory, and this nationalism could do. Logically the two concepts of nation – a body of citizens and a cultural collectivity – conflict. In practice, nationalism has been a sleight-of-hand ideology which tries to connect the two ideas together.[32]

Given this sleight of hand, as well as the political neutrality of the cultural identities to which nationalism appeals (which means they are available for many political uses), nationalism has taken a bewildering variety of forms. To move from this very general starting-point to the study of particular nationalist movements a typology is required as well as some concepts which draw attention to the different functions performed by nationalist politics. Having outlined these I will then try to show how these very general ideas can be used to make sense of particular cases of nationalism. I will draw upon examples from the Habsburg Empire, and also make some comparisons with the Ottoman Empire.

First, the arguments about the state as a body of citizens or as the political expression of a community need to be linked to the development of political movements. In a world where political legitimacy did not yet rest upon nationality, such movements were at first oppositional. It was only at a later stage that governments, either formed by the success of nationalist oppositions or taking on board the ideas of those oppositions, would themselves make nationalist arguments the basis of their claims to legitimacy.

Second, I distinguish between cases in which the nation on behalf of which the opposition claims to act is understood to form just part of the territory of the existing state, or is identical with that territory, or is larger than that territory. The distinctions give rise to three basic political strategies: *separation*, *reform*, and *unification*. There are complications to such a typology which I consider in my book and cannot enter into here.

Third, I distinguish three different functions which the use of nationalist ideas can serve. These are the functions of *coordination, mobilization,* and *legitimacy*. By coordination I mean that nationalist ideas are used to promote the idea of common interests amongst a number of elites which otherwise have rather distinct interests in opposing the existing state. By mobilization I mean the use of nationalist ideas to generate support for the political movement from broad groups hitherto excluded from the political process. By legitimacy I mean the use of nationalist ideas to justify the goals of the political movement both to the state it opposes and also to powerful external agents, such as foreign states and their public opinions.

Having outlined this framework I would now advance some hypotheses about the development of nationalism in the Habsburg and Ottoman empires.[33]

In the Habsburg Empire the internal functions of coordination and mobilization were of particular importance and the ideology of nationalism was highly developed. In the Ottoman Empire the external function of legitimacy was of much greater importance. Much of the elaboration of the nationalist argument was taken over from abroad (including from the Habsburg Empire) and in many cases, by comparison with the Habsburg Empire, it had a fairly crude and rudimentary form. Yet, the nationalist oppositions to the Ottoman Empire in Europe had far greater success by the end of the nineteenth century – if the achievement of national self-determination is the principal measure used – than did those of the Habsburg Empire. I will argue that my framework enables one to develop comparative analysis of the various cases involved as well as explanations of the differences involved.

There is not space here to go into descriptive detail. Let me just make a few brief claims. First, one needs to distinguish between the nationalist movements of dominant cultural groups such as the Magyars and the Greeks, and more subordinate groups such as the Romanians and Serbians. It is particularly useful, for the purposes of comparison, that Romanians and Serbians lived in both empires.

What is important in the Habsburg case is that it was a feudal state in which local power was devolved to privileged groups. This provided the Magyars with an institutional base on which a national opposition movement could develop. The process of political modernization, especially the Josephine reforms, threatened the Magyar position in various ways – through the official German language policy, through the extension of central bureaucratic power, and the attempts to reduce the role of privilege in such spheres as landownership or religious beliefs.

In these circumstances some Magyar aristocrats could come to see themselves less as privileged collaborators within a dynasty and more as the leaders of a nation threatened by a German-controlled state from above which, through its church, educational, and land reforms, was also (if inadvertently) stirring up unrest amongst subordinate Slav and Romanian groups.

I would stress the very faltering way in which this national reaction developed.[34] There was no sudden move to opposition; there was great reluctance to accept the implications of the national argument which would involve dismantling the inequalities of privilege within the Magyar nation (moving from coordination of noble, gentry and intelligentsia elites to mobilization of Magyar peasants); and the events of 1848 transformed and radicalized the shift towards nationalist opposition. But it was this shift which in turn generated nationalist movements amongst subordinate groups. These groups, lacking the diverse elite structure of the Magyars, were much more church- and intelligentsia-led peasant movements. Mobilization played a more important role than coordination. Although these movements did appeal to outsiders (one thinks, for example, of how Kossuth became a darling of American and Western European liberals and radicals after 1849), this was of limited importance. Indeed, the most significant external intervention was in 1849 by the Russians, and that in defence of the old dynastic order.

Obviously any detailed study would need to bring out the nature of religious differences, patterns of landholding, the character of the peasantry, the policy pursued by the Habsburg rulers faced with national oppositions which in turn conflicted with one another, and much else. A theory is not meant to provide such accounts, merely to outline a framework within which such accounts can be provided. But I would argue that the framework I have outlined does allow one to do this.[35]

In the case of the Ottoman Empire there was not a feudal structure with local aristocracies that largely exercised power under loose central supervision. Instead there was a patrimonial bureaucracy which did, however, accord autonomy to units of the Greek Orthodox Church. By the nineteenth century this patrimonial bureaucracy was in an advanced state of decay in its European territories, unable, for example, to pay its soldiers. Political opposition developed where state authority was at its weakest, for example in the Greek peninsula.

Such opposition was far less structured than in the Habsburg Empire, drawing upon Greek Orthodox priests and local notables (traders, landlords), often compelled to take more power because of the breakdown of Ottoman authority. There was little in the way of nationality conflict (although there were some communal massacres in towns where there had been a substantial Turkish settlement) because most regions did not possess the fairly clear relationship between language and privilege which one finds in parts of the Habsburg Empire.

Local autonomist movements with no dominant elite, without any social reform programme able to mobilize popular support, based on church institutions rather than privileges which themselves had ethnic dimensions – these could hardly give rise to nationalism. What did that was the role of outside governments – especially the tsarist government with its proclaimed Slav mission, and Western public opinion – the British, French and other Westerners' enthusiasm for the 'Greek' struggle for independence. For various reasons these governments supported some autonomy movements rather than seeking to prop up Ottoman authority or seeking to take direct control. Nationalist arguments provided legitimacy for this policy.

As a consequence, nationalism worked very differently in the two empires. Even when one is dealing with the 'same' nation, for example the Romanians, there are great differences. Ottoman Romanians were not reacting against a distinct and privileged cultural group, but rather formed a very limited autonomy movement led by the local rulers (*hospodars*). International intervention was crucial for the establishment of a Romanian state, and even compelled those in power to accept many of the ideas of the West (for example, concerning Jewish emancipation). However, a ruler could only be found by importing a Hohenzollern; and the constitution bore little resemblance to the traditional practices of local politics. On the other hand, the Romanian nationalist movement in the Habsburg Empire, reacting against Magyar domination, led by churchmen and secular intellectuals, advocating a programme of reform and autonomy, was a much more impressive oppositional movement. However, and closely linked to that, it confronted a much more powerful state, and one which had far more international support than the Ottoman Empire.

I would draw two major conclusions from these considerations.

First, it was a process of political modernization in the Habsburg Empire that shaped the development of nationalist opposition. That nationalist opposition could incorporate ideas developed elsewhere (for example, Herder's ideas about the Magyars as a nation threatened from both above and below) which seemed to make eminent sense of their situation, to bring together various elites, and to generate popular support. By contrast it was a process of political decay in the Ottoman Empire that stimulated the rise of autonomist movements in different areas. Only because of the prior development of nationalist ideas elsewhere could these movements come to employ such arguments, which never served important internal functions within the nationalist movements.

Second, this suggests to me that state modernization is crucial for the development of genuine and strong nationalist movements. Without such state modernization nationalism will simply be a rhetoric which provides one with little clue as to the real character of the movement. It will be dependent upon the prior development of nationalist ideas in other societies.

I would argue that the framework I have outlined, used to develop comparative analysis of nationalist movements, provides the best way of developing a general understanding of nationalism.

Conclusion

Summary

I will simply put these as a series of short propositions.

1. Nationalism needs to be understood as something peculiarly modern. Approaches to nationalism which do not have some theory of modernity at their heart cannot understand this key feature of nationalism.
2. Nationalism needs to be clearly defined.
3. This definition suggests three types of subject: doctrines, politics, and sentiments.
4. There are special advantages to making politics the focus of attention.
5. Once nationalist politics is made the centre of attention, the theory of modernity should focus on political modernization.
6. The central feature of political modernization is the development of the sovereign and bounded state, as part of a system of competing states. This in turn is part of a broader shift towards societies in which the major functions (political, economic, cultural) are concentrated into specialized institutions.
7. Nationalist politics is best understood as initially one kind of oppositional response to political modernization. To describe those responses one needs to distinguish between the different strategies of nationalist oppositions (separation, reform, unification) and the different functions of nationalist ideas within those oppositions (coordination, mobilization, legitimacy).
8. With this framework it is possible to compare and contrast different nationalisms. Such comparisons suggest that the more strongly developed is the process of political modernization, then the more strongly developed will be nationalist oppositions.

Concluding Remarks

The focus here has been on the late eighteenth and nineteenth century and the development of the first nationalist movements. Clearly by the early twentieth century the national idea had become the norm. This makes it increasingly difficult to theorize about nationalism. Once the modern, territorial and sovereign state had developed, there was an overwhelming tendency for the population of that state to identify with or against that state on national terms. By the time the nation-state was generalized through much of Europe – though as much because of lost wars and external interventions as because of the power of nationalist movements – then everyone had come to speak the language of nationalism. I have argued, with the Habsburg/Ottoman comparison in support, that merely speaking the language of nationalism can suit the interests of political movements that are not really national in any other respect. In a world where almost everyone is a nationalist in some way or another, it becomes more important to distinguish between nationalisms than to have a theory of nationalism.

When I published my book on nationalism more than a decade ago, I suggested that in most of the world nationalism as a genuine politics (rather than the rhetoric employed by all national governments) was disappearing.

I would still argue that case. But I did try to pinpoint exceptions. Of these, the first that I selected was Eastern Europe. I must confess I was not much of a prophet when I wrote:

> There are still areas of the world where the sort of situation which originally generated nationalism continues to exist. In eastern Europe one could envisage sections of the political community in countries other than the USSR moving towards a nationalist position, though the degree of political control and the need to use other ideological justifications than those of nationalism make it highly unlikely.[36]

I am trying to work out if the approach I have outlined can be fruitful in understanding contemporary European developments.[37] The modern state, as a specialized as well as sovereign institution, never developed in Russia. Instead there was a direct move from a top-heavy tsarist state to an even more powerful communist state. The institutions of civil society were arrested in their infancy – the market, voluntary societies, free churches. In the case of central Europe, what developments had taken place were pushed back with the imposition of communist rule after 1945.

Perhaps one could argue that the failure to modernize through the route of functional specialization set limits on the extent of both political and economic development. Those limits led eventually to crisis and reform. Many of those reforms – especially in the political sphere with attempts to increase political accountability – represented a belated attempt at modernization. But reform led to political collapse. To replace the crumbling order, an underdeveloped civil society has to build on whatever linkages there might be between elites (reformist communists, former dissidents, church leaders, technical and economic specialists, et cetera) and with broader strata of the population. Ethnic identity, especially in states where communist rule is linked to the dominance of one cultural group (the Russians, the Serbians) is an obvious and available way of making such links. It can lead to conflicts as well as cooperation (indeed the two go together as new collective forms of action are improvised). One should, however, not forget that there are other lines of conflict apart from those constructed on the basis of ethnic identity.

This process is going on in a very different situation from the nineteenth-century nationalist movements in dynastic multinational states. We now have industrial societies, mass literacy, modern techniques of communication, et cetera. Nevertheless, I would argue that there are also certain basic structural similarities. A mode of analysis developed to make sense of the Ottoman and Habsburg empires can have some application to the breakdown of the Soviet empire.

What I would certainly resist is the idea that Eastern and Central Europe are 'reverting' to age-old nationality identities and conflicts (the primordial explanation). Equally, although nationality clearly is being used in some cases as a tool of particular elites (for example, the Serbian communist leadership), one has to find a deeper explanation of why such a tool is available in the first place. I would, very tentatively, suggest that the kind of framework I have outlined could also be used in these contemporary cases.

Of course, whether the ideas I have outlined are useful, and whether the particular conclusions I have drawn from applying those ideas to certain cases are both valid and significant, is for others to judge.

Notes

1. Elie Kedourie, *Nationalism*, London 1960. Jacob L. Talmon, *The Myth of the Nation and the Vision of Revolution*, London 1981.

2. See for example, Carlton Hayes, *The Historical Evolution of Nationalism*, New York 1931.

3. See, for example, Hugh Seton-Watson, *Nations and States: An Enquiry into the Origins of Nations and the Politics of Nationalism*, London 1977.

4. This is close to, but not the same as, the 'core doctrine' developed in Anthony D. Smith, *Theories of Nationalism*, London 1971, p. 21. For further elaboration see John Breuilly, *Nationalism and the State*, Manchester 1985, pp. 3–18.

5. Kedourie, *Nationalism*, p. 9.

6. See Breuilly, *Nationalism and the State*, Introduction and chapter 1.

7. Anthony D. Smith, *The Ethnic Origins of Nations*, Oxford 1986. For a further application to modern history see also his more recent book, *National Identity*, Harmondsworth 1991.

8. Smith, *Ethnic Origins*, p. 32.

9. Ernest Gellner, *Nations and Nationalism*, Oxford 1983.

10. For the distinction between 'historic' and 'non-historic' nations, which was part of the political 'commonsense' of nineteenth-century Europe, see for example, Roman Rosdolsky, 'Friedrich Engels und das Problem der "Geschichtslosen Völker"', *Archiv für Sozialgeschichte*, vol. 4, 1964, pp. 87–282, and Charles C. Herod, *The Nation in the History of Marxian Thought: The Concept of Nations with History and Nations without History*, The Hague 1976.

11. Smith, *National Identity*.

12. Smith has performed the signal service of collecting numerous such statements from ancient and medieval history. Medieval historians often produce such collections which seem to give rise to interminable arguments about the existence or non-existence of nationalismus in their period. See, for example, Otto Dann, ed., *Nationalismus in vorindustrieller Zeit*, Munich 1986.

13. Breuilly, *Nationalism and the State*, chapter 1.

14. Ernest Gellner, *Plough, Sword and Book: The Structure of Human History*, London 1988.

15. I argue this at greater length in Breuilly, *Nationalism and the State*, chapter 3.

16. See Anthony D. Smith, *Theories of Nationalism*, London 1971, and introduction to Breuilly, *Nationalism and the State*.

17. I have tended to be dismissive of psychological accounts. However, my attention was drawn to a very careful and persuasive argument utilizing concepts from psychology: William Bloom, *Personal Identity, National Identity and International Relations*, Cambridge 1990. My thanks are due to Professor Lemberg for this reference.

18. This kind of argument, for example, was at the heart of Gellner's first theoretical account of nationalism: Ernest Gellner, *Thought and Change*, London 1964, pp. 147–78.

19. Presented most explicitly and generally in Gellner, *Plough, Sword and Book*.

20. There is a large critical literature on functional explanations. For a short introduction to some of the problems, I have found very useful Steve Rigby, *Marxism and History: A Critical Introduction*, Manchester 1987, pp. 84–91.

21. For some account of how the national, especially in the form of political history cast in narrative, came to figure in understanding the German past and also shaping the political culture of those historians see Georg Iggers, *Deutsche Geschichtswissenschaft. Eine Kritik der traditionellen Geschichtsauffassung von Herder bis zur Gegenwart*, Munich 1971; Thomas Nipperdey, *Deutsche Geschichte 1866–1918*, vol. 1: *Arbeitswelt und Bürgergeist*, Munich 1990, pp. 633ff; Bernd Faulenbach, *Ideologie des deutschen Weges: Die deutsche Geschichte in der Historiographie zwischen Kaiserreich und Nationalsozialismus*, Munich 1980.

22. This criticism of the narrative is based on rationalist, 'modernist' values – I am not casting doubt on this kind of historical account from the presently fashionable postmodernist position. I would also stress that I see nothing wrong with a 'teleological' approach in history, provided it is clear that the teleology furnishes only the questions (what, earlier in the process, contributed to what came later in the process?) and not the answers.

23. I developed this argument in critical style in John Breuilly, 'Nation and Nationalism in Modern German History', *The Historical Journal*, vol. 33, no. 3, 1990, pp. 659–75; and in a more positive way in: 'Introduction: The National Idea in Modern German History', in John Breuilly, ed., *The State of Germany: The National Idea in the Making, Unmaking and Remaking of a Modern Nation-State*, London 1992, pp. 1–28.

24. On the need to retain a sense of contingency in general social theory see Anthony Giddens, *The Nation-State and Violence*, Cambridge 1985, especially pp. 31–4. On some of the problems on how one combines a narrative with a sense of contingency, specifically in relation to the German revolutions of 1848 see Thomas Nipperdey, 'Kritik oder Objektivität? Zur Beurteilung der Revolution von 1848', in *Gesellschaft, Kultur und Theorie: Gesammelte Aufsätze zur neueren Geschichte*, Göttingen 1976, pp. 259–78.

25. Like many others I first became aware of Hroch's rigorous comparative approach from Miroslav Hroch, *Vorkämpfer der nationalen Bewegungen bei den kleinen Völkern Europas*, Prague 1968. It is unfortunate for English-language readers that the English version (*Social Preconditions of National Revival in Europe: A Comparative Analysis of the Social Composition of Patriotic Groups among the Smaller European Nations*, Cambridge 1985) is a much compressed and abridged account.

26. Benedict Anderson, *Imagined Communities. Reflections on the Origin and Spread of Nationalism*, London 1983. I have critically reviewed this book as well as Gellner, *Nations and Nationalism*, at length in John Breuilly, 'Reflections on Nationalism', *Philosophy of the Social Sciences*, vol. 15, 1985, pp. 65–75.

27. Gellner, *Plough, Sword and Book*.

28. See Timothy Blanning, *The Origins of the French Revolutionary Wars*, London 1986, on this particular case. On the meaning of a boundary in the French case see P. Sahlins, *Boundaries: The Making of France and Spain in the Pyrenees*, Berkeley 1989. For Germany see Alexander Demandt, ed., *Deutschlands Grenzen in der Geschichte*, Munich 1990. For a more theoretical consideration of the shift from a 'frontier' to a 'border' see Giddens, *The Nation-State and Violence*, pp. 49–53.

29. I develop this argument at length in Breuilly, *Nationalism and the State*, chapter 16.

30. See the collection of essays, Otto Dann and John Dinwiddy, eds, *Nationalism in the Age*

of the French Revolution, London/Ronceverte 1988.

31. For a cogent critique of liberalism from this perspective, see Michael Sandel, *Liberalism and the Limits of Justice*, Cambridge 1982.

32. These points are elaborated in the conclusion to Breuilly, *Nationalism and the State*.

33. Here I draw upon the arguments especially of chapter 3 in Breuilly, *Nationalism and the State*.

34. István Deak, *The Lawful Revolution: Louis Kossuth and the Hungarians, 1848–49*, New York 1979.

35. See the essay by András Vári in Eva Schmidt-Hartmann, ed., *Formen des nationalen Bewußtseins im Lichte zeitgenössischer Nationalismustheorien*, Munich 1994, in which he argues the case for elaborating the concepts I have already outlined, adding some concerned with the social composition of different kinds of nationalists, in order better to understand Magyar or Hungarian nationalism. I would not dispute that and Vári clearly uses these additional concepts effectively. My only reservation is a methodological one: as a tool of *general* analysis, there are distinct advantages to the multiplication of concepts in a theoretical approach. One simply ends up juggling too many balls. Given the focus on politics in my approach, I think it best that the concepts involved be confined to aspects of political action.

36. Breuilly, *Nationalism and the State*, p. 382.

37. I have developed some of these ideas in the revised edition of *Nationalism and the State*, Manchester 1993, especially the newly written chapter 17: 'Nationalism in Contemporary East-Central Europe'.

6

Nationalism and the Historians

Anthony D. Smith

The history of nationalism is as much a history of its interlocutors as of the ideology and movement itself. Exactly because it appears so protean and seems so elusive, nationalism reveals itself only in its various forms, or rather the forms given to us by its proponents and critics. That is why nationalism is so often considered a 'historical movement' *par excellence*. Not only did it emerge in a given epoch of European history, and not only does it manifest itself in specific historical situations. Nationalism is also profoundly 'historicist' in character: it sees the world as a product of the interplay of various communities, each possessing a unique character and history, and each the result of specific origins and developments.

But, beyond this, there is a more specific sense in which we may term nationalism a profoundly 'historical' movement. Historians figure prominently among its creators and devotees; but they have also led the way in seeking to assess and understand the phenomenon of nationalism. That historians should contribute in such large measure to so 'historicist' a movement is not surprising, given the common elements in early European nationalism and the historiography of the Romantic epoch. Michelet, Burke, Müller, Karamzin, Palàcky and many others provided the moral and intellectual foundation for an emerging nationalism in their respective communities. Along with the philologists, the historians have in many ways furnished the rationale and charter of their aspirant nations.[1]

Historians have also been among nationalism's sharpest critics and opponents, especially since the Second World War. Indeed, most of them have been sceptical of its ideological claims, if not downright hostile. They have attributed to nationalism a variety of harmful consequences,

ranging from absurd social and cultural policies to totalitarian terror
and global destabilization. This attitude has been conditioned by a number of widely held assumptions about the nature of the phenomenon.
Historians have generally seen nationalism as a doctrine or principle or
argument; it has been national*ism* rather than the nation that has exercised their imagination, with a few exceptions. This doctrine or principle
has often been regarded as an *idée fixe*, a motive force that remains constant beneath its many disguises. Alternatively, nationalism is equated
with 'national sentiment', a feeling of belonging to, and identification
with, the nation. The nation is then seen as serving individual and collective needs for warmth, strength and stability which assume much
greater importance once the ties of family and neighbourhood are loos-
ened. In that sense, nationalism may be functional for society in the
modern era.[2]

But the costs are high. There is no reason, for the critical historian,
why a group of human beings should not prefer to live, work and be governed together, perhaps on the basis of some cultural tie or shared
historical experiences; and they may be better governed by representatives of their own community than by others. But this liberal doctrine
must not be confused with the Continental and Romantic varieties of
nationalism, which treat individuals as members of immutable communities which can only be free if they are self-governing.[3] Such a doctrine
spells disaster for all, particularly in ethnically mixed areas, where it can
only exacerbate existing differences and historic antagonism.

Speaking generally, then, the historical understanding of the complex phenomenon of nationalism is grounded on a rather narrow
definition of the field and a similarly specific mode of explanation. The
latter is largely contextual, psychological and diffusionist. It insists, rightly
in my view, in locating nationalism and the concepts characteristic of
this movement in the context of European thought and history, at least as
far as the origins of nationalism are concerned; these concepts and ideas
can only be understood within that historical framework. Because modern Europe witnessed a breakdown in its modes of community, economy
and political order, the psychic advantages and aspects of nationalism are
emphasized; and the functions it performs for disoriented individuals
and dislocated communities receive special attention. Finally, the
favoured mechanism for explaining the spread of nationalism to Asia,
Africa and Latin America is a mixture of imitation and reaction: elites,
especially intellectuals, adopt and adapt Western ideas of the nation and
national regeneration. Nationalism flourishes in the specific circumstances of European imperialism and colonialism; but its diffusion is
largely self-propelled and self-reproducing, once a tiny stratum of intellectuals has made its appearance in the recipient country.[4]

Latterly, two other aspects of the historians' understanding of nationalism have become more visible, aspects which are shared by scholars from neighbouring disciplines. The first is the constructed nature of the nation. Not only is nationalism regarded as purely contingent and logically untenable: the nation itself, the object of every nationalism's endeavours, is artificial, a concept and model of social and cultural organization which is the product of the labours of self-styled nationalists bent on attaining power and reaping the rewards of political struggle. The nation is an invented category; it has roots in neither nature nor history. This leads into the second recent feature: the modernity of nations and nationalism. The past to which nationalists aspire is mythical: it exists only in the minds of nationalists and their followers, even when it is not cynically fabricated for present political purposes. The nation dates from the moment of nationalist success: it is a purely modern concept and the product of quite modern processes like bureaucracy, secularization, revolution and capitalism. Here the historians' understanding converges with the political scientist's, the sociologist's and the anthropologist's; except that, for the historian, the initial emergence of the ideology and movement of nationalism is fairly securely dated to the last quarter of the eighteenth century and the first decade of the nineteenth, the period from the Polish Partitions and American War of Independence to the Prussian and German reaction to the French Revolution and Napoleonic conquests.[5]

Three Historical Responses to Nationalism

Given the historical nature of their subject-matter and their own professional outlook, it would be surprising if historians did not conform to the general academic pattern, which discloses a close relationship between the ways in which scholars characterize and explain nationalism and their own *Sitz im Leben*, and that of their community; with ensuing differences in the basic meanings attached by each generation and group of historians to the concepts of nation and nationalism. This can be immediately seen in the typical early responses of historians and others to nineteenth-century nationalisms.

Early historians of the national idea tended to see the nation as a bulwark of individual liberty. This is of course the stance of Michelet in his *Historical View of the French Revolution*; writing in the mid nineteenth century, Michelet reaffirmed a Rousseauan vision of the return to nature and human sociability. The 'spontaneous organisation of France', born in 1789, had ushered in the era of fraternity, of 'Man fraternising in the presence of God', as Michelet put it. In the fraternity, 'there are no longer either rich or poor, nobles or plebeians; there is but one general table, and provisions are in common; social dissensions and quarrels have disappeared; enemies become reconciled; and opposite sects, believers and philosophers, Protestants and Catholics, fraternise together . . .'.[6]

This religion of patriotism is also the worship of man, and the motive force of modern French and European history. For the 'child upon the altar (of the festival of the confederation) is France, with all the world surrounding her. In her, the common child of nations, they feel themselves united . . .', and Michelet singles out Italy, Poland and Ireland, countries with nationalist movements belonging to the Young Europe movement of Mazzini, as fraternal sympathizers of France, even during the Revolution, revealing the power of an idea in modern history.

By the 1880s, nationalist principles were firmly entrenched in French politics, following the loss of Alsace-Lorraine in 1871. Renan, in opposing the principle of voluntary historical solidarity to that of an organic ethno-linguistic unity as the basis of the nation, remained true to the liberal spirit. 'Nations', he wrote, 'are nothing eternal. They had a beginning, they will have an end. The European confederation will probably replace them. But this is not the law of the century in which we live. At present, the existence of nations is good and even necessary. Their existence is a guarantee of liberty which would be lost if the world had only one law and one master . . .'. For Renan, the spirit of liberty was best embodied in a definition of the nation that was social-psychological, one that refused any kind of reduction, whether biological, linguistic, economic or geographical. 'Let us not abandon the fundamental principle that man is a rational and moral being before he is penned up in this or that language, before he is a member of this or that race, before he adheres to this or that culture.' So,

A nation is a soul, a spiritual principle. . . . A nation is a great solidarity, created by the sentiment of the sacrifices which have been made and of those which one is disposed to make in the future. It presupposes a past; but it resumes itself in the present by a tangible fact: the consent, the clearly expressed desire to continue life in common. The existence of a nation is a plebiscite of every day, as the existence of the individual is a perpetual affirmation of life.[7]

In trying to remain true to liberal principles in opposition to von Treitschke's militarism and racial nationalism, Renan may have overstated the voluntaristic aspects of the nation. What he really wants to affirm is the primacy of politics and shared history in the genesis and character of nations. Unlike the East, Western Europe saw the rise, after the demise of the Carolingian empire, of various nations which were fusions of populations. 'Even by the tenth century', he claims, 'all the inhabitants of France are French. The idea of a difference of races in the population of France has completely disappeared with the French writers and poets after Hugues Capet. The distinction between the noble and the serf is highly emphasised, but this distinction is in no way an ethnic distinction . . .' The important point for Renan is social and psychological: shared experiences and common memories (and forgotten things). He does not explain why the West evolved the kind of nation, which he thinks is new in history, based on shared experience and selective memory, while the East failed to do so and retained its pattern of ethnic distinctiveness.

A more conservative response to the proliferation of nationalism can be found in Lord Acton's essay criticizing Mazzini's ideal of political nationality, which he characterized as an expression of political idealism. While the English concept of libertarian nationality looks back to 1688 and tends 'to diversity and not to uniformity, to harmony and not to unity', the French ideal of racial collective nationality partakes of the character of 1789 and 'overrules the rights and wishes of the inhabitants, absorbing their divergent interests in a fictitious unity; sacrifices their several inclinations and duties to the higher claim of nationality, and crushes all natural rights and all established liberties for the purpose of vindicating itself'. For Acton, the theory of national unity 'makes the nation a source of despotism and revolution'; but the theory of liberty 'regards it as the bulwark of self-government, and the foremost limit to the excessive power of the State.'[8]

It follows that, for Acton, multinational empires are superior to nations, the Austrian Empire to France. 'A State which is incompetent to satisfy different races condemns itself; a State which labours to neutralise, to absorb, or to expel them, destroys its own vitality; a State which does not include them is destitute of the chief basis of self-government. The theory of nationality, therefore, is a retrograde step in history.' He concludes that 'nationality does not aim either at liberty or prosperity, both of which it sacrifices to the imperative necessity of making the nation the mould and measure of the state. Its course will be marked with material as well as moral ruin, in order that a new invention may prevail over the works of God and the interests of mankind'.

In fact, Acton has here slightly shifted his target, from the French theory of nationality to the nation itself. But what concerns us is Acton's sense of the constructed nature of the nation. Not only are its claims less important than those of traditional authority and individual liberty; it is really an outgrowth, a product of the denial of corporate rights by state absolutism. Acton is reacting against the movement for Italian unification; hence his focus on nationalism and a theory of unity rather than secession. Both his arguments and his historical analysis are tied to mid-nineteenth-century developments on the Continent; except for his conviction of the artificiality and modernity of the nation, they would evoke few chords in African or Asian states in the contemporary era. Yet his underlying assumptions continue to inspire academic analyses even today.

Not all conservative reactions were so hostile to nationalism. Max Weber, sociological historian and German nationalist, regarded nations as conflict groups and bearers of unique cultural values. Echoing Renan, Weber declares that 'A nation is a community of sentiment which would adequately manifest itself in a state of its own; hence a nation is a community which normally tends to produce a state of its own'.[9] The nation is also the focus of the cultural values that define its individuality: 'The significance of the "nation" is usually anchored in the superiority, or at least irreplaceability, of the cultural values that can only be preserved and developed through the cultivation of the individuality (*Eigenart*) of the community'.[10]

Like the other historians considered so far, Weber has left us with no historical account of the rise of nationalism, though he seems to have intended to do so. All we have are sections on ethnicity, the nation and nationalism in *Economy and Society*, in which his basic 'political' approach to the subject is evident. For, not only did Weber consider the state and the nation required each other in the modern world, as do the bureaucrats and intellectuals, the bearers of the respective concepts; it was political action, more than anything, which could transform ethnic communities into nations, as the case of Alsace with its French political memories so clearly demonstrated for Weber. As he put it,

> This can be understood by any visitor who walks through the museum of Colmar, which is rich in relics such as tricolors, pompier and military helmets, edicts by Louis Philippe and especially memorabilia from the French Revolution; these may appear trivial to the outsider, but they have sentimental value for the Alsatians. This sense of community came into being by virtue of common political and, indirectly, social experiences which are highly valued by the masses as symbols of the destruction of feudalism, and the story of these events takes the place of the heroic legends of primitive peoples.[11]

We cannot be sure how far Weber regarded nations as modern, let alone inventions or artificial. In his work, for perhaps the first time, we meet the problem of the relationship between ethnicity and nationalism which has exercised some latter-day scholars. This concern, however, was far from a third typical response to nineteenth-century nationalism, the socialist and Marxist historical evaluation. Not that Marx or Engels devoted any systematic attention to the phenomenon; their attitudes must be gleaned from passing references in articles on foreign policy or in revolutionary pamphlets or essays.[12] But their legacy to Marxist historians is clear in its main outlines: nations are communities of language and natural sympathies, as Engels put it; the great or 'leading' nations, furthest advanced on the road of capitalism, must be supported against reactionary absolutist states like tsarist Russia or small, backward nations like Serbia or the Czechs; the working class 'has no stake in the fatherland', though its struggle must first of all be with its own national bourgeoisie; and nationalism may only be supported by socialists where it hastens the overthrow of feudalism or, as in Ireland, bourgeois domination. To which Engels added, à propos Poland, that national independence is the pre-condition of social development, and that (as Hegel had claimed) only those nations which in the past had built their own states would be able to do so in the future, and so deserved the support of socialists.[13]

It was left to subsequent Marxist historians to take up these purely 'instrumental' positions and attempt to understand the phenomena of nations and nationalism in historical terms. Kautsky, Lenin and Luxemburg, despite their disagreements, extended the basically 'instrumentalist' analysis of Eastern European nationalisms as tools of the feudal or bourgeois classes and diversions from proletarian revolution, though Lenin was prepared to concede the popular reality of the Eastern nationalism with which he had to contend.[14] But it was left to Karl Renner and Otto Bauer to provide a more rounded Marxist account of nationalism.

Of course, theirs was also a programmatic statement. It was designed to meet the immediate needs of the Austrian Social Democrats, confronted with the problems of multinationalism within the empire and the party. To support their extra-territorial solutions and their concept of personal and cultural nationality, Renner and Bauer adopted definitions of the nation that led them away from the political and territorial conceptions of Marx and Engels. For Bauer, in particular, the nation was a 'community of fate', with its own character and culture. It was shaped by material factors, but close proximity and communication in a shared history and culture made the national bond even more powerful than class ties. Bauer, nevertheless, insisted on the individual's right to choose his cultural nationality, as the latter gradually evolved. In the case of the Germans, Bauer traced their national community back to the tribal horde living in isolation and sharing everything. With agricultural settlement, some parts of the horde broke away or fused with other groups; but the central stem was split in the Middle Ages on class lines, with the barons and clergy constituting the real nation. Later, with the rise of towns and a money economy, they were gradually enlarged by the addition of the bourgeoisie and educated middle class; and now socialism was broadening the national base still further through the inclusion of the working class. It was in this spirit that the 1899 Brunn Congress of the Austrian

Social-Democratic Workers' party called for a 'democratic federal state of nationalities', viewed as cultural-historical communities without territorial rights.[15]

Typologies and Evaluations

Bauer's is perhaps the first full-length study of nationalism, from an historical standpoint, albeit a political one dictated by very specific political circumstances. It reflects the growing importance of nationalism as a political ideology and movement, and as a subject of academic investigation in its own right. It was in the 1920s that Carlton Hayes and Hans Kohn began their close dissections of nationalist ideologies and attempted to order its varieties into definite, recurring types. Hayes's work is perhaps the first to adopt a more neutral stance, one that seeks to distinguish the various strands of nationalist ideology. If his distinctions between Humanitarian, Traditional, Jacobin, Liberal, and later Economic and Integral nationalism describe pure types rather than concrete trends or instances, which in practice mingle the different strands, they do sensitize us to the complexities of nationalist ideology. They also reveal, beneath the analytical discourse, the moralistic periodization of the first full-length histories of nationalism.[16]

A more influential typology, Hans Kohn's dichotomy of 'Western' voluntaristic and 'Eastern' organic nationalism, also discloses an underlying moral purpose. For Kohn, nationalism in England, France and America is rationalist, optimistic and pluralist. Couched in terms of the social contract, it answered to the aspirations for political community of the rising middle classes with their ideal of social progress. Across the Rhine, however, and eastwards into Russia and Asia, social backwardness and the weakness of the middle classes produced a much more emotional and authoritarian nationalism, based on the lower aristocracy and intelligentsia, and appealing to the folk instincts of the masses. Later, Kohn subdivided his Western type into 'individualist' and 'collectivist' subcategories, found respectively in the Anglo-Saxon countries and in France.[17]

As this last distinction suggests, it is the ideology of nationalism rather than the movement or community, that forms the object of Kohn's interest. This accords with our characterization of most historians' picture of nationalism, and the moralistic concerns which have often animated their research, concerns that were understandably pressing during the Second World War, when Kohn wrote his major study. Kohn does, however, attempt to link his ideological types with their social settings, albeit somewhat crudely; and to show some of the pre-modern group sentiments among Greeks, Jews and others, that went into the formulations of modern nationalism. In other words, Kohn's 'modernism' (the belief in the complete modernity of nations and nationalism) is tempered by his inclusion of pre-modern ethnic motifs; and this in turn implies a separate role for 'national sentiment', a role not attributable solely to nationalist ideologues. Indeed, even a cursory inspection reveals that Kohn's many books include not only detailed analyses of specific nationalist ideologies like Pan-Slavism, but studies of the social and political setting of a wider 'national consciousness' in Jacobin France, nineteenth-century Germany or early modern Switzerland.[18]

This wider consciousness seems also to form the object of the brief study *Nationalism and After* by Edward Hallett Carr.[19] Carr's attitude to nationalism is not wholly negative: he speaks of 'the development of that community of national thought and feeling, of political and cultural tradition, which is the constructive side of nationalism'. Generally, however, Carr, like Acton, whom he quotes at the outset, sees nationalism as a denial of individualism and democracy, of liberty and equality; though the nation, as an historical group, has a 'place and function in a wider society', it must not be allowed to impede its own supersession in an interdependent regional or world order.[20]

In his historical account, Carr distinguishes three periods of nationalism: an early modern epoch in which the new national unit was identified with the person of the monarch, international relations being simply the rules governing the intercourse of dynastic states, with 'mercantilism' as the characteristic economic policy; the era from the French Revolution till 1914, in which a popular and democratic political nationalism fathered by Rousseau was diffused throughout Europe under the aegis of an international economic order grounded on free trade, expansion and the financial dominance of London; and finally the period from the late nineteenth century to the Second World War, which saw the incorporation of the masses into the fully socialized nation, its growing economic nationalism, and the sheer proliferation of European nations, leading to totalitarian regimes and total warfare. Carr considers the prospects for a reversal of nationalism's appeal encouraging; his failure to allow for the possibility of a wave of anti-colonial nationalisms, or renewed European and Third World secession nationalisms, suggests again the moral and teleological basis of his penetrating analysis, as well as its Eurocentrism. Again, given the enormity of the issues at stake in the 1939–45 war, and his own social location, this is unsurprising.[21]

As long as fascism continued to be regarded as the logical denouement of nationalism, a European focus and a periodization in terms of moral progression seemed to make sense. But the moment a more global and less moralistic standpoint, which differentiated fascism from various kinds of nationalism began to be adopted, chronological typologies were seen to be inadequate. Thus, in his earlier work, Louis Snyder had opted for a common four-stage periodization, as follows:

1815–71   – 'integrative' nationalism
1871–1900– 'disruptive' nationalism
1900–45   – 'aggressive' nationalism
1945–?   – 'contemporary' world-wide nationalism.

In his later work, Snyder opts for a geographical typology, including a 'fissiparous' European nationalism, a racial black nationalism in Africa, a politico-religious nationalism in the Middle East, a messianic one in Russia, a 'melting-pot' one in the United States, and anti-colonial nationalisms in Asia and populist ones in Latin America.[22] It is not clear that such general, and necessarily over-lapping, regional types do more than point up the global diffusion of nationalism, but they serve at least to correct the Eurocentrism of earlier typologies.

This shift in geopolitical focus is apparent in a number of typologies proposed by historians and others, contrasting the European experience with that of the Third World, or parts of it. Here we may mention Kenneth Minogue's typology of European 'ethnic', Pan and diaspora, and 'underdeveloped' Third World nationalisms;[23] John Plamenatz's distinction between the nationalisms of those with a high level of cultural resources and education, like the nineteenth-century Germans and Italians, and those with poor cultural resources like the Slavs and Africans whose nationalism is therefore imitative and competitive;[24] E.K. Francis's contrast, taken from Meinecke, between 'ethnic' nations and nationalisms, based on a belief in common descent and identity, and 'demotic' nations which share administrative and military institutions and common territory and mobility.[25]

Perhaps the most influential of these recent typologies is Hugh Seton-Watson's distinction between, first, the 'old, continuous nations' like the English, French, Castilians, Dutch, Scots, Danes, Swedes, Poles, Hungarians and Russians, and the 'new' nations of the Serbs, Croats, Romanians, Arabs, Africans and Indians, whose national consciousnesses succeeded the spread of nationalism and were largely its products; and then, within this last category, three kinds of nationalist movement, secession, irredentism and 'nation-building' nationalisms. In his *Nations and States*,[26] Seton-Watson elaborates these distinctions (which Tilly had also used in relation to state-building) with a wealth of historical examples. They serve to organize his account, which shifts the object of interest away from nationalism as an ideology to the processes which encourage the formation of national consciousness, processes like geography, the state, religion and language.[27]

Nations as Nationalist Constructs

I said that historians generally aim to arrive at a contextual understanding of nationalism, that is, an understanding of the meanings which the participants attributed to the concept of the nation according to the concrete circumstances in which they were placed. For this reason, the problem of explanation is often seen as an attempt to grasp, first, the various traditions of nationalist thought and experience, and second, the manner in which such traditions are diffused to other peoples. An example of the first kind of attempt is Salo Baron's excellent analysis of the varieties of nationalist experience, at least in Europe, viewed in relation to different religious traditions such as Protestantism, Catholicism, Orthodox Caesaro-Papism and Judaism. If nations are modern and largely the product of the labours and ideas of rationalists, the latter can only be grasped in the context of definite traditions in which religion played the dominant role. However secular the nationalist doctrine, it cannot be understood in all its empirical variety outside this religious matrix, as many case studies were to demonstrate.[28] An example of the second type of attempt is Trevor-Roper's explanation of the diffusion of ideas from the 'historic' nationalisms of Germany, Italy and Hungary to the 'secondary' nationalisms of Czechs, Poles and Jews. Quite apart from the validity of the distinction itself, the imitative role of the East European intelligentsias who react against the West, but take up its nationalist ideas, requires further elucidation. Why should these particular ideas prove so attractive, and what accounts for the prominence of the intellectuals?[29]

An answer to both questions, and one which accords to religious traditions a determining role, is provided by the work of Elie Kedourie. In his initial study, Kedourie aimed at a contextual understanding of European nationalism from its invention in early-nineteenth-century Germany to its later diffusion by native intellectuals in Eastern Europe and the Middle East. Concentrating more on the varieties of nationalism than the growth of nations, Kedourie traces the evolution of notions of diversity, autonomy of the will, and linguistic purity, to the peculiar concerns of the European philosophical tradition from Descartes to Kant and Fichte, and the alienation of German-speaking intellectuals. The context, then, in which the example of the French Revolution and the ideals of the German Romantics captured the imaginations of the frustrated youth, was specifically modern and European, and it involved a radical breakdown of traditional communities like the family and church, and their accompanying political habits. Here the social-psychological base is apparent: nationalist movements, he argues, 'are seen to satisfy a need, to fulfil a want. Put at its simplest, the need is to belong together in a coherent and stable community.' So that nationalism here is treated as

the outcome of the spirit of an age in which old communities and traditions had fallen to the onslaught of Enlightenment doctrines and in
which disoriented youth craved the satisfaction of their need to belong.[30]

In a later work, *Nationalism in Asia and Africa*, Kedourie extended this
strictly 'modernist' analysis in two directions. The first was spatial and
sociological. In attempting to explain why native elites in Africa and Asia
adopted the Western ideals of nationalism, Kedourie developed a diffusionist model in which both Western institutions and ideas were spread to
other continents by the regimenting effects of modernizing colonialisms
and the Western education of indigenous intellectuals, who then suffered
discrimination at the hands of colonial administrations in their native
lands; Kedourie cites in particular the examples of Surendranath
Banerjea, Edward Atiyah and George Antonius. Imitation is here combined with psychological resentment at social rejection by the West. On
the other side, the original analysis is extended back in time. In returning
to the 'cult of the dark gods', African and Asian intelligentsias were nevertheless imitating not only the historicism of European intellectuals,
but also their revolutionary chiliasm, their belief in the perfectibility of
this world, which had its roots in the visions of Christian millennialism.
Tracing European nationalist ideals to their origins in the heterodox
doctrines of Joachim of Fiore, the Franciscan Spirituals and the
Anabaptists of Münster, whose activities Norman Cohn had so vividly
recorded, Kedourie is able to affirm that:

> We may say in short that the mainspring of nationalism in Asia and Africa is
> the same secular millennialism which had its rise and development in Europe
> and in which society is subjected to the will of a handful of visionaries who, to
> achieve their vision, must destroy all barriers between private and public.[31]

In tracing this particular lineage of nationalism, Kedourie does not mean
to imply that nations and nationalism are not peculiarly modern phenomena or that they have historical roots beyond the imaginings and
activities of nationalist intellectuals. Despite his respect for different historical traditions, the emphasis falls on the power of nationalism as a
doctrine to conjure the nation in place of decayed traditional communities, and on the activities of modern, rationalist intellectuals in serving as
creators and revolutionary agents of modern nations and nationalisms.[32]

This sense of the modernity and 'constructed' nature of the nation is
widely shared by contemporary historians of all persuasions, as well as by
scholars in other disciplines. Not all of them would, however, ascribe the
predominant role in the process of construction to the ideologues of
nationalism. John Breuilly, for example, restricts the definition of nationalism to political arguments designed to mobilize, coordinate and
legitimize support for the capture of state power. These arguments

presuppose the existence of the nation with its own peculiar character, seeking independence and possessing priority over every other interest or value. Such a doctrine emerges in opposition to state power, and becomes the basis for mobilizing and coordinating civil society during the early modern period in Europe, when the split between state and society became apparent. On this basis, Breuilly distinguishes three kinds of nationalist opposition, secession, unification and reform movements, each of which may emerge in nation-states and in states which do not define themselves as nations, for example, empires or colonies. This six-fold classification can then be used to compare the nationalist politics of both Europe and the Third World, in ways that illuminate the uses of nationalist arguments for elites and others in the struggle for state power. For Breuilly, the role of culture and intellectuals is supportive; national-ism is not primarily a matter of identity or communication, but simply a cultural mode of opposition (and more rarely governmental) politics, which equates the historicist notion of the unique nation with the polit-ical concept of the universal 'nation-state'. By this means, nationalists are able to tap all sorts of non-political resources in a society for the pur-pose of mobilizing political opposition. The nationalist solution to the problem of alienation which was the inevitable product of the growing division between state and society, was to regard each unique society or 'nation' as the natural (and only) basis of a territorial state, lest alien societies 'do violence to the unique national spirit'. Breuilly regards this fusion of a cultural and political concept of community as spurious, but acknowledges its wide appeal in all continents.[33]

This analysis is typical of the dominant 'modernist' and 'instrumen-talist' school of historical, and sociological, thought about nations and nationalism. Not only are nations recent constructs of partisan ideologues. Nationalism is also an instrument of legitimation and mobilization, through which leaders and elites stir up mass support for their competitive power struggle. Not only nationalists, but non-nationalists like Bismarck, can tap atavistic emotions and manipulate the fears and resentments of the masses by appealing to their chauvinism and heightening their sense of cultural difference. If Breuilly's political realism concedes rather less to intellectuals and their ideals among the upper and middle classes, he still reserves for them a place in igniting mass sentiment, which can be channelled for elite political ends.[34]

A similar 'instrumentalism' pervades the essays in the volume edited by Eric Hobsbawm and Terence Ranger, entitled *The Invention of Tradition*.[35] It must be said that not all the essays support the book's *leit-motif*, the novelty and even fabrication of traditions which masquerade as immemorial. It is, for example, clear from Prys Morgan's careful account of the revived *eisteddfodau* in the mid eighteenth century that new practices were meshed with much older customs and traditions; on the other hand, the incorporation of the neo-Druidic Gorsedd into the *eisteddfod* of 1819 was a stroke of pure invention on the part of Iolo Morganwg.[36] Hobsbawm, however, regards 'that comparatively recent historical innovation, the "nation", with its associated phenomena: nationalism, the nation-state, national symbols, histories and the rest', as closely bound up with 'invented traditions', and as resting on 'exercises in social engineering which are often deliberate and always innovative'. Nations are neither ancient nor natural: on the contrary, much of what 'subjectively makes up the modern "nation" consists of such constructs and is associated with appropriate and, in general, fairly recent symbols or suitably tailored discourse (such as "national history")'. In his concluding essay, Hobsbawm analyses the spate of invented traditions in late-nineteenth-century France, Germany and the United State – education manuals, public ceremonies, public monuments and buildings, the use of collective personifications like Marianne or the 'Deutsche Michel', commemorative anniversaries, the use of flags and anthems – and links them causally to the increasing rapidity of social change and in particular to the rise of mass political democracy. It was then that rulers and states discovered the uses of mass 'irrationality', though this does not mean that invented national traditions are themselves irrational responses to the breakdown in social structure and political hierarchies, for they clearly fulfil widespread social and psychological needs in the modern era.[37]

His conclusions are of a piece with Hugh Trevor-Roper's account of the invention of the Highlands tradition from the late eighteenth century, after the Jacobite defeat at Culloden. From Rawlinson's 'invention' of the small kilt in the 1730s, through Macpherson's 'rediscovery' of Ossian in the early 1760s and Walter Scott's creation of Scottish literary tourism to the 'clan' tartans published by Colonel David Stewart in 1822 and the *Vestiarium Scotium* (1842) and *The Costume of the Clans* (1844) of the 'Sobieske Stuart' brothers, who sought to revive an almost vanished medieval Scottish Highlands civilization, the threads of fabricated traditions were woven into the created new nation of Scotland, aided by Victoria's devotion to Balmoral and English bourgeois concern for the healthy pleasures of Highlands life.[38] The point, of course, is that any connection with life in the medieval Highlands, which till the seventeenth century under the MacDonald Lords of the Isles constituted a Hebridean variant of an overflow Irish culture, is purely fictitious: the traditions of the nations are as recent as the nation itself.

That is also the burden of Benedict Anderson's recent reflections on the origins and spread of nationalism, in his *Imagined Communities*. The nation is an abstraction, a construct of the imagination; it is a community which is imagined as both sovereign and limited. It emerges when the realms of church and dynasty recede, and no longer seem to answer to mankind's craving for immortality. The nation, with its promise of identification with posterity, can help us to overcome the finality of death and oblivion; but that only becomes possible when a new conception of homogenous, empty chronological time replaces medieval concepts of simultaneous time. Nations are created in the historical and sociological imagination, through identification with generalized communal heroes set in equally generalized but vividly detailed locations and times; though we can never meet them, we can 'know' our fellow-citizens, the members of our cultural nations, through these identifications and descriptions in newspapers, journals, novels, plays and operas. This has become a reality through what Anderson calls 'the technology of print-capitalism', which spawned the first real commodity, the mass-produced printed book. Together with the possibilities of travel and the 'administrative pilgrimages' of colonial elites, the rise of printed literature and the press has made it possible to 'narrate' the nation and imaginatively to 'construct' it. In different parts of the world and successive epochs, this process of construction took different forms, from the 'vernacular' literary and philological nationalisms of Europe to the 'official' nationalism of the authoritarian empires and the Marxist nationalism of communist states like Vietnam and China. But the underlying cultural and economic processes were broadly similar, and their result was everywhere the same basic model of imagined community we call the 'nation'.[39]

Identity and Continuity

This brief discussion of the work of some historians and a few others, who concerned themselves with the nature and history of nations and nationalism, has been necessarily selective and partial. I have been concerned to bring out the main lines of their treatment, rather than the historiographical detail. This has allowed us to grasp the stages of historical treatment, which correspond roughly, as I intimated at the outset, to the historians' own situation and epoch. The first of these periods or stages lasts, roughly, from the mid nineteenth century to the 1920s; with the exception of the full-length treatment of Bauer, who is not a historian in the strict sense, the treatments are in essay or section form, and addressed to particular nationalist situations in Europe. It is only in the second period that we encounter serious attempts by historians to concentrate on the field of rationalist phenomena, and to look closely at the varieties of ideology and the periodization of nationalism. On the whole, it is national*ism*, in the sense of an ideology rather than a sentiment, at the expense of nations, that preoccupies historians like Hayes, Snyder,

Kohn and Shafer; and the emphasis is less on systematic explanation of the rise and appeal of nationalism than on narration and classification of its sub-types. It is really only in the third period, since the 1950s, that historians have devoted greater attention to a rigorous search for situational or general factors that serve to explain the genesis and course of particular movements or of nationalism-in-general. In this period, too, there is a growing interest in national sentiment and the nation as explananda. Although some historians continue to devote their attention to the ideology, several others combine this with consideration of its role in creating nations or augmenting or fostering national consciousness. Equally, there is a growing interest in what might be termed sociological factors as possible causes of the origins and appeal of nationalism, and in cross-fertilization with other disciplines in approach and method.[40]

In the light of these different concerns and this variety of approaches, can we speak of an historical perspective on nationalism *tout court*? That would be going too far. What we can do is to list the main characteristics common to most historians' picture of nations and nationalism, and to ask how far the resulting image corresponds to, and helps to explain, the many facets of this complex phenomenon.

Of these characteristics, three stand out, especially in recent accounts by historians. The first is the scepticism, and even hostility, to nationalism which was mentioned at the outset. It takes the form of emphasizing the inherently absurd and destructive tendencies of nationalism. This is a motif that runs right through the three periods of historical investigation in the field. It is, of course, not peculiar to historians: scholars in political science and international relations also fasten on the destabilizing effects of nationalism for states and for inter-state order. Nevertheless, historians by and large appear to display greater scepticism and hostility than others, perhaps because they are keenly aware of the disturbing psychological aspects of national sentiment and nationalism. At times, this awareness makes them liable to the charge of psychologism, or reducing a phenomenon that manifests itself at several levels to just one, the social-psychological. But perhaps the more serious charge is that, by taking the ideology as their prime explanandum, they overlook or bypass the importance of processes of nation-formation which are to some extent independent of the activities of nationalist ideologues. If some sociologists have been guilty of missing out those activities, some historians have perhaps given them too much attention and explanatory weight.

One effect of this tendency among historians is to underplay some of the functional, even 'constructive', aspects of nationalist endeavours. Once those activities are placed within the context of a process of 'nation-formation' (not the same as 'nation-building'), which for various reasons may be under way, they may assume a greater validity and practical utility than is often conceded. It is not uncommon for this process to throw up a cultural renascence and a range of new communal ventures; if some of these border on the absurd or pernicious, others are clearly salutary and regenerative, notably in the fields of music, art and literature, and various fields of scholarship.[41]

Allied to the historians' general assumptions about the poverty of nationalism is their conviction that nations are artificial communities with largely fabricated ties. Hence the common enterprise of 'deconstructing the nation', shared with many anthropologists; and the need to uncover the ideological aims of nationalist manipulators who tap the atavistic emotions of the masses for their partisan ends. This is the subject of a lively debate between Paul Brass and Francis Robinson on the formation of Pakistan and the role of nationalist elites in forging, or reacting to, the Muslim sentiments of the masses in North India.[42]

But, as Hobsbawm concedes, only some traditions have mass resonance, and only some of them prove durable. The nation, as he points out, is the most important of the lasting 'invented traditions'.[43] If so, in what sense shall we regard it as 'invented' or 'constructed'? Why does this 'invention' so often and in such different cultural and social settings appear to strike such a deep chord and for so long? No artifice, however well constructed, could survive so many different kinds of vicissitude or fit so many different conditions. Clearly there is more to the formation of nations than nationalist fabrication, and 'invention' must be understood in its other sense of a novel recombination of existing elements.[44]

The so-called 'artificiality' of nations and nationalism is closely allied to the third characteristic of the historian's general image: the modernity of nations and nationalism. Now, the historians are surely correct in maintaining that national*ism*, as an ideology and a movement, seeking to attain and maintain autonomy, unity and identity for a social group deemed by some of its members to constitute an actual or potential 'nation', is a product of the late eighteenth century. It was then that a specifically nationalist doctrine arose, claiming that the world is divided into distinct nations, each with its peculiar character, that nations are the source of all political power, that human beings are free only insofar as they belong to an autonomous nation, and that international peace and security depend on all nations being autonomous, preferably in states of their own. It was only in the eighteenth century that such ideas gained currency, in the specific context of the European interstate system.[45]

Not all historians accepted, however, the correlate of this view, namely the modernity of the *nation*. An older generation of historian, particularly on the Continent, looked for and found nations even in antiquity, among Greeks, Jews, Persians and Egyptians.[46] Others were equally convinced of their presence among French and English, Scots and Swiss, in the Middle

Ages.[47] There are partisans of these views to this day, though their number is small.[48]

Today, however, most historians accept the modernity of the 'nation', and they differ only as to more detailed dating for the emergence of particular nations, and about the factors which facilitated their emergence. The nation is seen as an exclusively modern concept and type of social organization, requiring specifically 'modern' conditions of state bureaucracy, capitalism, secularism and democracy to bring it into being.

Three points can be made about this conception. The first is that it too contains a 'mythical' element, in the sense of a dramatic interpretation which is widely believed and which, while referring to past events, serves present purposes or future goals. The 'myth of the modern nation' refers back to a pre-modern era which is 'nationless', and dramatizes the narrative of modernization giving birth to nations; and the nations in this picture represent a more or less regrettable stage in human history, part of the radical break between traditional, agrarian and modern, industrial societies, to be superseded once full modernity is attained. Such a 'counter-myth' seeks to relativize nationalism and to dismiss and explain the claims and assumptions of the nationalist myth itself.[49]

The second point is that, even on the assumptions made by the 'modernist' conception of nationalism, there are important differences between groups of nations, both in type and in periodization. Of course, much depends on the definition of the 'nation' espoused. But let us suppose that by the term 'nation' we mean a *large, territorially bounded group sharing a common culture and division of labour, and a common code of legal rights and duties,* the kind of attributes which would be uncommon in antiquity and the early medieval era.[50] Even with such a 'modernist' definition, the kind of distinction that Hugh Seton-Watson and, in another context, Charles Tilly have drawn, between slowly emerging, continuous nations (and states) in western and northern Europe, and the later 'nations of design', created by and in the era of nationalism, must be observed. It is clear that in the West the process of 'nation-formation' was unforeseen and unintended, with states being forged around dominant ethnic communities, and in turn gradually becoming national states. Elsewhere such processes required external stimuli and planned activism.[51]

Of course, this must not be taken to imply that something like the 'nation' had already emerged in the fifteenth century in England, France and Spain; this was decidedly not Seton-Watson's claim. Rather, he was pointing to two quite different routes in the formation of nations, and to the need to trace the origins of one of these trajectories back into the Middle Ages, a trajectory that was not really completed (if it is ever complete) until the nineteenth century, as Eugen Weber has so well reminded us in the case of France and its regions.[52]

This leads to my last point. If it is conceded that some of the processes which enter into the formation of nations go back to the medieval era, and perhaps even earlier, then perhaps it becomes legitimate and necessary to inquire how pre-modern communities relate to what we call 'modern nations', in order to understand better why such nations have so wide an appeal in the modern world. The real trouble with the modernist picture of nationalism, assumed by so many historians and other scholars, is a certain historical shallowness. By locating the nation and nationalism exclusively in the transition to a modern era and treating them as products of 'modernity', one makes the task of explaining the return to the past and the felt continuities with an ethnic past more difficult. The balance between continuity and discontinuity has been upset, and this makes the modern quest for collective identity so baffling – unless of course one invokes a catch-all 'need to belong'. But as we said, that need is variable, and in any case it does not explain why it so often attaches itself to the 'nation' rather than other communities.

This is why it is so necessary and important to look at the cultural models of pre-modern community which may help to explain why so many people are drawn to the nation as their primary focus of loyalty and solidarity in the modern world. Not only may we point to specific continuities of the kind noted by John Armstrong in his study of medieval Christian and Islamic ethnic identities, notably in the realm of myth, symbol and historical memory which Renan singled out.[53] The fact that many parts of the world had been socially and culturally structured in terms of different kinds of ethnic community (or *ethnie*) in antiquity and the medieval era, as they continue to be to this day, and that *ethnies* share some elements with modern nations (myths of ancestry, memories, some cultural elements, perhaps a territory and a name), may afford a better point of departure for the study of the transformations and revivals involved in the formation of modern nations and the role played by nationalism in those processes. Even if elements of ethnicity are 'constructed' and 'reconstructed' and sometimes plainly 'invented', the fact that such activities have been operating for centuries, even millennia, and that several *ethnies* while changing their cultural character have nevertheless persisted as identifiable communities over long periods, suggests that we ignore the presence and influence exerted by such communities on the formation of modern nations at our peril.[54]

My purpose here has not been to fit every historian of nationalism into a preconceived framework, but only to draw out what I took to be the main points of an underlying argument to be found in many of their writings on this subject. Clearly, there are historians who do not subscribe to the currently dominant trends and for whom the nation is more than a modern construct and nationalism not only the genie of disruption which is often portrayed. Nevertheless, it is interesting that a wide spectrum of historians have and do subscribe to the general 'modernist' portrait which I have delineated, and share in the general scepticism and suspicion of nationalism, to which they attribute many of the world's ills.

Whether this verdict on so protean a phenomenon as nationalism is justified is an open question. But the underlying analysis from which it springs, while engendering many fascinating insights, poses as many problems as it resolves.

Notes

1. The role of nationalist historians in promoting nationalism has not, as far as I know, been the subject of a full-length study; but Hans Kohn's work has several chapters on the contributions of particular historians to specific movements, for example, Müller and von Treitschke in Hans Kohn, *The Mind of Germany*, London 1965; see also Kohn, *Prophets and Peoples*, New York 1961, on Michelet, and *Pan-Slavism*, 2nd edn, New York 1960, on Palàcky.

2. As for example in the Royal Institute of International Affairs' *Report on Nationalism*, Edward H. Carr, ed., London 1939, or the study by G. Michelat and J.-P. H. Thomas, *Dimensions du nationalisme*, Paris 1966. For a case study using such a definition, see S. Klausner, 'Why They Chose Israel', *Archives de sociologie des religions*, vol. 9, 1960, pp. 129–44.

3. For the Whig doctrine, see John Stewart Mill, *Considerations on Representative Government*, London 1872, and the comments on Lord Acton's critique, below.

4. M. Perham, *The Colonial Reckoning*, London 1963; Thomas Hodgkin, 'The Relevance of "Western" Ideas in the Derivation of African Nationalism', in J.R. Pennock, ed., *Self-government in Modernising Societies*, Englewood Cliffs 1964. For a social-psychological theory of European 'neo-nationalism', see Patricia Mayo, *The Roots of Identity: Three National Movements in Contemporary European Politics*, London 1974; for an evaluation of such approaches, Anthony D. Smith, 'The Diffusion of Nationalism', *British Journal of Sociology*, vol. 29, 1978, pp. 234–48.

5. A few historians, like E.D. Marcu, *Sixteenth-century Nationalism*, New York 1976, place the origins of national*ism* as an ideology in the sixteenth century; but most place it in the era of the 'democratic revolution', with R. Palmer, 'The National Idea in France before the Revolution', *Journal of the History of Ideas*, vol. 1, 1940, pp. 95–111, and J. Godechot, *France and the Atlantic Revolution of the Eighteenth Century, 1770–1779*, New York 1965; see Hans Kohn, *Prelude to Nation-States: The French and German Experience, 1789–1815*, New York 1967, and Eugene Kamenka, ed., *Nationalism. The Nature and Evolution of an Idea*, London 1976.

6. Jules Michelet, *Historical View of the French Revolution*, trans. C. Cocks, London 1890, Volume 3, chapters 10–12, pp. 382–403, cited in Hans Kohn, *Nationalism: Its Meaning and History*, Princeton 1955, pp. 97–102.

7. Ernest Renan, *Qu'est-ce qu'une nation?*, Paris 1882; Kohn, *Nationalism*, pp. 135–40.

8. Lord Acton, *Essays on Freedom and Power*, Illinois 1948, pp. 166–95.

9. Hans Gerth and C. Wright Mills, eds, *From Max Weber. Essays in Sociology*, London 1947, p. 176.

10. Max Weber, *Economy and Society*, ed. G. Roth and C. Wittich, New York 1968, vol. 3, chapter 3, p. 926.

11. Weber, *Economy and Society*, Volumes 1–2, chapter 5, p. 396. 'All history', Weber concludes, 'shows how easily political action can give rise to the belief in blood relationship, unless gross differences of anthropological type impede it' (p. 393).

12. Horace B. Davis, *Nationalism and Socialism : Marxist and Labor Theories of Nationalism*, London/New York 1967, chapters 1–3; Ian Cummins, *Marx, Engels and National Movements*, London 1980.

13. On Hegel's theory of the 'history-less peoples' and Engels's use of it, see Roman

Rosdolsky, 'Friedrich Engels und das Problem der "Geschichtslosen Völker", *Archiv für Sozialgeschichte*, vol. 4, Hannover 1964, pp. 87–282; more generally see V.C. Fisera and G. Minnerup, 'Marx, Engels and the National Question', in E. Cahm and V.C. Fisera, eds, *Socialism and Nationalism*, Volume 1, Nottingham 1978, and Walker Connor, *The National Question in Marxist-Leninist Theory and Strategy*, Princeton 1984.

14. Davis, *Nationalism*; Jacob L. Talmon, *The Myth of the Nation and the Vision of Revolution*, London 1980, Pt II, chapter 8 and Pts III & VI/2, p. 111.

15. Otto Bauer, *Die Nationalitätenfrage und die Sozialdemokratie (1908)*, Vienna 1924; Talmon, Pt III, chapter 7.

16. Carlton Hayes, *The Historical Evolution of Modern Nationalism*, New York 1931; Anthony D. Smith, *Theories of Nationalism*, London/New York 1967, especially chapters 5 and 7; Davis, *Nationalism*.

18. Hans Kohn, *Nationalism and Liberty : The Swiss Example*, New York 1957; *Pan-Slavism*; *Mind of Germany*; *Prelude to Nation-States*.

19. Edward H. Carr, *Nationalism and After*, London 1945.

20. Carr, II, p. 39; B.C. Shafer, *Nationalism, Myth and Reality*, New York 1955.

21. Carr, I.

22. Louis Snyder, *The Meaning of Nationalism*, New Brunswick 1954; *The New Nationalism*, Ithaca 1968, pp. 64–7.

23. Kenneth Minogue, *Nationalism*, London 1967, chapter 1.

24. John Plamenatz, 'Two Types of Nationalism', in Kamenka, ed., *Nationalism*.

25. Emerich Francis, 'The Ethnic Factor in Nation-building', *Social Forces*, vol. 68, 1968, pp. 338–46; also the distinction between 'ethnic' and 'political' nations in Yaroslav Krejci and V. Velimsky, *Ethnic and Political Nations in Europe*, London 1981; cf. Konstantin Symmons-Symonolewicz, *Nationalist Movements: A Comparative View*, Meadville, PA, 1970.

26. Hugh Seton-Watson, *Nations and States*, London 1977.

27. Hugh Seton-Watson, *Nationalism, Old and New*, Sydney 1965; *Nations and States*, chapters 1–2.

28. Salo W. Baron, *Modern Nationalism and Religion*, New York 1960, with an analysis of the founding fathers' views of the relationship between religion and nationalism.

29. Hugh Trevor-Roper, *Jewish and Other Nationalisms*, London 1961; Anthony D. Smith, *Theories*, chapter 2.

30. Elie Kedourie, *Nationalism*, London 1960, especially p. 101; the burden of his book, however, is to castigate nationalism as a doctrine of the Will, and one which is beyond the control even of its devotees.

31. Elie Kedourie, ed., *Nationalism in Asia and Africa*, London 1971, Introduction. See also Norman Cohn, *The Pursuit of the Millennium*, London 1957, on millennial movements in medieval Christendom. For some comments on the links between nationalism and millennialism, see Anthony D. Smith, *Nationalism in the Twentieth Century*, Oxford 1979, chapter 2.

32. Hence the anthology of nationalist writings collected in Kedourie, ed., *Nationalism in Asia and Africa*. On the role of intellectuals in nationalism, see Aleksandr Gella, ed., *The Intelligentsia and the Intellectuals*, Beverly Hills 1976, and Hugh Seton-Watson, *Neither War, Nor Peace*, London 1960, chapter 6. For class and nationalism, see B.C. Shafer, 'Bourgeois Nationalism in the Pamphlets on the Eve of the French Revolution', *Journal of Modern History*, vol. 10, 1938, pp. 19–38.

33. John Breuilly, *Nationalism and the State*, Manchester 1982, Introduction and Conclusion.

34. Breuilly, chapter 16. In this Breuilly is close to the position adopted by Tom Nairn in *The Break-up of Britain*, London 1977, chapters 2 and 9, on the intelligentsia.

35. Eric Hobsbawm and Terence Ranger, eds, *The Invention of Tradition*, Cambridge 1983.

36. P. Morgan, 'From a Death to a View: The Hunt for the Welsh Past in the Romantic Period', in Hobsbawm and Ranger, eds, *Tradition*. (Edward Williams was the real name of Iolo Morganwg.)

37. Eric Hobsbawm, 'Introduction: Inventing Traditions' (especially pp. 13–14) and chapter 7 (especially pp. 270–83) in Hobsbawm and Ranger, eds, *Tradition*. It is interesting

how attractive this idea of the nation fulfilling needs is to historians of all persuasions; it encourages the cautionary note.

38. Hugh Trevor-Roper, 'The Invention of Tradition: The Highland Tradition of Scotland', in Hobsbawm and Ranger, eds, *Tradition*.

39. Benedict Anderson, *Imagined Communities: Reflections on the Origin and Spread of Nationalism*, London 1983. I have included Anderson, though his account is as much sociological as historical, because of its attention to historical contexts and sequences of events; and his emphasis on the nation as a construct of the imagination accords well with the understanding of many historians today.

40. There is, of course, no hard and fast distinction between these three periods; and some elements, notably the sense of artifice in the phenomenon of the nation, echo throughout. Similarly, it is possible to find sociological elements in earlier periods, in Bauer, Kohn, Carr and of course Max Weber. For parallel sociological paradigms or approaches, see Anthony D. Smith, 'Nationalism and Classical Social Theory', *British Journal of Sociology*, vol. 34, 1983, pp. 19–38.

41. The term 'nation-building' really refers to a nationalist programme of building the institutions and roles of the 'nation-state'. In practice, it is more concerned with 'state-building' than 'nation-creation'. Whereas the term 'nation-formation' refers to all those processes, intended or not, that contribute to the emergence of the nation and national consciousness. These will normally include social and cultural activities of nationalists; but they may also cover the military and political activities of kings and ministers, the rates of population increase and urbanization, and the decline of churches and empires. All these may enter into a process of 'nation-formation', but not of 'nation-building'. On the role of the visual arts in late-eighteenth-century Western Europe in the formation of conceptions of the nation, see Robert Rosenblum, *Transformations in Late Eighteenth-century Art*, Princeton 1967, Robert Herbert, *David, Voltaire, Brutus and the French Revolution*, London 1972, and Anthony D. Smith, 'Patriotism and Neo-Classicism: The "Historical Revival" in French and English Painting and Sculpture, 1746–1800', unpublished Ph.D. thesis in the University of London.

42. David Taylor and Malcolm Yapp, eds, *Political Identity in South Asia*, London/Dublin 1979; T. Sathyamurthy, *Nationalism in the Contemporary World*, London 1983.

43. Hobsbawm and Ranger, eds, *Tradition*, especially pp. 6–7, 10–11, 13–14 and 303–5; also the essay by G. Mosse, 'Mass Politics and the Political Liturgy of Nationalism', in Kamenka, ed., *Nationalism*.

44. For this meaning of 'invention', see Joe Banks, *The Sociology of Social Movements*, London 1972.

45. For this statement of nationalist doctrine, and definition of nationalism as a movement, see Anthony D. Smith, 'Nationalism, A Trend Report and Annotated Bibliography', *Current Sociology*, vol. 21, no. 3, 1973, section 2. 'National sentiment' and consciousness of 'national' difference arose rather earlier, however, encouraged perhaps by the emerging European state system sanctioned by the treaty of Westphalia; see on this Aira Kemilainen, *Nationalism. Problems Concerning the Word, the Concept and Classification*, Yvaskyla 1964, and Charles Tilly, ed., *The Formation of National States in Western Europe*, Princeton 1975; see also Michael Howard, *War in European History*, London 1976.

46. For example, M.T. Walek-Czernecki, 'Le Rôle de la nationalité dans l'histoire de l'antiquité', *Bulletin of the International Committee of Historical Science*, vol. 2, no. 2, 1929, pp. 305–20; and, more critically, Moses Hadas, 'National Survival Under Hellenistic and Roman Imperialism', *Journal of History of Ideas*, vol. 11, 1950, pp. 131–9.

47. G.C. Coulton, 'Nationalism in the Middle Ages', *Cambridge Historical Journal*, vol. 5, 1935, pp. 15–40; M. Handelsman, 'Le Rôle de la nationalité dans l'histoire du Moyen Age', *Bulletin of the International Committee of Historical Science*, vol. 2, no. 2, 1929, pp. 235–46; Halvdan Koht, 'The Dawn of Nationalism in Europe', *American Historical Review*, vol. 52, 1947, pp. 265–80.

48. For example, Mario Attilio Levi, *Political Power in the Ancient World*, trans. J. Costello, London 1965; Johann Huizinga, 'Patriotism and Nationalism in European History', in *Men and Ideas: Essays on History, the Middle Ages and the Renaissance*, trans. J.S. Holmes and H. van Marle, New York 1970; and, more critically, Susan Reynolds, 'Medieval *Origines Gentium* and

the Community of the Realm', *History*, vol. 68, 1983, pp. 375–90, for whom the medieval kingdoms, though not nations in the modern sense, were based on communities of custom and descent and resembled 'ethnic states'; this is elaborated in Reynolds, *Kingdoms and Communities in Western Europe, 900–1300*, Oxford 1984.

49. Henry Tudor, *Political Myth*, London 1972; Anthony D. Smith, 'The Myth of the "Modern Nation" and the Myths of Nations', *Ethnic and Racial Studies*, vol. 11, no. 1, 1988, pp. 1–26.

50. For definitions of the 'nation', see Dankwart Rustow, *A World of Nations*, Washington DC 1967, chapter 1, and Smith, *Nationalism*, A Trend Report, section 2; for the 'modernist' and 'perennialist' images of the nation, see Anthony D. Smith, 'Ethnic Myths and Ethnic Revivals', *European Journal of Sociology*, vol. 25, 1984, pp. 283–305.

51. Seton-Watson, *Nations and States*, chapters 2–3; Tilly, *Formation of National States*, Introduction and Conclusion.

52. On processes of nation-formation in England and France, see J. Strayer, 'The Historical Experience of Nation-building in Europe,' in K.W. Deutsch and W. Foltz, eds, *Nation-building*, New York 1963; and more generally, Andrew Orridge, 'Separatist and Autonomist Nationalisms: The Structure of Regional Loyalties in the Modern State', in C. Williams, ed., *National Separatism*, Cardiff 1982. For France between 1870 and 1814, see Eugen Weber, *Peasants into Frenchmen*, London 1979.

53. John Armstrong, *Nations before Nationalism*, Chapel Hill 1982; and for the Irish case, see John Hutchinson, *The Dynamics of Cultural Nationalism; The Gaelic Revival and the Creation of the Irish Nation State*, London 1987.

54. As argued in Anthony D. Smith, *The Ethnic Origins of Nations*, Oxford 1986.

7

The National Imagination
Gopal Balakrishnan

Eric Hobsbawm, in the final chapter of a comprehensive survey on the history of nationalism, claimed that as a historical phenomenon it had passed its heyday.[1] Employing a Hegelian idiom he suggested that the nation-state was now on a declining curve of historical viability, the beginnings of its fossilization clearing the way for deeper explorations into its origins, impact, and possible futures. Subsequently, this statement has occasioned some amount of criticism on the part of those who think it flatly invalidated by the rebondissement of national causes in the former communist world. In fact Hobsbawm's statement was suitably qualified to take into account the outbreak and intensification of national conflicts in such contexts. His claim that the nation-state was no longer a vector of historical development meant only that the dominant trends of state formation, immigration, and economic life in the world's most dynamic societies were pushing beyond familiar national dimensions.

Despite the coquetting with Hegel, this vision of capitalism bypassing the nation-state is one of the central themes of classical Marxism. It has consistently held that capitalism's laws of motion would eventually 'break out' of the constricting frame of the national market by way of imperialism, ultra-imperialism or just plain old free trade. No doubt the thesis found in the *Communist Manifesto* is more complex: the claim that all that is solid, nationality included, melts into air is balanced by another: this same capitalism gives rise to the territorially fixed and juridically invariant structure of the modern bourgeois state. Although these two themes jostle with one another in the pages of the *Manifesto*, Marx and later Marxists believing that proletarian revolutions were imminent stressed the first over the second theme, for herein dialectically lay the possibility that the widening cosmopolitan scope of the market would throw up working classes of proportionate scale. The transnationalization of the productive forces that capitalism is now setting into motion is historically unprecedented. But, confounding Marx's expectations, its main thrusts seem to undermine the very bases of successful class struggle in advanced industrial societies, and unlike past defeats it is difficult to foresee the conditions under which organized working classes will rise up again 'stronger, firmer, mightier'.

The Site of Struggle

According to Marx the modern class struggle passes through a series of historical stages beginning with riots and machine-breaking and ending in nation-wide civil wars. As a preliminary condition for the successful conduct of the class struggle the unregulated competition of all against all must be suppressed within the ranks of labour. Historically this has only been accomplished by forcing the state to recognize that the purchase of labour-power on the national market will be to some significant degree the outcome of politically regulated class struggles and negotiations. The state, then, is not just the functional weapon of the possessing classes in Marx's theory, it is also the possibly unrecognized site and point of concentration of the struggle against those classes, ratifying its results. Far from opening the gates to more expansive working-class organization, the eclipse of the state has deepened its functional subordination to capital and threatens to dissolve the site and boundaries of sustainable collective action against it.

This development is difficult to understand from within the framework of Marxism – not only because of the strain it places on its theory of the state. The real challenge is rather to the anthropological basis of the Marxist theory of historical development. For Marx the irresistible scalar expansion of world capitalism could only temporarily leap beyond the dimensions of sustainable collective action against it. Capitalism's laws of motion, even while constantly pulverizing the cultural and material basis of all limited forms of membership (locality, nationality, religion), were supposed incessantly to recreate the bases of class solidarity at ever more cosmopolitan levels. No single Marxist idea is at present more discredited than this one, as even the semblance of such a dialectic has been overthrown.

Régis Debray has argued that the principal victories of the Left in this century emerged out of an unacknowledged liaison with the nation, and that the future of the Left depends on its ability to reinvent a national politics for the twenty-first century.[2] Behind this strategic assessment is the claim that the springs of political action are ultimately rooted in the pathos of national membership, for it is only in the form of a 'people' that the masses erupt into political life and make history. In this view, nations are like the 'fused groups' of Sartrean philosophy – in modern politics, existentially more gripping and decisive than class. This contrast of nation and class might at first appear to be sociologically artificial as they are not strictly comparable groups. Classes are groups which take shape around the dominant relations of exploitation which divide a society; nationality is a particular cultural or political form of existence which an entire society can assume. The argument that the proletariat emerged as a political force in modern history only as a national class certainly suggests that nation and class, far from being competing, mutually exclusive bases of organization, are, at the very least, complementary. An open conflict between the two emerged only for a brief period early this century at the level of a struggle between the competing 'myths' of national destiny and socialist internationalism. Mussolini, taking his cue from Sorel, maintained that the spectacular victories of the first over the second principle during those rare and decisive moments when they entered into open conflict, provided ample proof that international socialism was an 'inferior mythology'. This judgement, so seemingly plausible, conceals the actual reason why international socialism went under in 1914 and on other later occasions when it was put to this test: in contrast to nation-states, it has never had any substantial organizational basis, and those brief moments when it overcame this deficit will always, retrospectively, seem somewhat unreal.

The point that Debray raises does not concern the structural attributes of nations, as opposed to classes, but rather the spontaneous ideology behind peak levels of collective agency. The problem with Marxism, according to Debray, is that its central concerns do not enable it to grasp the enigmatic form which such collectivities assume, not just in the preconditions of the great *levées en masse*, but in the very possibility of organized social life.

As a characterization of Marxism this is only half true; there are in fact many rich insights into the material foundations of the pre-capitalist peasant community in the *Grundrisse*. In his intriguing sketches of what for him were the four basic types of agrarian civilization in Eurasia – Oriental, Slavic, Mediterranean and Germanic – Marx argued that the distinctive communal organization of entitlement, cooperation and exploitation formed the primordial social relationship of these pre-capitalist societies. Capitalism is premissed upon the epochal suspension and negation of the communal organization of the direct producers in their relation to nature, to each other and to their lords. Released from the semi-natural foundations of the communal provision of peasant subsistence, whole regions of the earth are plunged into an inescapable market dependence, setting in motion an incessant expansion of the productive forces.

For Marx, to the extent that social reproduction is dominated by exchange relations, the structure of society arises out of the spontaneous and anarchic interplay of market forces. In the *Philosophy of Right* Hegel argued that the modern sovereign state, while based on this condition of radical alienation, transcended it by imparting to peoples organized into political communities a higher sphere of ethical life, historical personality and collective agency. Marx, in his famous critique of this work, retorted that the political community constituted by the modern state was merely an 'imagined community', powerless and unreal. Marx conceived of this imagined community as the inverted expression of an alienated reality. In his essay *On the Jewish Question*, the modern state, 'the completed bourgeois state', is portrayed as a post-Christian community stripped of all particularistic vestiges. The elimination of ancient regime privileges and barriers to political participation made these states 'universal', that is, from a domestic perspective non-exclusive with regard to citizenship criteria. Marx did not address the obvious fact that, as long there is a multiplicity of such estates, there would have to be some particularistic principle which would legitimate citizenship in any given state, as well as delineating the boundaries between them.

Like Marx, Hegel had little sympathy for Romanticism with its celebration of customs, language, and 'authenticity'. The emphasis in Hegel is then mostly on the state, as with Marx, but its relationship to the cultural defined collectivity to which it gives form is maintained as a problem and source of tension, not extinguished as in the essay *On the Jewish Question*. 'Nations' in Hegel's theory express the phase structure of human history, each embodying in succession the unveiling of Reason taking concrete form in the customary, or what Hegel called the ethical, life of a people. In such a fashion there was a Chinese, Indian, Persian, Greek, Roman and finally German nation. The historically dominant mode of customary life contained core representations of nature, personality and freedom, and these, refracted onto a broader social structure, achieve final expression and coherence in the domain of political life. 'Nation' here is largely synonymous with civilization, that is, a largely non-ethnic and only vaguely geographic category. In fact the 'German nation' is probably *any* modern constitutional monarchy structuring market society through rational bureaucracy, estates representation and equality before the law, not Germandom in an ethnic sense. This German nation comes into its own, not when all German speakers get their own state (an objective that Hegel himself opposed after the dissolution of the empire) but rather when the plurality of Europe's leading states come to rest on this conception of modern constitutional monarchy. The diversity of peoples with respect to customs, institutions and beliefs is explained by a higher-order referent, but the connection between the low ethnographic fact and the high metaphysical passage of Reason's unfolding remains unintegrated: what is specifically 'German' about the German nation? The ethnically distinctive character of the nation is left as an opaque anthropological reminder in Hegel's theory of development.

In an early text, *The Positivity of the Christian Religion*, this problem was directly expressed. Hegel here defined the nation suggestively, if more conventionally, as a community of customs, memory and fate:

> Every nation has its own imagery, its gods, angels, devils or saints who live in the nation's traditions, whose stories and deeds the nurse tells her charges and so wins them over by impressing their imagination . . . In addition to these creatures of the imagination there also lives in the memory of most nations, especially free nations, the ancient heroes of their countries' history . . . Those heroes do not live solely in their nations' imagination; their history, the re-collection of their deeds is linked with public festivals, national games, with many of the state's domestic institutions or foreign affairs, with well-known houses and districts with public memorials and temples.[3]

The passage resembles contemporary theories, which, following the Romantic tradition, emphasize the role of myth, memory and symbol in the make-up of ethnic communities. But in contrast to all such Romanticisms, Hegel claimed that 'real' forward-moving history is not the history of such communities: world-historical progress brings with it massive erasures in the fabric of ethnic life, creating new peoples to accomplish new tasks. For Hegel the greatest transformation in history prior to the French Revolution was the rise of Christianity (or at least its Reformation). Those Germanic tribes drawn into the orbit of this Christian revolution were forever sundered from their shadowy and shapeless ethnic pasts:

> Christianity has emptied Valhalla, felled the sacred groves, extirpated the national imagery as shameful superstition, as a devilish poison and instead given us the imagery of a nation whose climate, laws, culture and interests are strange to us, whose history has no connection to our own. A David or Solomon lives in our popular imagination but our country's heroes slumber in learned history books.[4]

For the early Hegel such hybridization was lamentable, possibly reversible; later he saw it as a veritable iron law. The progressive nations in Hegel's schema have no real ethnic memories and no ethnic origins. They are the palimpsest of a radically discontinuous, nonetheless teleological history.

This excursus through Hegel is meant to reveal the tensions and displacements of emphasis involved in this interface of two images of the nation: as a general type of modern state or society, and in any given case as a particular 'ethnic' community whose outlines have been shaped by a historically ancient and ongoing intertwining of language, settlement, and religious life, a *Schicksalsgemeinschaft*. The utility of opening a discussion of nationhood with Hegel and Marx is that there is in both their theories of world history *a gap and tension between a law-like succession of general social structures and an underdetermined ethnography of peoples*. The lacuna indicated here is not specific to Marxism per se, as it in fact raises some of the central unresolved problems of classical social theory: (1) How are stable solidarities compatible with modern social relations, that is, with the normative indeterminacy and agonistic individualism associated with 'modernity'? (2) How are such collective identities experienced and reproduced? and finally (3) How do they shape the context of social and political action? Althusser once argued that the great contribution of Hegel and Marx to the understanding of history, was that they were able to conceive of it as a 'natural-historical process without a subject (telos)'. But one can not so easily eliminate the question of who are the subjects of this history and, relatedly, whether national mobilization or the class struggle is its motor.

Anderson and Imagination

Benedict Anderson's small book *Imagined Communities* is distinctive in the contemporary literature on nationalism in the centrality accorded to these issues. Composed in the shadow of the unexpected and disappointing aftermath of the victory of national liberation forces in Indo-China – the downward spiral of Cambodian genocide, Vietnamese intervention, and Sino-Vietnamese war – its melancholy reflections on the significance of these events must in retrospect be seen as uncannily clairvoyant. Published in 1983 when the Soviet bloc seemed glacially stable, Anderson came close to predicting its collapse along national lines. Viewing the Indo-Chinese tragedy as a culmination of two decades of hostility between 'actually existing socialisms', he noted that the belligerents in such conflicts were making fewer and fewer references to socialist ideology and increasingly more to 'sacred national interests'. He argued that this embrace of nationalism by regimes ostensibly committed to proletarian internationalism underlined the need for a fundamental re-evaluation of the whole problematic within which the Left had conceptualized the matter.[5]

In this Copernican spirit, Anderson suggests that nationalism should be seen not as an ideology like 'liberalism' but rather as the modern counterpart to kinship, with its own symbolically distinctive 'elementary forms'. But Anderson does not consistently stick with this association. He is also concerned to portray the nation as being open in a way that kin groups are not. To capture this openness he portrays the willingness of modern nations to absorb and 'naturalize' outsiders as analogous to the universalism of the great world religions with their enthusiasm for conversion. For most of the book, Anderson accentuates this universal side of the nation, at the expense of his original association of it with imagined kinship lineages. While this certainly makes nationalism seem more a positive thing, I will argue that it does so at the expense of neglecting its particularistic mystique – the more consistent source of its political power.

Anderson holds that nationalism, like religion, is not an 'ideology', being neither a coherent doctrine nor a form of 'false consciousness'. This foregrounding of the modern nation in older artefacts of religious community is based on a convocational experience that he sees as characteristic of both. 'All communities larger than primordial villages of face-to-face contact . . . are imagined. Communities are to be distinguished, not by their falsity/genuineness, but by the style in which they are imagined.'[6] The claim here is not that the social world is all will and representation, but that community is spontaneous ideology, impervious to theoretical debunking.

While modern liberalism has many partisans, it does not offer rich 'imagined' solutions to existential problems of suffering, sickness and death. For Anderson the enduring achievement of the great world religions was their ability to insinuate 'solutions' to these brute contingencies of existence in the modular style of the religious imagination, that is, by giving them shape and meaning in the narrative rituals of the life cycle. The frenzied devotion and disciplined asceticism which medieval Christianity could inspire had its sources in the collective ritual life of the corporately organized bodies of feudal society, not so much in its theological doctrine. Although intensely local in its identities, Christendom like Islam could be 'imagined' in its broader dimensions by the multitudes who flocked to its sacred centres and through the narratives of pilgrimage they brought back with them. But it was not pilgrimage, rather a thin stratum of Latin literati, that imparted a semblance of uniformity to the representations through which the medieval world experienced and conceptualized itself. Against a backdrop of a largely illiterate, dialect-divided agrarian civilization, this Latin language uniformity gave the church an impressive institutional cohesion, allowing it to rise above the power of all secular princes.

It is in the early modern breakdown of this encompassing ecclesiastic edifice that Anderson locates the cultural origins of the modern nation. The first spectacular crack, the Reformation, was made possible by the expansion of vernacular literacy from the fifteenth century. Protestantism used the vernacular to devastating effect in its pamphlet war against a church obstinately committed to Latin, allowing it to reach far beyond the thin social layer of Latin literates. And although doctrinally the writings of Luther, Calvin, and lesser publicists only occasionally raised any national issues, Anderson argues that in a sense the medium was the message. Literate civil societies were shaped and more sharply differentiated from one another as the mass-production techniques of early modern 'print-capitalism' standardized the norms and increased the density of social intercourse within particular vernacular languages.

But how do these cultural formations come to be imagined as 'nations' in Anderson's sense, that is, how do they appropriate the experience of the sacred attributed to world religion and give it civic and territorial shape? A recurring theme in the book is Marxism's failure to address the 'sacred' dimension of the nation – the longing for immortality becoming a will to membership in an imperishable collective. The sacred is held to be an anthropological constant of organized social life; the modern world is in this respect no exception, its novelty consisting only in the fact that the national form it assumes is essentially secular. While the sacred and the secular might seem to be antithetical orders, for Anderson they strikingly intersect in the peak symbolic artefact of the nation-state, the Tomb of the Unknown Soldier. This strange civic deity is the object of a ghostly communion reminiscent of an ancestor cult, but here intimacy is crossed with the anonymity of modern society – it does not seem to matter that there is no one in the vault.

However successfully, this linking of the national and the religious radically reverses Max Weber's verdict on modernity. Instead of an iron cage, the arrival of the modern social order gives rise to a collective re-enchantment specific to it. Anderson attempts to resolve the theoretical tension mentioned earlier between two conflicting images of the nation with the term 'imagined community': society is by necessity both a social structure and an artefact of the imagination, and not even the arrival of capitalism extinguishes this equation. From this, the significance of the term 'print-capitalism' becomes apparent: it is both a general structure – a capitalism – and a unique culture, one moreover that is imagined as sacred. This is not just Weber stood on his head; it is more strikingly a departure from the Marx of the *Manifesto* as well. Instead of capitalism, the great profaner of all that is sacred, there is print-capitalism, the matrix and crucible of its secular reconstitution.

How convincing is this attempted inversion? Its central argument is essentially correct. The thesis that bureaucracy and capitalism have effectively disenchanted the world fails to explain why people have been rather often willing to die for their nation. Anderson argues that this fact alone suggests that the modern social order can evoke powerful sacred imaginings. The national imagination deals, then, in high stakes; but the immortality that it offers seems rather pale in comparison to religion – a

monument to your heroic death at very best. Unlike prophets, nationalists cannot actually promise immortality. It might be thought that an
immortality which is only figurative, insinuated but never actually
promised, could not really motivate sacrifice. But if we move away from
the analogy to religion and instead consider the affective structure of kinship bonds, Anderson's argument seems immediately more plausible.
Unfortunately the latter analogy is only fitfully developed. If there is an
anthropologically invariant desire to overcome death through artefacts
which evoke social continuity, it is surely the family and not religion
which more universally fulfils this role. Despite the antiquity of ancestor
cults, the intensity and naturalness of the blood connection does not
rely on any belief in other-worldly rewards. Atheists, nationalists, and
Christians in equal numbers rush to save their children from burning
houses. Only quite late in the book does Anderson ground this equation
between kinship and the imagined affinities of the nation:

> While it is true that in the last two decades the idea of the family-as-articulated-
> power-structure has been much written about, such a conception is certainly
> foreign to the overwhelming bulk of mankind. Rather, the family has been tra-
> ditionally conceived as the domain of disinterested love and solidarity. So too,
> if historians, diplomats, politicians, and social scientists are quite at ease with
> the idea of 'national interest', for most ordinary people of whatever class the
> whole point of the nation is that it is interestless. Just for that reason, it can ask
> for sacrifices.[7]

While representations of the nation heavily depend on familial motifs,
the figure of the nation as an imagined kinship structure, as suggested
earlier, is in fact not compatible with the book's focus on religious community. It is important to remember that, despite the melancholic tone of
the introduction, Anderson has an almost uniformly positive view of
nationalism, maintaining that it is political love and solidarity which sustain it, not hate and invidious comparison to the Enemy. In contrast, the
narrower affinities of kinship seem too dependent on rigid genealogical
motifs to ground so generous a conception of the nation. The analogy to
world religion serves to convey better an image of the nation which is
open, even cosmopolitan in its horizons. Pointing to the affinities
between religious conversion and political naturalization, he suggests
that both are premised on conceptions of membership which *cancel* the
raw fatalities of birth, kinship, and race. Ironically, this rather positive
equation takes its terms from Lord Acton's famous polemic against
nationalism. Shaken by the Risorgimento, Acton argued that nationalism
represented a reversion to the unethical premises of the ancient world,
where 'merely natural' bonds of kinship and ethnic descent provided the
basis of political association. In contrast he held that 'Christianity rejoices

at the mixture of races.' For Anderson, it is modern nations which rejoice in a sort of imagined mixture of races.

This depiction of nationalism is certainly foreign to many on the Left who see its true face in the Nazi, the Khmer Rouge guerrilla or the Serbian militiaman. Circumventing such figures, Anderson relies instead on a strategy often less than convincing, of rummaging through nationalist poetry and anthems to demonstrate that 'it is astonishing how insignificant the element of hatred is in these expressions of national feeling'.[8] The sharp distinction he draws between nationalism and fascism relies not simply on this charitable hermeneutic of the themes of patriotic fraternity, but in his very selection of case studies. These draw heavily on the eighteenth- and nineteenth-century creole revolts in the Americas with their constitutions and high republican ideals. The principle if not the practice of this classical republicanism constitutes for him the paradigmatic and essential form of nationhood. These were societies which despite their tremendous ethnic and racial diversity and division were imagined as national communities, and invented broad and inclusive genealogies to match their civic and territorial dimensions:

> The son of an Italian immigrant to New York will find ancestors in the Pilgrim Fathers . . . Spanish-speaking mestizo Mexicans trace their ancestries, not to Castilian conquistadors, but to half-obliterated Aztecs, Mayans, Toltecs and Zapotecs . . . San Martín's edict baptizing Quechua-speaking Indians as 'Peruvians' – a movement that has affinities with religious conversion – is exemplary. For it shows that from the start the nation was conceived in language, not in blood . . .[9]

But there are several ways in which nations are not 'conceived in language'. Throughout the world the boundaries of nation-states and the boundaries of linguistic distributions rarely overlap – many nations share the same language; many states are officially multilingual; in some the most official language is no one's mother tongue. If the first point raises no insurmountable difficulties for Anderson's claim, the second and particularly the third suggest that language is only one dimension of the 'nationality principle'. More problematically it raises the question as to whether there are *any* cultural attributes which uniformly designate nationhood.

Language is stressed by Anderson because it defines membership in ways that are fundamentally connected to his specific conception of the nation. Language is intimate and natural; it is thus very deeply associated in the minds of an overwhelmingly monoglot humanity with who one essentially is. Added to this, the fixity and palpability of these cultural formations generate an image of the nation as an eternal collective. (Very few conceive of even a distant future in which their language is not spoken, and more interestingly, because simply false, may have difficulty imagining a past in which their language did not exist.) And yet, despite this intimacy, it defines a form of collective membership which, unlike race or even possibly ethnicity, can be acquired:

> If every language is acquirable, its acquisition requires a real portion of a person's life: each new conquest is measured against shortening days. What limits one's access to other languages is not their imperviousness but one's own mortality. Hence a certain privacy to all languages . . . Seen as both a *historical* fatality and as a community imagined through language, the nation presents itself as simultaneously open and closed.[10]

More than even our position in the relations of production, it is language which circumscribes our existence, and it is for this reason, Anderson argues, that print-capitalism has been the principal determination of social being in the modern world.

The Nation in Arms

The problem for Anderson's thesis is that the cultural affinities shaped by print-capitalism do not in themselves seem sufficiently resonant to generate the colossal sacrifices that modern peoples are at times willing to make for their nation. It is relatively easy to see why people might be willing to die for their religion – weightier issues than mere life on this earth hang in the balance. It is rather harder to see how civil societies conducting their affairs in a vernacular could ever inspire the same pathos. If societies are imagined in sacred idioms, then vernacular sociability seems to offer very little in this department when compared to religion. Anderson attempts to address this by claiming that the social organization of language in the modern world (schools, newspapers, novels) gives rise to a belief in the antiquity and imperishability of the nation. His argument is not as strong as it seems, as such a belief could not be the basis of a compulsion to make sacrifices for my nation. I could after all believe that French will be spoken in the twenty-fifth century, but this is not the same thing as making the more affectively weighty statement 'France is eternal'. Only the latter evokes a project, a struggle and a call to arms, and all this has arguably little to do with language.

'Collective sacrifice', 'fatality', 'the Tomb of the Unknown Soldier' – this is the language and imagery of war. But the relationship of war to the pathos of national membership is only fitfully addressed by Anderson, no doubt discomfited by its implications.[11] This is not because the state is absent from Anderson's treatment of the 'cultural roots of the nation'. In fact, there is a lengthy discussion of the role of absolutist state formation in shaping the cultural grid of what would later become nations. But here the rule of the state is strictly analogous to that of print-capitalism. The mushrooming bureaucracies of early modern Europe were simply an alternate path to the vernacular sociability which elsewhere emerged out of the Reformation and the market. The state, then, stirs the national imagination merely by giving territorial shape to a language of public life. But just as it is doubtful whether the cultural affinities produced by print-capitalism could be sufficient to generate resonant, let alone sacred, idioms of collectivity, so the same is arguably true of these strangely pacific states. Without the possibility of sacrifice it is doubtful whether the nation evokes the affective peaks of collective belonging that Anderson attributes to the national imagination.

Weber, always sensitive to the role of domination and force in history, formulated the relation between state and national identity differently, and more realistically:

> The political community is one of those communities whose action includes, at least under normal circumstances, coercion through jeopardy of life and freedom of movement. The individual is expected ultimately to face death in the group interest. This gives to the political community its particular pathos and raises its enduring emotional foundations. The community of political destiny, i.e. above all of common political struggle of life and death, has given rise to groups with joint memories which have often had a deeper impact than the ties of merely cultural, linguistic, or ethnic community. It is this 'community of memories' which constitutes the ultimately decisive element of national consciousness.[12]

For Weber, like Hegel, the modern state possesses a historical purpose and collective meaning because it organizes a community into a sovereign polity ready for war. It is during war that the nation is imagined as a community embodying ultimate values. The claim that the nation is an imaginatively resonant cultural artefact is compelling, but are nations always so stirring? During times of peace, if someone were to make the claim that his imminent death had ceased to trouble him because 'France is eternal', many people would think he'd gone mad. If he formulated the same high-minded and dramatic sentiments en route to battle, few would point out the fault in his logic, as in this context, and perhaps only in this one, such a statement becomes, miraculously, sensible. Ironically, after a positive portrayal of nationalism as the great political passion and love of the modern age, Anderson concedes that in fact war is the great test of its social imagination:

> [T]he great wars of this century are extraordinary not so much in the unprecedented scale on which they permitted people to kill, as in the colossal

numbers persuaded to lay down their lives . . . The idea of the ultimate sacrifice comes only with the idea of purity, through fatality . . . Dying for one's
country, which usually one does not choose, assumes a political grandeur
which dying for the Labour Party, the American Medical Association, or perhaps even Amnesty International cannot rival, for these are all bodies one can
join and leave at easy will.[13]

In this passage there are two themes which cut against the general tenor
of Anderson's idea of the nation. Instead of the uplifting spectacle of
peasants becoming Frenchmen, or Quechuas becoming Peruvians, the
power of nationalism is by implication linked to the perpetuation of a sort
of state of nature between nations. And the purity and fatality of national
imaginings do not arise spontaneously from the social organization of
vernacular language, but through the risks of membership in a 'community of life and death'. Imagined nationhood, with its sacral affinities to
religion, does not always seem to be deeply rooted in the everyday life of
modern society. Under normal conditions, individuals belong to, and
identify with, a vast number of overlapping associations, membership in
which can be, to some degree, instrumentally evaluated. This means that
most of the time the experience of national membership is faint and
superficial. Only in struggle does the nation cease to be an informal, con-
testable and taken-for-granted frame of reference, and become a
community which seizes hold of the imagination. This is not simply a
question of militarism. Anderson is right to argue that the history of
nationalism cannot be reduced to what he describes as its official, state-
sponsored versions. The mobilization of a people on a national basis has
just as often played the decisive role in the more subaltern history of
struggle against colonialism and foreign occupation. The era of Great
Power nationalism with its inter-imperialist wars came to an end around
1945; thirty years later anti-colonial nationalism as a force in world politics peaked. While these developments have not made the nation-state
irrelevant, they have made the future of a political imagination which sees
both power and emancipation in national terms more uncertain.[14]

In contemporary Western Europe after fifty years of a thorough pacification of interstate relations, it is difficult to imagine the nation in
sacred terms. Squabbles over tariffs, agricultural subsidies and an occasional football riot are no substitute for the nation in arms. The postwar
settlement stripped what had once been Great Powers of empires, institutionally distinctive designs and full geopolitical sovereignty. Even as
that settlement now comes undone its institutional legacy is probably
irreversible – the neutralization of any danger of war in this theatre has
closed off the sources of the great political enchantments of the previous
period. It is not just, then, the unleashing of capitalism on continental
and planetary scales which has put a question mark over the future of the

nation-state; the social and cultural atmosphere after such an unprecedently long peace is unable to sustain themes of high drama in the political sphere. In a Europe where 'coercion through jeopardy of life and freedom of movement' is a fate reserved only for the immigrant worker, new social and cultural divisions have come to replace national ones.[15]

But for Anderson, the vector of historical development does not bring a kinder and gentler world. The transnationalization of the productive forces does not extinguish the desire for stable, clear and authentic 'identities'. As the patterns of contemporary cultural and economic life relentlessly frustrate the desire and need to live in communities, these become 'imagined' only in the bad sense, that is, disconnected from any sense of social reality, civic commitment and the possibility of transformative collective agency. No longer based on any substantial experiences of a shared political destiny, the longing for national identity becomes a taste for a pseudo-archaic ethnicity cranked out in made-to-order forms by the heritage industry. Anderson explains how such pastiches can evoke a sense of ersatz belonging, despite their superficiality:

> [C]onsider the well-known photograph of the lonely Peloponnesian *Gastarbeiter* sitting in his dingy room in, say, Frankfurt. The solitary decoration on his wall is a resplendent Lufthansa travel poster of the Parthenon, which invites him, in German, to take a 'sun-drenched holiday' in Greece. He may well never have seen the Parthenon, but framed by Lufthansa the poster confirms for him and for any visitor a Greek identity that perhaps only Frankfurt has encouraged him to assume.[16]

We began by pointing out that Marxism lacked a concrete conception of a *people*, a political anthropology. Does this now cease to be a deficit if nationalism itself becomes something increasingly unconcrete, 'spectral'? Unfortunately, this would only be true if, to paraphrase Marx, such spectres did not weigh so much. While the implied claim that there was once an authentic nationalism free of sentimental dross or ideological manipulation may be questionable, Anderson challenges those who would too easily see the bypassing of the nation-state as the long-awaited coming of the 'open society' – liberal, tolerant and multicultural. It is argued that there are in fact limits to how 'open' society can be: beyond these limits the imagination and solidarity falter. Anderson began his book by contrasting cosmopolitan ideologies like liberalism and socialism with the elementary forms of social community. But these ideologies have always tacitly relied on an image of society as an ultimately finite association. The successes, failures and compromises of both traditions stem in large measure from the fact that these communities are imagined as nations in the modern world, and that the only versions of these creeds which have any measure of practical success are those which have tailored their message to the limited sympathies of nations. Anderson's book is a reminder that, at its best, imagined nationhood in all its crudity has been the entry ticket for the wretched of the earth into world history. This is because the nation state is the place in which the stakes of this century's great class struggles were defined. The reason why it took place in nation-state frameworks, I argued, was a matter of the scale of effective collective agency. But there is another way of approaching the same problem which Benjamin suggested in his Twelfth Thesis on History:

> Not man or men but the struggling oppressed class itself is the depository of historical knowledge. In Marx it appears as the last enslaved class, as the avenger that completes the task of liberation in the name of generations of the downtrodden. This conviction, which had a brief resurgence in the Spartacist group, has always been objectionable to Social-Democrats . . . Social-Democracy thought fit to assign to the working class the role of the redeemer of future generations, in this way cutting off the sinews of its greatest strength. This training made the working class forget both its hatred and spirit of sacrifice, for both are nourished by the image of enslaved ancestors rather than liberated grandchildren.

Although Benjamin wanted to harness this memory of the past to Spartacism, it is clear that when one speaks of one's dead ancestors one is talking about the nation and not international socialism. Even so, this was not Benjamin's last word on the subject of memory and revolutionary agency. He also suggested that the Revolution could not be simply conceived of as a retrieval of a fragmented mythical past in Thesis 14 where he compares the bourgeois (and in this context I think it is appropriate to say 'national') to the proletarian revolution.

> The French Revolution viewed itself as Rome incarnate. It evoked ancient Rome the way fashion evokes costumes of the past. Fashion has a flair for the topical, no matter where it stirs in the thickets of long ago; it is a tiger's leap into the past. This jump [i.e. the bourgeois or national revolution] however takes place in an arena where the ruling class gives the commands. The same leap in the open air of history is the dialectical one, which is how Marx understood the revolution.

The nation became a central figure in the radical political imagination of the twentieth century. When, in the next century, people once again begin to imagine society transformed, nationality will likely play a less conspicuous role. Will the claim that the working class is still the decisive agent of any radical politics seem even less plausible than now? The point of citing Benjamin in this context is to suggest that references to the Owl of Minerva in predictions about the nation-state, or class politics, might turn out to be premature, confounded by some unforeseen dialectical surprise.

Notes

1. Eric J. Hobsbawm, *Nations and Nationalism since 1788*, London 1990.

2. Régis Debray, 'Marxism and the National Question', *New Left Review* 105 (September–October 1977), p. 33.

3. Cited after Shlomo Avineri, *Hegel's Theory of the Modern State*, Cambridge 1974, p. 21.

4. Ibid., p. 20.

5. Benedict Anderson, *Imagined Communities*, first edn, London 1983; revised and extended edn, London 1991.

6. *Imagined Communities*, revised edn, p. 6.

7. Ibid., p. 131.

8. Ibid., p. 129.

9. Ibid., pp. 133, 140, 133.

10. Ibid., pp. 135, 133.

11. His examples on this point are revealing. As indicated earlier, he draws very heavily on anti-colonial and national liberation struggles, in which it is claimed that fraternal love of one's country trumps hatred of the colonizing people and their culture, as the source of national solidarity. But if this is true (and Franz Fanon for one thought that in even these cases the record was mixed), can the same be said of war between states? The introductory reflections on the bewilderingly abrupt passage in the Indochinese theatre from anti-imperialist struggle to interstate conflagration suggests that powerful hatreds and powerful loves are not so easily separated.

12. Max Weber, *Economy and Society*, Berkeley 1978 p. 903.

13. *Imagined Communities*, p. 132.

14. This is not to say that national cultures are necessarily militaristic. The nation is imagined most often in defensive postures, however far this may be from the truth. Of course many states today are utterly incapable of waging war or, more rarely, are truly pacific. But even in these cases, ancient battles loom large in the national imagination.

15. Does the rise of the far Right signal a reversal of these developments? The striking thing here is the degree to which older national animosities have effectively disappeared from within their ranks, replaced now by a common hatred of the non-European immigrant. But this hatred of the culture of foreigners, not 'redeemed' by love of one's own – is it nationalism?

16. Benedict Anderson, 'Exodus', *Critical Inquiry*, winter 1994, p. 322.

8

Whose Imagined Community?

Partha Chatterjee

Nationalism has once more appeared on the agenda of world affairs. Almost every day, state leaders and political analysts in Western countries declare that with 'the collapse of communism' (that is the term they use; what they mean is presumably the collapse of Soviet socialism), the principal danger to world peace is now posed by the resurgence of nationalism in different parts of the world. Since in this day and age a phenomenon has first to be recognized as a 'problem' before it can claim the attention of people whose business it is to decide what should concern the public, nationalism seems to have regained sufficient notoriety for it to be liberated from the arcane practices of 'area specialists' and made once more a subject of general debate.

However, this very mode of its return to the agenda of world politics has, it seems to me, hopelessly prejudiced the discussion on the subject. In the 1950s and 1960s, nationalism was still regarded as a feature of the victorious anti-colonial struggles in Asia and Africa. But simultaneously, as the new institutional practices of economy and polity in the postcolonial states were disciplined and normalized under the conceptual rubrics of 'development' and 'modernization', nationalism was already being relegated to the domain of the particular histories of this or that colonial empire. And in those specialized histories defined by the unprepossessing contents of colonial archives, the emancipatory aspects of nationalism were undermined by countless revelations of secret deals, manipulations, and the cynical pursuit of private interests. By the 1970s, nationalism had become a matter of ethnic politics, the reason why people in the Third World killed each other – sometimes in wars between regular armies, sometimes, more distressingly, in cruel and often protracted civil wars, and increasingly, it seemed, by technologically sophisticated and virtually unstoppable acts of terrorism. The leaders of the African struggles against colonialism and racism had spoiled their records by becoming heads of corrupt, fractious, and often brutal regimes; Gandhi had been appropriated by such marginal cults as pacifism and vegetarianism; and even Ho Chi Minh in his moment of glory was caught in the unyielding polarities of the Cold War. Nothing, it would seem, was left in the legacy of nationalism to make people in the Western world feel good about it.

This recent genealogy of the idea explains why nationalism is now viewed as a dark, elemental, unpredictable force of primordial nature threatening the orderly calm of civilized life. What had once been successfully relegated to the outer peripheries of the earth is now seen picking its way back toward Europe, through the long-forgotten provinces of the Habsburg, the tsarist, and the Ottoman empires. Like drugs, terrorism, and illegal immigration, it is one more product of the Third World that the West dislikes but is powerless to prohibit.

In light of the current discussions on the subject in the media, it is surprising to recall that not many years ago nationalism was generally considered one of Europe's most magnificent gifts to the rest of the world. It is also not often remembered today that the two greatest wars of the twentieth century, engulfing as they did virtually every part of the globe, were brought about by Europe's failure to manage its own ethnic nationalisms. Whether of the 'good' variety or the 'bad', nationalism was entirely a product of the political history of Europe. Notwithstanding the celebration of the various unifying tendencies in Europe today and of the political consensus in the West as a whole, there may be in the recent amnesia on the origins of nationalism more than a hint of anxiety about whether it has quite been tamed in the land of its birth.

In all this time, the 'area specialists', the historians of the colonial world, working their way cheerlessly through musty files of administrative reports and official correspondence in colonial archives in London or Paris or Amsterdam, had of course never forgotten how nationalism arrived in the colonies. Everyone agreed that it was a European import; the debates in the 1960s and 1970s in the historiographies of Africa or India or Indonesia were about what had become of the idea and who was responsible for it. These debates between a new generation of nationalist historians and those whom they dubbed 'colonialists' were vigorous and often acrimonious, but they were largely confined to the specialized territories of 'area studies'; no one else took much notice of them.

Ten years ago, it was one such area specialist who managed to raise once more the question of the origin and spread of nationalism in the framework of a universal history. Benedict Anderson demonstrated with much subtlety and originality that nations were not the determinate products of given sociological conditions such as language or race or religion; they had been, in Europe and everywhere else in the world, imagined into existence.[1] He also described some of the major institutional forms through which this imagined community came to acquire concrete shape, especially the institutions of what he so ingeniously called 'print-capitalism'. He then argued that the historical experience of nationalism in Western Europe, in the Americas, and in Russia had supplied for all subsequent nationalisms a set of modular forms from which nationalist elites in Asia and Africa had chosen the ones they liked.

Anderson's book has been, I think, the most influential in the last few years in generating new theoretical ideas on nationalism, an influence that of course, it is needless to add, is confined almost exclusively to academic writings. Contrary to the largely uninformed exoticization of nationalism in the popular media in the West, the theoretical tendency represented by Anderson certainly attempts to treat the phenomenon as part of the universal history of the modern world.

I have one central objection to Anderson's argument. If nationalisms in the rest of the world have to choose their imagined community from certain 'modular' forms already made available to them by Europe and the Americas, what do they have left to imagine? History, it would seem, has decreed that we in the postcolonial world shall only be perpetual consumers of modernity. Europe and the Americas, the only true subjects of history, have thought out on our behalf not only the script of colonial enlightenment and exploitation, but also that of our anti-colonial resistance and postcolonial misery. Even our imaginations must remain forever colonized.

I object to this argument not for any sentimental reason. I object because I cannot reconcile it with the evidence on anti-colonial nationalism. The most powerful as well as the most creative results of the nationalist imagination in Asia and Africa are posited not on an identity but rather on a *difference* with the 'modular' forms of the national society propagated by the modern West. How can we ignore this without reducing the experience of anti-colonial nationalism to a caricature of itself?

To be fair to Anderson, it must be said that he is not alone to blame. The difficulty, I am now convinced, arises because we have all taken the claims of nationalism to be a *political* movement much too literally and much too seriously.

In India, for instance, any standard nationalist history will tell us that nationalism proper began in 1885 with the formation of the Indian National Congress. It might also tell us that the decade preceding this was a period of preparation, when several provincial political associations were formed. Prior to that, from the 1820s to the 1870s, was the period of 'social reform', when colonial enlightenment was beginning to 'modernize' the customs and institutions of a traditional society and the political spirit was still very much that of collaboration with the colonial regime: nationalism had still not emerged.

This history, when submitted to a sophisticated sociological analysis, cannot but converge with Anderson's formulations. In fact, since it seeks to replicate in its own history the history of the modern state in Europe, nationalism's self-representation will inevitably corroborate Anderson's decoding of the nationalist myth. I think, however, that, as history, nationalism's autobiography is fundamentally flawed.

By my reading, anti-colonial nationalism creates its own domain of sovereignty within colonial society well before it begins its political battle with the imperial power. It does this by dividing the world of social institutions and practices into two domains – the material and the spiritual. The material is the domain of the 'outside', of the economy and of statecraft, of science and technology, a domain where the West had proved its superiority and the East had succumbed. In this domain, then, Western superiority had to be acknowledged and its accomplishments carefully studied and replicated. The spiritual, on the other hand, is an 'inner' domain bearing the 'essential' marks of cultural identity. The greater one's success in imitating Western skills in the material domain, therefore, the greater the need to preserve the distinctness of one's spiritual culture. This formula is, I think, a fundamental feature of anti-colonial nationalisms in Asia and Africa.[2]

There are several implications. First, nationalism declares the domain of the spiritual its sovereign territory and refuses to allow the colonial power to intervene in that domain. If I may return to the Indian example, the period of 'social reform' was actually made up of two distinct phases. In the earlier phase, Indian reformers looked to the colonial authorities to bring about by state action the reform of traditional institutions and customs. In the latter phase, although the need for change was not disputed, there was a strong resistance to allowing the colonial state to intervene in matters affecting 'national culture'. The second phase, in my argument, was already the period of nationalism.

The colonial state, in other words, is kept out of the 'inner' domain of national culture; but it is not as though this so-called spiritual domain is left unchanged. In fact, here nationalism launches its most powerful, creative, and historically significant project: to fashion a 'modern' national culture that is nevertheless not Western. If the nation is an imagined community, then this is where it is brought into being. In this, its true and essential domain, the nation is already sovereign, even when the state is in the hands of the colonial power. The dynamics of this historical project is completely missed in conventional histories in which the story of nationalism begins with the contest for political power.

I wish to highlight here several areas within the so-called spiritual domain that nationalism transforms in the course of its journey. I will confine my illustrations to Bengal, with whose history I am most familiar.

The first such area is that of language. Anderson is entirely correct in his suggestion that it is 'print-capitalism' which provides the new institutional space for the development of the modern 'national' language.[3] However, the specificities of the colonial situation do not allow a simple transposition of European patterns of development. In Bengal, for instance, it is at the initiative of the East India Company and the European missionaries that the first printed books are produced in Bengali at the end of the eighteenth century and the first narrative prose compositions commissioned at the beginning of the nineteenth. At the same time, the first half of the nineteenth century is when English completely displaces Persian as the language of bureaucracy and emerges as the most powerful vehicle of intellectual influence on a new Bengali elite. The crucial moment in the development of the modern Bengali language comes, however, in midcentury, when this bilingual elite makes it a cultural project to provide its mother tongue with the necessary linguistic equipment to enable it to become an adequate language for 'modern' culture. An entire institutional network of printing presses, publishing houses, newspapers, magazines, and literary societies is created around this time, *outside* the purview of the state and the European missionaries, through which the new language, modern and standardized, is given shape. The bilingual intelligentsia came to think of its own language as belonging to that inner domain of cultural identity, from which the colonial intruder had to be kept out; language therefore became a zone over which the nation first had to declare its sovereignty and then had to transform in order to make it adequate for the modern world.

Here the modular influences of modern European languages and literatures did not necessarily produce similar consequences. In the case of the new literary genres and aesthetic conventions, for instance, whereas European influences undoubtedly shaped explicit critical discourse, it was also widely believed that European conventions were inappropriate and misleading in judging literary productions in modern Bengali. To this day there is a clear hiatus in this area between the terms of academic criticism and those of literary practice. To give an example, let me briefly discuss Bengali drama.

Drama is the modern literary genre that is the least commended on aesthetic grounds by critics of Bengali literature. Yet it is the form in which the bilingual elite has found its largest audience. When it appeared in its modern form in the middle of the nineteenth century, the new Bengali drama had two models available to it: one, the modern European drama as it had developed since Shakespeare and Molière, and two, the virtually forgotten corpus of Sanskrit drama, now restored to a reputation of classical excellence because of the praises showered on it by Orientalist scholars from Europe. The literary criteria that would presumably direct the new drama into the privileged domain of a modern national culture were therefore clearly set by modular forms provided by Europe. But the performative practices of the new institution of the public theatre made it impossible for those criteria to be applied to plays written for the theatre. The conventions that would enable a play to succeed on the Calcutta stage were very different from the conventions approved by critics schooled in the traditions of European drama. The tensions have not been resolved to this day. What thrives as mainstream public theatre in West Bengal or Bangladesh today is modern urban theatre, national and clearly distinguishable from 'folk theatre'. It is produced and largely patronized by the literate urban middle classes. Yet their aesthetic conventions fail to meet the standards set by the modular literary forms adopted from Europe.

Even in the case of the novel, that celebrated artifice of the nationalist imagination in which the community is made to live and love in 'homogeneous time',[4] the modular forms do not necessarily have an easy passage. The novel was a principal form through which the bilingual elite in Bengal fashioned a new narrative prose. In the devising of this prose, the influence of the two available models – modern English and classical Sanskrit – was obvious. And yet, as the practice of the form gained greater popularity, it was remarkable how frequently in the course of their narrative Bengali novelists shifted from the disciplined forms of authorial prose to the direct recording of living speech. Looking at the pages of some of the most popular novels in Bengali, it is often difficult to tell whether one is reading a novel or a play. Having created a modern prose language in the fashion of the approved modular forms, the literati, in their search for artistic truthfulness, apparently found it necessary to escape as often as possible the rigidities of that prose.

The desire to construct an aesthetic form that was modern and national, and yet recognizably different from the Western, was shown in perhaps its most exaggerated shape in the efforts in the early twentieth century of the so-called Bengal school of art. It was through these efforts that, on the one hand, an institutional space was created for the modern professional artist in India, as distinct from the traditional craftsman, for the dissemination through exhibition and print of the products of art and for the creation of a public schooled in the new aesthetic norms. Yet this agenda for the construction of a modernized artistic space was accompanied, on the other hand, by a fervent ideological programme for an art that was distinctly 'Indian', that is, different from the 'Western'.[5] Although the specific style developed by the Bengal school for a new Indian art failed to hold its ground for very long, the fundamental agenda posed by its efforts continues to be pursued to this day, namely, to develop an art that would be modern and at the same time recognizably Indian.

Alongside the institutions of print-capitalism was created a new network of secondary schools. Once again, nationalism sought to bring this area under its jurisdiction long before the domain of the state had become a matter of contention. In Bengal, from the second half of the nineteenth century, it was the new elite that took the lead in mobilizing a 'national' effort to start schools in every part of the province and then to produce a suitable educational literature. Coupled with print-capitalism, the institutions of secondary education provided the space where the new language and literature were both generalized and normalized – outside the domain of the state. It was only when this space was opened up, outside the influence of both the colonial state and the European missionaries, that it became legitimate for women, for instance, to be sent to school. It was also in this period, from around the turn of the century, that the University of Calcutta was turned from an institution of colonial education to a distinctly national institution, in its curriculum, its faculty, and its sources of funding.[6]

Another area in that inner domain of national culture was the family. The assertion here of autonomy and difference was perhaps the most dramatic. The European criticism of Indian 'tradition' as barbaric had focused to a large extent on religious beliefs and practices, especially those relating to the treatment of women. The early phase of 'social reform' through the agency of the colonial power had also concentrated on the same issues. In that early phase, therefore, this area had been identified as essential to 'Indian tradition'. The nationalist move began by disputing the choice of agency. Unlike the early reformers, nationalists were not prepared to allow the colonial state to legislate the reform of 'traditional' society. They asserted that only the nation itself could have the right to intervene in such an essential aspect of its cultural identity.

As it happened, the domain of the family and the position of women underwent considerable change in the world of the nationalist middle class. It was undoubtedly a new patriarchy that was brought into existence, different from the 'traditional' order but also explicitly claiming to be different from the 'Western' family. The 'new woman' was to be modern, but she would also have to display the signs of national tradition and therefore would be essentially different from the 'Western' woman.

*

The history of nationalism as a political movement tends to focus primarily on its contest with the colonial power in the domain of the outside, that is, the material domain of the state. This is a different history from the one I have outlined. It is also a history in which nationalism has no option but to choose its forms from the gallery of 'models' offered by European and American nation-states: 'difference' is not a viable criterion in the domain of the material.

In this outer domain, nationalism begins its journey (after, let us remember, it has already proclaimed its sovereignty in the inner domain) by inserting itself into a new public sphere constituted by the processes and forms of the modern (in this case, colonial) state. In the beginning, nationalism's task is to overcome the subordination of the colonized middle class, that is, to challenge the 'rule of colonial difference' in the domain of the state. The colonial state, we must remember, was not just the agency that brought the modular forms of the modern state to the colonies; it was also an agency that was destined never to fulfil the normalizing mission of the modern state because the premiss of its power was a rule of colonial difference, namely, the preservation of the alienness of the ruling group.

As the institutions of the modern state were elaborated in the colony, especially in the second half of the nineteenth century, the ruling European groups found it necessary to lay down – in law-making, in the bureaucracy, in the administration of justice, and in the recognition by the state of a legitimate domain of public opinion – the precise difference between the rulers and the ruled. If Indians had to be admitted into the judiciary, could they be allowed to try Europeans? Was it right that Indians should enter the civil service by taking the same examinations as British graduates? If European newspapers in India were given the right of free speech, could the same apply to native newspapers? Ironically, it became the historical task of nationalism, which insisted on its own marks of cultural difference with the West, to demand that there be no rule of difference in the domain of the state.

In time, with the growing strength of nationalist politics, this domain became more extensive and internally differentiated and finally took on the form of the national, that is, postcolonial, state. The dominant elements of its self-definition, at least in postcolonial India, were drawn from the ideology of the modern liberal-democratic state.

In accordance with liberal ideology, the public was now distinguished from the domain of the private. The state was required to protect the inviolability of the private self in relation to other private selves. The legitimacy of the state in carrying out this function was to be guaranteed by its indifference to concrete differences between private selves – differences, that is, of race, language, religion, class, caste, and so forth.

The trouble was that the moral-intellectual leadership of the nationalist elite operated in a field constituted by a very different set of distinctions – those between the spiritual and the material, the inner and the outer, the essential and the inessential. That contested field over which nationalism had proclaimed its sovereignty and where it had imagined its true community was neither coextensive with nor coincidental to the field constituted by the public/private distinction. In the former field, the hegemonic project of nationalism could hardly make the distinctions of language, religion, caste, or class a matter of indifference to itself. The project was that of cultural 'normalization', like, as Anderson suggests, bourgeois hegemonic projects everywhere, but with the all-important difference that it had to choose its site of autonomy from a position of subordination to a colonial regime that had on its side the most universalist justificatory resources produced by post-Enlightenment social thought.

The result is that autonomous forms of imagination of the community were, and continue to be, overwhelmed and swamped by the history of the postcolonial state. Here lies the root of our postcolonial misery: not in our inability to think out new forms of the modern community but in our surrender to the old forms of the modern state. If the nation is an imagined community and if nations must also take the form of states, then our theoretical language must allow us to talk about community and state at the same time. I do not think our present theoretical language allows us to do this.

Writing just before his death, Bipinchandra Pal (1858–1932), the fiery leader of the Swadeshi movement in Bengal and a principal figure in the pre-Gandhian Congress, described the boarding-houses in which students lived in the Calcutta of his youth:

> Students' messes in Calcutta, in my college days, fifty-six years ago, were like small republics and were managed on strictly democratic lines. Everything was decided by the voice of the majority of the members of the mess. At the end of every month a manager was elected by the whole 'House,' so to say, and he was charged with the collection of the dues of the members, and the general supervision of the food and establishment of the mess. . . . A successful manager was frequently begged to accept re-election; while the more careless and lazy members, who had often to pay out of their own pockets for their mismanagement, tried to avoid this honour.
>
> . . . Disputes between one member and another were settled by a 'Court' of the whole 'House'; and we sat night after night, I remember, in examining these cases; and never was the decision of this 'Court' questioned or disobeyed by any member. Nor were the members of the mess at all helpless in the matter of duly enforcing their verdict upon an offending colleague. For they

could always threaten the recalcitrant member either with expulsion from
the mess, or if he refused to go, with the entire responsibility of the rent being
thrown on him. . . . And such was the force of public opinion in these small
republics that I have known of cases of this punishment on offending members, which so worked upon them that after a week of their expulsion from a
mess, they looked as if they had just come out of some prolonged or serious
spell of sickness. . . .

   The composition of our mess called for some sort of a compromise between
the so-called orthodox and the Brahmo and other heterodox members of
our republic. So a rule was passed by the unanimous vote of the whole
'House,' that no member should bring any food to the house . . . which outraged the feelings of Hindu orthodoxy. It was however clearly understood
that the members of the mess, as a body and even individually, would not interfere with what any one took outside the house. So we were free to go and have
all sorts of forbidden food either at the Great Eastern Hotel, which some of us
commenced to occasionally patronise later on, or anywhere else.[7]

The interesting point in this description is not so much the exaggerated
and obviously romanticized portrayal in miniature of the imagined political form of the self-governing nation, but rather the repeated use of the
institutional terms of modern European civic and political life (republic,
democracy, majority, unanimity, election, House, Court, and so on) to
describe a set of activities that had to be performed on material utterly
incongruous with that civil society. The question of a 'compromise' on
the food habits of members is really settled not on a principle of demarcating the 'private' from the 'public' but of separating the domains of the
'inside' and the 'outside', the inside being a space where 'unanimity' had
to prevail, while the outside was a realm of individual freedom.
Notwithstanding the 'unanimous vote of the whole House', the force
that determined the unanimity in the inner domain was not the voting
procedure decided upon by individual members coming together in a
body but rather the consensus of a community – institutionally novel
(because, after all, the Calcutta boarding-house was unprecedented in
'tradition'), internally differentiated, but nevertheless a community
whose claims preceded those of its individual members.

   But Bipinchandra's use of the terms of parliamentary procedure to
describe the 'communitarian' activities of a boarding-house standing in
place of the nation must not be dismissed as a mere anomaly. His language is indicative of the very real imbrication of two discourses, and
correspondingly of two domains, of politics. The attempt has been made
in recent Indian historiography to talk of these as the domains of 'elite'
and 'subaltern' politics.[8] But one of the important results of this historiographical approach has been precisely the demonstration that each
domain has not only acted in opposition to and as a limit upon the other

but, through this process of struggle, has also shaped the emergent form of the other. Thus, the presence of populist or communitarian elements in the liberal constitutional order of the postcolonial state ought not to be read as a sign of the inauthenticity or disingenuousness of elite politics; it is rather a recognition in the elite domain of the very real presence of an arena of subaltern politics over which it must dominate and yet which also had to be negotiated on its own terms for the purposes of producing consent. On the other hand, the domain of subaltern politics has increasingly become familiar with, and even adapted itself to, the institutional forms characteristic of the elite domain. The point, therefore, is no longer one of simply demarcating and identifying the two domains in their separateness, which is what was required in order first to break down the totalizing claims of a nationalist historiography. Now the task is to trace in their mutually conditioned historicities the specific forms that have appeared, on the one hand, in the domain defined by the hegemonic project of nationalist modernity, and on the other, in the numerous fragmented resistances to that normalizing project.

This is the exercise I wish to carry out. Since the problem will be directly posed of the limits to the supposed universality of the modern regime of power and with it of the post-Enlightenment disciplines of knowledge, it might appear as though the exercise is meant to emphasize once more an 'Indian' (or an 'Oriental') exceptionalism. In fact, however, the objective of my exercise is rather more complicated, and considerably more ambitious. It includes not only an identification of the discursive conditions that make such theories of Indian exceptionalism possible, but also a demonstration that the alleged exceptions actually inhere as forcibly suppressed elements even in the supposedly universal forms of the modern regime of power.

The latter demonstration enables us to make the argument that the universalist claims of modern Western social philosophy are themselves limited by the contingencies of global power. In other words, 'Western universalism' no less than 'Oriental exceptionalism' can be shown to be only a particular form of a richer, more diverse, and differentiated conceptualization of a new universal idea. This might allow us the possibility not only to think of new forms of the modern community, which, as I argue, the nationalist experience in Asia and Africa has done from its birth, but, much more decisively, to think of new forms of the modern state.

The project then is to claim for us, the once-colonized, our freedom of imagination. Claims, we know only too well, can be made only as contestations in a field of power. Studies will necessarily bear, for each specific disciplinary field, the imprint of an unresolved contest. To make a claim on behalf of the fragment is also, not surprisingly, to produce a discourse that is itself fragmentary. It is redundant to make apologies for this.

Notes

1. Benedict Anderson, *Imagined Communities: Reflections on the Origin and Spread of Nationalism*, London 1983.

2. This is a central argument of my book *Nationalist Thought and the Colonial World: A Derivative Discourse?*, London 1986.

3. Anderson, *Imagined Communities*, pp. 17–49.

4. Ibid., pp. 28–40.

5. The history of this artistic movement has been recently studied in detail by Tapati Guha-Thalkurta, *The Making of a New "Indian" Art: Artists, Aesthetics and Nationalism in Bengal, 1850–1920*, Cambridge 1992.

6. See Anilchandra Banerjee, 'Years of Consolidation: 1883–1904'; Tripurari Chakravarti, 'The University and the Government: 1904–24'; and Pramathanath Banerjee, 'Reform and Reorganization: 1904–24', in Niharranjan Ray and Pratulchandra Gupta, eds, *Hundred Years of the University of Calcutta*, Calcutta 1957, pp. 129–78, 179–210 and 211–318.

7. Bipinchandra Pal, *Memories of My Life and Times*, Calcutta 1932, reprinted 1973, pp. 157–60.

8. Represented by the various essays in Ranajit Guha, ed., *Subaltern Studies*, vols 1–6, Delhi 1982–90. The programmatic statement of this approach is in Ranajit Guha, 'On Some Aspects of the Historiography of Colonial India', in Guha, ed., *Subaltern Studies* vol. 1, Delhi 1982, pp. 1–8.

9

Whither 'Nation' and 'Nationalism'?

Katherine Verdery

Nation and Nationalism: What are They?

During the 1980s and 1990s, the scholarly industry, built up around the concepts of nation and nationalism, became so vast and so interdisciplinary as to rival all other contemporary foci of intellectual production. I take 'nation', anthropologically, as a basic operator in a widespread system of social classification. Systems of social classification not only classify; in institutionalized form, they also establish grounds for authority and legitimacy through the categories they set down, and they made their categories seem both natural and socially real. Nation is therefore an aspect of the political and symbolic/ideological order and also of the world of social interaction and feeling. It has been an important element of systems of social classification for many centuries. This is not surprising, given its root meaning, 'to be born' – an idea crucial to making any system of categories appear natural. As the historian Eric Hobsbawm, among others, reminds us, however, it has had many different meanings historically: it has been employed in reference to guilds, corporations, units within ancient universities, feudal estates, congeries of citizens, and groupings based in ostensibly common culture and history.[1] In all cases, it was a sorting device – something that lumped together those who were to be distinguished from those with whom they coexisted[2] – but the criteria to be employed in this sorting, the thing into or for which being born mattered, such as the transmission of craftsmanship, aristocratic privilege, citizenly responsibility, and cultural-historical community, varies across time and context.

In the modern period, nation has become a potent symbol and basis of classification within an international system of nation-states. It names the relation between states and their subjects and between states and other states; it is an ideological construct essential to assigning subject positions in the modern state, as well as in the international order. That is, nation is crucial to the way a state is linked to its subjects, distinguishing them from the subjects of other states, and to the state's larger environment. As a symbol, nation has come to legitimate numerous social actions and movements, often having very diverse aims. It works as a symbol for two reasons. First, like all symbols, its meaning is ambiguous. Therefore, people who use it differently can mobilize disparate audiences (both internal and international) who think that they understand the same thing by it. Second, its use evokes sentiments and dispositions that have been formed in relation to it throughout decades of so-called nation-building.

Nationalism, in this perspective, is the political utilization of the symbol nation through discourse and political activity, as well as the sentiment that draws people into responding to this symbol's use. Nationalism is a quintessentially homogenizing, differentiating, or classifying discourse: one that aims its appeal at people presumed to have certain things in common as against people thought not to have any mutual connections. In modern nationalisms, among the most important things to have in common are certain forms of culture and tradition, and a specific history.

But modern nationalisms have operated in the name of at least two major meanings of nation as a state–subject relation. Eric Hobsbawm identifies the two principal senses of nation in modern times as: a relation known as citizenship, in which the nation consists of collective sovereignty based in common political participation, and a relation known as ethnicity, in which the nation comprises all those of supposedly common language, history, or broader cultural identity.[3] The latter is the one most often invoked with the term nationalism, but it is not the only meaning. The confusion and overlap of these meanings in politics has confounded scholarship whenever it takes nation and nationalism to mean only one thing. We can identify additional meanings of nation that have insinuated themselves into political discourse, such as the state–subject relation attempted under state socialism, emphasizing a quasi-familial dependency I call *socialist paternalism*.[4] Any of these (or other) meanings, or some combination of them, might apply in a particular use of the symbol nation; its meaning cannot simply be presumed.

These observations suggest three pitfalls that scholarship on nation might strive (and has often not managed) to avoid. First, it should explore which sense of nation is apt to the context in question, rather than imposing a modern sense on a medieval reality, a French sense on

a Kenyan reality, or a nineteenth-century sense on the evolving reality of
today. Second, it should treat nation as a symbol and any given nationalism as having multiple meanings, offered as alternatives and competed
over by different groups manoeuvring to capture the symbol's definition
and its legitimating effects. This means we should not treat nationalism
itself as a social actor and ask whether it is good or bad, liberal or radical,
or conducive to democratic politics. Rather we should ask: What is the
global, societal, and institutional context in which different groups compete to control this symbol and its meanings? What are the programmes
of the different groups? Radical? Liberal? Reactionary? What are the
social conditions that predispose towards success for one group and one
programme over another? This approach takes the 'ism' out of nationalism and lodges agency back in human beings, constrained by social
structures. It also leads us to wonder if the term nationalism is adequate
to the inflation of its meanings and uses. Third, given the crucial ideological role of nation in linking states with their subjects, scholarship
should make a concerted effort not to be conned by the terms of national
ideologies: not to treat nations as actually defined, for example, by culture, or descent, or history. We should take those terms instead as objects
of study and ask: What is the context in which one or another definition
or symbolization of nation operates? What is it accomplishing? Is it doing
work for arguments aimed elsewhere rather than at national questions
per se? This third point can be illustrated by exploring five possible areas
for inquiry into nations and nationalism.

How Should We be Studying Nations and Nationalism Now?

What Underlies the Notion of Identity?

We tend to write about national identity as if the second term were not
problematic, as if everyone ought to have identities or to have certain
kinds of identities, and not too much of some of them. Where has the
notion of identity come from, and why has it become important for
human beings to possess them? What specific notion of person or human
being is implied in the concept of identity, and what is the historical
specificity of this concept? By what political, economic, social, and symbolic context is it informed? How are identities socially constructed, and
how are persons made who have identities?

This inquiry overlaps with the notion of 'possessive individualism' –
with the historical rise of monads called individuals for whom possessing
was to be a defining trait – and it joins the matter of nation because
nations are conceived as collective individuals.[5] Since at least the writings
of the German philosopher and theologian Johann Gottfried von

Herder, nations are conceived – like individuals – as historical actors, having spirits or souls, missions, wills, geniuses; they have places of origin/birth (cradles, often, in the national myth) and lineages (usually *patri-lineages*), as well as life cycles that include birth, periods of blossoming and decay, and fears of death; they have as their physical referent territories that are bounded like human bodies. Nations, like individuals, are thought to have identities, often based in so-called national characters. National identity thus exists at two levels: the individual's sense of self as national, and the identity of the collective whole in relation to others of like kind. What is this peculiar concatenation of ideas all about? What is the socio-historical efficacy of the notion of identity, with its seemingly contradictory root meanings of same, as an identical, and unique – root meanings that, like national ideologies, simultaneously homogenize and differentiate?

How Do People Become National?

How is a sense of self as national developed? We might call this the problem of national subjectivities – in the plural, because we cannot assume that there is only one form of self-experience as national. This issue relates directly to the preceding one: it asks how the homology between the nation and the individual becomes internalized and is assimilated by the individual, entering his or her 'inside'. My phrasing presupposes, of course, that a notion of inside is socio-culturally available. Not all human societies have thought of people as having a separate realm of the inside.[6]

Exceedingly helpful here is a distinction the anthropologist John Boreman makes between nationalism and nationness, the former referring to conscious sentiments that take the nation as an object of active devotion, the latter to daily interactions and practices that produce an inherent and often unarticulated feeling of belonging, of being at home.[7] These practices and routines may range from the relatively mundane rituals of courtship and family-making, as influenced by the policies of the state,[8] to the relatively rare and spectacular, such as participation in warfare, which may have been essential to building devotion to the nation during the early-modern period so that such devotion could be presupposed by war-makers later on.[9] Beneath this inquiry rests a Foucauldian premise about the creation of modern subjects through the often invisible practices (what Foucault calls microphysics) of power. To research it would direct attention away from the noisy and visible rhetorics of nationalists and toward the techniques through which receptive dispositions have been quietly laid down in those to whom they appeal.

How Variously is Nation Symbolized?

What do we gain by seeing the nation as a symbol rather than as a thing? In recent anthropological writings, a concern with nationalism has given way to seeing national rhetorics as plural, as elements in larger contests to define the meaning of national symbols and to define the nation-as-symbol itself. For such an objective it no longer makes sense to use the term national*ism*, for the point is to see how a single symbol, nation, takes on multiple meanings. Groups orienting to it all take the nation to be the paramount symbol, but they have different intentions for it. Various things enter into their conflicts – contrasting ideas about authenticity, about the nation's true mission, about cultural patrimony or heritage, about national character, and so forth.[10] This research asks how ideas about nation and identity are produced and reproduced as central elements in a political struggle. It sees nation as a construct, whose meaning is never stable but shifts with the changing balance of social forces, and it asks what kind of leverage this construct has afforded certain groups – and why those groups rather than others.

To take seriously the use of nation as a symbol means a close inspection of the social tensions and struggles within which it has become a significant idiom – a form of currency, used to trade on issues that may not be about the nation at all. For example, in postsocialist Eastern Europe there is widespread stereotyping and scapegoating of Gypsies, seen as lazy and thieving. If one thinks ethnographically about these stereotypes, it becomes apparent that people use Gypsies to symbolize the dislocating introduction of markets into the former socialist bloc. Gypsies are not the only ones engaged in trade, yet responsibility is assigned to them for much that people find confusing and upsetting in the new postsocialist order. This kind of approach helps to account for why group boundaries of categorizations can persist even in the absence of members of the group in question, as with anti-Semitism in many Eastern European countries having scarcely any Jews.[11]

National symbolization includes as well the processes whereby groups within a society are rendered visible or invisible. For the project of nation-building, nonconforming elements must be first rendered visible, then assimilated or eliminated. Some of this can occur quite physically, through the violence most recently associated with 'ethnic cleansing' in Bosnia-Herzegovina. But short of this are other, symbolic violences through which difference is highlighted and then obliterated. Notions of purity and contamination, of blood as a carrier of culture, or of pollution are fundamental to the projects of nation-making. They merit more attention than scholars have accorded them.

How Can We Understand the Intersection of Nation with Other Social Operators?

Ethnicity, race, gender, and class can be seen, like nation, as aspects of identity formation, but they are also at the same time axes of social classification, which often appear alongside one another, interacting in complex ways. In a brilliant review article, the anthropologist Brackette Williams discusses how the projects and policies of state-making implicate many of these different axes in the homogenizing process basic to the modern nation-state's form of rule.[12] She sees the state as the encompassing frame within which symbolic conventions are established and fought over, legitimacies striven for, group relations and the distributions associated with them fixed. The state is the frame for producing visibility, the anchor for what prove to be politically effective notions such as culture, authentic, tradition, common/shared, or barbarian. As she writes, 'concepts of race, ethnicity, locality, and nationality competitively label different aspects of [the identity-forming] process'; their context is a state that motivates differences as it inscribes boundaries, demarcating inside from outside, self from other.[13]

Following Williams, we should see the modern state as produced through a totalizing process that entails a relentless press toward homogeneity, which is simultaneously a process of exclusion. Such homogeneity is not necessarily pursued for its own sake; it may serve various ends, such as creating a common foundation of skills for a workforce or a space amenable to managing the state.[14] In the latter case, a homogenizing thrust creates the nation as all those the state should administer, because they all supposedly have something in common. States vary in the intensity of their homogenizing efforts, partly as a function of the power held by political elites and the resistances they encounter. This equation may explain why certain, especially Third World, states pursue less radical homogenizations than do others.[15]

Nevertheless, to institutionalize a notion of commonality is to render visible all those who fail to hold a given feature in common. Thus, by instituting homogeneity or commonality as normative, state-building renders difference socio-politically significant – that is, it creates the significance of differences such as ethnicity, gender, locality, and race, each of them defined as particular kinds of differencing with respect to the state's homogenizing project. The most comprehensive possible agenda for the study of nationalism is, therefore, the study of historical processes that have produced a particular political form – nation-states – differently in different contexts, and of the internal homogenizations that these nation-states have sought to realize in their different contexts. In each case, they pursued their homogenizations within locally varied understandings of same and different that implicated class, gender, ethnicity, and race – but did so variously in each place.

How Does the Dissolution of the Nation-State Affect the Viability and
Deployment of Nation as a Legitimating Symbol in Politics?

In the world of today, participation is legitimated by the idea of nation –
nation-states – even when a given empirical case realizes the classic
nation-state form only imperfectly. Yet scholars and others have begun to
suspect that the modern state form is, if not dying out, undergoing a
major reconfiguration.[16] The international weapons trade has made a
mockery of the state's supposed monopoly of the means of violence.
Capital's extraordinary mobility means that as it moves from areas of
higher to areas of lower taxation, many states lose some of their revenue
and industrial base, and this constrains their ability to attract capital or
shape its flow. Capital flight can now discipline all nation-state governments.[17] The increased flow of capital – and of populations, in its wake,
producing the much commented phenomenon of transnationalism –
calls into question in an unprecedented way all those arbitrary, taken-for-
granted nation-state boundaries.[18] The result is both real-world changes
in those boundaries – as with the break-up of the Soviet Union, Czechoslovakia, and Yugoslavia, not to mention the threatened secession of
Quebec from Canada, of the Celtic Fringe from Great Britain, and so
forth – and also frenzies of national re-legitimation, both where the
boundaries are in question and elsewhere as well.[19] On this reading, the
turmoil in former Yugoslavia merely sets in bold relief what it means to
create a nation-state, with all the most violent forms of homogenizing and
purification and the forcible imposition and legitimation of boundaries.

But all this is happening, paradoxically, at a moment when the nation-
state form itself is being superseded. If, as geographer and social theorist
David Harvey claims, the new world order is one in which finance capital
rather than bounded nation-states will play the chief coordinating role,[20]
what might be the consequences of this for the legitimating significance
of nation as a symbol in international politics? Is nation, too, headed for
the exit, as Eric Hobsbawm argues?[21]

I have my doubts. It seems more likely that nation is once again changing its referent (as well as its articulation with capital), a sign of this
change being the novel grounds for which it is now being proposed,
such as the Arab Nation or Queer Nation. The size requirements of viable
nationhood are decreasing. In addition, persons are being compelled
into single identities – alternatives are being stripped away from those
who would have multiple allegiances (think of the offspring of mixed
marriages in former Yugoslavia, for example) – while xenophobia and
multiculturalism normalize these identities as the basic elements in socio-
economic competition and conflict. This suggests that although the idea
of nation with which we have been familiar may indeed be past its peak,

being born into something as a natural condition will remain fundamental to human experience and to scholarship, even if in new ways.

Acknowledgement

My thanks to Pamela Ballinger, Kira Kosnick, and Michel-Rolph Trouillot
for improving this essay.

Notes

1. See Eric Hobsbawm, *Nations and Nationalism since 1780: Programme, Myth, Reality*,
Cambridge 1990, pp. 16–24.

2. Ibid., p. 16.

3. Ibid., pp. 18–20.

4. This form of state–subject relation was referred to, in the Romanian case, as the
'socialist nation'. Instead of emphasizing political rights or ethnocultural similarity, socialist paternalism posited a moral tie linking subjects with the state through their rights to
share in the redistributed social product. Subjects were presumed to be neither politically
active, as with citizenship, nor ethnically similar to each other: they were presumed to be
grateful recipients – like small children in a family – of benefits their rulers decided upon
for them. The subject disposition this produced was dependency, rather than the agency
cultivated by citizenship or the solidarity of ethnonationalism.

5. See C.B. Macpherson, *The Political Theory of Possessive Individualism: Hobbes to Locke*,
Oxford 1962; Louis Dumont, 'Religion, Politics, and Society in the Individualistic Universe',
Proceedings of the Royal Anthropological Institute of Great Britain and Ireland, London 1970, pp.
31–45; and Richard Handler, *Nationalism and the Politics of Culture in Quebec*, Madison, Wis.,
1988.

6. The notion of an 'inside' relates to the historical rise of a notion of personality,
among other things; this emerging inside was provided by the psychological investigations
of Freud and others, who discovered the notion of the unconscious. See Hannah Arendt,
The Origins of Totalitarianism, New York 1958.

7. John Borneman, *Belonging to the Two Berlins: Kin, State, Nation*, Cambridge 1992,
p. 339 n. 19.

8. This is the focus of attention in Ibid.

9. This point is made by Charles Tilly, among others. See the papers in Charles Tilly,
The Formation of National States in Western Europe, Princeton 1975.

10. See, for example, Virginia Dominguez, *People as Subject, People as Object*, Madison,
Wis., 1990; Handler, *Nationalism and the Politics of Culture in Quebec*; Katherine Verdery,
National Ideology under Socialism: Identity and Cultural Politics in Ceauşescu's Romania,
Berkeley/Los Angeles 1991; and Brackette F. Williams, *Stains on My Name, War in My Veins:
Guyana and the Politics of Cultural Struggle*, Durham, NC 1991.

11. For more on this point, see Katherine Verdery, 'Nationalism and National Sentiment
in Post-Socialist Romania', *Slavic Review* 52 (summer 1993).

12. See Brackette F. Williams, 'A Class Act: Anthropology and the Race to Nation Across
Ethnic Terrain', *Annual Review of Anthropology*, 18, 1989, pp. 401–44.

13. Ibid., p. 426. See also David Campbell, *Writing Security: United States Foreign Policy and
the Politics of Identity*, Minneapolis 1992, p. 8.

14. Cf. Ernest Gellner, *Nations and Nationalism*, Ithaca 1983.

15. This point emerged from dialogue with Michel-Rolph Trouillot.

16. See Hobsbawm's predictions at the end of *Nations and Nationalism since 1780*, and any
number of the writings of Charles Tilly, such as 'Prisoners of the State', *International Social
Science Journal*, vol. 44, 1992, pp. 329–42, and *Coercion, Capital, and European States, A.D.
990–1990*, Oxford 1990.

17. David Harvey, *The Condition of Postmodernity: An Enquiry into the Origins of Cultural Change*, Oxford 1989, p. 164.

18. For consistency's sake, this ought to be called 'trans-statism'.

19. Kira Kosnick, 'Boundaries and the Production of National Identity', manuscript, author's files.

20. Harvey, *The Condition of Postmodernity*, pp. 164–5.

21. Hobsbawm, *Nations and Nationalism since 1780*, pp. 181–3.

Woman and Nation

Sylvia Walby

Introduction

Literature on nations and nationalism rarely addresses the question of gender, despite a general interest in the differential participation of various social groups in nationalist projects. A key issue in the analysis of nation has been the conditions under which an ethnic group can claim and possibly achieve the status of nation and then of nation-state.[1] Nationalist movements necessarily draw upon their relevant constituency in uneven ways, and there has been much analysis of the differing class compositions of such movements, their levels of education, and a variety of socio-economic and cultural variables. However, this body of literature has engaged but little with the differential integration of women and men into the national project. Most texts on nationalism do not take gender as a significant issue.[2] Rare and thus important exceptions to this absence are Enloe, Jayawardena, and Yuval-Davis and Anthias.[3]

There has been a revival of interest in the related concept of citizenship, which historically has formed a link between 'nation' and 'state'. 'Citizenship' has been introduced in the context of macro-societal comparisons in order to facilitate discussions of the social conditions under which different forms of democracy have been attained.[4] It is of interest here because of its link with 'nation' and the possibility that the concept offers assistance in dealing with degrees of integration into the national project. However, the existing literature, despite this potential, deals with neither gender nor, perhaps even more surprisingly, with ethnicity and 'race'.

There are five main positions on the issue of the intersection of gender with citizenship, ethnicity, nation and 'race'. Firstly, there is the argument that gender, while existing, does not affect the nature of citizenship/ethnic/national/'race' relations.[5] This is sometimes expressed via a suggestion that there is patriarchy or there is not, with little attempt to use or build the necessary concepts for a more sophisticated position.[6] Secondly, there is a symmetrical argument that citizenship/ethnic/nation/'race' do not significantly affect the nature of gender relations.[7] This is the argument that gender inequality has common features in all societies and all historical periods, and that women share a common oppression despite their documented differences of ethnicity/nationality/'race'. This position is not to be confused with the notion that ethnicity is irrelevant to the analysis of social relations. Thirdly, there is the argument that these systems of social relations should be added together so as, for instance, to talk of the double burden that black women suffer from both racism and sexism. This also suggests that racism is an extra layer of oppression some women have to bear and produces differences and inequalities between women. Fourthly, there is the argument that ethnic/national/'race' differences mean that the institutions which are central for white women's oppression are not central to those of women of other ethnicities.[8] For instance, the family can be considered to have different significance for gender relations in different ethnic groups. This means that there is not a common form of gender differentiation and inequality across different ethnic groups. Fifthly, there is the argument that gender and ethnic/national/'race' relations affect each other, leading to dynamic analyses of the shifting forms of gender and of ethnic/national/'race' relations.[9] This entails an analysis of the causal interconnections between gender and ethnic/national/'race' differentiation and inequality. Overlying all of these five positions is a further variable of the different significance of class and capitalist relations within each of these analyses. This varies independently of the five perspectives.

Gender, Nation and Nationalism

While many texts on the nation have ignored gender there have been several very important contributions which have addressed this issue: Yuval-Davis and Anthias, Jayawardena and Enloe.[10]

In the introduction to their volume,[11] Anthias and Yuval-Davis suggest that there are five major ways in which women are involved in ethnic and national processes:

1. as biological reproducers of members of ethnic collectivities;
2. as reproducers of the boundaries of ethnic/national groups;
3. as participating centrally in the ideological reproduction of the collectivity and as transmitters of its culture;

4. as signifiers of ethnic/national differences – as a focus and symbol in ideological discourses used in the construction, reproduction and transformation of ethnic/national categories;
5. as participants in national, economic, political and military struggles.[12]

The papers in the collection excellently illustrate these themes. They provide evidence that women and gender relations are indeed used in the ways that the editors suggest. They show that gender is important for ethnic/national practices and ethnic/national practices are important for gender relations.

The volume shows the significance of demographic factors such as birth-rate for some ethnic/national projects, and hence the pressure placed, in historically specific moments, on women to breed or not to breed 'for the good of the nation/"race"'. Klug convincingly illustrates both pressures in her case study of Britain,[13] and de Lepervanche in hers of Australia, where white women have been encouraged to produce more children and black women not to,[14] and Yuval-Davis shows similar issues in the programmes of both Israeli and Palestinian nationalists. The flexibility of the discourse of motherhood rather than its biological fixity is the theme of Gaitskell and Unterhalter's comparison of the changes in the idea of motherhood for Afrikaner nationalism and the African National Congress over the course of the twentieth century.[15]

Anthias suggests that women were used as symbols of national identity in the case of Greek-Cypriot nationalism. This theme is continued by Kandyoti writing on the case of Turkey, although she also raises the question of whether women will always be passive symbols rather than actively engaging themselves in 'the woman question'.[16] Here she raises the question of the extent to which one idea of gender is used by nationalism, and the extent to which the woman question has a dynamic which shapes history itself. In Obbo's paper on Uganda women appear to have their interests as women under attack, not only as a pawn in a nationalist project.[17] This again suggests that it is insufficient to think of nationalism affecting gender in a one-way relationship. Finally, in Afshar's paper, women unequivocally leave the world of symbols and appear fighting for their gendered interests in the context of Islamic revival in Iran.[18]

Thus Anthias and Yuval-Davis's five major roles of women in ethnic/national processes have empirical support from papers in the book. However, there is a question as to whether these five encompass all the major ways that gender and ethnic/national relations intersect. While they are important, some additions should be made.

Firstly, this categorization privileges the ideological or cultural level in three out of the five practices; of the other two, one is biological, the other is 'national economic, political and military struggle'. The division of labour is curiously absent from this list, unless it is considered to be subsumed under biology or culture. Is the specificity of the gender division of labour in different ethnic/national groups considered to be relevant to ethnic/national divisions only at the symbolic level? Or is the category 'biological reproducers' meant to carry an analysis of women's labour? This latter is surely difficult, since birthing is only one part of women's labour, albeit a significant one.

A second and related point which gets underemphasized in this summary is that conflict, and the maintenance of boundaries, between ethnic/national groups is also a conflict between different forms of social hierarchies, not only different cultures. Even the most cohesive ethnic/national group almost always entails a system of social inequality, and one where the dominant group(s) typically exercise(s) hegemonic control over the 'culture' and political project of the 'collectivity'. It is a sociological orthodoxy that societies typically have a system of social inequality and that the dominant group tries to exercise hegemonic control over the ideas current in that society. Ethnic/national conflicts, then, may be expected to benefit the interests of the members of that grouping differentially. Different genders (and classes) may therefore be differentially enthusiastic about 'the' ostensible ethnic/national project, depending upon the extent to which they agree with the priorities of 'their' political 'leaders'. It may be that there is unanimity on 'the' ethnic/national project by members of both genders and all social classes, but this is unlikely, and at least it is a question to be investigated.

Indeed, the volume itself contains evidence of the varying commitment of women, and indeed of different groups of women differentiated by class, education, urban/rural residence and so forth, to the ethnic/national project of 'their' community leaders. Some of the strongest papers are about this tension between (highly differentiated) gender groupings and the ethnic/national project, as in the case of Afshar on Iran. Sometimes, the gender discourse would shift as nationalist movements shifted ground (as in the case of Gaitskell and Unterhalter's analysis of the changes in Afrikaner nationalism and the African National Congress).

While Anthias and Yuval-Davis emphasize the participation of women in the ethnic/national project, albeit in different ways, I have suggested emphasizing the question of women's differential involvement. The national project may differentially affect women and men (and subgroups of these) and hence engender different degrees of enthusiasm.

The significance of feminist demands in the shaping of nationalist demands is discussed by Jayawardena.[19] She argues that feminists were active in pushing for the emancipation of women in Third World nationalist movements at the end of the nineteenth and beginning of the twentieth centuries. She shows that there have been important feminist components of nationalist movements in Third World countries in the late nineteenth and early twentieth centuries. She discusses evidence of the interconnections between feminism and nationalism from Egypt, Iran, Afghanistan, India, Sri Lanka, Indonesia, the Philippines, China, Vietnam, Korea and Japan. All these countries had been subject to imperialism, and the feminism that she finds is bound up with anti-imperialist nationalist movements.

Jayawardena discusses the suggestions from Third World writers that feminism is merely Western, decadent, foreign, suitable only for the bourgeoisie, and a diversion from the struggle for national liberation and socialism. She also discusses the parallel view from the West that feminism is a product of Europe and North America and that if it is to be found elsewhere then it is merely an imitation. She argues against both these positions that feminism had endogenous roots in Third World countries, and that it is not imposed from the West. However, she does not want to deny that the impact of the West was important in creating social changes which indirectly led to feminism:

> feminism was *not* imposed on the Third World by the West, but rather . . . historical circumstances produced important material and ideological changes which affect women, even though the impact of imperialism and Western thought was admittedly among the significant elements in these historical circumstances. Debates on women's rights and education were held in 18th-century China and there were movements for women's social emancipation in early 19th-century India; the other country studies show that feminist struggles originated between 60 and 80 years ago in many countries of Asia.[20]

Jayawardena wants to argue that feminism should not be reduced to Westernization, but that this does not mean that Westernization was not relevant. She goes on to argue that women's emancipation movements were conducted in the context of nationalist struggles. They were

> acted out against a backdrop of nationalist struggles aimed at achieving political independence, asserting a national identity, and modernizing society.[21]

> struggles for women's emancipation were an essential and integral part of national resistance movements.[22]

The organization of women around their own demands was closely interrelated with the nationalist movements. They rarely organized autonomously, but more usually as wings or subsidiaries of male-dominated nationalist groups.[23]

In a similar manner Jayawardena argues that the expansion of capitalism was an important factor in the creation of the material circumstances which led to both the movement of women into the public sphere and to feminism, but that it did not simply cause feminism. Rather it created the conditions under which feminist demands were possible.

> The basic reforms that involved the freeing of women from pre-capitalist social constraints of various kinds, giving them freedom of mobility, bringing them out of seclusion and facilitating their work outside the home, were in keeping with strategies of capitalist forms of economic production and capitalist ideology. In many countries, the periods of reform coincided with attempts to develop capitalism and to harness the supply of cheap female labour into factory production and the service sector of the economy.[24]

Jayawardena is clear that there are significant class variations in the way that these economic and social changes affected women. It was the women of the bourgeoisie and petty bourgeoisie who benefited most from the development of education and the opening of the professions to women.

Hence Jayawardena is arguing not only that feminist and nationalist movements were closely interconnected, but that they cannot be understood outside of an understanding of imperialism and both local and international capitalism.

It is interesting to note, although Jayawardena does not make this point, that many Third World countries granted formal suffrage to women at the same time as men, at the point of national independence. The histories of Third World democratic practices are thus very different from those in the First World, where men's and women's suffrage were typically separated by several decades. Citizenship and nationalism and gender are closely interconnected.

While Jayawardena and Yuval-Davis and Anthias focus on the relationship of woman to nation, Enloe focuses on the significance of gender for the relations between nations. She examines both the international order and transnational entities and demonstrates how they cannot be fully understood outside of an analysis of gender relations. Enloe makes her argument by examining the gendered nature of the institutions which make up the international order.

Enloe looks at sex and the international tourist trade, arguing that the forms of the development of tourism cannot be understood outside of the various constructions of gender and sexuality which affect practices ranging from package tours for 'the respectable woman' to sex tourism for men.[25]

Enloe examines the way the hierarchical relations between nations and the construction of gendered cultural forms mutually affect each other. For instance, images of women in colonized countries were often constructed and purveyed in a manner which simultaneously eroticized and exoticized them while justifying imperial domination in the name of 'civilization'. 'Oriental' women 'needed' male European 'protection'.

> European 'Orientalism' nurtured an appreciative fascination with these cultures while justifying European rule in the name of 'civilization'. The image of the tantalizingly veiled Muslim woman was a cornerstone of this Orientalist ideology and of the imperial structure it supported.[26]

Enloe is arguing that support for a particular kind of gender relations was used as a justification for colonial domination. The notion of 'civilization' was saturated with ideas about correct gender relations and forms of sexual relations.

> Ladylike behaviour was a mainstay of imperialist civilization. Like sanitation and Christianity, feminine respectability was meant to convince both the colonizing and the colonized peoples that foreign conquest was right and necessary.[27]

Not only was femininity an imperial issue, so also was masculinity. Enloe suggests that British leaders were concerned to ensure appropriate forms of masculinity to sustain the empire. In particular she suggests that the Crimean and Boer wars led to initiatives to 'improve' the forms of masculinity. The founding of the Boy Scouts in 1908 by Robert Baden-Powell was to counter the spread of venereal disease, intermarriage of the races and falling birth-rates which were allegedly leading to the decline of the British Empire:[28] 'Baden-Powell and other British imperialists saw sportsmanship combined with respect for the respectable woman as the bedrock of British imperial success.'[29]

Enloe shows that nationalist movements have often grown out of men's rather than women's experiences: 'nationalism has typically sprung from masculinized memory, masculinized humiliation and masculinized hope'.[30] She suggests that nationalisms would be different if women's experiences were foregrounded in the building of this culture and project. She goes further to suggest that, if this were to happen, then the nature of the relations between states, and the international order itself, might be different: 'If more nation-states grew out of feminist nationalists' ideas and experiences, community identities within the international political system might be tempered by cross-national identities.'[31]

Enloe discusses the international division of labour in which women's labour in the Third World is constructed as cheap. She examines the various patriarchal practices which make women's labour 'cheap', such as maintenance of 'family' relations and the suppression of women's unions. The international significance is demonstrated by an examination of the uses to which this labour is put by transnational corporations. National boundaries are becoming less significant for multinational capital and hence for women as workers.

Enloe's argument about the significance of gender to issues of nation and the international is often conducted through an analysis of sexuality. This is the case when she discusses the international tourist industry, Hollywood cinema, the role of women on military bases who work as prostitutes, and the women who are wives of diplomats. This is not always the case, however, as in Enloe's discussion of women workers in the world factories of Asia and as domestic servants. Her conclusion is that the personal is not only political, but also international. The personal and gender are everywhere, even in the international order.

Enloe's argument that gender is pertinent to nations and to the international order is convincing at both a theoretical and an empirical level. She is able to show how the building blocks of the international order are gendered, and how this affects international relations.

Implicit in her analysis are theories both of the international order and of gender. In her account Enloe appears to privilege the sexual and cultural levels, with the sexual division of labour taking a lower level significance. In as far as Enloe includes all of paid work, housework, sexuality, culture, violence and the state in her analysis of women and the international order, I am in agreement with her. I hesitate at the apparent privileging of the sexual and cultural levels rather than the economic. A fuller account might also have discussed the gender structuring of the international institutions themselves. These were curiously absent apart from occasional reference to the IMF.

To What Extent do Women Share the Same National Project as Men?

In the second half of this essay I shall discuss the extent to which women share in the same group identity as men, and in particular the same national project. By national project I mean a range of collective strategies oriented towards the perceived needs of a nation which include nationalism, but may include others. I shall argue that there are often differences between men and women on these issues and I shall suggest some reasons for this.

First I shall make some suggestions for conceptual development to facilitate comparison of gender relations between different nations and ethnic groups. Debates in this area have been held back for lack of simple macro concepts which grasp the significant distinctions between patterns of gender relations at a societal level.

Secondly, I shall discuss the reasons why women and men have different identifications with national projects and may have different commitments to different types of macro-level groupings. This will be approached in three stages. First, via a discussion of the extent to which and conditions under which national projects are simultaneously gender projects. Secondly, via a discussion of the interconnections and distinctions between nationalism, militarism and gender. Thirdly, via a discussion of whether gender relations share the same spatial ordering as class and ethnic relations, and whether women and men have commitments to social phenomena which have different spatial scales. This last will be discussed with the assistance of two examples: gender, the nation and the EEC; feminism, nationalism and Westernization.

Concepts for Analysing Different Forms of Gender Relations

We need to be able to conceptualize and theorize different forms of gender relations. At the moment most writers argue one of three positions: first, that there is only one main form of gender relations and that differences are trivial;[32] secondly, that the range of different practices is so great that every instance is unique, so we cannot theorize gender (the postmodernist position); thirdly that either there is patriarchy or there is not.[33] The first is empirically incorrect; the second is defeatist and abandons the social science project altogether; the third is unsophisticated and incorrect. I take an intermediate position, that the development of middle-range concepts is an important part of the sociological enterprise, and argue that there are differences in the forms of gender relations, and that those differences can be grouped into major types.

One of the major problems with many theories of patriarchy is that they suggest that there is only one base to patriarchal relations, and that this is determinant of other aspects of gender. The base itself varies between different theorists but the base-superstructure model is shared. It is this that makes the analysis of gender relations so static and makes it so difficult to analyse changes except by stepping out of the framework.[34]

The solution to this problem is to theorize gender relations as composed of analytically separable structures. There are six: household production, employment, the state, violence, sexuality and culture. These structures can articulate in different ways, so creating different forms of patriarchy. Two main forms can be distinguished: private and public. Private patriarchy is characterized by the domination of the patriarchal relations in the household. Public patriarchy is dominated by employment and the state. In private patriarchy the mode of expropriation of the woman is individual, by the woman's husband or father. In public patriarchy it is collective, by many men acting in common. In private patriarchy the dominant strategy can be characterized as exclusionary, as women are excluded from activities in the public domain, and thereby constrained to the domestic. In public patriarchy the dominant strategy is segregationist whereby women are allowed to enter all spheres, but segregated and subordinated there.[35]

The form of patriarchy is separate from the degree of gender inequality. This point is important since it enables us to make comparisons of the form of gender relations, without automatically presuming that the difference is related to inequality. That is another, and important, question. Entry into the public sphere may entail greater freedom for women, such as the freedom to earn an independent wage and to dissolve an unhappy marriage; however, alternatively it may only mean an extra job on top of domestic work and the possibility of abandonment at a husband's whim.

Nineteenth-century Britain largely accorded to the private model, while Britain in the 1990s has moved towards the public form. But there are divisions between ethnic groups in Britain. Afro-Caribbeans have the most public form, Asians the most private, with whites in between. Iran may be considered to have moved from a private form, temporarily towards a public form under the Shah, and now back to the private form under Islamic fundamentalism.

There are sub-types of these forms of patriarchy, depending on the relationship of the other structures to the dominant one. Public patriarchy can be divided into a market-led form and a state-led form. The USA is a market-led form of public patriarchy, while the Soviet Union is a state-led form, with Western Europe in between.

With these concepts it is possible to engage in comparative analysis. These following analyses draw upon these concepts.

Nationalism and Women

Are women as committed to national/ethnic/'racial' projects as men? Is their project the same one as men's? Do women's nationalist/ethnic/ 'racial' and other large-scale social projects have the same, or more global, or more local boundaries than those of men?

Anthias and Yuval-Davis are concerned with the way that women are part of the national project, especially how women are differently but equally engaged in this project, sometimes voluntarily, sometimes eagerly involved in the struggle (role number 5 – see discussion of Anthias and Yuval-Davis above), sometimes coerced, as sometimes happens when they are considered to be the breeders of the 'race' (role number 1), most often in a day-to-day way, as reproducers of the culture via socialization of children (numbers 2–3), sometimes passively as symbols (number 4). It appears that Anthias and Yuval-Davis argue that women are just as committed to the national/ethnic project as men, but they sometimes do it in different ways.

I have queried this. Sometimes it may be the case, sometimes not. Sometimes women may support a different national project from that of men. There is a struggle to define what constitutes *the* national project, and women are, typically, heard less than men in this. Thus gender relations are important in determining what is constituted as *the* national project. Where the national project includes women's interests, then women are more likely to support it. Jayawardena's work on feminism and nationalism in the Third World in the early twentieth century shows how integrated these projects can be, though only as a result of women's struggles.

Is there reciprocal impact between gender and ethnicity/nation/ 'race'? While Yuval-Davis and Anthias have clearly shown the impact of nation on gender, I think there is a mutual influence (see the discussion below of militarism and nationalism). Further, women's differential commitment to the ethnic/national project affects the project itself, and its relationships with other ethnic/national groups.

The question of *whose* national project has already been discussed in relation to the work of Enloe. In the example which follows I am arguing for a re-casting of the theorization of 'nation formation' in order to take this point into account.

Critical Period of State Formation or Rounds of Restructuring?

One of the assumptions behind the work of Mann[36] and of Turner[37] is that there is a critical period of nation formation (or state formation or nation-state formation). This is a key to Mann's discussion of the societal variations in the development of what he considers to be the key political institutions which constitute democracy. It is also a key assumption in Turner's discussion of the moments of formation of different forms of citizenship.

I am arguing that there is often no one key period of nation formation. In many countries citizenship did not arrive at one moment for all people, but different groups gained different aspects of this in different periods. That countries vary as to whether white men, white women, men and women of minority ethnic groups, gained citizenship at the same time or not. Mann and Turner falsely universalize from white men's citizenship experiences. As Smith has shown there is a very long period of formation of the ethnic groups which go to make up a nation.[38]

Turner seems to suggest that in the US when white men won suffrage in the 1840s citizenship and democracy were won. Yet black men did not get the vote technically until the 1880s and in practice, given the Jim

Crow laws, not until after the civil rights movement at the end of the 1960s. White women did not get the vote until 1920 and black women, while technically getting the vote in 1920, had to wait until further rounds of struggle brought them the franchise in practice at the end of the 1960s together with black men. The history of the citizenship rights of the native American Indians, of course, is one of loss of citizenship after conquest. Thus there are five significant dates: the conquest period, the 1840s, the 1880s, 1920 and the late 1960s, each with an associated period of social struggle. Do we have several stages in nation-building? It remains true of course that the formal institutional structure that constitutes the apparatus of democracy in the US was set up in the second wave of struggle, but these empty institutions do not a democracy make.

In most First World countries there is a period of several decades between the granting of political citizenship to men and to women. This is quite different from the circumstances of many Third World countries, where women won the franchise at the same time as men at the moment of national independence from colonial power. The winning of civil citizenship, while completed for most First World men before political citizenship, is barely completed for women in these countries, since only recently have women won control over their own bodies, the ability to disengage from marriage and the right to engage in all forms of employment. That is, for First World women political citizenship is typically achieved before civil citizenship, the reverse of the order for men. This exists in direct contradiction of Marshall's thesis.

Rather than this notion of one critical period of 'nation formation' it is more appropriate to talk of 'rounds of restructing' of the nation-state. I borrow the term from Massey's work on economic restructuring.[39] It is useful in carrying the notion of change built upon foundations which remain, and that layer upon layer of change can take place, each of which leaves its sediment which significantly affects future practices.

It matters whether the 'citizenization' of society involves all adults at once or only a fragment of them at a time. In the US the gap ranges over well over one hundred years from 1840 to the late 1960s. In Britain the gap was shorter; a few decades separated adult men's suffrage from that of all women in 1928. In many newly independent African and Asian societies these were granted simultaneously at the time of independence in the 1950s and 1960s. It is perhaps salutary to remember that in the early 1960s some African and Asian states had full universal suffrage while that in the US was only partial. Indeed the granting of full citizenship to all was one of the ways in which previously dominated colonies could make a claim to a nationhood.

The restructuring of states in terms of degrees of democracy has some interesting global patterns. Most European and North American states granted citizenship by degree to different layers of the population between the eighteenth and mid twentieth centuries. Most postcolonial states granted full citizenship at once in the mid twentieth century. Some countries have lost democracy. This usually occurs all in one go, as when there is a military coup in which all people lose the right to vote simultaneously. However, since 1979 there has been a serious exception to this situation, with the loss of civil and political rights to women alone, with the rise of Islamic fundamentalism where the Islamic priesthood has taken power, for example in Iran.

Women, Militarism and Nationalism

The relations between gender and nationalism may be mediated through the differential relations of women and men to militarism. The most famous linking of these themes is by Virginia Woolf in *Three Guineas* where a female pacifist says: 'As a woman I have no country. As a woman I want no country. As a woman my country is the whole world.'[40] Women are frequently, though by no means universally, thought to be more pacifist and less militaristic than men.[41] Some writers have argued that women's greater pacifism is a result of a specific aspect of gender ideology.[42] Whether or not this is the explanation, empirally the fact remains that there is a difference in the extent to which men and women take up arms for nationalist projects, support peace movements and support politicians who favour military build-up.[43] The issue here is whether there is a connection between this lesser militarism and support for nationalism. Does women's greater non-violence have an effect upon their view of the 'national' project, in that they are less prepared to pursue nationalist goals by force than men? Does this then make them appear less nationalistic, in that they are less prepared to use a particular means of pursuing that goal, and does this mean that they are actually less nationalistic? That is, is women's lesser militarism a cause of lesser nationalism? Or does it mean that women support a different nationalism? Or that women are greater supporters of transnational projects?

A leading example which suggests a link between women's non-violence and greater internationalism is that of the women's peace camp at Greenham Common in the 1980s, which was part of a loose international grouping of women's peace camps opposed to nuclear weapons, war and the social systems which breed militarism. Women's peace initiatives here may be seen to affect the nature of the national project. Another contemporary example of a group which links anti-militarism with internationalism is that of the Green movement. This is a political grouping, finding expression in both parliamentary and other political arenas, which is committed to ecologically sound policies and which

includes a feminist programme as an integral part of their politics. They
are seriously internationalist in outlook, finding voices in both the Third
World[44] and the First – the Green Party fought EEC elections as a
European party to a greater extent than any other political grouping.
Here, ecological politics, feminism and internationalism converge into a
unitary political programme. Further evidence of the link between
women and pacifism is to be found in opinion polls which regularly show,
at least in Britain and the US, that women are less likely to support militaristic defences of the nation.[45]

Another possibility is that the link between nationalism and militarism
works the other way around. Here women's greater commitment to peace
and opposition to militarism might be thought to be linked to their lesser
commitment to 'their' nation. Do women less often think war for nationalist reasons is worth the candle because they have fewer real interests in
'victorious' outcome, since it would make less difference to their place in
society than that of men? While some men will move from being the
rulers to being subordinate, that is likely to be true of next to no women.
Conversely is the gap between women and men's militarism less marked
in societies where women have a greater stake as a result of less gender
inequality?

There are a number of ways in which gender and nationalism are
mediated by women's typically lesser support for militarism. We see here
women's greater commitment to international peace and cooperation
than to militaristic nationalism. The Green slogan of 'Think globally, act
locally' is very close to typical feminist and women's practice.

Boundaries for Gender Relations

Women's political activity can thus be on a different spatial scale to that
of men. I am suggesting that women's political activities are typically
more local than those of men, and less nationalist. I shall explore the differential significance of a number of large-scale political entities for
women and men, in order to discuss this issue further.

Women are less often than men to be found in formal electoral politics. Women are more likely to be found in the elected assemblies of local
rather than national government. In Britain women constituted 6.6 per
cent of Members of the House of Commons after the 1987 election,
while they formed 19 per cent of local councillors after the 1985 elections. Indeed it is popularly believed that women do not engage in
large-scale national organizations. However, there are such women's
organizations. There are mass, national women's organizations, for
example Women's Institutes, Townswomen's Guilds, Mothers' Unions.
So the argument about the different spatial scales of men's and women's

political organizations should not be exaggerated. It is, nevertheless, often thought that women are more active on a smaller territorial scale than men.

I have been using a variety of concepts and categories to differentiate between different social patterns and groups – the notions of ethnic group, 'race' and nation. There are also a number of others – religion, empire, common language. These have been largely used to differentiate between groups of men. The question in relation to gender is then logically – are the concepts which denote difference between men the same as the concepts which usefully denote difference between women? Are men and women divided up in identical or different ways? Are women as attached to and defensive of 'their' ethnic, or other, group as men?

There are a number of possible answers to this. First, if it is held that men and women have identical interests, then there would be little possibility of separation. However, this is a largely discredited idea. Men and women do occupy different social positions and thus do have different interests. But do these differences make for differences at the level of ethnic/nation/'race'? Secondly, if women suffer from ethnic domination or benefit from ethnic dominance to the same extent as men, then they may have similar ethnicity/nation/'race' interests. Thirdly, different ethnicity/nation/'race's have different patterns of gender relations, some of which may be seen as preferable to others. This is likely to give rise to different gender opinions as to the merits of a given ethnicity/nation/'race' project. This is still dependent upon the same ethnicity/nation/'race' boundaries as those experienced by men, but may entail differential evaluation of the ethnicity/nation/'race' projects by men and women (or, more likely, some men and some women). Fourthly, given that ethnicity, nation, 'race', religion, language and other signifiers of boundaries between social groups often overlap, but are not usually co-terminous, then there is the possibility that some of these boundaries may have more salience for women and some for men. One example of this is that a religious signifier might be more important to women than a 'national' signifier, but not for men, so that if those two systems are in conflict, then men and women may diverge. Issues of militarism and nationalism may be affected here. Fifthly, different gendered discourses may hold a greater or lesser commitment to large or small groups. (Gilligan has suggested that women have different criteria of moral evaluation.[46])

Women, Nation and Europe

The shifting relations between a state, the UK, and a supranational body, the EEC, illustrates the issue of different bounded units having varying gender relations. It also demonstrates the importance of not considering a state to have only one critical period of formation, as was argued above. Gender, ethnicity and class have different relationships to the 'nation', the state and to supranational state-like institutions. This is because the determinants of gender, class and ethnicity are different. Hence the nation-state has a different place in their construction.

An example of this can be seen in the development of the EEC. The central EEC institutions have long supported the practice of 'equal opportunities'.[47] This was formally built into the EEC in the Treaty of Rome, which operates effectively as a constitution for the supranational EEC. These formal rules have been brought into effective operation partly by the actions of some of the officials of the EEC. It is also obviously the case that it is not in the interests of those countries which have instutionalized equal opportunities practices to allow others to continue to use subordinate female labour which could undercut their industries. Recalcitrant nation-states have been brought into line by the use of rulings from the European Court and directives from EEC Commissions, with consequent changes to national legislation.

The UK state has not passively accepted these changes but has a long and complicated history of resistance interleaved with compliance. For instance, the UK government's representatives on the EEC bodies have typically resisted the expansion of equal opportunities policies. They have used their right of veto to prevent the EEC extending equal opportunities policies to parental leave, and part-time workers. Hence the UK government's preferred policies on gender have affected the workings of the EEC. Nevertheless, many policies have been imposed on a reluctant UK government. One of the most important was the 'equal value' amendment to the equal pay legislation. This significantly widened the ways a woman could claim equal pay. No longer did she have to find a man doing the 'same or similar' work, which was very difficult given the extent of occupational segregation. Now she could claim equal pay with a man whose work was of the same value as hers (usually to be determined by some method of job evaluation). In the US in those places where such policies have been introduced it has often led to 20 per cent increases in women's pay. Tens of thousands of these cases are currently wending their way through the British industrial courts.

Here we see a supranational body challenging and changing the gender relations of a nation-state. There are two key elements in the explanation of this. First, the differential representation of women's interests at the level of the supranational body, the EEC, as compared to the national, for example the British state. Secondly, the relations between the EEC and the British state.

Gender relations in Britain today cannot be fully understood outside of an analysis of the relations between the British state and the EEC, that is, issues of 'nation' and 'state' are significant determinants of the changes in contemporary British gender relations. The greater the loss of the independence of the British state *vis-à-vis* the EEC, the greater has been, and is likely to be, the strengthening of equal opportunities legislation and practices. Women have an interest in the loss of British sovereignty on this issue.

Feminism, Nationalism and Westernization

Another example of a transnational category which is of relevance to gender relations is that of 'Westernization'. The issue of whether there is a link between feminism and Westernization is important for issues of political mobilization around nationalist projects and feminist and anti-feminist ones.[48] Is feminism transnational or is it nationally or ethnically specific?

Third World critics of feminism have often suggested, first, that it is Western in origin, and secondly that this renders it less relevant than if it were nationally endogenous. There are really two further questions here. Is feminism a transnational political movement? Is it Western in origin?

It is the case that the kinds of demands which are called for by feminists are not nationally specific. It is also the case that feminists have typically read the work of feminists in other countries. But it is also the case that a lot of feminist writing originated in the West.

However, this is not to say that feminism is not generated by local conditions. Indeed Jayawardena argues strongly that feminism movements in the Third World have been generated by Third World women in their own interests, as was discussed above.[49] Evans shows that the first wave of feminism was not only to be found in many European countries including Russia, and also in Australia and North America, but that there were international feminist organizations as well.[50]

The question, of course, is whether women share similar forms of subordination in different countries. If they do, then it is likely that women in many countries will articulate similar demands. It is then logical that literature written and tactics generated in one country will be pertinent in another. That is, there are internationally valid forms of feminism. The evidence from writers such as Jayawardena and Evans is that feminists across the world have believed that there are such commonalities. That is, feminism and patterns of gender relations have significant transnational aspects.

However, the significance of the 'accusation' that feminism and the movement of women into the public sphere are Western should not be underestimated. In this case whether it is true or not does not necessarily diminish the significance of this assertion in the context of national struggles. Whether or not male elites have the ability to characterize women's public presence as Western is often a matter of local struggle. Further, the meaning of 'Western' is variable. Sometimes the epithet 'Western' has been conflated with that of 'modern' (as in the case of Turkey under Ataturk, and Iran under the Shah), in which case it has assisted the implementation of policies likely to increase the public presence of women. On other occasions the epithet 'Western' is conflated with that of 'hated alien and imperialist oppressor', in which case it has assisted policies likely to hinder the presence of women in public (for example Iran under Khomeini). Thus the conflation of feminism or the public presence of women with 'Western' may assist or hinder such a change, depending on other circumstances. An analysis of which circumstances lead in which direction needs not only an analysis of gender, but also of ethnicity/nation/'race' and the international order.

Conclusions

Gender cannot be analysed outside of ethnic, national and 'race' relations; but neither can these latter phenomena be analysed without gender. It is not a case of simply adding these two sets of analyses together, but rather that they mutually affect each other in a dynamic relationship.

Patterns of gender relations sometimes take the same spatial units as those of class and ethnicity, nation and 'race', but often they do not. It appears, from the available evidence, as if women's political activities have tended to be both more global and more local than men's as a proportion of their total political activity. However, this conclusion must remain tentative in the light of the limited evidence. Women have less often than men engaged at the level of the nation. Commonalities in the nature of gender relations sometimes transcend national frontiers and ethnic and 'radical' specificity. At the same time, the 'personal' is as political as ever.

The relationship between feminism and nationalism is crucially mediated by militarism, since men and women often, but not always, have a different relationship to war. This may mean that women are simultaneously both less militaristic and less nationalistic because militarism is often seen as an integral facet of a national project.

A national or ethnic project will have been struggled over by social forces differentiated in many ways, especially by class and by gender. Thus relations between nations are partly the outcome of many locally specific gendered struggles.

The struggle for citizenship is today a democratic project. In popular political discourse it entails the full participation of all adults regardless of 'race', ethnicity, sex, or creed. It is also a national project and indeed a project by which the 'nation' seeks to obtain legitimacy as a project in the eyes of both that country's inhabitants and the 'international community'. Social scientists should pay regard to the new meaning of the term citizen, rather than the limited notion utilized in ancient Greek city-states from which women, slaves and 'aliens' were excluded.

Notes

1. See Anthony D. Smith, *Theories of Nationalism*, London 1971, and *The Ethnic Origins of Nations*, Oxford 1986.

2 See Ernest Gellner, *Nations and Nationalism*, Oxford 1983; Elie Kedourie, *Nationalism*, London 1966; Smith, *Theories of Nationalism* and *Ethnic Origins of Nations*.

3. Cynthia Enloe, *Bananas, Beaches and Bases: Making Feminist Sense of International Politics*, London 1989; Kumari Jayawardena, *Feminism and Nationalism in the Third World*, London 1986; Nira Yuval-Davis and Floya Anthias, eds, *Woman-Nation-State*, London 1989.

4. See Michael Mann, 'Ruling Class Strategies and Citizenship', *Sociology*, vol. 21, no. 3, 1987, pp. 339–54; Brian Turner, *Citizenship and Reformism: The Debate over Reformism*, London 1986, and 'Outline of a Theory of Citizenship', *Sociology*, vol. 24, no. 2, 1990, pp. 189–217.

5. E.g. Michael Mann, 'A Crisis in Stratification Theory? Persons, Households/Families/Lineages, Genders, Classes and Nations', in Rosemary Crompton and Michael Mann, eds, *Gender and Stratification*, Cambridge 1986.

6. Cf. Michael Mann, *Gender and Stratification*, and *A History of Power from the Beginning to A.D. 1760*, Volume 1, *The Sources of Social Power*, Cambridge 1986; Bryan Turner, *The Body and Society*, Cambridge 1987.

7. E.g. Mary Daly, *Gyn/Ecology: The Metaethics of Radical Feminism*, London 1978.

8. E.g. bell hooks.

9. E.g. Enloe, *Bananas, Beaches and Bases*; Jayawardena, *Feminism and Nationalism*; Floya Anthias and Nira Yuval-Davis, Introduction, *Woman-Nation-State*.

10. Yuval-Davis and Anthias, eds, *Woman-Nation-State*; Jayawardena, *Feminism and Nationalism*; Enloe, *Bananas, Beaches and Bases*.

11. Anthias and Yuval-Davis, Introduction, *Woman-Nation-State*.

12. Ibid., p. 7.

13. Francesca Klug, '"Oh to be in England": The British Case Study', in Yuval-Davis and Anthias, eds, *Woman-Nation-State*.

14. Marie de Lepervanche, 'Women, Nation and State in Australia', in *Woman-Nation-State*.

15. Deborah Gaitskell and Elaine Unterhalter, 'Mothers of the Nation: A Comparative Analysis of Nation, Race and Motherhood in Afrikaner Nationalism and the African National Congress', in *Woman-Nation-State*.

16. Floya Anthias, 'Women and Nationalism in Cyprus', in *Woman-Nation-State*; Deniz Kandyoti, ed., *Women, Islam and the State*, London 1991.

17. Christine Obbo, 'Sexuality and Domination in Uganda', in *Woman-Nation-State*.

18. Haleh Afshar, 'Women and Reproduction in Iran', in *Woman-Nation-State*.

19. *Feminism and Nationalism*.

20. Ibid., pp. 2–3.

21. Ibid., p. 3.

22. Ibid., p. 8.

23. Ibid., p. 259.

24. Ibid., p. 256.

25. Cf. Swasti Mitter, *Common Fate, Common Bond: Women in the Global Economy*, London 1986; John Urry, *The Tourist Gaze*, London 1990.

26. Enloe, *Bananas, Beaches and Bases*, p. 44.

27. Ibid., p. 48.

28. Ibid., pp. 49–50.

29. Ibid., p. 49.

30. Ibid., p. 44.

31. Ibid., p. 64.

32. E.g. Daly, *Gyn/Ecology*.

33. Cf. Mann, *Gender and Stratification* and *Sources of Political Power*; and Turner, *Body and Society*.

34. See the analysis of Firestone in Sylvia Walby, *Theorizing Patriarchy*, Oxford 1990.

35. See Walby, *Theorizing Patriarchy*, for a fuller account.

36. Mann, 'Ruling Class Strategies'.

37. Turner, 'Theory of Citizenship'.

38. Smith, *Ethnic Origins of Nations*.

39. Doreen Massey, *Spatial Divisions of Labour: Social Structures and the Geography of Production*, London 1984.

40. Virginia Woolf, *Three Guineas*, London 1938.

41. See Erika Cudworth, 'Feminism and Non-Violence: A Relation in Theory, in Herstory and Praxis', unpublished MSc dissertation, London School of Economics, 1988; Sybil Oldfield, *Women Against the Iron Fist: Alternatives to Militarism, 1990–1989*, Oxford 1989.

42. See Sara Ruddick, *Maternal Thinking*, Boston 1989.

43. Beatrix Campbell, *The Iron Ladies: Why do Women Vote Tory?*, London 1987: Cudworth, 'Feminism and Non-Violence'; Hester Eisenstein, *Contemporary Feminist Thought*, London 1984; Cynthia Enloe, *Does Khaki Become You? The Militarization of Women's Lives*, London 1983.

44. See Vandana Shiva, *Staying Alive: Women, Ecology and Development*, London 1989.

45. See Zillah Eisenstein, *Feminism and Sexual Equality: Crisis in Liberal America*, New York 1984.

46. Carol Gilligan, *In a Different Voice: Psychological Theory and Women's Development*, Cambridge, Mass., 1982.

47. See Jeanne Gregory, *Sex, Race and the Law: Legislating for Equality*, London 1987; Catherine Hoskyns, 'Women's Equality and the European Community', *Feminist Review*, 20, summer 1985, pp. 71–88.

48. See Jayawardena, *Feminism and Nationalism*.

49. Ibid.

50. Richard J. Evans, *The Feminists: Women's Emancipation Movements in Europe, America and Australasia 1840–1920*, London 1977.

11

Ethnicity and Nationalism in Europe Today

Eric J. Hobsbawm

I speak to you not simply as a historian who has been interested in the development of nationalism and has written something about it, but as part of my subject. For historians are to nationalism what poppy-growers in Pakistan are to heroin addicts: we supply the essential raw material for the market. Nations without a past are contradictions in terms. What makes a nation *is* the past; what justifies one nation against others is the past and historians are the people who produce it. So my profession, which has always been mixed up in politics, becomes an essential component of nationalism. More so even than the ethnographers, philologists and other suppliers of ethnic and national services who have usually also been mobilized. In what terms do Armenians and Azeris argue about who has the right to Mountain Karabakh which, I remind you, is in Azerbaijan, but inhabited mainly by Armenians? In terms of arguments about the Caucasian Albanians, a people which no longer exists but which in the Middle Ages inhabited the disputed region, were they more like or unlike the Armenians who are there now? This is essentially a problem for historical research, in this case endlessly speculative historical debates. (I take this example from Nora Dudwick of the University of Pennsylvania.) Unfortunately the history that nationalists want is not the history that professional academic historians, even ideologically committed ones, ought to supply. It is a retrospective mythology. Let me repeat yet again the words of Ernest Renan in his famous lecture 'What is a Nation?' in 1882: 'Forgetting history, or even getting history wrong [*l'erreur historique*], is an essential factor in the formation of a nation, which is why the progress of historical studies is often dangerous to a nationality.' So a historian who writes about ethnicity or nationalism cannot but make a politically or ideologically explosive intervention.

Let me begin with a semantic query. If there is any standard criterion today of what constitutes a nation with a claim to self-determination, that is, to setting up an independent territorial nation-state, it is ethnic-linguistic, since language is taken, wherever possible, to express and symbolize ethnicity. But of course it is sometimes not possible, because historical research demonstrates conclusively that the kind of standard-ized written language which can be used to represent ethnicity or nationality is a rather late historic construction – mostly of the nine-teenth century or even later – and in any case quite often it does not exist at all, as between Serbs and Croats. Even then, however, the ethnic dis-tinction, whatever it may signify, is made. I spend my holidays in a cottage in Wales which is administratively and legally less distinct from England than Connecticut is from New York State. Yet even though in my part Welsh has not been spoken for a long time, and indeed the natives have even forgotten the Welsh pronunciation of our Celtic place-names, it would not cross my neighbours' minds that just living there makes me Welsh. Of course I must add that the concept of ethnicity is available to them, as it would not be available to my neighbours if I bought a cottage in Suffolk, unless they were anti-Semitic. There I would be just as much a stranger, but they would have to define themselves against me as natives against incomers, or in terms of social classification. This would probably be a less effective form of making collective distinctions than 'ethnicity', but I am by no means clear why.

Every separatist movement in Europe that I can think of bases itself on 'ethnicity', linguistic or not, that is to say on the assumption that 'we' – the Basques, Catalans, Scots, Croats, or Georgians are a different people from the Spaniards, the English, the Serbs or the Russians, and therefore we should not live in the same state with them. This is not, by the way, the case as yet in most of Asia, Africa and the Americas south of the Canadian border. I shall return to this point later.

Why then do we need two words, which help us to distinguish *nation-alism* from ethnicity, though both are so closely identified today? Because we are dealing with different, and indeed non-comparable, concepts.

Nationalism is a political programme, and in historic terms a fairly recent one. It holds that groups defined as 'nations' have the right to, and there-fore ought to, form territorial states of the kind that have become standard since the French Revolution. Without this programme, real-ized or not, 'nationalism' is a meaningless term. In practice the programme usually means exercising sovereign control over a, so far as possible, continuous stretch of territory with clearly defined borders inhabited by a homogeneous population that forms its essential body of citizens. Or rather, according to Mazzini, it includes the totality of such a population: 'Every nation a state and only one state for the entire nation.' Within such states a single language, that of the 'nation' in question, is dominant, or rather enjoys privileged official status or monopoly. I observe in passing that probably not more than a dozen or so out of the 170-odd political entities in the world conform to even the first half of the Mazzinian programme, if nations are defined in ethnic-linguistic terms.

Nationalism, or rather, to use the more lucid nineteenth-century phrase, 'the principle of nationality', assumes 'the nation' as given, just as democracy assumes 'the people' as given. In itself it tells us nothing about what constitutes such a nation, although since the late nineteenth century – but not, commonly, much before then – it has increasingly been defined in ethnic-linguistic terms. However, I must remind you that earlier versions of the principle of nationality, which I describe in *Nations and Nationalism since 1780* as the 'revolutionary-democratic' and 'liberal', are not so based, although there are overlaps. Neither language nor ethnicity is essential to the original revolutionary nationalism, of which the USA is the major surviving version. Classical nineteenth-century liberal nationalism was the opposite of the current search for a definition of group identity by separatism. It aimed to *extend* the scale of human social, political and cultural units: to unify and expand rather than to restrict and separate. This is one reason why Third World national liberation movements found the nineteenth century traditions, both liberal and revolutionary-democratic, so congenial. Anti-colonial nationalists dismissed, or at least subordinated, 'tribalism', 'communalism' or other sectional and regional identities as anti-national, and serving the well-known imperialist interests of 'divide and rule'. Gandhi and Nehru, Mandela and Mugabe, or for that matter the late Zulfikhar Bhutto who complained about the absence of a sense of Pakistani nationhood, are or were not nationalists in the sense of Landsbergis or Tudjman. They were on exactly the same wavelength as Massimo d'Azeglio who said, after Italy had been politically unified: 'We have made Italy, now we have to make Italians', that is, out of the inhabitants of the peninsula who had all sorts of identities, but not one based on a language they did not speak, and a state that had come into existence over their heads. There was nothing primordial about Italianness, just as there is not about the South Africanness of the ANC.

Ethnicity, on the other hand, whatever it may be, is not programmatic and even less is it a political concept. It may acquire political functions in certain circumstances, and may therefore find itself associated with programmes, including nationalist and separatist ones. There are plenty of good reasons why nationalism thirsts for identification with ethnicity, if only because it provides the historical pedigree 'the nation' in the great majority of cases so obviously lacks. At least it does so in regions of ancient written culture like Europe, where the same names of ethnic groups persist over long periods, even though they may describe quite different and changing social realities. Ethnicity, whatever its basis, is a readily definable way of expressing a *real* sense of group identity which links the members of 'us' because it emphasizes their differences from 'them'. What they actually have in common beyond not being 'them' is not so clear, especially today, and I shall return to this point. Anyway ethnicity is one way of filling the empty containers of nationalism. Thus Sabino Arana invents the name Euskadi for the country of the people who had long given themselves, and been given, a collective name (Basques, Gascons or whatever) but without feeling the need for the sort of country, state or nation Arana had in mind.

In other words, nationalism belongs with political theory, ethnicity with sociology or social anthropology. It can take the state or any other form of political organization or it can leave it alone. If it becomes political, it has no special affinity for ethnically labelled politics. All it requires is that the political label, whatever it is, should make a disproportionately strong appeal to the members of the ethnic group. An extreme case, now long forgotten, is the appeal of the passionately non-ethnic Bolshevik party in the revolutionary period to the inhabitants of what has become Latvia. The prominence of some Lettish names in the last days of Soviet communism is a reminder of the days when the Lettish riflemen were to Lenin what the Swiss Guards are to the Pope. There is Colonel Alksnis on the hard-line side and Otto Latsis of *Kommunist* and *Izvestia* on the reforming side.

If this is so, why then the general European mutation of ethnic politics into nationalist politics? This mutation takes two forms, which have little or nothing in common except the need or desire to control state policy: national separatism and national xenophobia, that is, being against foreigners by setting up 'our' own state, and being against them by excluding them from 'our' already existing state. The second variant I find more difficult to account for than the first, for which there are both specific and general explanations today.

But before I try to answer these questions, let me remind you once again that there are vast areas of the globe where ethnic politics, however embittered, are not nationalist, sometimes because the idea of an ethnically homogeneous population has been abandoned at some time in the past, or never existed – in the USA – or because the programme of setting up separate territorial, ethnic-linguistic states is both irrelevant and impractical. The USA is once again a case in point, but the situation also arises in the majority of the decolonized Third World states. Whatever the bitterness of interethnic and ghetto conflicts in the USA, separatism is not a serious option, and serves no purpose for any ethnic or other groups.

To return to the main question. The specific reason for the wave of nationalist separatism in Europe today is historical. The chickens of World War I are coming home to roost. The explosive issues of 1989–91 are those created in Europe and, I am tempted to add, in the Middle East, by the collapse of the multi-cthnic Habsburg, Ottoman and Russian empires in 1917–18, and the nature of the postwar peace settlements in respect of their successor states. The essence of these, you may recall, was the Wilsonian plan to divide Europe into ethnic-linguistic territorial states, a project as dangerous as it was impracticable, except at the cost of forcible mass expulsion, coercion and genocide which was subsequently paid. Let me add that the Leninist theory of nations on which the USSR was subsequently constructed (and Yugoslavia) was essentially the same, though in practice – at least in the USSR – supplemented by the Austro-Marxist system of nationality as an individual choice, which every citizen has the right to make at the age of sixteen wherever he or she comes from.

I do not want to document my thesis at length, but I will just remind you that Slovak conflict with Czechs, Croat conflict with Serbs, could not exist before 1918 when these peoples were put into the same states. Baltic nationalism, which had been the least of the tsar's political worries and barely existed in 1917, was nurtured by setting up independent little states as part of the quarantine belt against the Bolshevist infection. Conversely, national issues which *were* serious or even explosive before 1914 have receded: I am thinking of the famous 'Macedonian Question', the Ukraine, or even the demand for the restoration of historic Poland. Ukraine (except in the formerly Habsburg part) and Macedonia showed no signs of wanting to break away until the USSR and Yugoslavia had been destroyed by other hands, and they found they had to take some action in self-defence.

It is therefore more important than ever to reject the 'primordialist' theory of ethnicity, let alone of national self-determination. Since this is an audience of anthropologists I hope that I may assume that this is an uncontroversial statement. It is the historians who need to be reminded how easily ethnic identities can be changed, as witness the nationalist animus against 'assimilation', so familiar in Jewish debates about Judaism. Early-twentieth-century Europe was full of men and women who, as their very names indicate, had *chosen* to be Germans or Magyars or French or Finns, and even today the names of President Landsbergis and a number of prominent Slovenes suggest German parents opting for another collective identity. Conversely, a German anthropologist, Georg Elwert, reminds us that the concept of the *Volksdeutsche*, the ethnic German who, by the constitution of the Federal Republic, has a 'right of return' to his homeland as Jews have in Israel, is an ideological construct. Some of those who have, like the East European Mennonites, were not Germans by origin at all (unless all speakers of Germanic languages are counted), but Flemings or Frisians. And the only East European settlers from Germany who actually saw themselves, among other things, as cultural and linguistic Germans – to the point of organizing German schools teaching the standard German language – do not enjoy the 'right of return' except to Israel. They were the upper- and middle-class eastern Jews, whose very choice of surnames – Deutscher, Ginsburg, Shapiro – echoes unforgotten origins. Elwert even notes that there are Transylvanian villages where High German (as distinct from the Teutonic dialects actually spoken) was known before the Hitler period as 'Judendaitsch'. Such are the paradoxes of primordial ethnicity.

And yet there is no denying that 'ethnic' identities which had no political or even existential significance until yesterday (for instance being a 'Lombard', which is now the title of the xenophobic leagues in North Italy) can acquire a genuine hold as badges of group identity overnight. In my book *Nations and Nationalism since 1780* I suggest that these short-term changes and shifts of ethnic identities constitute 'the area of national studies in which thinking and research are most urgently needed today', and I maintain this view.

There are good reasons why ethnicity (whatever it is) should be politicized in modern multi-ethnic societies, which characteristically take the form of a diaspora of mainly urban ghettoes, combined with a sharp increase in the occasions for friction between ethnic groups. Electoral democracy produces a ready-made machine for minority groups to fight effectively for a share of central resources, once they learn to act as a group and are sufficiently concentrated for electoral purposes. This gives ghettoized groups a lot of potential leverage. At the same time, for reasons both of politics and ideology, and also of changing economic organization, the mechanism for defusing interethnic tensions by assigning separate niches to different groups, atrophies. They now compete not for comparable resources ('separate but equal', as the phrase went) but for the *same* resources in the same labour or housing or educational or other markets. And in this competition, at least for the disadvantaged, group pressure for special favours ('affirmative action') is the most powerful weapon available. Where, for whatever reason, participation in elections is low, as in the USA today, or traditional mass support weakens, as in the US Democratic and the British Labour parties, politicians pay even more attention to minorities, of which ethnic groups are one variant. We can even see pseudo-ethnic groups being invented for political purposes, as in the attempt by some on the British Left to classify all

Third World immigrants as 'black' in order to give them more leverage within the Labour Party for which most of them vote. So the new 'black sections' of the party which have been set up will include Bangladeshis, Pakistanis, West Indians, Indians and presumably Chinese.

Yet the core of ethnic politicization is not instrumental. What we see very generally today is a retreat from social into group identity. It is not necessarily political. One thinks of the familiar nostalgia for 'roots' which makes the children of assimilated, secularized and anglicized Jews redis-cover comfort in the ancestral rituals and sentimentalize the memories of the *shtetl* which, thank God, they have never known. Sometimes when it calls itself political it is so only by semantic innovation, as in the phrase 'the personal is political'. Yet, inevitably it has a political dimension. But under what circumstances does it become politically separatist?

Miroslav Hroch has tried to answer this question for contemporary Central and Eastern Europe by comparison with nineteenth-century small-nation linguistic nationalism. One element he stresses in both cases is that it is a lot easier to understand language demands than the theory and institutions of democracy and constitutional society, especially for people who lack both political education and political experience. But more crucially he stresses social disorientation:

> in a social situation where the old regime was collapsing, where old relations were in flux and general insecurity was growing, the members of the 'non-dominant ethnic group' [in English in the original German text] would see the community of language and culture as the ultimate certainty, the unam-biguously demonstrable value. Today, as the system or planned economy and social security breaks down, once again – the situation is analogous – lan-guage acts as a substitute for factors of integration in a disintegrating society. When society fails, the nation appears as the ultimate guarantee.

The situation in the ex-socialist societies and especially in the ex-USSR is clear. Now that both the material framework and the routines of every-day life have broken down, now that all the established values are suddenly denied, what *is* the citizen of the USSR? What can he or she believe in?

Assuming the past is irrecoverable, the obvious fall-back positions are ethnicity and religion, singly or in combination. And ethnicity turns into separatist nationalism for much the same reasons as colonial liberation movements established their states within the frontiers of the preceding colonial empires. They are the frontiers that exist. Only more so, for the Soviet constitution itself had divided the country into theoretically ethnic territorial sub-units, ranging from autonomous areas to full federal republics. Supposing the union fell to pieces, these were the fracture lines along which it would naturally break. It is a curious joke of history that it was Stalin who gave Lithuania its capital city (between the wars it was in Poland), and Tito who, in order to weaken Great Serbian chauvinism, created a much larger Croatia with a much larger Serbian minority.

However, let us not – or not yet – infer mass nationalism from separatist movements in all cases. So far the Yugoslav civil war has been waged mainly by activist minorities plus the professionals. Has it yet become a real peoples' war? We don't know, but there are at least 2.8 million Yugoslav families – those who produced the 1.4 million mixed marriages, mostly Croat-Serb – for whom the choice of an exclusive ethnic identity must be a complex matter.

If the roots of ethnic politics in social disorientation are plain in the ex-socialist countries, the same social disorientation is found for other reasons elsewhere. Is it an accident that Quebec separatism became a major force at the end of a decade during which the Quebec birth-rate had virtually halved and (for the first time) fallen well below that of Canada?[1] The decades since 1950, the forty most revolutionary years in the history of human society, should lead us to expect a massive disintegration of old values, a collapse of old certainties. The 'nation' is not as obvious a fall-back position everywhere as it is in those parts of the globe whose frontiers were drawn on Wilsonian-Leninist lines after 1918, and neither is that old-time religion. But it is one such position, and the demonstration effect of central and eastern Europe naturally encourages it, where local conditions are favourable.

However, separatism is exceptional in Europe outside the ex-Soviet zone. National xenophobia shading into racism is almost universal. And it poses a problem which I cannot solve. What exactly is being defended against 'the other', identified with the immigrant strangers? Who constitutes 'us' poses less of a problem, for the definition is usually in terms of existing states. 'We' are French, or Swedes, or Germans or even members of politically defined sub-units like Lombards, but distinguished from the invading 'them' by being the 'real' Frenchmen or Germans or Brits, as defined (usually) by putative descent or long residence. Who 'they' are is also not difficult. 'They' are recognizable as 'not we', most usually by colour or other physical stigmata, or by language. Where these signs are not obvious, subtler discriminations can be made: Québecois who refuse to understand anglophones who talk in a Canadian accent will respond to anglophones who talk with a British or US intonation, as Flemings who claim not to understand French spoken with a Belgian accent understand French French. I am not sure how far, without these visible or audible marks of strangeness, 'they' would be recognized by cultural differences, though in racist reactions much is made of such things: how good Frenchmen are insulted by the smells of North African cooking, or good Brits by that of curry emanating from their neighbours. In fact, as the global expansion of Indian and Chinese restaurants suggests, xenophobia is directed against foreign people, not foreign cultural imports.

It would be tempting to say: what is being defended against strangers is jobs, and there is a certain truth in the proposition. The major social base of European racist movements such as the French National Front appears to be in the native working-class, the major activists or such movements appear to be working class young men – skinheads and the like – and a long era of full or virtually guaranteed employment ended, in Western Europe during the 1970s, in Central and Eastern Europe at the end of the 1980s. Since then Europe is once again living in societies of mass unemployment and job uncertainty. Moreover, as I have already observed, the social mechanisms which assigned each group different and non-competitive niches are eroding or are politically unacceptable. The relatively sudden rise of xenophobic parties, or of the xenophobic issue in politics, is largely due to this.

Nevertheless, this is clearly only part of the answer. What is being defended is not simply the position of individuals in group A against challenge by outsiders. If this were so we would not find the genuine uneasiness about an influx of strangers (or outside influences) which cannot in any realistic sense threaten the members of the group as *individuals*, for instance the insistence by sections of US citizens that English – of all languages – has to be given protection against immigrant languages by the grant of an official monopoly of public use. In some sense it is the idea of 'us' as a body of people united by an uncountable number of things 'we' have in *common* – a 'way of life' in the widest sense, a *common* territory of existence in which we live, whose landscape is familiar and recognizable. It is the existence of *this* which the influx from outside threatens. Virtually every single item on the list of what 'we' as English, French, Germans or Czechs are said to have in common can be acquired by immigrants who wish to do so, except physical appearance, where this differs very markedly from the norm of the receiving population. (This is one of the things that make racism so hard to eradicate.) Moreover, some of the countries where xenophobia has been politically mobilized very powerfully are, like France, also countries which in the past received, even encouraged, and successfully assimilated mass immigration to an extent almost comparable at times to the USA: Italians, Spaniards, Poles, even North Africans. Some countries which are very much exercised about the alien danger actually have very little immigration. Indeed they do their best not to have any. This the case of the Scandinavian countries – I am thinking of Finland and Iceland in particular – though the prevailing liberal ideology in those parts makes it embarrassing to admit to this form of intolerance. Finland virtually makes permanent immigration impossible, but until the collapse of the USSR it could hardly be described as a clear and present danger. On the contrary, Finland is, as it has long been, a country mass-producing emigrants.

I am not, of course, denying that societies may exist within a specific set of habits and ways of life, which may be destroyed or transformed by, among other things, excessive immigration. Emotionally, most of us can understand the sentiments of the Pyrenean village which decided to block its public water-fountain, so that not even the thirsty cyclists touring the region should have any incentive to pass through it. It would be disingenuous, even for those of us who take another view, to pretend that we do not know what made an intelligent British traditionalist like Enoch Powell call for a halt to mass immigration some twenty-five years ago, and what made British governments of both parties follow his lead. What is more, all of us apply the same criteria when it comes to saving our own favourite environments, human or non-human, from 'being ruined' by too many people or the wrong kind of people. The point is not whether some places, or even some regions and countries, should be, or could still be, protected from the disruption by change of their ancient collective character, but whether this is what modern political xenophobia is actually trying to do.

In fact, fear of the alien today is rarely a traditional nationalist defence of old ways of life against the foreign virus. This form of cultural xenophobia was indeed common in the 1950s, mainly in anti-American versions – some of us remember the campaign against 'Coca-colonization' – but that battle has long been forgotten. Culturally, the most militant gangs who beat up immigrants in the name of the nation belong to the international youth culture and reflect its modes and fashions, jeans, punk rock, junk food and all. Indeed, for most of the inhabitants of the countries in which xenophobia is now epidemic, the old ways of life have changed so drastically since the 1950s that there is very little of them left to defend. It actually takes someone who has lived through the past forty years as an adult to appreciate quite how extraordinarily the England of even the 1970s differed from the England of the 1940s, and the France, Italy or Spain of the 1980s from those countries in the early 1950s.

And this seems to me to be the clue. This is the point of contact with separatism, or the rush into fundamentalism (as we see it, for instance, in Latin America). All are comprehensible as symptoms of social disorientation, of the fraying, and sometimes the snapping, of the threads of what used to be the network that bound people together in society. The strength of this xenophobia is the fear of the unknown, of the darkness into which we may fall when the landmarks which seem to provide an objective, a permanent, a positive delimitation of our belonging together disappear. And belonging together, preferably in groupings with visible badges of membership and recognition signs, is more important than ever in societies in which everything combines to destroy what binds human beings together into communities. A recent documentary film, *Paris is Burning*, presents a population of the most marginalized, excluded, anomic individuals imaginable: black drag queens in New York. Nothing is more touching and sad than to see how these people – cast out and despised by everyone including their kin, living in and for their regular 'balls' where they compete to dress up to act out, for a moment, the roles they would like to play in real life, and know they cannot – reconstruct their own human groups. In these so-called 'families', each with an invented family name, each with a senior 'mother' who takes responsibility for the rest of the group, individuals can feel that they are not entirely weak and alone.

But for those who can no longer rely on belonging anywhere else, there is at least one other imagined community to which one can belong: which is permanent, indestructible, and whose membership is certain. Once again 'the nation', or the ethnic group, 'appears as the ultimate guarantee' when society fails. You do not have to do anything to belong to it. You cannot be thrown out. You are born in it and stay in it. As Eugene Roosens says in *Creating Ethnicity*, the book which, with Frederik Barth's *Ethnic Groups* I have found particularly helpful: 'After all, nobody can change "the past" from which one descends, and nobody can undo who one is'.[2] (Well, of course you can change, or at least invent a past – but they don't know it.) And how do men and women know that they belong to this community? Because they can define the others who do not belong, who should not belong, who never can belong. In other words, by xenophobia. And because we live in an era when all other human relations and values are in crisis, or at least somewhere on a journey towards unknown and uncertain destinations, xenophobia looks like becoming the mass ideology of the twentieth-century *fin de siècle*. What holds humanity together today is the denial of what the human race has in common.

And where does that leave you anthropologists whose very name commits you to some conceptual universalism'? And us historians, who are being told not only that only blacks or whites or Basques or Croats can properly understand the history of these respective groups, but to invent the sort of history that they want to 'understand'? At least it leaves us – it should leave us – the freedom to be sceptical. No good will come of it, but it won't last for ever.

Notes

1. Gerald Bernier, Robert Boily et al. *Le Québec en chiffres de 1850 à nos jours*, Montreal 1986, p. 28.

2. Eugene Roosens, *Creating Ethnicity*, Newbury Park 1989, p. 16.

12

Internationalism and the Second Coming

Tom Nairn

Navigation of the seas beyond the end of history requires new bearings. 'Internationalism' is one of the most important of these. It is important that it not be taken for granted, yet it often is. The concept we have inherited was the reverse of the medal of first-wave (nineteenth- and earlier twentieth-century) nationalism. Even then it was more wielded than analysed, and not often considered in its own right. It tended to be the background music which helped to form attitudes rather than the foreground story. Now we badly need a change of tune.

Much of this was borne in upon me recently at an event I attended in Glasgow.[1] I was presenting the case for national self-determination in a suitably broad sense – nationalism as the least bad answer, or in any case inevitable – and opposing the new international pessimism, what I guess we have come to call the theory of the Ethnic Abyss. Afterward a well-known theorist of the (old) New Left said to me:

> *Merci, mon cher Nairn, merci, très intéressant, mais* . . . allow me to observe, with-out giving undue offence. . . . It seems to me that you are arguing the way you do because, being a nationalist, you have to.

What I believe he meant is that I distorted everything to suit my parochial bias. He was, of course, far too kind to employ phrases like 'dressing up your personal prejudices' or 'special pleading'. But the point was that history, whether ended or reborn, had to be rewritten to make it fit the inescapable necessity that Scotland be free and have her own government.

I, in turn, was too polite to make the obvious reply: he also might have prejudices to enrobe and interests to defend. His own contribu-tion, an austerely revised version of an internationalist credo focusing on

racism, could equally be viewed as a belief system of a particular group –
a group speaking (or implicitly claiming to speak) for science and civilization as such.

The bias of nationalism (even generalized nationalism) is indeed easy
to detect. However, that of internationalism is less so. A nationalist (even
a pan-nationalist) by definition speaks from somewhere; the internationalist speaks (or claims to speak) from nowhere in particular.

Of course, it is ridiculous that the truth on such matters should be
seen as merely a clash of such interests. I am not arguing for any kind of
half-witted relativism here. The dialogue is what counts, and the question
is how to continue it more fruitfully, or less one-sidedly. I believe that may
be an important part of the post-1989 change. Nationalism and hence
internationalism are now beginning to appear in a different light: one
kinder to both sides, but which makes it clearer that the truth belonged
exclusively to neither.

Internationality

The key distinction is between internationalism and what I am afraid
must be referred to as 'internationality'. This is an uncomfortable term,
at least in the English language, and is not in common use. However it
does exist and, more importantly, it does mean something.[2]

'Of course, a French race-course is not like an English one.
Internationality is not yet so perfect.' This was the *Oxford English
Dictionary*'s authority from the 1864 *Daily Telegraph*. It also expressed the
scarcely veiled great nation chauvinism which, as the years went by, was
destined to be a notable part of the internationalist orchestra.
Racecourses were growing more alike over the world as civilization
advanced. So were factories, shops, high streets, farms, and even people.
Given enough time, would they not become indistinguishable?

Such would be the fulfilment of 'internationality'. A recent high note
of the same chorus was struck by Alexander Cockburn. When the communists gave up in Russia, he predicted with a certain sourness that Pizza
Hut would soon be setting up in Red Square, quite possibly in Lenin's
mausoleum if only they could remove 'the old stiff'. Though a fully sub-
scribed internationalist of the old school, Cockburn was definitely
unhappy about this – maybe because he detected the hand of the
American empire in such a triumph of internationality. Internationalism
has always suffered from such problems.

There is, of course, nothing remotely left-wing about internationality.
It denotes all the things which were so conspicuously hymned in *The
Communist Manifesto*: the majestic revolutionary tide of capitalist expan-
sion dissolving all traditions and effacing every frontier; the lineaments of

that right-wing world which would very soon be taken over and purified by the Left. I do not need to elaborate on the stages of tidal progress that are in review here, from Manchester Free Trade via the 'international trusts' to their more powerful successors, the multinational corporations. The message has always been much the same, whether delivered as a hymn or as a curse.

One hundred and twenty-six years later, we hear essentially the same tune from Jacques G. Maisonrouge, a former executive of the multinationalist International Business Machines:

> For business purposes the boundaries that separate one nation from another are no more real than the equator. They are merely convenient demarcations of ethnic, linguistic and cultural entities. . . . Once management accepts this world economy, its view of the marketplace – and its planning – necessarily expand. . . .[3]

The views of many representatives of convenient entities (not invariably delighted to see their boundaries treated like the equator, whether by computer salesmen, revolutionaries, or cocaine vendors) have expanded as well. Since then IBM has discovered that it does not rule the globe.[4] Small is not only beautiful but has teeth too (speaking both technically and politically).

The dignified point is, however, that internationality has never in any case implied internationalism, or at least not in any straightforward sense. Marx and Maisonrouge were equally mistaken. There have been, and there still are, constant, recurrent, and simplistic arguments to the effect that the one leads inevitably to the other. As protagonists of medieval particularism (as Lenin loved to call it), we nationalists find ourselves from time to time belaboured by those in love with the communication and information revolutions or overawed by economic scale. Technological determinism is as inescapable as the weather. 'How (they say) can you small-time extras and understudies go on pretending you have a starring future, when your own kids come home every day to stuff themselves with Big Macs while they watch programmes like *Neighbours* or *L.A. Law* beamed down from a satellite?'

In fact, the overwhelmingly dominant political by-product of modern internationality so far has been nationalism. Not the implacably prescribed common sense of internationalism, but the nonlogical, untidy, refractory, disintegrative, particularistic truth of nation-states. Not swelling or supine unity but 'Balkanization', a world of spiky exceptions to what ought to have been the rule but clearly is not. Even before 1989 it was clear that medieval particularism still had a future. Only after that year could it be more convincingly argued that it had *the* future too.

I fail to see how one can avoid suspecting that there is some connection here. It cannot simply be a chain of accidents, as internationalists pretend. Political Marxism may be in the grave, but in my book historical materialism lives on. All those Big Macs and IBM salesmen must have actually (materially) fostered or created this result, no doubt unintentionally. 'Balkanization' must not be a doomed and mindless resistance to the advance of progress, but that progress itself. It must be what actually happens, as distinct from the ideological virtual reality offered up by the determinists, the multinational salesmen, and the internationalists. Ah yes, we always thought we knew that the poor Macedonians would have to resign themselves to progress – to the erosion of their antique and colourful ways, to becoming more like everybody else. Now, we also know that progress must resign itself to being Macedonian.

Ethic and Doctrine

An analogy may be in order here. It is now a commonplace of the theory of nationalism that it bears no simple relationship to nationality. The '*ism*' does not spring out from the brute facts of difference or singularity. There are nationalities without nationalism. I happen to come from one. In Scotland in the 1950s, everyone knew that they were Scottish, but almost no one believed that they would later require the troublesome '*ism*' as well. Actually, we thought our *ethnos* had been in some blessed and British way sublimated, carried over into a postpolitical state as a reward for being so good. Around 1970, however, the truth began to catch up with us.

The general belief here is that nationalism arose from the specific developmental conjuncture described by Ernest Gellner and his school of thought.[5] It was industrialization which did the trick. The ragged, uneven march into modernity, in which certain peoples led or dominated others and transformed them (instead of merely sitting on them), squeezed nationalism out of nationality, and made it into the general political climate of world development. Nationalism is not a reflection, a mirror of ethnic variety. It is a set of levers (which are sometimes weapons) through which ethnos is driven into a new salience in human affairs.

But, in a very broad sense, the same could be said of internationalism. It is not a mirror of internationality, but a complex range of reactions to nationalism: part defence, part disguise, and part staged adaptation. It is a constituent of the same nationalist universe. Since the fall of Napoleon's empire, these two world views have existed in a permanent, uneasy tension with one another, the Siamese twin brothers of a single world-historical process.

This is, incidentally, why internationalism bears only a somewhat tortured and distant relationship to universalistic beliefs of the past. It is easy to see resemblances between these spiritual doctrines of man's nature and the kind of preaching internationalists admire. But I doubt if this will take us far. The religious verities are counterposed to sin and evil, in the framework of a mainly unchanging universe. Internationalism has arisen against the convulsions of the post-1776 or -1789 world: the endemic betrayals wrought by industrial and democratic development. The latter's devils are more powerful: contingency, particularism (medieval or otherwise), and a nativist darkness which has been triumphant. Priestly evil, on the other hand, was installed by a deity, who could be envisaged as an ultimate arbiter. Internationalists have no such consolation.

There is not a strong rapport between internationalists and cosmopolitans either. The latter were a pre-industrial elite, convinced they had a vanguard role for civilized internationality. This was to be disseminated from the more elevated centres. Edmund Burke noted that there existed in his day 'a system of manners and education that was very nearly similar to all in this quarter of the globe', such that by the 1780s 'no citizen of Europe could be altogether an exile in any part of it' and no one 'felt himself quite abroad'.[6]

Now internationalists often fancy themselves as cosmopolitans. Sometimes a city, a region, or a person may be described as 'cosmopolitan', meaning it or he is agreeably open to outside cultural influences and that foreigners (most often intellectuals) easily feel at home with it or him. There are also actual cosmopolitans, in the sense of individuals or families from culturally mixed or transplanted backgrounds who genuinely feel that they could choose to settle anywhere.[7] The same description, of course, leaves them open to attack by nativist spokesmen for vices such as rootlessness, lack of allegiance, and so on.

However, I think such categories are really marginal. The more important point is that the whole thrust of nationalist-governed development has been against civilization being disseminated out and downwards from the appropriate centres, by those equipped with the right manners and education. Do-it-yourself replaced the metropolitan schoolteacher. But one can only do it oneself – in one's own language, via one's own resources and mistakes – by vigorously rejecting what the citizens of Europe are saying. This happened in 1776, and then again after the 1790s. 'Never trust a citizen of Europe' became the prevalent slogan. In other words: 'Join on our own terms, not theirs.'

Cosmopolitanism slid into troubling confusion in the post-1789 world. It became more difficult to distinguish from imperialism, as waves of metropolitan civilization imparters began to work, each one convinced of his innate right to uplift and lead the way. Great Powers make internationalism their own by a sleight of hand which seems perfectly natural when one happens to be holding most of the good cards. Paris, London, Vienna, New York, Moscow are out in front with the aces and jokers; the peasants, therefore, have the rubbish. For the latter not to let themselves be civilized by the former is rash, presumptuous, crass, vulgar, hopelessly ill-advised, and self-defeating. It is quite nationalist in fact.

Very fortunately, as Gellner noted in *Thought and Change*, there have been enough nativist fools around consistently to thwart imperialism.[8] Otherwise, one form or another of the empire would have to get its boots permanently on humanity's windpipe – a fate uncomfortably close in the years from 1939 to 1942.

In this era of imperialist and nationalist struggles, internationalism was kept going as an ethic mainly by a single doctrine: the belief in an alternative vehicle of civilized development, neither imperial nor national. It was the idea that class could become a developmental vector in its own right. The proletariat, by opposing the empire and transcending nationality, might step forward and itself assume the Enlightenment mantle. By uniting, the workers of all lands could escape from the vicious contradictions of capitalist progress. They could make themselves into citizens of the world, not just of Europe. Though for the moment confined to national stages, the working class should conduct its battles there in the appropriate spirit – the internationalist spirit looking to a wider horizon of emancipation, to the freeing of national enemies as well as friends.

Although lacking a social basis in the sense of Burke's educated cross-border caste, this secular faith did have a composite and shifting foundation. Part of it came from what George Steiner, in a 1987 television lecture on Vienna, called the 'Judaic intelligentsia' (especially after the end of the Habsburg Empire); part from the working-class movement of different countries, as self-educated cadres adopted internationalism in opposition to what they felt as the oppressive cultures of their own schools; and part from metropolitan or Atlantic Left cliques whose influence was (or seemed) big enough to make them feel for a time like the centre of the world.

The Small Battalions

Internationalists knew defeat was coming well before 1989. In 1977, Eric Hobsbawm morosely concluded that 'The United Nations Organization . . . is soon likely to consist of the late 20th century equivalents of Saxe-Coburg-Gotha and Schwarzburg-Sondershausen.'[9] He was trying to defend two things at once: Leninist internationalism and Great Britain – the latter as a remaining exemplar of sane multinational values (if only Scottish and Welsh separatism could be exorcised). The big battalions, with all their faults, were already giving way to ever smaller ones (whose faults would be worse). He felt even then that internationalism was not going to reverse this trend. However, it could still be cautioned and contained. As long as some functioning multinational states like the United Kingdom, the Soviet Union, and Yugoslavia survived, all was not lost.

From that point of view, all *was* lost in 1989. The last shards of the doctrine dropped through the grating, as the Eastern working class opted decisively for a mixture of 'bourgeois democracy' and nationalism. The key overarching states fell apart. The United Kingdom is still there, true, though much worse afflicted than in the 1970s. So are China and India. Yet one need only cite this short list to see how hopeless the position may soon be. The internationalist ethic had survived only by being preserved in the Cold War aspic along with so much else.

Its great day had been the previous one – that of the struggles against pathological variants of nationalism in the interwar years. This too followed on the great defeat represented by the explosion of World War I in 1914. Nonetheless, Leninism, the Third and Fourth Internationals, and the anti-fascist battles restored a certain salience and impact to the credo, for which, incidentally, one may perfectly well be grateful today, even while doubting most of what it stood for. After all, it stiffened resistance to the most deadly kind of imperialism. But we should not forget either that it did so (and won) only by allying itself to nationalism – that is, to those nonpathological forms of the creed which counterattacked fascism and brought about its destruction.

In that period, internationalism found justification as a heroic defensive morale. Yet, even at that time it remained simultaneously a way of adapting to the nationalist world. It often accomplished this by minimizing and deprecating nationality, on the assumption that *ethnos* was tolerable only because it was near history's exit door.

At its worst, the assumption could become a rigid sectarian conviction that the world is quite other than it was, that the exit door was standing wide open, as it were, with the masses already straining to get out. All they had to do was understand the patent map for getting there. This was the late, millenarian form of the internationalist belief structure. It remained a force until the 1970s, particularly in Italy and Germany. As it lost political ground it tried for a time to make up for it with a mixture of intellectual terrorism and armed force.

By 1989 this too was already a memory. The relatively small battalions were taking over for good. The longer-term process mentioned earlier, by which globalization seems to engender fragmentation, attained a climax, namely, the liberal end of history. The Saxe-Coburgs and Sondershausens began queuing up at the UN's door. Slovenia was free; Andorra voted for full self-government; Denmark briefly wrecked the European Community, then changed its mind in May of 1993 and (even more revealing) saved it. At least in the old sense, internationalism was no more: the well-born ghost was homeless, doctrineless, and reduced to pious moralizing of the kind that Christian and other religions do far better. Since so many in the UN queue were and are still trying to kill one another, people feel a certain nostalgia for order and stability. But what intellectual content can that possibly have?

All Nationalists Now

Socialism has to find new, post-1989 bearings, although some may find this a charitable description of its plight. Its new bearings will take it through capitalism, not against it, even if socialists still want, eventually, to alter everything. The alternative lies within what used to be the enemy, not outside it or in alienated global contraposition to it. If market-governed development is the only kind that there is, then this implies that there will be – or perhaps, more *obviously* will be – different kinds of capitalism. Once unfrozen and uncongealed from permanent contraposition to a supposed alternative, it is the immense variety, the contradictions, and the unevenness of industrialization that will be both intellectually evident and more practically important.

But the same is true of nationalism and internationalism. Here also the alternative lies through (not against) a finally nationalized world. Any new bearings lie beyond the Ethnic Abyss (except that there is no abyss, in the hysterical-liberal sense). Are the fragmentation and anarchy really so bad? Some parts may be, but here we are inevitably talking on the whole – trying to hold the whole spectrum in view and to judge it accordingly. And, as I have argued elsewhere, in that general sense the new disorder is much better than the stand-off of imperiums which came before.[10] The first has brought a murderous threat to certain border populations; had it endured, the second would have ended by murdering everybody.

On both counts – capitalism and nationalism – the other interpretation is to say we are now merely facing the real, longer-term trajectory of development 'with sober senses', as Marx liked to say. If this is all for the best and not just a spasmodic response to communism's collapse, then socialists will have to decide what type of capitalists they will become, and internationalists will have to decide what sort of nationalists they will become.

Some may regard this choice as the hangman's noose, but I believe they are wrong. It is wrong if we attend to the generous, imaginative side of the old internationalist credo, rather than to its rigid, elitist, quasi-metropolitan side. The post-Yugoslav war has given a momentary boost to old-style Atlantic Leftism, but I doubt it will last long. For the former, by contrast, new navigation lights are perfectly possible and some of them are becoming visible. Internationalism can only be built upon a certain style of nationalism whose construction rests more upon democracy than upon *ethnos*. A durable and bearable disorder will rely more upon chosen identities and less upon the classical motifs of language, folk custom, and 'blood'.

Some of the bearings are intellectual. They rest upon a rereading of nationalism and its doctrines. Recently, in Prague, I heard Roman Szporluk of Harvard University give an address on the history of nationalist ideas. He described how, often under the sway of internationalism, scholars tended to misinterpret the story of uneven development and even its principal theorists, like Herder and Friedrich List. Nationalism was in fact the first genuinely secular 'world view' outside the natural sciences: its '*ism*' denoted the universal factor, the aspiration at its heart.

In the disturbed metropolitan perspective, *ethnos* has always figured as the spoilsport, the eruption in what would otherwise be a neat garden. But what they want is their own garden, a figurative place within the grander landscape of modernity. Szporluk also shows how List compares quite favourably as an analyst with, for example, Marx and Engels, and how he has fared incomparably better as a prophet. In one sense, it was clearly the Listian world which re-emerged after 1989.[11]

Beyond Dystopia

We need a new sense of the future as well as a revised history. As is so often said in the United Kingdom these days, one clings to nurse because of the fear of something worse – in this case, 'the Abyss'. But what is this black hole which we are supposedly being pulled into? Its profile is familiar enough; it has been frequently described in theory. The most up-to-the-minute example that I have is a paper written by Ernest Gellner.[12]

Gellner has always had a sociologist's weakness for incomprehensible diagrams. This new work contains two superb displays of agrarian (pre-nationalist) and industrial (or nationalist) society, respectively – civilization reconfigured for modernity. For Gellner, history tends to be the mildly annoying stuff which happens between one sociological model and another. Composed in 1991, the second has what feels like a post-1989 addendum:

> Society must be homogenized, *gleichgeschaltet*; and the only agency capable of carrying out, supervising or protecting this operation is the central state.

Given the competition of various states for overlapping catchment areas, the only way a given culture can protect itself against another one . . . is to acquire one of its own. Just as every girl should have a husband, preferably her own, so every culture should have a state, preferably its own. The state-cultures live in competition with one another. So this is the end-product: a mobile, atomized, egalitarian society with a standard culture where the culture is a literate, 'high' one, and where its dissemination, maintenance and boundaries are protected by a state. . . . One culture, one state. One state, one culture.[13]

So here is the Abyss indeed: a universe of armed Leibnizian monads drunk both with their own cultures and with a dislike of neighbours, as well as rootless cosmopolitans. Progress across a future Europe or even over the North American Free Trade Area might soon, on this reckoning, become like crossing Bosnia today. Every few miles a band of ruffians, uniformed or otherwise, would be waiting to dispose of enemies and to inflict their miserably depreciated currency upon hapless travellers.[14]

Civilization is certainly incompatible with this. But, of course, Gellner is typically half tongue-in-cheek about the vision of dread. He concludes that, while it looks 'virtually Euclidean in its cogency', not everyone agrees. 'As a matter of regrettable fact an astonishing number of people fail to accept this theory even when presented with it.' I am one of that number. It may fit Bosnia-Herzegovina, but Bosnia-Herzegovina does not (fortunately) fit very closely anywhere else. The general dystopia is false. There are no monads, nor is there any likelihood that a small-battalion, nationalized universe will look much like that.

By way of a suggestive counter-example, let us look briefly at another small zone within the same general area of post-Cold War Europe: Trieste. Here is a classical specimen of an 'overlapping catchment area' of incorrigibly mixed populations: Italian, Slovene, Friulian, Croat, Austro-German, and Jewish. This artificial city-state would be doomed if the isomorphic state-culture norm were enforced (more or less what the Italian Fascists tried to do between 1926 and 1945).

Having nearly been strangled by 'homogenization', most Triestines do not want a repeat performance. Nor is there any pressure for it from the side of the new Slovenia. The latter shows no signs whatever of wishing to redeem its catchment area, in spite of the fact that most people in this great city have either a Slovene grandparent or (often unconfessed) Slovene skeletons in either the backyard or the nearest cemetery.

At the same time, the live political forces in Trieste know that there is no escape from nationalism in a political sense. There can only be independence – a city-state independence or autonomy, through which sovereignty can be established inside the advancing new disorder. Since the place is inherently multi-ethnic, this implies that such self-government will have to have a democratic rather than a natural foundation. It will have to be a chosen identity, and in a sense a synthetic one which embraces elements of everything from the Habsburgs to the *Lega Nord*, currently in the ascendant.

But that too would be part of the new nationalist system – every bit as much as a cleansed Greater Serbia or a purified Schwarzburg-Sondershausen. The new order will and should be an order of bastards, mongrels, odd interstices, and breathing spaces, as well as 100 per cent isomorphs like Slovenia and Poland. What is disorderly about it may be what is best, as well as what is worst. In fact, I suspect any such system will need its buffers, zones of confluence, no-man's-lands, and enclaves in order to function tolerably at all. Andorra, the Isle of Man, Sarajevo, Singapore, and Gibraltar may be as important in it as the more neatly theorizable ethnic building blocks.

The old internationalism was often uncomfortably close to 'all-the-same-ism'. I feel confident that this will never be said of post-1989 nationalism. Internationalism will find a far more natural foothold there as a moderating tendency of the system, rather than as a futile holding operation against its realization. Democracy has been the midwife of the post-1989 order, and remains its general interest. The anarchy in that is, in part, merely admitting that metropolitan grandeur and pretensions have shrunk out of sight and are unlikely ever to return. However, anarchy ought also to have a more positive function, which the new style of internationalism should take to heart.

Anarchist Internationalism

In the post-1989 world, an odd thing has happened. While the Atlantic Left gloom traders see mainly atavism and warfare, utopia is advancing on other fronts. Earlier I mentioned some work relevant to the general revision of ideas about nationalism. But it may also be worthwhile recalling some other notions which, when they first appeared in print, were dismissed as roseate ruminations, visions of an almost inconceivably remote future.

For example, let us consider the theory put forward by Professor Jane Jacobs in *Cities and the Wealth of Nations*.[15] It is not true, as so often is said, that nobody foresaw the collapse of the Soviet Union. Jacobs did, and she lucidly described the 'transactions of decline' which were then destroying it, as well as other 'profoundly stagnated and pitiable fragments of empires, both old and recent'. She concluded that the world would be better if it were smaller, economically and in every other way. But the problem was the existing frozen character of the international nation-state system which did not easily permit 'the multiplication of sovereignties'.

Existing national states (especially the bigger ones) were based on 'the gruesome glamour of human sacrifice' so that betraying their unity meant rendering 'the most glorious pages of national history mere sound and fury'.[16] This sounds (incidentally) very similar to the speeches that London government ministers delivered in Scotland during the British general election campaign of 1992. They were, basically, 'How dare you?' As well as that, an international order has been maintained on the principle of inviolability – the sacredness of every existing frontier, as lodged in the protocols of the United Nations and the European Community. Although this may sometimes protect the weak from the strong and hungry, it also defends the strong from the weak and hungry, in the sense of secessionists, new sovereignties, and the new patterns created by population movements.

An internationalism founded on these ideas alone is therefore profoundly disabled, and out of touch with what Jacobs saw as the living trends and possibilities of any new order. These will, she argued, depend primarily on the multiplication of political sovereignties by democratic means. They involve a radical freeing of international relations from the winding sheets of the Cold War and its pitiable assorted imperial fragments. How is this to be attained? Jacobs somewhat hesitantly suggests the following formula: for former empires or large national states, the alternative to 'transactions of decline' would simply be to countenance break-up:

> for a political unit not to try to hold itself together. The radical discontinuity would thus be division of the single sovereignty into a family of smaller sovereignties, not after things had reached a stage of breakdown and disintegration, but long before while things were still going reasonably well. In a national society behaving like this, multiplication of sovereignties by division would be a normal, untraumatic accompaniment of economic development itself, and of the increasing complexity of economic and social life. Some of the sovereignties in the family would in their turn divide as evidence of the need to do so appeared. . . . In this utopian fantasy, young sovereignties splitting off from the parent nation would be told, in effect, 'Good luck to you in your independence!'[17]

Lugubrious economists from both the Left and the Right see this as a calamitous course with chaos, a multiplication of currencies, and a breaking of all the rules to follow. In 1984, Jacobs pointed out that if there was any truth at all in matching theories of the information revolution and the computerization of the globe, then the multiplication of both sovereignties and currencies ought in fact to become for the first time quite easy. Such new tools could allow smaller economic units to cease deranging international trade and affairs. Again, globalization would bring about and actually encourage the proliferation of smaller, competing entities, rather than wipe them off the map.

I should perhaps add that anarchist internationalism and urbanology in Jacobs's sense have little to do with the well-remembered slogan 'Small is Beautiful.' She knows that small is not necessarily or invariably beautiful. It can be suffocating, hopeless, and a nuisance. Her point was not to praise gnomic worlds as such, but to envisage a general order within which small could cease to be perceived as a nuisance and start to deliver: an internationality more favourable to mini- and micro-units, where these in turn could be open, functioning parts of the greater world.

It seems that only several years later Jacobs's utopian prospect is less improbable: utopia has rushed towards us in the sense that what then looked like an eccentric fantasy is at least conceivable in practical terms.

But here I am once again blatantly arguing for a break-up, for new nations and a general international disorder only because, as a representative of the United Kingdom, I must. Let me stop with some closing words from *Cities and the Wealth of Nations*. In the past, imitative and would-be states 'have ignored the Icelandic and Isle of Man parliaments, but heeded Britain's parliamentary system' at a cost. What if things were different?

> Since it does seem that sooner or later human beings get around to trying everything within their capacities, no doubt somewhere, sometime, in some culture or civilization this alternative form of discontinuity will be tried – if it really is within human capacities to divide large sovereignties before they have reached a dead end of disarray.[18]

Five years after Jacobs wrote this, the great discontinuity appeared, unplanned and mostly unforeseen. We are still learning about life and the principles of anarchy. One of them will be a new kind of internationalism.

Notes

1. The occasion was a conference on nationalism organized in March of 1993 at the Caledonian University of Glasgow (formerly Glasgow Polytechnic). I would like to thank the organizers of that event, as well as the Friedrich-Ebert-Stiftung and the organizers of a subsequent conference at Cornell University in New York, where I delivered the paper upon which this essay is based.

2. 'Internationality' first appeared in the *Oxford English Dictionary* in 1864, conveniently enough the year when Marx founded his First International and modern left-wing internationalism along with it.

3. As quoted in Richard J. Barnet and Ronald E. Muller, *Global Reach: The Power of the Multinational Corporations*, New York 1974, pp. 14–15.

4. *The Economist*, 22 May 1993, carries a probing piece about the proposed break-up of IBM to make it more efficient, and recoup its record losses of 1991–92.

5. The *opus classicus* is of course Ernest Gellner, *Nations and Nationalism*, Ithaca 1983; a

less well-known but still very important *locus ultra-classicus* is Ernest Gellner, 'Nationalism' in Ernest Gellner, *Thought and Change*, Chicago 1965.

6. Thomas J. Schlereth, *The Cosmopolitan Ideal in Enlightenment Thought*, Notre Dame, Ind., 1977, p. 2.

7. The ones I happen to know have all been Russian, or partly Russian. I know one who is happy only living in hotels, and justifies this with a complex philosophy of exile as the natural, if often unrecognized, human condition. Buying a house and 'settling down' merely makes him feel in exile from everywhere else.

8. Gellner, *Thought and Change*.

9. Eric J. Hobsbawm, 'Some Reflections on the Break-up of Britain', *New Left Review* 105 (September–October 1977).

10. See my article in the *London Review of Books*, February 1993.

11. Roman Szporluk, *Communism and Nationalism: Karl Marx Versus Friedrich List*, New York 1988.

12. Ernest Gellner, 'The Coming of Nationalism, and Its Interpretation: The Myths of Nation and Class'; see chapter 4 this volume.

13. Ibid.

14. Some time ago, a friend on his way from Zagreb to Belgrade was halted and, after the usual hassles and warnings, 'invited' to pin on a lapel badge. It read, 'I Love Serbs'. He declined the honour, pointing out that he had not had the time to discover whether he loved them or not. This reply was met with gales of laughter: 'Just what a Serb would say!' roared one of the banditti.

15. Jane Jacobs, *Cities and the Wealth of Nations: Principles of Economic Life*, New York 1984, pp. 212–14.

16. Ibid.

17. Ibid., pp. 214–20 passim.

18. Ibid., pp. 212–14.

13

The European Nation-state – Its Achievements and Its Limits.
On the Past and Future of Sovereignty and Citizenship

Jürgen Habermas

As the name of the 'United Nations' already reveals, the world society today is politically composed of nation-states. This is by no means a trivial fact. The historical type of that state which first appeared with the French and American revolutions has spread world-wide. After World War II a third generation of nation-states emerged from the processes of decolonization. The trend continues since the implosion of the Soviet empire. The nation-states proved superior to both the city states (or their federations) and the modern heirs of the old empires (the last of which, China, we just observe undergoing a process of deep transformation). This global success of the nation-state is, in the first place, due to the advantages of the modern state as such. Let me start, before I deal with the formation of nation-states, with separate commentaries on each of the two components: on what we today understand by 'state' and by 'nation'.

In the German tradition 'state' is a legal term that refers at the same time to *Staatsgewalt*, an executive branch securing internal and external sovereignty, to *Staatsgebiet*, a clearly delimited territory, and to *Staatsvolk*, the totality of citizens. The latter is the symbolic carrier of the legal order that constitutes jurisdiction within the limits of the state territory. From a sociological point of view, one would add that the institutional core of this modern state is formed by a legally constituted and highly differentiated administrative apparatus which monopolizes the legitimate means of violence and obeys an interesting division of labour with a market society set free for economic functions. With the support of military and police, the state maintains its autonomy inside and outside; sovereignty means that the political authority maintains both law and order within the boundaries of its territory and the integrity of these boundaries against an international environment, where competing states recognize each other under international law. Because of the institutional differentiation between political and economic functions, state and society mutually depend on each other. The administrative state is dependent on taxes, while the market economy relies on legal guarantees, political regulations and infrastructural provisions. To put it in a nutshell, the immense historical success of the nation-state can partly be explained by the fact that the modern state, that is, the tandem of bureaucracy and capitalism, has turned out to be the most effective vehicle for an accelerating social modernization.

All of us live today in national societies which owe their identity to the organizational unity of such a state. But modern states had existed long before 'nations', in the modern sense, came about. It was not until the late eighteenth century that both elements, the modern state and the modern nation, melted into the shape of a nation-state. Certainly, in legal and political contexts we normally use 'nation' and 'people' as interchangeable terms. Yet besides its straightforward legal and political meaning, the term 'nation' carries connotations of a community shaped by common descent, culture and history, often by a common language, too. Members of a state form a 'nation' in terms of a particular form of life. It is not by chance that the concept of 'nation' ambiguously refers to both a *Volksnation* and a *Staatsnation*, a prepolitical nation and a nation of legally empowered citizens.

These two concepts could merge all the more easily because of the roots which the concept of the *Volksnation* already had in two different pre-modern strands. The modern term 'nation' inherited its meaning from the ambivalent history of a cultural as well as a political meaning of 'nation'. Allow me a brief digression into conceptual history.

In the classical usage by the Romans, *natio* like *gens* functions as the opposite of *civitas*. Here, nations are initially communities of people of the same descent, who are not yet integrated in the political form of a state but hang together just by settlement, common language, customs and traditions. This usage of the word reaches through the Middle Ages up to early modern times and applies here to all those situations in which natio and lingua were taken to be equivalents. Thus, for example, students at medieval universities were divided up into nations depending on the regions they came from. Even back then, the national origin *ascribed to you by others* was already in a conspicuous way linked with the pejorative demarcation of the foreign from your own: nationalities, with certain negative connotations, were attributed to foreigners.

At the same time the term 'nation' gained, in a different context, another meaning. This new political meaning carried positive connotations. In the course of the Old German Empire the feudal system had given way to a stratified political society of corporate states. *Stände* in the political sense were based on contracts (like the famous Magna Carta) in which the king or emperor, who was dependent on tax and military support, granted the aristocracy, the church and the towns privileges – that is to say limited participation in the exercise of political power. These ruling estates, which met in 'parliaments' or 'diets', represented the country or 'the nation' *vis-à-vis* the Court. As 'nation' the aristocracy gained a political existence, which the mass of the population, the 'private subjects', at that time did not yet enjoy. This explains the revolutionary implication of the slogan 'King in Parliament', in England, and that of the identification of the Third Estate with 'the nation', in France.

The democratic transformation of the *Adelsnation*, the nation of the nobility, into a *Volksnation*, a nation of the people, required a deep mental change on the part of the general population. This process was inspired by the work of academics and intellectuals. Their nationalist propaganda unleashed a political mobilization among the urban educated middle classes, before the modern idea of a nation met with broader resonance. To the extent that this idea, during the course of the nineteenth century, seized the imagination of the masses it soon became clear, however, that the transformed *political* concept of the nation had borrowed also connotations from its older *pre-political* twin concept – precisely that ability to generate stereotypes which had been associated with 'nation' as a concept of origin. The new self-understanding as a nation often functioned to ward off all things foreign, to debase other nations and to discriminate against or exclude national, ethnic and religious minorities, especially the Jews.

The two components of the concept of the nation-state, state and nation, refer to convergent but different historical processes – the formation of modern states and the building of modern nations. The classical nation-states in the west and north of Europe evolved within existing territorial states, while the 'belated' nations, Italy and Germany, took a course that then became typical for central and eastern Europe: here, the formation of the state only followed the traces of a national consciousness crystallizing around common languages, cultures and histories. The categories of actors who initiated and carried the process of either state- or nation-building differ significantly. With regard to the formation of modern states, mainly lawyers, diplomats and officers engaged in the construction of an effective bureaucracy, while on the other side writers, historians, and journalists preceded the diplomatic and military efforts of statesmen (like Cavour and Bismarck) with the propagation of the – at first imaginary – project of a nation unified on cultural terms. Both developments led to that European nation-state of the nineteenth century which in any case provides the context from which the present normative self-understanding of the constitutional state derives. In what follows I will disregard the different patterns of national histories, which in fact had an impact on the strength or weakness of liberal political cultures. Democratic regimes proved more stable in countries where a national identity developed hand in hand with revolutionary fights for civil liberties within existing territorial states, while democracies turned out to be less stable wherever national movements and wars of liberation against a foreign enemy had first to create borders for nascent national states.

In this study I would like to explain the specificity and particular achievement of the national state. I will then analyse the tension between republicanism and nationalism built into it. This provides us with a key for a brief discussion of two problems the nation-state has to cope with today. The challenges that arise from the multicultural differentiation of civil society and from trends towards globalization throw a light on the limits of this historical type.

Let me first explain what the modern state gained by its unique fusion with the homogenizing idea of the nation. This first modern form of collective identity had a catalytic function for the transformation of the early modern state into a democratic republic. The national self-consciousness of the people provided a cultural context that facilitated the political activation of citizens. It was the national community that generated a new kind of connection between persons who had been strangers to each other, so far. By this, the national state could solve two problems at once: it established a democratic mode of *legitimation* on the basis of a new and more abstract form of *social integration*.

Briefly stated, the first problem came up in the wake of religious wars. The conflict between confessions and denominations led to religious pluralisms that undermined any claim to the divine legitimation of the kings and in the end required the secularization of the state. Political authority was in need of a legitimation other than that derived from a shared religious world view. The second problem, that of social integration, was a consequence of various modernization processes. The population was pulled out of the traditional relationships and freed from the corporate ties of early modern societies and thereby faced the alienating experience of becoming at the same time mobilized and isolated. The nation-state countered both of these challenges with a political activation of the people. The new kind of national identity allowed the combination of a more abstract form of social integration within a changed pattern of the political process: those who had been subjected to a more or less authoritarian rule now gained, step by step, the status of citizens. Nationalism stimulated this move from the status of private subjects to citizenship.

Certainly, it took a long time before political rights would include the population as a whole. But in the course of this spread of political participation, there emerged a new level of a *legally mediated solidarity* among citizens, while the state, by the implementation of democratic procedures, at the same time tapped a new secular source for *legitimation*. The innovation is best explained in terms of 'citizenship'. Of course, there never was a modern state that did not define its social boundaries in terms of citizenship rights which regulate who is, and who is not, included in the legal community. But being a member of a particular state just meant being subjected to its authorities. With the transition to a democratic national state this legally *ascribed* organizational membership changed its meaning: now, citizenship gained the additional political and cultural meaning of an achieved belonging to a community of empowered citizens who actively contribute to its maintenance. This surplus in meaning must be differentiated, however, according to the political and the cultural aspects of this demanding citizenship, in which the strands of republicanism and nationalism run together.

Viewed from the distance of early modernity, we may say that the absolutist, for the sake of simplicity let us say the Hobbesian, state was constituted already in forms of positive or enacted law, which invested private subjects – the contracting members of a growing market society – with some legal powers of their own. Due to the developing civil law, they already enjoyed, in terms of a set of yet unequally distributed rights, to a certain extent private autonomy. With the republican shift from royal to popular sovereignty, these paternalistically conferred rights were transformed into human and civil rights. These rights are supposed to grant equally civic as well as private autonomy. Participation rights and public autonomy now supplemented private autonomy. The constitutional state is conceived as a political order which is voluntarily established by the will of the people, so that the addressees of legal norms can at the same time understand themselves as the authors of law.

But there would have been no driving force for such a transformation, and there would have been a lack of impetus even within a formally constituted republic, if a nation of self-conscious citizens had not been emerging from the people of subjects, at least in the long run. For this political mobilization an idea was required that could have an appeal to the hearts and minds of the people stronger than those somewhat abstract ideas on human rights and popular sovereignty. This gap was filled by the modern idea of a nation, which first inspired the inhabitants of a shared territory with the sense of belonging to the same republic. Only the awareness of a national identity, which crystallizes around common history, language and culture, only the consciousness of belonging to the same nation, makes distant people spread over large territories feel politically responsible for each other. Citizens thus come to see themselves as parts of the same whole, in whatever abstract legal terms this whole may be constituted. This kind of national self-consciousness refers to the *Volksgeist*, the unique spirit of the nation, which was carefully constructed by intellectuals in terms of romantic myths, histories and literary traditions, and which became widely communicated through the channels of the mass media of the time. This cultural identity provides the socially integrating substrate for the political identity of the republic.

This explains why citizenship is spelled out in a double code: it extends beyond the legal status, defined in terms of civil rights, to the membership of a culturally defined community. Both aspects are first complementary. Without this cultural interpretation of political membership rights, the European national state in its initial period hardly would have had the strength to reach what I have described as its main achievement: namely, to establish a new, more abstract level of social integration in terms of the legal implementation of democratic citizenship. There are few counter-examples. The example of the United States shows that the national state might well retain its republican form without the support of a culturally homogenized nation; here the shared civic religion was, however, maintained on the base of an unquestioned majority culture – at least until recently.

So far, I have talked about the achievement of the national state; the reverse side of this accomplishment is an uneasy tension between a nationalist and a republican self-understanding. The fate of democracy depends on which one dominates the other. With the rise of the national state and the implementation of democratic citizenship, the notion of sovereignty changes too. This affects, as we have seen, the notion of internal sovereignty – the shift of sovereignty from the king or emperor to 'the people'. But the change has an impact on the perception of external sovereignty as well. When national states emerge, the old Machiavellian idea of strategic self-assertion against potential enemies gains the additional meaning of an existential self-assertion of 'the nation'. Thereby a third concept of 'freedom' is introduced, besides the liberties of private persons and the political autonomy of citizens. While these individual freedoms are granted by universal rights, the freedom of the nation is of a different, a particularistic nature – it refers to a collectivity, the independence of which must be defended, if necessary, with the blood not of mercenaries but of the 'sons of the nation'. The interpretation of the nation as a prepolitical entity allows it to uphold an unchanged early modern image of external sovereignty that is but imbued with national colours, as it were. This is the place where the secularized state preserves a residue of sacred transcendence: in times of war the national state imposes on its citizens the duty to risk and sacrifice their lives for national liberty. Since the French Revolution general conscription has gone with civil rights; the willingness to fight and die for one's own country is supposed to express both national consciousness and republican virtue.

This double code is revealed by the inscriptions of the collective memory: political milestones in the fight for civil rights join together with the military ceremonies in memory of soldiers killed in action. Both these traces mirror the ambiguous meaning of 'the nation' – the voluntary nation of citizens, who generate democratic legitimation, and the inherited or ascribed nation of those, born into it, facilitating social integration. *Staatsbürger* or citizens are supposed to constitute themselves as an association for free and equal persons by choice; *Volksgenossen* or nationals *find* themselves formed by an inherited form of life and the fateful experience of a shared history. Built into the self-understanding of the national state, there is this tension between the universalism of an egalitarian legal community and the particularism of a cultural community bound together by origin and fate.

This tension can be solved on the condition that the constitutional principles of human rights and democracy give priority to a cosmopolitan understanding of the nation as a nation of citizens over and against an ethnocentric interpretation of the nation as a prepolitical entity. Only under a non-naturalist description can the nation be smoothly combined with the universalistic self-understanding of the constitutional state. The republican idea can then operate as a constraint on particularistic value-orientations; it can then penetrate and structure the sub-political forms of life according to universalist patterns. The very achievement of the constitutional state was to substitute the integrative force of democratic citizenship for outworn traditional forms of social integration. But this republican core of the national state is in danger as soon as the integrative force of the nation, which was meant only to support democratization, is led back to a prepolitical fact, to the quasi-natural features of a historical community – that is to say to something given independently of the political opinion and will-formation of the citizens themselves. There are two obvious reasons why this danger, in the course of the nineteenth and twentieth centuries, surged again and again – the first conceptual, the second empirical.

There is a conceptual gap in the legal construction of the constitutional state which invites a naturalist interpretation of the nation to be filled in. The scope and borders of a republic cannot be settled on normative grounds. In purely normative terms one cannot explain how the universe of those who originally join ranks in order to form an association of free and equal persons, and to regulate their common life by means of positive law in a fair or legitimate way, should be composed – who should or should not belong to this circle. From a normative point of view, the territorial and social boundaries of a constitutional state are contingent. In the real world it is up to historical contingencies, to the accidental course of events, normally to the arbitrary outcomes of wars or civil wars, who finally seizes power and thereby gains the power for defining the territorial and social boundaries of a political community. It is a mistake, one that dates back to the nineteenth century, to assume that this issue can again be answered in theory with reference to a right of national self-determination. Nationalism found its own practical answer to the issue which must remain unresolved in theory.

It may very well be that national consciousness, which jells around a common descent, language and history, is itself mainly an artefact. It nevertheless *projects* the nation as an imaginary entity that is grown and which, in contrast to an artificial order of enacted law, presents itself as a matter of course needing no justification beyond its sheer existence. This is why the recourse to a nation with organic roots is able to conceal the contingency of what has happened to become state borders. Nationalism confers on these borders, and on the actual composition of the political community, an aura of imitated substance and inherited legitimacy. The naturalized nation can thus symbolically fasten and fortify the territorial and social integrity of the nation-state.

Another reason for the dominance of such a naturalist interpretation is more trivial. Because national identities have been intentionally fabricated by the intellectual efforts of writers and historians, and because national consciousness has been spread through the modern mass media from the start, national sentiments can be more or less easily manipulated. In modern mass-democracies nationalism is a rather cheap resource from which governments and political leaders can draw on occasions, when they are tempted to exploit a well-known psychological mechanism for the purpose of turning the attention of citizens away from internal social conflicts and gaining support for foreign policy issues instead. The history of European imperialism between 1871 and 1914, and moreover the integral nationalism of the twentieth century, not to speak of the racist policies of the Nazis – all these developments prove the sad fact that in Europe the idea of the nation did not so much promote loyalty to the constitution but more often served, in its ethnocentric and xenophobic version, as an instrument for securing mass mobilization for policies, in view of which opposition, if not resistance, would have been the right course of action.

The normative conclusion from the history of the European nation-states is obvious: the national state must get rid of that ambivalent potential of nationalism which was originally the vehicle for its success.

We can nevertheless still learn from the very achievement of the national state how to provide a frame for an abstract kind of legally mediated solidarity. Once more: with the institution of egalitarian citizenship, the nation-state did not only provide democratic legitimation but created, through widespread political participation, a new level of social integration as well. In order to fulfil this integrative function democratic citizenship must, however, be more than just a legal status; it must become the focus of a shared political culture. This raises the sceptical question, whether this idea can still work under the present conditions of more and more complex and diverse societies.

Originally, a more or less homogenized nation facilitated, as we have seen, the cultural extension of the legally defined nation of citizens. This contextualization was necessary if democratic citizenship was also to knot social ties of mutual responsibility. But today, all of us live in pluralist societies that move further away from the format of a nation-state based on a culturally more or less homogeneous population. The diversity in cultural forms of life, ethnic groups, world-views and religions is either huge already, or at least growing. Except for policies of ethnic cleansing, there is no alternative to this route towards multicultural societies. Here, we have not even the option of moving the burden of coping with social disintegration away from the level of political will formation and public communication to the level of a supposedly homogeneous nation, as was the case in nineteenth- and early-twentieth-century Europe. Hidden behind such a façade of cultural homogeneity, there would at best appear the oppressive maintenance of a hegemonic majority culture. If, however, different cultural, ethnic and religious subcultures are to coexist and interact on equal terms within the same political community, the majority culture must give up its historical prerogative to define the official terms of that *generalized* political culture, which is to be shared by all citizens, regardless of where they come from and how they live. The majority culture must be decoupled from a political culture all can be expected to join. The level of the shared political culture must be strictly separated from the level of subcultures and prepolitical identities (including that of the majority) which deserve equal protection only once they conform to constitutional principles (as interpreted in this particular political culture).

   Such generalized political cultures have as their points of reference the national constitutions, but each of them differently contextualizes the same universalist principles, popular sovereignty and human rights, from the perspective of its own particular history. On such a basis, nationalism can be replaced by what one might call constitutional patriotism. But compared with nationalism constitutional patriotism for many people appears too thin a bond to hold together complex societies. So the pressing question remains, under which conditions a liberal political culture shared by all citizens can at all substitute for that cultural context of a more or less homogeneous nation in which democratic citizenship once, in the initial period of the nation-state, was embedded.

This is today a problem even for classical countries of immigration like the United States. By comparison, the civic culture of the United States did provide more space for the peaceful coexistence of citizens with widely diverging cultural identities, allowing each of them to be at the same time a member and a stranger in his or her own country. But the surging fundamentalism and terrorism (such as in Oklahoma) are alarming signs that the safety curtain of a civil religion, interpreting a constitutional history of two hundred years, may be about to break. My suspicion is that a liberal political culture can hold together multicultural societies only if democratic citizenship pays in terms not only of liberal and political rights, but of social and cultural rights as well. Democratic citizenship can stand on its own feet and yet extend beyond a merely legal status only if it is cashed out in the use values of social welfare and the mutual recognition among the existing varieties of forms of life. Democratic citizenship develops its force of social integration, that is to say it generates solidarity between strangers, if it can be recognized and appreciated as the very mechanism by which the legal and material infrastructure of actually preferred forms of life is secured.

This kind of answer is, at least partly, suggested by a kind of welfare state, which was able to develop in Europe during a short period after World War II under favourable conditions which, however, no longer hold. At that time, the particularistic batteries had been overcharged with the worst possible consequences of integral and racial nationalism. Under the umbrella of a nuclear balance struck between the superpowers, borders ceased to be an issue. Moreover, the European countries – and not just the two Germanys – were denied a foreign policy of their own. Internal conflicts now ceased to be hidden behind the primacy of foreign policy. Given such conditions, it became possible to uncouple the universalistic understanding of the constitutional state from its enveloping in the traditional mode of power politics motivated by national interests. Despite the hostile image of a communist enemy, there was gradually a move away from the conceptual linkage of liberties and civil rights with the ambitions of national self-assertion. National liberty was not the prevailing topic, not even in West Germany.

This trend towards what could to a certain extent be termed a 'postnational' self-understanding of the constitutional state may have been a bit more pronounced in the former Federal Republic of Germany – given its special situation and the fact that it had, after all, been even formally deprived of its external sovereignty. However, the welfare state's pacification of class antagonisms had created a new situation in most European countries. Be it under socialist or conservative governments, systems of social security were erected or expanded everywhere, policies of equal opportunities were implemented, reforms carried out in areas such as schooling, the family, criminal law and the penal system, data protection, and so on. These reforms strengthened and expanded the substance of citizenship and, what is important in our context, made the general public more keenly aware of the priority to be attached to the issue of the implementation of basic rights. The citizens themselves could more and more realize the relevance of the priority the real nation of different people must preserve over and against the naturalist image of a homogeneous nation of *Volksgenossen* – of those who identify each other by origin and collectively close themselves off from those who appear to them to be different or alien.

If under such favourable circumstances the system of rights is elaborated and extended, each citizen can perceive, and come to appreciate, citizenship as the core of what holds people together, and of what makes them at the same time dependent on, and responsible for, each other. They perceive that private and public autonomy each presupposes the other in maintaining and improving necessary conditions for preferred ways of life. They intuitively realize that they only succeed in a fair regulation of their private autonomy if they make an appropriate use of their civic autonomy, and that they are in turn empowered to do so only on a social basis that makes them, as private persons, sufficiently independent. They learn to conceive citizenship as the frame for that dialectic between legal and actual equality from which fair and convenient living conditions for all of them can emerge.

Looking back at the past few decades of the wealthy European societies, we have to admit that this dialectic has come to a stand-still. If we want to explain this, we must cast a glance at those trends that are currently receiving attention under the heading of 'globalization'.

Globalization signifies transgression, the removal of boundaries and thus a danger for a nation-state which almost neurotically watches its borders. Anthony Giddens has defined 'globalization' as 'the intensification of worldwide relations which link distant localities in such a way that local happenings are shaped by events many miles away, and vice versa'. Global communication takes place either in natural language (most often via electronic media) or in special codes (this is, above all, the case with money and law). From this process spring two opposed trends, since 'communication' has a double meaning here. It promotes as well the expansion of (individual or collective) actors' consciousness as the differentiation and range of systems, networks (such as markets) or organizations. The growth of systems and networks enhances the multi-plication of possible contacts and information; but it does not per se stimulate the expansion of an intersubjectively shared world. Today it is unclear whether an expanding consciousness, that depends on higher order intersubjectivities in an ever wider universe of shared meanings, will be able to span the extending systems, or whether instead the sys-temic processes, having taken a life of their own, will rather lead to the fragmentation of a multiplicity of global villages unrelated to each other.

The nation-state did indeed provide a framework within which the republican idea of a community, consciously influencing itself, could be articulated and institutionalized. Now, however, the globalization of those same trends which originally spawned the nation-state, calls its sover-eignty in question. Let me first focus on internal sovereignty. Individual states are less and less able to control the national economies as stocks of their own. Of course, capitalism has developed from the start in the dimensions of a 'world-system' (Wallerstein); and for centuries the dynamics of accumulation has rather strengthened the position of the European national states. Sovereign states can well live with zones of free trade, too. But they benefit from their economies only as long as these develop within the format of national economies which governments can effectively influence in terms of economic, financial and social poli-cies. Yet the scope for such policies is shrinking. With the international-ization of financial, capital and labour markets, national governments are increasingly aware of the gap between their limited scope for action, on the one hand, and, on the other, the imperatives stemming, not primar-ily from world-wide trade relations, but from globally networked pro-duction relations. These more and more escape interventionist policies, not only of monetary redistribution, but of industrial promotion, credit subsidies, tariff protection and so on. The national legislation and admin-istration have no longer an effective impact on transnational actors, who take their investment decisions in the light of comparing relevant pro-duction conditions on a global scale.

While the world economy operates largely uncoupled from any political frame, national governments are restricted to fostering the mod-ernization of their national economies. As a consequence, they have to adapt national welfare systems to what is called the capacity for interna-tional competition. So they are forced to allow the sources of social solidarity to dry up still further. An alarming signal is the emergence of an underclass. More and more marginalized groups are gradually seg-mented off from the rest of society. Those who are no longer able to change their social lot on their own, are left to their own. Segmentation does not mean, however, that a political community can simply shed a 'superfluous' section without facing the consequences. In the long term, there are at least three of them (which are already becoming obvious in countries like the US). First, an underclass creates social tensions that can only be controlled by repressive means. The construction of jails is becoming a growth industry. Second, social destitution and physical immiseration cannot be locally confined; the poison of the ghettos spreads to the infrastructure of cities and regions, permeating the pores of the whole society. Finally, and in our context most relevant, the segmentation of minorities who are robbed of an audible voice in the public sphere brings an erosion of morality with it, something that certainly undermines the integrative force of democratic citizenship. Formally correct decisions which reflect both status anxiety and xenophobic self-defence of endangered middle classes must undermine the legitimacy of the procedures and institutions of the constitutional state. On this route, the very achievement of social integration via political participation of citizens will be gambled away.

This is one scenario, which is far from being unrealistic, but only one among several perspectives. There are no historical laws, and human beings, even societies, are capable of learning. A way out of the impasse I have described is indicated by the emergence of supranational regimes within the format of the European Union. We must try to save the republican heritage by transcending the limits of the nation-state. Our capacities for political action must keep up with the globalization of self-regulating systems and networks.

In the light of this analysis, the decision of the German Supreme Court on the Maastricht Treaty reveals a tragic irony. The court has based its strong reservations about further extension of the European Union on the argument that the constitutional state requires a certain cultural homogeneity of the people. This argument is symptomatic of a defensive attitude which in fact accelerates that erosion of citizenship it intends to counter. In view of both the growing pluralism inside national societies and the global problems national governments face from the outside, the nation-state can no longer provide an appropriate frame for the maintenance of democratic citizenship within the foreseeable future. What generally seems to be necessary is the development of capacities for political action on a level above and between nation-states.

Whereas in the field of international relations and security policies at least some outlines for some sort of the required 'world domestic politics' can be traced, present policies seem to be almost wholly impotent in the face of the world economy. I cannot deal with these complex problems here, but I would like to finish with a somewhat more hopeful remark. If we look at the agenda of the four last Earth summits arranged under the auspices of the UN – ecological risks in Rio, human rights in Vienna, social problems and poverty in Copenhagen, climate in Berlin – we

certainly do not get the feeling that this temporary, yet world-wide, pub-
licity has an immediate effect on the governments of the Great Powers;
what we get, however, from this panorama is a sharpened consciousness
of global risks, the impact of which almost nobody will escape, if those
global trends are not stopped and reversed. In view of the many forces of
desintegration within and beyond national societies, there is this fact
that points in the opposite direction: from an observer's point of view, all
societies are already part and parcel of a community of shared risks perceived as challenges for cooperative political action.

14

Nation-states in Europe and Other Continents:
Diversifying, Developing, Not Dying
Michael Mann

Many believe we have now reached the old age of the nation-state. Since 1945, they say, its sovereignty has been outreached by transnational power networks, especially those of global capitalism and postmodern culture.[1] Some postmodernists take the argument further, asserting that this jeopardizes the certainty and rationality of modern civilization, one of whose main props is a secure, unidimensional notion of absolute political sovereignty lodged in the nation-state. In the historic heartland of modern society, the supranational European Community (EC) seems to lend especial credence to the argument that national-political sovereignty is fragmenting. Here, the actual death of the nation-state has sometimes been announced – though perhaps a graceful retirement would be the more apt life-cycle metaphor for such a view. The political scientist Philippe Schmitter has argued that, though the European situation is unique, its progress beyond the nation-state has more general relevance, since 'the contemporary context systematically favours the transformation of states into either confederatii, condominii or federatii in a variety of settings'.[2] Most current writers probably do not have such decided views as these. Nonetheless, most – and almost all of those whom I later cite – believe that the nation-state is declining in Europe and that this signals a more general retirement.

It is true that the EC, to which I devote most attention, is developing new political forms, somewhat reminiscent of much older political forms, as Schmitter's Latin tags imply. These force us to revise our notions of what contemporary states and their interrelations must be. But I will also briefly examine the other two major regions of advanced capitalism and the less developed world. I will conclude that Western European weakenings of the nation-state are slight, ad hoc, uneven, and unique. In parts of the less developed world, would-be nation-states are also faltering, but for different, essentially 'pre-modern' reasons. Across most of the globe, nation-states are still maturing, or they are at least trying to do so. Europe is not the world's future. The states of the world are many and they remain varied, both in their present structures and in terms of their life-cycle trajectories. The few that are near death are not old but are still in their cots.

The European Historical Background

The sovereign, territorial nation-state is very young. Most political theorists and international relations specialists date the birth of 'unidimensional' territorial state sovereignty to the sixteenth or seventeenth centuries.[3] This is because the theorists pay too much attention to the claims of monarchical ideologists and because international relations specialists are interested only in sovereign powers over foreign policy, which arrived earlier than most other aspects of modern sovereignty. But in real socio-logical terms, territorial state sovereignty was born more recently and matured even more recently.

There has been an enormous growth in state size and scope over the last three centuries. Before the eighteenth century, entities we call 'states' had shared political functions with other agencies – local lords, churches, and other corporate bodies. Whole swathes of social life were not penetrated by states or indeed by any political agency. States prior to the eighteenth century did very little. They conducted diplomacy and small foreign wars; they erratically administered only the highest level of internal justice and repression. Monarchs might have proclaimed ambitious projects but they achieved very little. It was only when entwined with churches that they penetrated much of social life outside of their 'Home Counties'.

Nonetheless, between the thirteenth and eighteenth centuries, European states gradually came to monopolize the single function of military violence. In the eighteenth century, however, this military function exploded. Around 1700, states absorbed perhaps 5 per cent of the GNP in peacetime, 10 per cent in wartime.[4] By 1760, this had risen to between 15 and 25 per cent; by 1810, to between 25 and 35 per cent. At this point, the armies were comprised of about 5 per cent of the total population. These 1810 extraction rates are *identical* to those of the two world wars of the twentieth century and to the highest rates in the world today, those of Israel and Iraq.

Such figures and comparisons enable us to appreciate the scale of the eighteenth-century transformation. From being fairly insignificant, states suddenly loomed large in the lives of their subjects, taxing them, conscripting them, attempting to mobilize their enthusiasm for its goals. States were becoming cages, trapping subjects within their bars. Masses were thus aroused out of their historic political indifference. They were empowered by the contemporary development of a capitalist civil society, which in Europe, North America, and Japan always accompanied the rise of the modern state. They demanded changes in the conditions of their cages. They demanded political citizenship and exhibited new nationalist ideologies – first males, the bourgeoisie, and dominant religious and ethnic groups, then females, the peasantry, the working class, and minorities.

Foreign wars eased in the nineteenth century, but citizenship then combined with industrial capitalism to produce demands for a whole range of new state services for burgeoning civil societies. States first sponsored major communication systems, then mass education systems. Both contributed to the consolidation of a series of civil societies partly bounded by the territories of states. Next, states organized health systems, followed by the first stirrings of modern welfare systems. The national integration of the United States lagged behind that of most European countries, since it went through a civil war, was a large continent, and had a rather weak federal government during this period. Massive twentieth-century wars then expanded nationalism further and encouraged a deepening of economic planning and a widening of national welfare systems. Through the compromise of class struggle, citizenship became social as well as political, to use T.H. Marshall's famous terms. Citizens – often led by labour movements – became true zoo animals, dependent on and emotionally attached to their national cages. The widening of political citizenship and the emergence of social citizenship occupied a period centred on the early twentieth century. This is when the first true nation-states, mostly in Europe, were born. Others emerged more recently, especially in a sudden great wave affecting all continents after 1945. To date, even the oldest have enjoyed only a normal human life span; most are much younger, and many are still struggling to be born.

In the last twenty-five years, we have seen neoliberal and transnational reversals of some nation-state powers. Yet some of its other powers are still growing. Over this same recent period, states have increasingly regulated the intimate private spheres of the life cycle and the family. State regulation of relations between men and women, family violence, the care of children, abortion, and personal habits that used to be considered private, such as smoking, is still growing. State policies for consumer protection and the environment continue to proliferate, and feminists and 'green' activists demand still more state intervention. Through the twentieth century, central government has also been increasing far more than local government. Apart from a few 'subnations' – the Catalonias and Quebecs – local and regional barriers have declined inside the nation-state. National education systems, mass media, and consumer markets are still subverting localism and homogenizing social and cultural life into units which are, at their smallest extent, national. When watching the Olympic Games or other events transformed into displays of emotional nationalist pageantry, it is difficult to believe that the nation-state is finished.

The nation-state is thus not in any *general* decline, *anywhere*. In some ways, it is still maturing. However, even if it were declining in the face of the supranational forces that I will shortly analyse, it is still gaining at the expense of the local, the regional, and especially the private forces. The modern nation-state remains a uniquely intense conception of sovereignty. Militarism, communications infrastructures, economic, social, and familial regulation, and intense feelings of national community attachment have been fused into a single caging institution. There is a reality lying behind the facile assumption made by so many social scientists in the recent past that the 'society' that they were studying was the nation-state.

But out 'society' has *never* been merely national. It has also been transnational – involving relations that freely cross national boundaries. And it has also been geopolitical – involving the relations between national units. Transnational relations are not merely 'postmodern': they have always undercut the sovereignty of all states. Geopolitical relations restrict the sovereignty of states which are parties to binding agreements, and they more persistently undercut the sovereignty of weaker states.

Neither the capitalist economy nor modern culture has ever been greatly constrained by national boundaries. Capitalism was especially transnational in its early industrial phase, with virtually free mobility of capital and labour and with most of its growth zones located in border or cross-border areas, like the Low Countries, Bohemia, and Catalonia. Though industry went through a more national phase between about 1880 and 1945, finance capital usually remained highly transnational. The cultural identity of this 'civil society' was not just – or even primarily – 'Britain', 'France', and 'Spain'. It was also 'Christendom', 'Europe', 'the West', and 'the white race'. Cultural artefacts also diffused transnationally as 'the Romantic movement', 'the realist novel', the 'Victorian' furniture style, the symphony orchestra, opera and ballet, 'modernism' in art and design, and now soap operas, jeans, rock music, and postmodern architecture. National sovereignty was always undercut by both capitalist and cultural transnationalism.

But since 1945 both economic and cultural transnationalism have undeniably increased. Capitalism has become, in Susan Strange's words, 'casino capitalism', its funds slushing rapidly through the world in a

complex web of institutions which partially elude the economic planning capacities of states and partially 'internationalize' them.[5] Mass
transportation and electronic media have almost confirmed Marshall
McLuhan's prophecy of a 'global village' – at least Coca-Cola, Benetton,
and Charles and Di are momentarily universal. Capitalism and culture
merge into what the Marxist cultural critic Fredric Jameson has termed
'postmodern hyperspace',[6] diffused without regard to nationality or territory, fragmented, but united by the logic of capitalist profit-taking. As
we shall see, Europe, a small, densely settled area of essentially similar
countries, has been especially penetrated and homogenized.

The postwar geopolitical transformation has also been momentous,
coming in two sudden spurts at the beginning and end of the Cold War.
It was knife-edged: the Cold War might have destroyed us all, but did not.
But war exhaustion in 1945, followed by the Cold War, made the West
extraordinarily pacific in its internal relations, while the collapse of the
enemy in 1989–91 has resulted in a unique absence of any threat from
outside. War between the Great Powers, and especially between the major
European Powers, seems a long way off. This has reduced that aggressive
mass-mobilized nationalism so destructive of the twentieth century,
though it remains around the fringes of the West and in a more symbolic
aggression, requiring few commitments from citizens, directed against
hate figures in the less developed world. The absence of a threat is also
reducing the military size of Western and some former communist
regimes, an important and hopeful reduction in the strength of the
nation-state.

But this geopolitical transformation has gone to quite unique lengths
in Europe. Europe may show us the future of a more pacific world,
should that indeed transpire. Eurocentric events, such as two 'world'
wars and the Cold War, finished off the region's traditional Great Power
aspirations. Since 1945, West European sovereignties have been undercut
geopolitically by their voluntary dependence upon the United States,
and Eastern European sovereignties were undercut by their involuntary
dependence on the Soviet Union. Since 1945, Europe has not defended
itself. West Germany, its major economic power, has had 350,000 foreign
troops occupying great swathes of its territory for forty-five years. Few
Germans have minded; they complain only when the troops get drunk.
But other European NATO members do not have much representation
in its High Command. All depend on an American defence of Europe
over which they lack ultimate control. Thus, Western Europeans could
run military expenditures averaging approximately 3 per cent of GNP –
half of both the United States' and the whole world's levels and very
small in historical terms. Their states hunkered down together in pacific
harmony, living without what was historically the main state function and

the main source of aggressive nationalism – a military power adequate to defend themselves. This regional peculiarity greatly assisted their drive toward cooperation.

The European Community

The EC occupies a much smaller area than the United States, but with a substantially bigger population. Its numerous countries (twelve at present, soon to increase to perhaps twenty) are essentially similar, being advanced capitalist, Christian, and liberal democratic, virtually all ranging centre-left social democratic parties against centre-right conservative or Christian parties. The transnational and geopolitical forces noted above ripped unhindered through them, enabling much closer cooperation than has occurred in any other part of the globe.

Cooperation began in the new geopolitical core of Europe, France, West Germany, and the Benelux countries. Their Iron and Steel Community widened to become the European Economic Community (EEC), gradually expanding its membership and scope. Its task remained economic: to liberalize trade and permit more integrated industrial production. It was successful in this endeavour, though partly through bribing the protectionist, unintegrated agricultural sector every step of the way.

Until the 1980s, the EC was almost entirely compatible with the nation-state. It was merely an extreme example of the peaceful geopolitical negotiations that have characterized the capitalist world order after 1945. Under such arrangements, the representatives of constituent governments sit in committees and work out agreements which are taken back to be ratified or rejected by the sovereign national governments. In fact, EC history has been something of a two-Power initiative. As Perry Anderson emphasizes, bilateral agreements between Germany and France essentially provided all its forward surges.[7] Since France and especially Germany were offering resources, most countries willingly accepted their leadership. Nation-states were still following sovereign interests, sacrificing nothing. But, through the 1980s, EC political regulation began to cut more directly into member state sovereignties. What were these subverting political functions?

The Political Functions of the European Community

The Treaty of Maastricht, signed in December 1991, gives a simple answer: it declares EC control over virtually all policy areas. A cursory reading might give the impression that the EC is indeed a superstate. This text was aired before the Danish and French voters in 1992, and they did not like it. Most of its clauses are mere rhetoric. It is an oddity of the EC that most of its staff become committed federalist Europeans. They write federalist-sounding documents which are then signed by national politicians, many of whom do not share their values. To assess real EC functions, we must look at those Maastricht clauses which are actually implemented by sizeable institutions. These reveal three main undercuttings of national sovereignties.[8]

Law. Most EC law is known as 'secondary law', since originally it largely supplemented national legislation. But, in the 1980s, member governments passed beyond merely recognizing each other's laws and administrative regulations and began to 'standardize' them – a process involving considerable revisions of the national laws. Governments now routinely announce to their parliaments that a particular national law contravenes Community law and needs revision. The EC also denounces violations by member states, though this does not always lead to changed behaviour. Secondary law has somewhat undercut state sovereignty, though almost always through its technical details rather than through sweeping legal declarations.

More general Community law rests in the rulings of the European Court of Justice. These have expanded in scope, again largely through detail, and they will probably continue to expand since social life and culture in the member countries are gradually becoming more similar. But these rulings are binding only because of the voluntary commitment of the states, and they are administered, rather variably, by the individual states.

The content of European law, especially of the secondary law, overwhelmingly concerns the EEC's two original purposes: trade liberalization and production integration and standardization. It regulates in great detail the nature of commodities bought and sold in the Community, gradually extending this to include labour as a commodity, especially regulating occupational qualifications. Its core thus remains economic policy, expanding as initially limited economic activities spilled over more broadly into economic life. This resulted as capitalism expanded into more differentiated consumer markets with a more occupationally differentiated labour force. The advanced capitalist economy turns more of life into commodites, and the EC became this region's way to regulate them.

The Single Market.[9] The Single European Act of 1986 laid out a timetable for the removal of all impediments to the flow of persons, goods, and services throughout the EC. It was to be fully implemented by 31 December 1992. Although implementation has lagged a little, it is largely

complete – though the free flow of persons and animals has been delayed
by the British, Irish, and Danish governments (the new French government is currently also advising delay). The Act virtually eliminates
internal borders. Reinforced by Maastricht clauses, it supposedly confers a common European citizenship. It may also lead to a new European
Police Authority. When a state no longer has arbitrary power over its
own borders, its sovereignty has indeed eroded. Again, the core of the
erosion was economic policy, expanding across the lives of Europeans as
producers and consumers.

The European Monetary System (EMS). The drive toward a single monetary
system, culminating in a single currency, represents an important loss of
the key traditional state sovereignty over coinage. It also undercuts the
kind of macro-economic planning which states claimed to have exercised
during most of the twentieth century, though this is also being undercut
by transnational capitalism. Its rules for the convergence of currencies
have also implied a deflationary economic strategy contrary to the social
Keynesianism and/or competitive devaluations espoused by many
twentieth-century governments. This drive resulted partially from near
unanimity between the member states and partially from geopolitical
relations of influence between them. Wayne Sandholtz notes that its path
was paved by the earlier separate decisions of virtually all the states to
abandon traditional Keynesianism.[10] Indeed, in countries like Italy and
Spain, currency union allows governments to blame unpopular monet-
arist policies on the exigencies of membership in a desired 'modern'
Europe. Geopolitically, Germany has also led the monetary system, believing it to be in its own national interests.

Now, however, some states are wavering in their commitment to monetary union. Many Germans have come to predict a loss of national
sovereignty if the EMS goes further, and this significantly lessens their
commitment. Britain and Italy have been permitted to bolt out of the
EMS, Denmark has been allowed that privilege in the future, and Spain
and Ireland have stretched its rules by decisions that resemble old-style
competitive devaluations. The European Monetary Union's (EMU)
single currency was intended to be reached in the period from 1997 to
1999. This is not now possible, and many believe it will never be reached.
Before it can happen without disaster, there probably must be a general
economic recovery plus far more standardization of economies and economic policies than yet exists – though there are also substantial
disagreements between 'economists' and 'monetarists' over this issue.
Of course, the core of the progress actually made is again economic.

Overall, these three activities have undoubtedly eroded the sovereignty
of the individual member state. This has been reinforced by Maastricht's

major constitutional change. The treaty greatly extended the scope of the 'qualified majority' voting system at the expense of unanimity. Fifty-four of the seventy-six member votes are required to make a new ruling, with no country having more than ten votes. A ruling now needs three big countries and more smaller ones to block legislation. Of course, a country's votes are always cast as a single national bloc, leading toward stable geopolitical power relations between states, not toward a single 'transnational' superstate.

The EC thus remains fundamentally an economic planning agency. It has expanded with the broadening of Europe's product-market range, its complex web of consumer regulations, its diversified occupational structure, and its intricate set of financial instruments. All of this regulation is highly technical and capitalistic. Euro-institutions are arcane, and they are dominated by the lobbying of business enterprises and trade associations. Union and professional organizations are much weaker, and lobbying by churches and other secondary institutions is virtually nonexistent. The direct impact of EC policies on everyday politics in the member countries is rather limited. Regulations about markets and products rarely reach a mass audience, except for the rampaging of French farmers and for the EC's jokes over who can sell products labelled with words like sherry, champagne, or ice cream. The most important Acts, about free movement and currencies, have great implications. When these become apparent, they cause dissension. While the European economy was booming, the states found near unanimity relatively easy. They rarely defined erosions as 'loss' – economic growth was the whole point of the EEC, and is still the central policy object of the EC. Yet, in recessions, their negotiations tend to stall. Future progress seems dependent on growth, the trade-off for the erosion of sovereignty.

The state as a whole is not, as Marx asserted, an organization for managing the collective affairs of the bourgeoisie; the state does far more than this. The EC, however, is. Throughout the twentieth century, political parties and national states, aided by the results of two world wars, have managed to institutionalize relations between the social classes. What remained more problematic as capitalism continued to expand across the world was the relations between the national and the transnational. Since 1945, a group of institutions has emerged to regulate these relations. the EC is a stronger regional equivalent of these institutions – the global corporation, the International Monetary Fund (IMF), the World Bank, and the General Agreement on Tariffs and Trade (GATT). Europe is the biggest market in the smallest area of the three main capitalist regions. It is divided into many similar, pacific states. The EC became more sovereignty-constraining-by-consent than its comparable global institutions. But it has largely extended the same types of functions.

There are several areas, however, where the EC shows little interest. It provides a few communications infrastructures, one traditional (and usually a relatively uncontentious) mainstay of state activity. If Europe comes out of recession, these might be expanded. It interferes in nationalized industries only when they are subsidized monopolies offering goods in competition with other countries' enterprises, that is, a few state enterprises in southern Europe. The bulk of the state sector (whose size varies greatly between countries) is unaffected. EC expenditure is important only for the agricultural sector and is dwarfed by national state expenditure. The EC has not moved into class or other group relations, such as the regulation of labour relations, public order, religion, or the welfare state, though where welfare and the labour market meet in national educational policy, it is active. It does not regulate moral issues, the family, or gender relations – this would be impossibly divisive if attempted. Regional policies began to be scaled down when they appeared to be redistributive. There has otherwise been no attempt at social redistribution. True, there is the fairly vacuous 'Social' Chapter 8 of the Treaty of Maastricht, but the Thatcher government refused to sign even this and EC did not compel it. Britain is not bound by it, a sign of the low priority social issues have for the EC. Indeed, the deflationary rigour of the EC's requirements for fiscal convergence are overwhelming any real social objectives. The EC can hardly point to Britain alone as the home of 'social dumping'.

The EC does not really cultivate a real sense of European identity or citizenship. The Strasbourg parliament has few powers, an attendance rate of less than 50 per cent, and little salience for Europeans. Polls show that Brussels, the seat of executive power, is seen as a bureaucratic Leviathan. This is unfair in one sense, since the administration is small, only seventeen thousand – less than Madrid's municipal government – and one-quarter are translators. But it is accurate in another sense: it is a technicist apparatus uninterested in commanding sentiments or affections from Europeans. There is a diffuse cultural sense of being 'European' which is widespread across the member countries and which is reinforced in everyday life by myriad 'town-twinnings', student exchanges, professional and scientific conferences, and vacationing arrangements. This cultural identity exists alongside strong and enduring national loyalties, whose only major 'weakening' appears to be a substantial reduction in aggressive xenophobia. To be 'European' today means to be nice, gentle, and civilized. Such a European identity could be mobilizable for 'pan-European' politics and social purposes. But these are absent. Most national politics concern taxes, incomes policy, welfare policies, moral issues and foreign crises. These are not perceived to be, and are not, the province of the EC. Thus the political parties are still entirely national in organization and almost entirely national in orientation. Even referenda supposedly about Europe have tended to turn into confidence votes on the national performance of governments.

Moreover, there are two functions, central to the modern state and to almost all other states today, which the EC has not acquired. As a Belgian minister remarked during the Gulf War, the EC is an economic giant, a political dwarf, and a military worm. There is no collective defence and not much foreign policy-making. Under Maastricht rules, there is inter-governmental policy-making and it is decided by unanimity, not by a qualified majority. The French and German governments are developing a small joint defence force, but in bilateral negotiations. The American creature, NATO, has different, though overlapping, members to the EC. The Western European Union might house a European defence agency, but its members differ yet again – Denmark, Greece, and Ireland are not members. Some Europeans favour broader defence commitments, but the two nuclear Powers, France and Britain, refuse to share control of these weapons and jealously preserve their individual UN Security Council seats. The individual states largely maintain their own military and foreign policies. Yet fiscal pressures and the lack of an external threat continue to reduce European militarism. The English sociologist Martin Shaw predicts the end of popular militarism, institutionalized in con-scription. Militaries, he argues, will become smaller, hi-tech, professional, somewhat removed from civil society.[11] Yet the only geopolitical agency capable of coordinating a defence remains the United States. At little cost to themselves, most European states tagged along in the Gulf War. But where is their response when the United States has (so far) been less interested, to the convulsions on their own border, in Yugoslavia? Things have certainly changed since the assassination in 1914 of a single archduke! Defence arrangements are not only outside of EC scope, they are also a bit of a mess.

Thus Europe is not moving toward a single state or even toward a fed-eral state. Different political arrangements for three main types of state function may be distinguished. First, for most economic policy, sover-eignty is divided between the EC and the nation-states, though not according to clear, 'federal' or 'confederal' constitutional principles. Second, in other civilian policy areas, sovereignty remains largely, though not entirely, in the hands of the nation-state. Third, in defence and for-eign policy, very little effective sovereignty is located anywhere. Overall sovereignty is now divided and messy. The EC is diplomatically recog-nized by many states and is an accredited observer at the United Nations, but so is the Vatican. The EC itself has no single seat or place of sover-eignty for what it does control. In democracies, this resides in an elected executive and in a sovereign parliament. Europe is far short of either. Europe does not in effect possess a constitution, clearly regulating these complex institutional relations. The major encroachments on national sovereignty are not really constitutional – the replacement of one sovereignty by another. Instead, they are the practical, surreptitious, and delayed implementations of decisions taken by the Council of Ministers, whose decision-making processes reflect partly consensus and partly the geopolitical influence of the various member Powers. The encroachments are routinized, constraining practices like the dense web of product regulations or the narrow band of currency fluctuations permitted by the EMU. These Powers do not add up to a single, organized state-like whole. In controversial areas, the EC works not according to supranational principles, but according to geopolitical ones – agreements and alliances between Powers.

Recently, Britain, Denmark, and France have claimed a damaging right. They have identified a major EC policy as 'of vital interest' to themselves and so claim the right not to conform. The British government declares that it is in principle opposed to monetary union; the French government is at odds over agricultural tariff policy. We do not know where these disputes will end. But in December 1992, the Danish government was allowed disassociation from monetary policy and formal citizenship. There is a formidable sanction available to the majority against the dissident state: expulsion. It has not yet been wielded. If it is, we will know that the EC is a powerful new political entity, over its admittedly narrow sovereign range of policy. Largely toothless, the EC regulates only the capitalist activity of a region. It provides a genuinely 'European' regulation – but only for areas agreed on by traditional geopolitics. It is not yet a state, nor is it replacing states.

The Future of the European Community

What will happen in the future? The EC might weaken or it might strengthen. Contraction, or worse collapse, seems unlikely, as the economic consequences for all would be disastrous. No present member can sensibly withdraw and the momentum now is toward gaining more members. At the other extreme, the nation-states and the EC *could* eventually form a single federal whole. But where are the pressures for this? The EC was developed for economic harmonization. Its 'spillovers' into other state functions have been limited. Even in the economic sphere, the existence of core and periphery regions and the difficulty in reaching monetary union is producing a Europe of 'different speeds'. Europe has been led since the 1950s by the core Franco-German alliance, loyally backed by Benelux countries whose economies are inseparable from theirs. But the British are still puzzled when they examine the map. Are we in Europe, they ask, or are we in the Atlantic? Italy remains a dual entity, North and South, with a quite distinctive system of government (to put it mildly). The other Southerners are poorer and bring future problems of integration with the North; the Scandinavian neighbours with Austria are as rich as Germany, and they will soon enter the EC. Yet many favour more progressive domestic and foreign policies than most of its present members. Europe has a problematic eastern periphery. It has no clear eastern boundary, and the EC has no clear vision or policy for this area. Its activities in the countries of Eastern Europe are insignificant when compared with those of a single member state, Germany. And, finally, Germany, recently united, with an economy nearing the size of the former Soviet Union's, with massive influence in Eastern Europe, now has another option: to play the Great Power. It seems unlikely that German governments would choose this rather than the EC. But present indications imply that Germany might resist further erosion of its national sovereignty. Without German leadership, there would have been no EC; without German leadership, the EC will not deepen. As Felipe González, the president of the Spanish government, has stated, 'If Germany fails we will all fail as well.'[12]

Thus, it is more likely that for the members, arrangements will either stall or there will be a Europe of differential convergencies and speeds, encouraged by the entry of new members and ad hoc associations with other neighbours creating a widening but not a deepening. Ad hoc cooperation agencies may proliferate within and across its new borders. A pan-European Environmental Agency will hopefully appear, stretching at least to the Urals (Chernobyl taught a very broad geography lesson). Less territorially and functionally unified political alternatives seem more likely than federalism.

Europe is not headed toward singular political arrangements. Indeed, it may be headed back to political arrangements resembling, though in far denser forms, those of earlier feudal times. As then, Europe has no single locus of sovereignty. It has different political institutions regulating different functions in its EC core, and it contains Powers of greatly differing strengths. Europe has ad hoc institutional solutions to particular problems, such as defence and the environment, devising stronger agencies according to present combinations of functional and geographical need. There are committed federalists. But dilemmas of defence, currency, and Eastern Europe are slowing these federalists down and increasing pragmatism and ad hoc solutions.

Proliferating pragmatism may seem sensible, but it has raised the issue of a 'democratic deficit' in EC institutions. These tend to be bureaucratic rather than democratic. Can democracy control them? Clearly not, since democracy itself arose as the sovereign nation-state. Democracy was the achievement of the state as a single, representative place. The federal version of democracy requires a clear division of sovereignty between plural institutions – as in the US Constitution, between the states and the federal government, and between the president, the two houses, and the Supreme Court. Making the EC democratic without transferring some specialized formal sovereignties to it is impossible. Such an act of transference is unlikely.

Do we need to bother? We only need bother if states remain the cages they became in the eighteenth, nineteenth, and early twentieth centuries, and if they threaten their own citizens or their neighbours, as many of those states did.

The European nation-state has lost some economic functions to the EC and some defence functions altogether, while gaining functions in what had previously been more private and local spheres. Overall, the bars of the cage may not have changed very much. Citizens still need to deploy most of their vigilance at the national level and most accountable sovereignty should remain there.

But Euro-institutions do exploit. They are only responsible in a rather indirect, cumbersome way. And since the EC is essentially a capitalist club, it is part of the growing postwar ability of the capitalist class to outflank other classes organized overwhelmingly at the level of the nation-state. Twentieth-century, not nineteenth-century, socialists have concentrated virtually all their activities on the nation-state, greatly strengthening it in the process. Now their social Keynesian achievements are threatened, and their social democratic governments and union federations are simply unable to resist the economic logic imposes by a more globally organized capitalism. Clearly, socialists and other dissidents should organize more in Euro-institutions. But, as long as they can only mobilize their forces on policy issues which remain overwhelmingly the province of the nation-state, it is also a reason for them to be wary of more sovereign powers transferred to the EC. European socialists have been feeble in response to the fiscal conservatism of the Bundesbank-led EC. But their humbling by fiscal conservatism occurred first within their individual nation-states. European leftists need to renew their sense of purpose, and this can only occur through international cooperation. European institutions provide one locus of cooperation, of which they must take full advantage. But it is not the only locus, since they have been outflanked by global, not European, capitalism.

European states no longer threaten each other. Europeans had been long nurtured on negative evaluations of each other. I, for example, was brought up in postwar Britain as deeply anti-German, resenting the French, mildly despising Italians, Greeks, and Spaniards, and making malicious Irish jokes. The Swiss, I was led to believe, were tidy and repressed, the Belgians messy and fat, and the Scandinavians and Dutch were nice because they were totally harmless. I hope they reciprocate with anti-British sentiments. But the polls show that negative national stereo-types have almost vanished. National rivalries now largely consist of Eurovision Song Contests, football cups, and contests in servility to attract global corporations. Western Europe has no military governments and virtually no authoritarian Right. The greatest political transformation of twentieth-century Europe is not the decline of socialism but the defeat of authoritarianism of both the Right and the Left. Centre-right conser-vatives, Christian Democrats, and centrist Social Democrats dominate European politics. And what some carelessly call resurgent fascism is nothing of the sort: it is racism focused on immigration, appealing (as fas-cism rarely did) almost exclusively to the working class on the material issues of jobs, housing, and schools.

The new Europe is harmless. It is also unthreatened. Europe has the geopolitical security it has always wanted, as well as client states and even supplicant states, between itself and any threat coming out of the East. And the Americans remain to defend it. Europe has little need for effi-cient geopolitical decision-making. Pacific muddling can do little harm. Its sins are the lesser ones of omission. If this is postmodernity, it is closer to being a utopia than a crisis.

The EC also enjoys fairly amiable relations with the other two trilater-alists: the United States and Japan. It is true that they have unending trade disputes about protectionism regarding automobile spare parts, semiconductors, and rice, but they also show a capacity for finally com-promising on these. Capitalism is not so transnational that it can dispense with political regulation, and trilateralism fits the bill. Cultural solidarities across the Atlantic are also strong, reinforced by a capitalism and a con-sumerism that blur both national and continental identity. Americans may know that Jaguar cars are now American. But do they know that Burger King and Winchells Donuts are British? Spaniards may know Seat cars are German and Pryca supermarkets French, but not that Texas Homecare stores are British and not American, that half their clothes are Dutch, and that Massimo Duti fashion clothes are not Italian but Spanish, more precisely Catalan.[13] Perhaps one-half of the television programmes shown in mainland European countries originate from America, but they are dubbed. Do Clint Eastwood, Sylvester Stallone, and the *Dallas* and *Beverly Hills 90210* casts remain American when speaking Portuguese or German slang? Do the cartoon characters of *Dragonball* remain Japanese? Europeans seem capable of ingesting American and even Japanese identities.

The EC must also be viewed favourably by its neighbours since – from Iceland to the entire Baltic and Mediterranean littorals – they want in. The EC has had a benign effect on some of its neighbours by making democracy a condition of membership. Greeks and Spaniards have cause to be grateful for this, and East Europeans and Turks might in the future.

But there is a potential European threat to its neighbours: the immigration issue, with a potential for strengthening Euro-racism. This is linked to the broader issue of 'fortress Europe', especially whether Europeans will show much interest in the less developed countries to their east and south. The fortress would revive Europe's identity as Christendom and 'white'. Whether Slavs would be members or aliens remains unclear, and this would affect the exact nature of the European racial and religious identity. The fact that some Slav groups have their own ethnic conflicts adds to the potentially heady brew. In fact, all three of the trilateral regional hegemonies, Europe, the United States, and Japan, now have relations with the developing world on their doorsteps and within their thresholds which have ethnic implications. Racism may no longer be 'the American dilemma' since America has experience and achievements in this area. Racial geopolitical conflict may be more the European and the Japanese dilemma. Who knows what riots, terrorism, and even war this might bring to global geopolitics in the twenty-first century? If it brought much violence, then there would surely be a resurgence of European state sovereignty. Would this be a move back to the nation-state or forward to the United States of Europe? The nation-state, reinforced by European-wide immigration and counterterrorism policies, seems the more likely outcome, in line with the pragmatic political developments I charted earlier. European nation-states are neither dying nor retiring; they have merely shifted functions, and they may continue to do so in the future.

The American and Japanese States

What of the other two trilateralists? In contrast to Europe, they are still dominated by single nation-states, which have given no hint of retirement, let alone of death. The Americas are dominated by the United States. The continent's other states are varied and most live with threats to their security from neighbours and dissidents from within. They are in this respect typical emerging nation-states, with fairly secure territorial scope, fairly stable, large state administrations but contested and volatile political regimes. However, as dependent economies, they also lack the degree of economic sovereignty possessed by most European states of the nineteenth century. Now the US hegemony helps to police the continent.

The United States is itself a nation-state, though never such a right little, tight little nation-state as the European type. The United States has had more ethnic diversity and a weaker, more federal government, reducing national homogenization and centralization. Yet, it is a virtual continent. Its size, ecological variety, and historic isolation have ensured that its economy has remained more self-sufficient than its rivals'. The value of national trade has always greatly exceeded that of international trade in the United States, and that is not true of its major competitors. Its capitalism is more nationally owned than is the capitalism of any European country. Despite the growth of Japanese investment, the largest single foreign investor remains, as it has always been, Europe's offshore island, Britain. We can find a faint echo of the European Common Market in the free-trade agreements between the United States, Mexico, and Canada, but none of the parties is under any illusions as to who is the dominant partner.

Indeed, the life cycle of the American nation-state has differed, maturing more recently. In the 1930s, the federal government took major welfare functions away from the individual state and municipal governments. Its military might dates only from World War II; this finally enabled the federal government to exceed the size of the state and local governments. Unlike most civilian state functions, military power is wielded by the federal government to exceed the size of the state and local governments. Unlike most civilian state functions, military power is wielded by the federal government and by the president as Commander-in-Chief. Thus, its militarism resonates amid symbols and institutions of the nation-state. The phrase 'the American people' is constantly used to legitimate foreign and military policies. Around the mid-century there was also social homogenization as immigration slowed and the South ended its isolation. Regional homogenization has been laggard but it is still continuing in areas such as mass media or banking. Immigration is now going through another great burst and this may bring a distinctive role within the United States for Latino and Asian cultures. But overall the United States seems still to be maturing as a nation-state, and not declining. Of course, it is declining as an economic power relative to Europe and Japan, and I suspect that the consequent loss of national confidence accounts for much of the popularity of postmodern relativism in American intellectual circles.

The second region, East Asia and much of the Pacific, is also a varied region dominated economically, though not yet politically, by a single Power, Japan. Japan is the least economically self-sufficient of the three regional superpowers and is the most isolated from the others. Its state, though formally small, tightly coordinates its national capitalism, especially through the patron–client relations of its single ruling party, the Liberal Democratic Party, and through its dominant economic Ministry of International Trade and Industry (MITI). The ownership of its capitalism remains overwhelmingly Japanese. Foreign raiders have found takeovers and subsequent management extremely difficult to accomplish.

All of this is reinforced by dense and cohesive social and familial relations of a type unique in the advanced capitalist world.

Like Europe, Japan has not been a 'full state' since 1945, lacking control of its defence and foreign policy. But the size of the American army stationed in Japan, just over 50,000, is small. Though the constitution restricts military spending to 2 per cent of GNP, the size of that GNP has become so large that Japan now has the fourth largest armed forces in the world. Though the Japanese remain divided and cautious about their rising power, and though Japanese foreign policy remains weak, Japan is objectively a Great Power once again. Most Japanese are quite nationalistic and share a racial myth of common descent – though their actually varied physiognomies derive from many East Asian stocks. Abroad, Japanese 'internationalism' is tinged with economic imperialism, with a tendency to impose particularly exploitative labour relations in the less developed countries of its own Asia-Pacific region.[14]

Japan remains a cohesive nation-state, despite playing a very large role as both a transmitter and receiver of capitalist and cultural transnationalism. As a nation-state, Japan was an unruly and militaristic adolescent. Its maturation has now resumed – though with very recent intimations of relative economic decline.

So European talk of the death of the nation-state should sound odd in the other two main capitalist regions. The new Euro-institutions are probably not a pattern for the future. It is difficult to see why the United States or Japan should enter into major sovereignty-pooling or sovereignty-shedding with other states or political agencies. They will continue to negotiate with their neighbours and with Europe as single Great Powers.

States in the Less Developed World

The less developed world presents different and more varied state problems. Most states date their birth or rebirth from after 1945, when decolonization imposed an ostensibly similar nation-state form on all countries, despite massive differences in the real infrastructural capacities of states and civil societies. The UN Charter and the Cold War tended to freeze these often artificial political arrangements. But this short era is now over. States must depend on their own, sometimes limited, power capacities. Few possess the infrastructures and mobilization capacities of true nation-states. In this 'outer rim', many states confront an essentially 'Hobbesian' problem of order, unlike states in the 'Lockeian heartland'.[15] Along with the former communist states, many face severe internal dissidence, sometimes combined with threats from their neighbours to their national security. Nowhere else is there a region enjoying the tranquillity of Western Europe. As the sociologist Charles Tilly notes, for several decades most states in less developed countries have not been following the European path of military development.[16] There militaries did not decline in size once they reached a certain level of economic development – as happened in Europe. They have remained large, expensive, and modern, and are likely to remain so for some time. Such countries may spend another century struggling over political and social citizenship, regional and ethnic autonomies, and boundary disputes with neighbours. These are very different political agendas to those of Europe, North America, or Japan, and they may strengthen nation-states rather than weaken them.

But state scenarios in the less developed world are also very varied. At one extreme, mostly in Africa, we find collapsing Hobbesian states whose regimes are unable to penetrate their territories to provide even minimal social order – let alone to pursue the development goals required by the new global culture of instant gratification. In their ineffectual violence, the warlords of Somalia, Liberia or Zaire resemble the vast majority of political regimes throughout pre-modern history. They are not monsters but reflections of our own past – though armed with automatic weapons and Swiss safe deposits. Their problem is not postmodernism, but the absence of a genuinely diffused modernism in their civil societies. This problem lessens as we proceed through the rest of Africa and the less developed South Asian countries, then to Latin American, the former Soviet and the more advanced South Asian countries, and finally to the most successful East European and East Asian countries. By the time we reach Hungary, the Czech lands, South Korea, Singapore, or Taiwan, we encounter civil societies with solid economic and cultural infrastructures, effective state penetration of territories, and political battles over political and social citizenship that are undeniably 'modern', in the sense that they resemble the recent history of Western Europe, North America, and Japan (though East European countries also have their own distinctive political battles). In between the Somalian and South Korean poles, a multitude of semi-effective states are coping with uneven modernity – unevenly developed or enclave capitalisms, religious or ethnic identities sometimes dividing, sometimes strengthening them, bulging militaries keeping order and oppressing, bulging state administrations sponsoring development and dispensing corruption. Some of the problems of such regimes are indeed distinctively postmodern – they are subverted by the global reach of capitalism and the global culture of instant consumer gratification. But their basic political problem is that formally modern political institutions cannot compensate for the weakness of the other modernizing prerequisite: an evenly diffused civil society. They confront a crisis of modernity, not of postmodernity. This is their own crisis, and their diverse solutions will not reproduce the histories of Western Europe, North America, or Japan. But like these histories, they will centre on the struggle to create civil societies and nation-states.

Conclusion

States became important in the modern world for providing five services of varying utility to humanity: (1) they became capable of waging massive, routinized war; (2) they provided communications infrastructures for both militarism and capitalism; (3) they became the site of political democracy; (4) they guaranteed social citizenship rights encroaching into the private sphere; and (5) they invented macro-economic planning. All five functions were connected and entwined with the rise of modern civil society. In the twentieth century, they have fused tremendous powers on the sovereign nation-state. Some of these powers are now declining, but others are still growing.

There is no necessary reason why all these functions should be located within the same political agency. For most of history, they were not. States shared some political functions with lords, with churches, and with private corporate associations. Other functions were not pursued collectively at all, but were considered essentially private activities. In one part of the world, in Western Europe, such functions have again partially separated. This is undoubtedly a world historical change, since it stemmed an apparently unstoppable growth of the nation-state. Europe has created new political institutions of divided, confused sovereignty, and this may spread to some adjacent countries. But since this development was largely a response to a particular regional situation, it may not be a blueprint for the world. Twentieth-century states seem highly varied.

The more global sources of contemporary change, from which some have also predicted the death of the nation-state, actually bring more mixed and varied political implications. Military changes, especially the advent of nuclear and biological weapons, have made major war between the Great Powers irrational, and this logic may also spread downward to lesser Powers. Since the modern state, and much of the nation-state, was conceived in war, this might be interpreted as signalling its eventual death. Yet, after its birth, the modern nation-state found other things to do and is still finding them. In any case, societies are not governed by rationality. Modern wars have been intensified by ferocious ideologies purporting to solve social conflicts. Ethnicity and religion entwined with 'First World' versus 'Third World' social conflict might be a fertile new source of ideologies capable of keeping states violent. It is thus particularly important that Europe, the United States, and Japan cope humanely with their immigration, border, and regional problems. If, instead, they invoke racist-religious identities, they too will suffer the consequences, in violence and in expenditures, of terrorism and counterterrorism. As far as war and violence are concerned, it is easier to see what should be done than what will be done.

Capitalist and cultural transnationalism do not merely undermine states. The increasing density of global society gives states new geopolitical roles. Tariffs, communications, and environmental issues are already notable generators of geopolitical negotiations between states and these may be expected to grow and be joined by many other issue areas. We might see, for example, more global 'Social Chapters' (hopefully, unlike the Maastricht one, with teeth) regulating labour relations or setting common standards of public health or educational and professional qualifications. In the recent past, such negotiations, in or out of agencies like the United Nations or GATT, have been typically led by two great nation-states, the United States and Japan, by more ad hoc arrangements for representing 'Europe' (sometimes all the above are replaced by the Group of Twelve states), and by ad hoc representation of 'the Third World' by one or more states, with a more erratic Soviet/Russian and an occasional Chinese presence.

And so we reach a curious paradox. Transnationalism and the EC have so far been largely capitalist. Yet capitalism seems to be near its state-subverting limits. Capitalist profit-taking has resulted in not quite Fredric Jameson's 'postmodern hyperspace'. Though capitalism has reduced the social citizenship powers of the nation-state, and in association with military and geopolitical trends has also reduced the military sovereignty of most states, it still depends on continuous negotiations between sovereign states in a variety of ad hoc agencies. Capitalism will not further reduce the nation-state. Yet, if socialism, of the democratic Western variety, is to survive, it has to take up this very task. When even Swedish social democracy is being undermined by transnational fiscal conservatism, the message should become totally transparent: unless socialists lift their gaze from inside their own nation-states to exercise power at the international level, they will have precious little to offer the voters. Throughout its life cycle, the nation-state has been entwined with class conflict. But the class movement which historically most strengthened the nation-state should now begin to subvert it. Whether it will recognize this destiny and whether it has the capacity to achieve it are open questions.

For now and for the foreseeable future, ad hoc associations of capitalism and nation-states stride dominant across most of the world, especially the most advanced ones. In the less developed world, states are varied. Some are in crisis, and a few are near death. Their crisis is not of postmodernity but of insufficient modernity. Where countries lack an effective nation-state, they would dearly like to have one. The nation-state is not hegemonic, nor is it obsolete, either as a reality or as an ideal.

Notes

1. Earlier versions of this essay were given as lectures under the titles: 'The End of the Nation-State?' at *Instituto Juan March*, Madrid, 11 December 1992, and 'The End of the Nation-State? Prospects for Europe and for the World', in the Wendy and Emery Reves Lecture Series, 'Beyond the Nation-State', at The College of William and Mary, 15 February 1993.

2. Philippe Schmitter, 'The European Community as an Emergent and Novel Form of Political Domination,' *Instituto Juan March*, Working Paper No. 26, 1991, p. 15.

3. For example, John G. Ruggie, 'Territoriality and Beyond: Problematizing Modernity in International Relations', *International Organization* 47 (1) (1993).

4. All figures on state finances and manpower, and all generalizations about state activities prior to 1914, are drawn from the research I have conducted on the history of five states – Austria-Hungary, France, Great Britain, Prussia/Germany, and the United States – reported in Michael Mann, *The Sources of Social Power*, Volume 2: *The Rise of Classes and Nation-States, 1760–1914*, New York 1993, chapters 11–14.

5. Robert Cox, *Production, Power and World Order: Social Forces in the Making of History*, New York 1987.

6. Fredric Jameson, 'Postmodernism, or the Cultural Logic of Late Capitalism', *New Left Review* 146 (1984) and Fredric Jameson, 'Marxism and Postmodernism', *New Left Review* 176 (1989).

7. Perry Anderson, 'The Development of the European Community', unpublished paper, Center for Social Theory and Comparative History, University of California at Los Angeles, 1992.

8. Two of the major EC activities – agriculture and regional policy – do not undercut national sovereignties. The labyrinthine agricultural policies (still absorbing 65 per cent of the EC budget) have resulted from intergovernmental agreements, especially between France and West Germany. In the 1970s, regional policy seemed to be moving toward undercutting sovereignties, but the entry of poorer southern European states as members reversed this. Most regional conflicts now pit northern against southern states rather than richer against poorer regions regardless of state boundaries (though German unification has provided an exception to this, since the regions of the former GDR qualify for regional funds). And the geopolitically dominant northerners were successful in late 1992 in keeping development funds down to 1.25 per cent of the European Community's GNP rather than the 5 per cent earlier envisaged for them.

9. The literature on the single market and the European Monetary System is vast. Informative, provocative discussions of recent developments are available in articles in Otto Holman, ed., *European Unification in the 1990s: Myths and Reality*, special issue of the *International Journal of Political Economy* 22 (1) (Spring 1922).

10. Wayne Sandholtz, 'Choosing Union: Monetary Politics and Maastricht', *International Organization* 47 (1) (1993).

11. Martin Shaw, *Post-Military Society*, Cambridge 1991.

12. Interview with Felipe González, *El País*, 23 February 1992.

13. Nor can I guarantee that this information will remain accurate even to the time of the publication of this article – since global corporations buy and sell individual enterprises with great zeal and rapidity.

14. Anthony Woodiwiss, 'Human Rights, Labour Law and Transnational Sociality around the Pacific Rim (with Special Reference to Japan and Malaysia)', unpublished paper, Department of Sociology, University of Essex, 1992.

15. K. van der Pijl, 'Ruling Classes, Hegemony and the State System: Theoretical and Historical Considerations', *International Journal of Political Economy* 19 (1989).

16. Charles Tilly, *Coercion, Capital and European States*, Oxford 1990.

Acknowledgements

'Nationality', by Lord Acton, was first published in *The Home and Foreign Review* 1, July 1862, pp. 146–74.

'The Nation', by Otto Bauer, was first published as chapter 1 of *Die Nationalitätenfrage und die Sozialdemokratie*, Vienna 1924.

'From National Movement to the Fully-formed Nation: The Nation-building Process in Europe', by Miroslav Hroch, was first published in *New Left Review* 198, March–April 1993, pp. 3–20.

'The Coming of Nationalism', by Ernest Gellner, was first published in *Storia d'Europa*, vol. I, Turin 1993.

'Approaches to Nationalism', by John Breuilly, was first published in *Formen des nationalen Bewußtseins im Lichte zeitgenössischer Nationalismustheorien*, ed. Eva Schmidt-Hartmann, Munich 1994, pp. 15–38.

'Nationalism and the Historians', by Anthony D. Smith, was first published in the *International Journal of Comparative Sociology* XXXIII, 1–2, 1992, pp. 58–80.

'The National Imagination', by Gopal Balakrishnan, was first published in *New Left Review* 211, May–June 1995, pp. 56–69.

'Whose Imagined Community?', by Partha Chatterjee, was first published as chapter 1 of *The Nation and its Fragments: Colonial and Post-colonial Histories*, Princeton 1993.

'Whither "Nation" and "Nationalism"?', by Katherine Verdery, was first published in *Daedalus* 122, summer 1993, pp. 37–46.

'Woman and Nation', by Sylvia Walby, was first published in the *International Journal of Comparative Sociology* XXXIII, 1–2, 1992, pp. 81–100.

'Ethnicity and Nationalism in Europe Today', by Eric J. Hobsbawm, was first published in *Anthropology Today* 8, 1, February 1992.

'Internationalism and the Second Coming', by Tom Nairn, was first published in *Daedalus* 122, 3, summer 1993, pp. 155–70.

'The European Nation-State – Its Achievements and Its Limits. On the Past and Future of Sovereignty and Citizenship', by Jürgen Habermas, was first published in *Ratio Juris*, vol. 9, no. 2, July 1996.

'Nation-States in Europe and Other Continents: Diversifying, Developing, not Dying', by Michael Mann, was first published in *Daedalus* 122, 3, summer 1993, pp. 115–40.

The editor and publishers gratefully acknowledge permission to reproduce the essays in this volume.

Index

319